The Golden Woman

Peter J. Seymour
(photograph by Anthony Mattina)

The Golden Woman

THE COLVILLE NARRATIVE
OF PETER J. SEYMOUR

Edited by Anthony Mattina

Translated by Anthony Mattina
and Madeline deSautel

The University of Arizona Press
Tucson, Arizona

THE UNIVERSITY OF ARIZONA PRESS

Copyright © 1985
The Arizona Board of Regents
All Right Reserved

Manufactured in the U.S.A.

Library of Congress Cataloging in Publication Data

Seymour, Peter J.
The golden woman.

Bibliography: p.
1. Colville Indians — Legends. 2. Indians of North
America — Northwest, Pacific — Legends. I. Mattina,
Anthony.   II. Title.
E99.C844S49   1985   398.2′08997   85-1156

ISBN 0-8165-0915-8

Contents

Acknowledgments   vii

Introduction   1

The Golden Woman (Continuous translation)   19

Analysis of the Tale   53

The Colville Text and Interlinear Translation   69

The Golden Woman   75

Appendix I   233

Appendix II   282

Appendix III   284

Appendix IV   289

Appendix V   294

Organization of the Glossary   301

Glossary   303

Bibliography   355

Acknowledgments

My research on the Colville language and literature has been sponsored by the National Science Foundation, the National Endowment for the Humanities, the Melville and Elizabeth Jacobs Fund of the Whatcom Museum, and the Universities of Montana, Hawaii, and Kansas. I am grateful for this support. I am indebted to my mentors Drs. M. Dale Kinkade and Laurence C. Thompson, professors of Salish linguistics, and Drs. Ernest Baughman and Richard Bauman, professors of folklore and anthropology for their guidance and assistance. I am also indebted to many colleagues, friends, and students who have read drafts of my work and made valuable suggestions of form and substance, especially my two anonymous reviewers, Ann Campbell, Barry F. Carlson, Ivy Doak, Lee Drummond, Larry Evers, Robert Hausmann, Ernest Jack, Nancy Kryder, Herbert Luthin, Timothy Montler, Douglas Purl, LaVonne Brown Ruoff, and James Welch. Special thanks go to Timothy Montler, who directs all the computer programming done at our Linguistics Laboratory. All errors and shortcomings of this work remain exclusively mine.

I have quoted Leslie Silko's work with her publisher's permission.

I am grateful to the Colville tribal Council for its endorsement of my work, and to other Colville Tribal officials who have supported my efforts, particularly Mike Somday, Adeline Fredin, and Andy Joseph. Most of all I want to thank the Colvilles who over the years have trusted me to work with them: Sophie MacDonald (deceased), Mary Lemery, Nelly Toulou (deceased), George Quintasket, Albert Louie, Charlie Quintasket, Suzanne Louie, Dora DeSautel (deceased), Ada Holford, and Tillie George. This book is dedicated to the memory of Madeline DeSautel and Pete Seymour, friends and respected elders.

Introduction

Peter J. Seymour narrated *The Golden Woman* in three installments
on August 2, 5, and 6, 1968, and I recorded it on six and one half
45-minute tapes. At the time I did not understand the language,
and I was, moreover, uninterested in any but the grammatical facts
of the narrative. I never thought of quizzing Seymour about the
meaning, form, and function of the story. I wish I could say that
I was silent because I knew that a rule of Colville conversational
interaction forbids direct, premature, or untimely questions--it was
just lack of interest. I recorded none of its contextual details.
It wasn't until two or three years later that, having transcribed a
considerable number of Colville texts, I became interested in them
as literary productions. Still later I began to appreciate them as
performances in the context of a culture in transition. This work
is an attempt at making public Seymour's version of *The Golden
Woman*, framed in its historical, cultural, and linguistic contexts, a
prerequisite to formal and structural analysis. Several other Colville
narratives, by Seymour and others, await similar treatment.

I tried without success to publish a collection of Colville stories.
While reviewers praised the intrinsic worth of the texts, they
lamented the lack of contextual information. I had failed, it seems,
to answer the many questions that the narratives raise. But the
reviews helped crystallize my realization that linguistics without
context would interest only the grammarian, and that I would have
a small audience if I went beyond the sentence without being fluent
in one of the dialects of sociolinguistics. This was at once a
sobering and a liberating discovery. Though I am quite secure as
a syntactician who could devote a lifetime to the problems raised
by fragments of sentences, I am also willing to explore past the
sentence without expecting returns in my sentence-level syntax.
In other words, my notion that autonomous linguistics is a perfectly
legitimate field of study has remained intact, and I have a newly
acquired sense of what I've been missing.

Unfortunately, my new good will at recording texts "properly" is not retroactive, and my reviewers will have to be content with my work from memory and secondary sources. And even though this will sound self-serving, let me add that I am certain that, had I organized a story-telling session with audience, atmosphere, and the works, Seymour wouldn't have performed. When I met him, Seymour sensed that his children, grandchildren and great-grandchildren wouldn't or couldn't be interested in any marathon story-telling session, and he had grown to refer to captíkʷl (story telling)[1] as "BSing".[2] For one thing, the household was too busy to listen to stories in the middle of haying season; for another, elders outside the household were not receptive to meeting for the purpose of listening to Pete's stories. I had tried that, and Pete found himself interrupted and eventually ignored. This wasn't due to rudeness, but rather it stemmed from Seymour's speech being not clearly audible beyond three or four feet. His raucous bass did not carry well and became a rumble a short distance away. I used to take Pete for rides to visit old acquaintances of his, so I could hear conversational Colville. On many occasions I watched him participate fully in the conversation the first few minutes, only to lose his audience as he started relating an episode, usually health-related, about himself. Three times I heard him tell a wonderful story about his heart that, except for me, went unheard. Seymour, apparently, had just undergone a doctor's examination--whether routine or emergency I cannot remember. He would tell how the doctor had

[1]captíkʷl refers primarily to "Coyote" stories, but applies to all mythological and fictional narrative. (Cf. p. 14 for Commons' discussion of the term and my comments.) While the art of "story telling" is valued as highly as the art of fine speech making, oratory, it is quite distinct from it--and occasions for speech making are different from story-telling occasions. This description of Paschal Sherman, a highly educated full-blooded Colville (A.B., A.M., Ph.D., LL.B., MPL [Master of Patent Law]) gives an idea of what may be cause for rhetorical displays, in this case a Western religious feast: "The tribal chiefs on Corpus Christi, with the throng foregathered on the campus beneath Japanese lanterns, delivered addresses on signal from father de Rouge. I was thrilled by these addresses, delivered in different Indian dialects, eloquent, some fierce and forceful in manner, always inspiring and moving in the sentiments and counsel so warmly proceeding from the heart" (p. 373). The setting for Indian oratory, obviously, has changed as much as the setting for story-telling, and it deserves the same study that story-telling is attracting.

[2]Seymour only used the acronym form. I never heard him use obscene language (in English), or any of the so-called four-letter words which many people indulge in, particularly while drinking beer--something that Pete and I enjoyed doing together.

listened to his heart through a stethoscope, only to find it "out of place." He would then report the doctor's prognosis and his recommendations, which included, much to Seymour's chagrin, no more horseback riding.

It wasn't much different with a white crowd. I had occasion to host him at my house in Missoula, 350 miles away from his home, for two weeks. One Friday afternoon I took Seymour and my linguistic field methods class to The Big Barn, a local tavern, for happy hour. Margaret Woo, a student of Chinese descent from Havre, Montana, was with us, and eventually Seymour, mistaking her for Indian, asked her her tribal affiliation. Margaret, amused, explained she was Chinese and not Indian, and Seymour assured her with a few words that it is honorable to be Chinese. After that episode I heard Seymour give at least half a dozen accounts of that exchange that took place at the Big Barn. Each time it was to a white audience, and each time it went unheard after the first few sentences. The story goes approximately as follows: "Well, here the other day, my school boy [Mattina] took me to the Barn. No..., it wasn't the kind you think... barn, it used to be. Now it's a tavern, but still looks like a barn [various elaborations]. Well, here's this breed [one who seems to have Indian blood] sitting across from me. So I asked her, 'Say, what tribe are you?' Well, that girl lowered her head..., she said 'Mmm... I'm ashamed to tell you... I'm ashamed to tell you... but I'm no Indian..., I'm Chinee [čayní].' 'Well,' I said, 'there's nothing to be ashamed of. My grandfather was part Chinee.' [Final elaborations and comments.] The story never drew a response. The reason, again, must have been that one had to strain to follow all Seymour said, which most people weren't willing to do. (Seymour paid us all back, so to speak. When I elicited paradigms he claimed poor hearing, and would evade my questions. I once took him to an ear specialist in Spokane, Washington, who examined him and could find nothing wrong with his hearing. He concluded essentially that Seymour's "deafness" was selective. That diagnosis is, perhaps, confirmed by the fact that he could "hear" much better when spoken to in Colville than in English.)

Peter Seymour, when I first met him, would not admit that he spoke his ancestors' language,[3] but once I befriended him, he de-

---

[3] I find this reticence to admit expertise in one's Indian language widespread. The reasons are to be found in the Indians' profound respect for the tongue of their ancestors. All the Colvilles I know who are not yet elders (a respectful

monstrated that he knew how to use it with consummate ease. Over a period of several summers we spent countless hours talking while driving the dirt roads of the beautiful Colville Reservation. He loved horses and hunting--and I heard many a story about horse racing and deer hunting. But he never talked with me about Indian spiritual matters. He avoided subjects like vision quests, medicine practices, and supernatural beliefs. He never offered any information or opinions on these subjects, and I never pried. He was very stingy with his "Indianness", which he must have considered his private and inviolate possession, and he was unwilling to talk about it. He never explained what it meant to sweat, for example, but the reverence with which he uttered the word "sweathouse", and the way his eyes glittered, showed me that he held the practice sacred. The Indian wisdom he had accumulated over the years became dignified acceptance of the disintegration of his ancestors' ways. This stance about Indian things is reflected in the stories he told.

Seymour was born May 1, 1896, and died September 26, 1979. He married Lina Camille and remained with her until her death in 1967. Together they had eleven children, one short of an even dozen, as he would say. Toward the end of his life he suffered hardening of the arteries, and without warning he would sometimes wander off in the woods, in the direction of Smoke Ranch, around Kewa, where he had once lived. The last time I saw him Pete was in a nursing home in Colville. He did not show any signs of recognizing me.

How does a story mean? When children hear their grandparents tell a story, they focus on the content of the story. They might ask

term that denotes age but connotes wisdom) apologize for their limited linguistic fluency. Another facet of this is the derision with which they greet learners' feeble attempts at Colville speech. This reticence is not only real, but deep-rooted. Cline (in Spier 1938) reports the story of a woman who acts strangely by walking on the dancing ground and then breaking a taboo. Subsequently four Indian doctors attend to her, trying to cure her. "While they were doctoring, she sat up and spoke Okanagon, which she had never spoken before… It was [someone else] speaking through this woman… It seems … that when one is bewitched in this way one speaks a foreign language plainly." This happened around 1922, and the woman was from Nespelem, where they do speak Colville, which is southern Okanagan. This probably means that the woman knew the language, but spoke it so seldom that nobody knew of her fluency.

questions about the story, and these also focus directly on the story: 'What did the man do? I didn't understand that. Did he really kill the girl? Is the girl still dead? Did she really do it?' Extended exposure to grandpa's stories will have a long term impact on the children of a community, an impact assumed to be largely uniform. Individual syntheses of the materials, however minutely different, must be sufficiently similar to each other to warrant classification in collective terms, even after children mature into adult individuals. Leaving aside for the moment questions of genres, styles, historical developments, and so on, we can and do talk about Coyote Stories of the Colville Indians, myths of the Kwakiutl, Wishram legends, etc., because we take for granted that these narratives mean essentially the same thing to all the members of the particular community. If we asked the members of these communities to "explain" these stories, we would get a variety of surprised looks, all showing that these stories, at least on the surface, are taken literally. Whatever the subconscious integration of these stories into a collective psychological interpretation may be, such interpretation is very difficult and always subject to question. In any case, the lay members of these communities do not normally verbalize their abstractions of their literatures. Rather, it is only literary critics, anthropologists, social psychologists, folklorists, and various other scholars who indulge in speculations about the significance of these literatures. Given individual scholars' backgrounds and preferences, they will focus on certain aspects of these literatures, emphasizing whatever falls within the perimeter of their scrutinizing glass, and ignoring the rest.

There is always a tug-of-war between the generalists and the specialists, and it is becoming increasingly difficult to be a generalist. This is true of humanists as well as of scientists and social scientists. The amount of scholarly material available on any given topic multiplies daily, and to be an expert on something means to have very little time for other explorations. The Renaissance Man, the Jack-of-all-trades is an anachronism. What is more likely to happen is that a scholar with a single specialty develops another specialty, typically one bordering on the first. In the case of literary texts, a linguist develops an interest in folklore, a folklorist develops an interest in linguistics, a literary critic develops an interest in anthropology, and so on.

There is another tug-of-war, that between the universalist and the nominalist. This has to do with inherent personality needs:

simplistically put, given datum A and datum B, a universalist, convinced of platonic ideals, will concentrate on finding out what they have in common, what is similar in A and B; a nominalist will concentrate on discerning every detail that might differ between A and B. Pushed far these are aberrations, perversions; otherwise they are but tendencies. Thus, it seems to me, ethnography, the study of different cultures, attracts more nominalists than universalists, literature (in the classical sense) more universalists than nominalists, and generative linguistics more universalists than nominalists. And then myriad misunderstandings take place. The anthropologist calls one who disagrees "ethnocentric", the sociolinguist calls a competence-oriented linguist a visionary reductionist, and so on. We are enlightened to the point of blindness.

Is it then impossible to analyze a text avoiding the specialist's narrowness, the generalist's shallowness, the universalist's overgeneralizations, and the nominalist's near-sightedness, while retaining, at the same time, broad perspective and depth, and perceiving universal principles and distinctive detail? Such would be perfection, and not of humans. What I think is possible is to define well one's own particular perspective, and then present that view.

I became acquainted with Pete Seymour at the end of July, 1968, when he agreed to teach me some Colville. On Tuesday, July 30, we met and I elicited about 300 items from him, mostly isolated words, phrases, and a few sentences. He didn't particularly enjoy this work, and soon he offered to tell me a story in Colville titled Black Pig--a Colville version of Cinderella. I noticed right away that Seymour enjoyed telling stories, and we arranged for another session on Friday, August 2. That afternoon, in an abandoned farm house near Inchelium, with me as his only audience, he started narrating The Golden Woman. We recorded two 45-minute tapes, Parts I and II. We continued Monday, August 5, when we recorded two more 45-minute tapes, Parts III and IV; and we finished Tuesday, August 6, when we recorded two and one half more tapes, parts V, VI, and VII. The same day he finished The Golden Woman he started telling me another story, which he called Coyote and His Family.[4] At the

---

[4]This is another very long narrative that breaks very naturally into a prologue (Coyote receives special powers, and in exchange he will rid the earth of

end of each tape Seymour would "take a five," roll and smoke a cigarette, chat in English, and then pick up the story where he remembered to have left off.

THE GOLDEN WOMAN

The Golden Woman is a tale of European origin that goes as follows: A king has four sons, the three eldest of whom go off to see the world. They happen upon a man-eater's house, where they become guests for the night, scheduled to be decapitated while sleeping. The youngest brother, with the aid of a magic horse, rescues them, in spite of golden birds that act as the man-eater's sentries. The four brothers leave and arrive at a town where they obtain jobs, and the three eldest boys, jealous of their little brother's power, plot to have him killed. In the name of their little brother they offer to capture the man-eater's golden birds as a gift to the king, sure that the man-eater would take revenge on him and kill him. With the horse's help the little boy captures the birds and brings them to the king. Then the three offer in their brother's name to capture the Golden Woman, a strange and powerful sea-creature, which the boy instead manages to do. The king wants to marry the beautiful Golden Woman, but she has fallen in love with the boy who captured her, and schemes to dispose of the king and marry the boy. Her plot involves having the Golden Birds tell their life story, apparently for the purpose of awakening the boy to the Golden Woman's love. The Golden Birds' life story is nothing but the story of the boys who set out to see the world and are saved by their little brother. In the end the Golden Woman poisons the king and marries the boy, who takes her back to his original home. His brothers also return home and remain unpunished, while the magic horse disappears from the scene altogether.

As soon as the birds start telling their story, the narrative becomes a "round" (Aarne-Thompson type 2320), a story which begins "over and over again, and repeat[s]." At least twice in his narrative

man-eaters); three episodes, in each of which Coyote kills one or more man-eaters; and an epilogue, a statement about the conditions of the world at the conclusion of Coyote's deeds.

Seymour became caught in a circle, so to speak, and spun his story over and over. How conscious Pete Seymour was of having repeated himself more than once I cannot say, but at the beginning of the fourth tape he said (in English) "I gotta think. I've been BSing and I haven't started telling the story." This could be paraphrased as 'I had better concentrate and get to the point." Seymor liked to tell stories, and he enjoyed being listened to--even if in August, 1968, I could not understand a word of what he was saying--and therefore I am not surprised that he went on and on as he did.

So much for how the story was told. I didn't videotape it, and I can't begin to reconstruct what movements of the hands, head, eyes, and body he used as props. I remember very, very few. The recordings show an even tone without obvious dramatic pauses, loud peaks, whispers, and other theatrical devices, except for the pan-Salishan phenomenon of extra long vowels[5] pronounced in falsetto.

This is how I recorded *The Golden Woman*. The rest of that summer and for the next two I recorded more stories from Seymour (and a few from other Colvilles also). In 1969, 1970, and in the years following I began transcribing them and discovered how good they were. Seymour did not have the patience or interest to do transcription work, but he introduced me to his cousin, Mary Madeline DeSautel, who eventually became my most helpful consultant. Like Seymour, Madeline DeSautel was at first reluctant to work with me, but in the summer of 1970, a full year after I had met her, she agreed to help me transcribe Colville texts. We developed a close and warm relationship. She visited me in Honolulu for six weeks during winter, 1971, and for three weeks in Missoula in 1974. She treated me as a member of her family, and I did the same with her. She was born on March 4, 1888, and had four children, all of whom she outlived by a good twenty years. Her energy was boundless and into her eighties she still chopped her own wood for fuel. She was

---

[5]These are marked with double length (two raised dots) in the Colville text. I have marked the loudest sentence stress with an acute accent and other word stresses with grave accents. Thompson and Thompson (forthcoming) describe the analogous phenomenon of *rhetorical lengthening* in Thompson as "extra-long vowel with high pitch (sometimes with falsetto)", and label its function "colorful emphasis." Hymes 1977 discusses "lengthening of vowels for emphasis" among other Chinookan 'presentational forms.'

a prayer leader at Indian funerals and attended as many wakes as she could. She died on December 4, 1979.

The way we transcribed Colville texts is, I suppose, the usual--stretches of tape are played over and over, and each sentence (or fragment) repeated until correctly transcribed. Then it would be translated phrase by phrase by Madeline, but with frequent interruptions when I could beat her to the translation. The thrill at being able to understand what is being said in Colville has never palled for me. It was an exciting game to transcribe and translate, to understand the various syntactic constructions and the morphological make-up of words, and to test new forms and constructions. Madeline's translations were loose--certainly not morpheme by morpheme, and not even word by word. She translated Colville into the English she normally spoke, and I wrote it the way she spoke.

For convenience let us call the English dialect spoken by Madeline DeSautel "Red English." I don't think it would be an overgeneralization to state that Red English is a pan-Indian phenomenon, with various subdialects, of course. Some scholars object to printing this Red English because they think that many lay readers see this dialect as a sort of impoverished and inferior English that perpetuates the perception of the American Indian as a backward sort. A comment by one of my anonymous reviewers expresses this view eloquently, and I quote it here: "I feel strongly (indeed violently) that common oral English should be preferred to what looks like incompetence at language. This is not to argue that Indian-English itself is an 'impoverished' language; at least, I need to make clear that I make no value judgment about grammar, propriety, usage, and so on in and of themselves. But much of the reading audience will already believe in that old stereotype of the semi-articulate (or primitive, or 'backward') Indian, and I see no reason to strengthen that idea..." The objection, however, I find unconvincing, for the problem of perpetuating a stereotype of backward Indians is not inherent either in the Indians or in the way they talk; the problem, rather, resides in those who judge Indians by their speech habits. Rather than changing the way Indians talk, I advocate educating those who hear Indians talk. This is an old problem, plenty discussed with reference, for example, to Black English. Some will die thinking that Reds and Blacks better talk the way we do, by God; some will die shaking their heads.

There is another two-pronged argument in favor of a translation into "careful" English. The first prong of this argument correctly assumes that the Colville of Seymour's story is elegant and formal, and therefore insists that the language of translation be equally elegant and formal. The other insists that the language of translation should reflect carefully the subtleties and complexities of the Colville original, even at the risk of stilting English. My colleague Douglas Purl, a literary scholar who espouses the formal English cause, and impatient with my Red English, has gone so far as to retranslate one of Seymour's stories to conform to his notion of a good story. My collaborator Clara Jack, a native speaker of Okanagan with linguistic training, insists on careful literal translations. However, my choice of Red English as the language of translation has its real justification not in the first polemic argument I made (don't judge people by how you think they should talk), nor in the second (translate formal texts only into formal language), but in the slowly emerging tradition of artistic (hence respectable and appropriate) published Red English.

I translate *The Golden Woman* into the Red English of Madeline DeSautel, because a Red English translation matches better than another kind of English the function of the original Colville narrative.

To my knowledge the earliest and longest document of Colville English is the transcript of the United States congressional hearings of 1965 on Colville termination. The hearings were held in Washington, D.C.; Spokane, Washington, and Nespelem, Washington, on the Colville Reservation. That 600-page document contains a very large number of statements and letters of Colville Indians. I don't doubt that these have been edited at least to some extent to conform to standard English usage. Nevertheless, they show nicely many of the strategies used by Colvilles in public speaking: for example, when to ask rhetorical questions, when to repeat, when and how to stray from the central point, when to conclude and how, and so on. There is enough material for several sociolinguistic analyses. The form of these statements ranges from standard English to something close to Red English, as is shown by these excerpts from the statement of Mr. Louis Camille, who was, incidentally, Pete Seymour's wife's brother.

> Well, my name is Louis Camille. I am a member of the Colville Tribe… If this here bill was to go through, we, us Indians, would be lost. Maybe the counties get rich, other people surrounding the reservation, but the Indians would be lost and it would be just another burden to the Government… We don't want that, we are proud. We have many of the reservation here but it is still tied down. I think if the reservation was

thrown open that would be our loss... There is no other man in this whole world has the privilege, the rights, that the Indians got. Why should I step down one step to be equal with the rest of the citizens of the United States? I am above. I owned this whole country at one time, my ancestors did. Before the white man come here Mr. Indian was living well, and I can take any of you white men right out here and put us out here in these mountains with nothing to eat and I'll starve you out. I can find something to eat out there where you couldn't find nothing. That I know.

Like I say, I am 74 years old, I have no education, but I have experience. Now, the north half was taken away from us. Colville valley was taken away from us. All we get is promises. Now, I still stand, just the way I put it out in District of Columbia there, that I am opposed to S. 1413 or any other bill like it, and, furthermore, at that time they drew the line that we can only just speak on the subject and nothing more so there was not much more that we could say, but this time, the way it looks to me like, I could sit here all day and talk to you with no limit, it seems like...

Like I say, that's all I got is experience...

I don't have any children, I don't have no future, it won't be very long and I will be shoving off, but I have grandchildren from my niece and nephews and I would like to see them enjoy what I enjoyed, and I have got a boy in the Army now back there fighting somewheres now. Last summer he come home for a furlough and just the day before he left again I visited him and I told him that I am going to stand pat on trying to hold this land for you. You are out there fighting for your land and here while you are gone I am not going to sell it out from under you. I want you to come home and you will have a home and you will have a reservation. I will do my damndest to try and save it for you. That's what I told the young fellow and he thanked me for it. He may be dead now for all I know.

I thank you. (pp. 223-4)

This speech in Red English is every bit as effective as any of Winston Churchill's war speeches in British English.

Another document that is witness to the legitimacy of Red English as perfectly beautiful poetic language is Dorothea Kashube's *Crow Texts*. The texts, recorded in 1953 and published in 1978, include such gems as

Right now the push-dance song.
It's a different kind of dance,
the words in the song,
lots of these songs,
I was lonesome for you.
Was you lonesome for me when you went away. (p. 70-1)

The two documents from which I have quoted are verbatim transcripts--the editor of the congressional hearings transcripts makes no comment whatever, and Kashube says that the English of Pretty-On-Top (the Crow Indian who volunteered the Red English translation of her own text) is "more vivid than would be the English translation of Crow by a linguist."

There are more recent works that flaunt, and not just report, Red English, as well they should. I'll give three examples that, again, attest to the adequacy of Red English as a vehicle for poetic language and for journalistic language, and in these cases the authors make no apologies and give no explanations. The first piece, lack of subject-verb agreement and all, is an excerpt from Mary Augusta Tappage, a Shuswap woman born three weeks before Madeline DeSautel:

> I used to help at times of birth, yes,
> I used to help all the women around here.
> I learned it from my book, my blue doctor's book.
> I used to read it all the time.
>
> I made up my mind that if she needs help,
> I will help her. I'm not scared.
> You've got to be awfully quick. There's two lives there.
> The baby and the mother.

This piece, published in 1973, was recorded by Jean E. Speare, who does not tell us how and to what extent she edited these lines. The second is an excerpt from a 1980 newspaper article that appeared in the *Tribal Tribune* of October 30 by William M. Charley Sr., entitled "Traditional Values," which goes as follows:

> Today what I have on paper is my life and have learn this the true Indian-way years ago as the child my parents my Father the Chief from the Methow-band and my dear Mother she is from the Wenatchee-band my language the native the two bands mention above and did not know English, the self-taught and feel the true self-made Indian and my knowledge is gain word by mouth from my elders, as did not read about the fine Indian culture from the book-store.
> Such as life we do not live this day by day, here we learn for our selves from the past to make mistakes and as this old world turns the same picture shall come before us to let our mind wander back to the past yesterdays as we did this before and why, would this work the second time around, when the first time we fail...

And finally, an example from Leslie Marmon Silko's *Storyteller*. This book, an Indian writer's telling of Indian story-telling, shows us how an educated and widely published Indian artist repeats and reports stories that Indians tell--and these are not just Indian mythologies, but all kinds of stories. One excerpt, substandard expressions, ungrammatical conjunctions, elliptical sentences and all, goes:

> Seems like
> it's always happening to me.
> Outside the dance hall door

```
late Friday night
in the summer time,
and those brown-eyed men from Cubero,
smiling
They usually ask me
"Have you seen the way stars shine
up there in the sand hills?"
And I usually say "No. Will you show me?" (p. 97)
```

Why is it necessary to talk at such length about Red English? Because it is silly to hope that anyone other than a native speaker of Colville can appreciate Seymour's *The Golden Woman* in the original, and because the odds are overwhelming that any formal study of *The Golden Woman* would be based not on the Colville original, but on the translation, or, at best, on a combination of the two, in the style, for example, of Dell Hymes. The point is that Seymour's *The Golden Woman* is a great story not because it's a story told in Colville, but because it is an artistic production, told before a white audience of one by an Indian who had deep roots in his Indian land, but whose realm was shrinking from the relentless encroachment of aliens. It is a near miracle that the story you're about to read got told at all.

We do not know very much about ancient Colville story telling practices. Neither Teit nor Ray says anything on the subject in their respective ethnographies. We do have the following report by Rachel Commons (in Spier 1938):

> Stories were told at any time, although the confined leisure of winter evenings made this season best for recounting legends. Suszen stated: "Stories are always told at night in the winter because whoever tells stories in the daytime or in summer, gets bald. That is why only old men and women and women can tell stories in the daytime and in summer." Anyone might tell them, but in each family or village one or two old men or women were recognized as having the greatest talent and the largest repertoire of tales. Such an individual would entertain a group, often invited for the purpose, throughout an evening, recounting one myth after another. Sometimes guests at the gatherings brought small gifts for the story-teller.[6]

[6]Cf. Silko's remarks:

"I remember Grandpa telling us that story—
We would *really* laugh!
He wouldn't begin until we gave him
something real good to eat—

...

That's what you're supposed to do, you know,
You're supposed to feed the storyteller good things" (p. 110).

There was no distinction between tales for men and women, adults and children. However, Billie Joe said that his grandfather used to send his sisters away because certain tales were considered unfit for girls to hear. Probably each individual was familiar with all of the tales and could tell them on occasion, yet this familiarity did not lessen the eagerness with which a story was received at any telling. Favorite legends were those in which Coyote, the hero-trickster, was the chief actor. A Coyote myth invariably evoked interest and laughter, no matter how often it had been told.

Stories were told to adults chiefly in the evening. During the day, children would gather around an old man or woman for hours, demanding tales. These were seldom for the purpose of pointing a moral. Many tales contained educational matter, such as directions for making tools, houses or clothing, the preparation of food, technique of the hunt, or rules for playing games; but these points were not emphasized. Ideas of cosmology and ethical concepts were all implicit in the myths and were doubtless absorbed by everyone in childhood through the medium of the story-teller; yet there was no formalization of tales, no ritual of myth, no secrecy or sacredness.

A story was sometimes ended with a little formula. At the conclusion of the tale, the teller spat upward (spraying the moisture instead of a solid stream) and said, "Rain a little; clear up again; get warm; Sun, shine and let the children play around outside." This was considered as a prayer to Qwulencolten [kʷl—əncutn̩], "God"] but was not requisite for story telling. All stories were concluded, however, with a formal phrase, "Then I came back" (xoɬxEntsxai or xike'kike'nsplak). The individual tale-teller sometimes elaborated on the formal ending, as "Then I left them [the characters in the myth] and came back, and I have been living here ever since," or I told him I would leave him; so I came back," or the like.

Several types of tale are distinguished: tcapti`klah (?), myth; insim'a`pEluks, "French" fairy tale; kumaixi`ts, a narrative of a recent event. (p. 185)

To study this passage carefully means to make several inferences that leave us with some idea of the cultural norms that regulated story telling, and with more questions than answers. In the first paragraph, with her statement that "stories were told at any time," Commons contradicts her own source's report of the interdiction against day- and summer-time story telling and the attendant retribution for the violation. I would not discount Suszen's warning, and would surmise that Colvilles are forbidden to tell *some* stories in the daytime and in the summer--most likely some sacred stories. Commons' concluding paragraph identifies captíkʷɬ as myth, insim'a`pEluks (səma?-ápəlqs) as "French" fairy tale (sáma? *French, European*); and kumaixi'ts (kʷu may?-xít-s *he tells me*) as narrative of a recent event. It is probably only captíkʷɬ that should be told exclusively on winter nights, very likely a rule enforced for some, but waived for others. My inference of the sacredness of some captík^{w}ɬ is contradicted directly in Commons' text: "there was no formalization of tales, no ritual of myth, no secrecy or sacredness." Yet the statement cannot be accepted literally. There *were* sacred stories, and the telling of these storied *had* to be highly structured, including certain formulas similar to the ones Commons mentions in her third paragraph, or else there couldn't have been sanctions against infractions of these rules. And while I recognize neither the first formula nor the ritual of the spit-spray, I cannot be sure that these are older forms now forgotten, or deficiencies of my corpus.

A scholar by the name of John Fahey wrote a book on the Flathead Indians, cousins of the Colvilles. He perused enormous amounts of data, and then reconstructed his perception of the people. About story telling he says: "venerable men told stories. The old women talked among themselves and recited tales for young children."[7]
If he read Commons' second paragraph he certainly didn't swallow her story. And he also guessed that "traditional tales [were] often spun in contests to determine the best story tellers," but that sounds too much like a county fair event to me, and I would add that such contests would involve no formal judging, however structured they otherwise might be.

I want to bring up a couple of questions that have tantalized me for a while. The first has to do with the length of the narrative sessions. We have already seen that story telling could go on all night. But how long was each story? Coyote stories were by their very nature as long as the narrator wanted to make them, and I have a feeling that the longer he was able to make them while keeping his audience awake, the better a storyteller he was. Coyote was given some special power in exchange for some tasks he was assigned to complete for the benefit of the sqílx^w, the People, the Indians. Each deed is told in an episode that blends into the next at the discretion of the teller--and that's why and how you could tell stories all night, taking turns, with the audience par-

---

[7]There is at least another place where the strong implication is made that men and not women typically tell stories. Mrs. S. S. Allison in her *Account of the Similkameen Indians of British Columbia* says, "There are numerous other stories that the old men are fond of relating while sitting round their camp fires" (p. 314). Mrs. Allison had, in her words, "lived alone among these people for years (sometimes not seeing a white face for three months)" (p. 317).

ticipating fully, the best story tellers talking, the others enjoying, the youngest ones learning.

While the length of these sessions has been mentioned or implied by several people, no one has spilled too much ink on the topic. Listen to what Hill-Tout had to say about the Thompson Indian story of NTLAKAPAMUQ: "This story is the longest in my collection" (p. 39); "it was originally so long that those listening to it went to sleep before it was concluded" (p. 21). I remember Pete Seymour telling me several times how Joe Boyd had put him to sleep one night, half a century earlier, telling stories. It was one of the episodes Pete went back to and talked about. He smiled about it, but to have fallen asleep was a source of mild embarrassment to him. He could smile about it because had events slowed down for just a generation, his grandchildren would have been the ones to fall asleep while he told stories, and the balance of the life-cycle restored. Youngsters are the most likely to fall asleep while they still don't comprehend fully that the stories told by their elders contain principle by principle the secrets of how to be Colville--what it means to have been preceded in life by Coyote, by the other animals of their land, and by the birds of their sky, and by the fishes of their water.[8]

It is not uncommon nowadays to hear middle-aged Colvilles lament the short attention span of their youth, when their grandparents were still alive and talking to them winter nights, but also at other times. The problem now is the same that chagrined the editor of

---

[8]Silko reports:

> she said her grandchildren had brought home
> a library book that had my "Laguna Coyote" poem in it.
>> We all enjoyed it so much,
>> but I was telling the children
>> the way my grampa used to tell it
>> is longer."
> "Yes, that's the trouble with writing," I said,
> "You can't go on and on the way we do
> when we tell stories around here.
> People who aren't used to it get tired." (p. 110)

Hymes (1977) reminds us of the many factors that contribute to variation in narrative performance: "sometimes a speaker capable of full performance does not feel comfortable in providing it, not knowing the hearer well enough, being tired, missing native conditions for such display, whatever" (p. 441). He also suggests that "narrative performances varied on [the] dimensions ... of explicitness and length. An admired narrator could spin out a story to any length desired by filling in detail, but could also convey the essence of a story in brief. Some people emphasize the latter ability in expressing admiration for narrators they have known--ability to tell everything yet keep it short" (pp. 441-2).

Jimmy Teit's work in 1904, 1908 and 1909: "the ancient customs have disappeared to such an extent that direct observation is impossible." (p. 25).[9]

We'll never know exactly how the Indians used to do it, but a revival of story-telling is happening, and an article in the *Vancouver Sun* of March 18, 1974, tells how Selina Timoyakin and her son Larry Pierre, Okanagan Indians from Penticton, recount Coyote stories in a Cariboo Community College classroom: "Selina sticks to Okanagan while Larry does the translating. At the start her presentation is a little wooden, but as she warms up to the story of Coyote, the past becomes the present and she is as animated as a guest conductor anxious to catch the next flight out of town. Larry is a bit of an embellisher as well as translator, so the end result is a joint mother-son account of Coyote, who was sent by the Great One and is not to be confused with 'the coyote you see running around breaking into chicken houses.'" And so cultures have their quiet way of changing, sensitive to the impulses that keep them alive. I am glad that we have some tapes and transcripts of Seymour's stories and DeSautel's translations, however imperfectly they may record a stretch of Colville tradition.

[9]The editor is Franz Boas, who is often criticized as one who (in Maud's words, for example) "was not constitutionally inclined to make friends with his informants nor spend more time with them than the serious business of science demanded; and he elevated this trait into a theory: an informant is a spokesman for the tribal past, and one cannot inject prying questions or pleasantries without contaminating the medium" (p. 11). I've always liked to think that Boas objected to befriending Indians as a *means* of obtaining information.

The Golden Woman: Continuous Translation

1. One tribe of people was sitting around, it's one town, one big town, but I don't know the name of the town. It's nothing but a fairy tale. And they have a chief in that town, they have a big chief, and he's important, and he's got more than one son, four of them, all boys. It's early spring and the snow is all gone, school was over, and the three oldest ones went to see their father.

2. They told him: "Father, you're the chief, and we're going to tell you what we're thinking. Well, father, we're going to leave you." Their father said to them: "And why, is there something you're angry about and then you're leaving us? I thought I treat you children real good, I respect your feelings, you're not hard up, and I baby you. And now you're thinking of leaving me."

His sons told him: "No, don't think that way. It's for good [reasons] that we're leaving you, we're not mad at anything. Now we're out of school, and it'll be some time before we get back to school. We're done with with this here grade school, and even if we stay here, we'd be staying here with you, and we won't learn nothing that way, just books. All you do is baby us, coax us around, you never send us to do anything for us to learn how to work. We're going to have our own experience, whatever we learn. We don't know yet what we're going to experience, but maybe if we travel around the world we'll look for a job, and maybe we'll learn work, and we'll practice, and that's why we ask permission to travel around."

And their father asked them: "And where will you be going?" And they told their father: "You know that we never get out of your sight since we's born. We don't know anything about the country, and we'll just go, for nothing, no direction, in the open country, we'll get somewhere. Wherever we are facing, that's the direction

-19-

we're taking. But this is what we are telling you, it'll be exactly one year the same day that we're gone, and if we're still alive we'll come back. Not yesterday, but today next year, when it's exactly a year, we'll come back, me and my brothers. We don't know where we're going, and we don't know what we'll do, maybe we'll be all together when we get a job, or maybe not, we'll scatter and get a job each by himself. If one of us doesn't come back, that's the sign he's dead. If we're lucky we'll stay in one place and then we'll see one another in the evening. We're still together yet." Their father said: "OK, if that's what's going to please you, and this is what you want, travel around, go on."

3. Then he told his working man: "Go tie the very best of my horses, three saddle horses, and put saddles on and bridles, the very best saddles and bridles of mine, fur chaps, or fringed chaps, bat-wing chaps, spurs, a quirt whip, rope, so they won't be hard up, everything good, the best that's useful." And he told the store keeper: "Give to my boys the very best clothes you got, and shoes, what they're going to wear. They'll take everything from my warehouse, but the money from my bank I'll give it to them myself, I'll open it for them. That's my orders."

His wife heard him and asked him: "What's the matter, why, these are your best outfits and you're giving them to your children?" And he told her: "If they go someplace, or anybody sees them, and then they'll get stuck on them, their lips'll get dry. 'Gee, but they got expensive things, their parents must sure be powerful, and that's why they got such good things.' They'll brag on them. But if they're poorly dressed, and if their horses are pitiful, their saddles ugly, the people might say, if they find out their father is a king, 'Gee, but he's awful poor this chief, their father, or maybe he's awful stingy, look at what ugly outfits they have.' That's why I gave them good outfits."

The working man ran out, in a while he got all that. They got the horses there, they're all saddled up, they got clothes, all expensive, shoes, hats, it was all there.

4. Then he got his bank over, one whole trunk, because at that time there was no bank, and he keeps his own money, and it's all gold and silver, he didn't have no greenbacks, and he started counting. He put it in three piles, one, and another, and another. One for the oldest one, and he put it down, and for the in-between one, and he put it down, and for the last one, and he put it down.

I don't know how many tens and how many hundreds. Twenties, gold pieces. Until he got enough. Then he put silver down. That's change.

Then he told the oldest one: "You're the oldest one and I'll give you this for your lunch." He told the middle one, "I'll give you this for your lunch too." And he told the youngest one, "This is for you, for your lunch."

He told them: "You don't know where you're going, and you don't know the country, and then you won't know the people when you get there, and maybe you might get hungry. And this is what I give you for your grub. And if you get to a town then you'll have money, and if you go to a eating place you can eat, and you can camp at a hotel, and you can put your horses in a barn. You have some money and you can pay for that. But if you don't have money you'll have a bad time."

He went on: "Don't think that I gave you too much money. It won't be just as you get out of sight that you'll get a job. No. You'll travel far before you might see a town, and people. You might get hard up. This is for your eats, for your sleeps, or you'll get dirty and this'll buy new clothes. That's what the money will be for." He's got them all fixed up. The boys put their money in their pockets. They got on their horses and left. And I guess their country is level for a long ways, it's quite a ways before they get out of sight.

5. And then the youngest one wanted to go along, but he was small. His father told him, "No, you stay home. You're too small, you'd give your brothers something to worry about, you might do something your brothers'll be responsible for. You just as well stay here. Take care of us old people. You'll be setting down with us."

But no, he wouldn't listen because a little boy just ain't got no sense. And then he cried.

6. Then his mother pitied him, and she told her man: "Pity our boy's feelings, even if he's only one child we got left. It's a pity he's just a baby. That might do the boy some harm if you always refuse him. He might get sick, get lonesome, maybe die.

Now I'm going to give you something to think about. You send somebody to tie him an old horse, a good horse, but old, and not able to travel or to run. A horse that all he does is walk. Tie that one, and put the saddle on, put everything, and then put him on his back, give him some money, just a little, he doesn't know what money is, tell him 'That's for your eats', and he'll be happy. That old horse won't go far, won't take him far, he might go over there, maybe get out of sight and maybe not, his horse'll just stand there he's so tired. He'll try, and he'll just ride around there, he'll try to whip him, and then he'll turn back, he'll never overtake his brothers. He won't get lost, he can't go far. And then he won't get feeling bad, he won't get sick over it. He'll be in good humor and then he'll come home."

7. Her husband said to her: "You sure think up good things. It's a pity you're my wife, I have whatever you tell me." So he told his working man: "Go and get that old horse, that laziest one. The one that we don't use any more, just feed. It was a good horse at one time, and that's why we still take good care of him, and he'll die by himself, of old age, and he'll have a good death. What good will it do if we kill him? Well, tie that one up. Get any old saddle, even if it's an old one, put it on, and put a bridle on him. It's for my youngest boy, he's just going to ride it around here."

Then the working man went and tied the old horse, and saddled it and came back with it. Then his father gave him some money, maybe just pennies, some silver just to satisfy him, he told him "this is for your eats." The boy got really tickled, put his money in his pocket. He shook hands with his mother and father, they kissed him. His father put him on the horse, and the boy's happy. And he's got spurs, and he had a whip. And they never thought he'd get away and follow them, he couldn't follow even to catch up with his brothers, his horse can only walk, and they're already out of sight.

8. He turned his horse around, he whipped him on the back, whipped him until his arm got tired, and he spurred him to boot. But he's too old, he can only walk, he couldn't even trot this here horse, he just slowly walks. The boy didn't go far, he had just got out of sight, and his horse lay down. He was plum give out. The boy jumped down, landed on the ground and started to cry. And he got angry at his horse, started fighting his horse, whipped it, hit him on the body, hit him on the head. All at once his horse talked to him, he tried to stop him, he said: "Please have pity on me little boy, I'm not doing this on purpose. It's not my fault I'm to the limit with oldness, my breath is all out of me, and I'm weak-boned. That's the best I can do, I can't even make another step, and that's why I lay down, I can't lift myself up. Don't whip me on the head, you might accidentally put my eye out, and then

I'll get blind, bust my eye."

But the boy kept it up, he was angry and he was crying while he's fooling around like that. It was in the afternoon, going towards evening.

9. All at once something spoke to him from above: "Leave that poor thing alone, pity your horse, I'll pity you." He raised his head, gee, he seen a beautiful horse, pretty as a picture. Gee, the saddle brand new, and the bridle, and chaps with fringe hanging on them. Complete. That beautiful horse told him: "Hurry, get on, or you'll be too late to save your brothers. They're just getting to the man-eater, and he's going to kill them, they're just about dead, or we might be in time. If you take your time they'll be dead. You keep staring at me. Let's get close to their heels. Hurry and get on."

And because it's fairy tale, then his father helped him when he first got on the horse, now he puts his foot in the stirrup and gets on. The horse told him: "Hang on tight. You don't have to guide me or whip me, I'm the one that's going to guide you. I know the way where you're going, you don't know where you're going. Hold on tight and don't get scared. I'm going through the air, right next to the sky, if we go by ground we'll be too late. Don't be uneasy, let the reins loose. You just hold on and if you get dizzy in the head, shut your eyes and keep your lids down. And when we hit the ground that's when I'll tell you what to do, if we get to your brothers in time."

The horse started rising himself, he went up in the air. It doesn't feel like his feet left the ground, the horse was weaving around, rocking from side to side, like it didn't move ahead. You can tell when a horse is running. He was going to get scared and he shut his eyes. And then all he could feel is the wind in his face. Then he tried to peek. Sure enough they were off the ground. He don't see the country, all he can see is the sky. This horse is flying. His eyes is starting to turn, then he shut his eyes tight, then he hung on, then he just shut them lightly. They went. And I don't know what time then got started, but he's way behind. And then the day started changing, the sun went down.

10. Late in the evening the horse struck the ground. He told the boy: "Put down in writing what I'm going to tell you, don't forget it. Just when you make a mistake you'll die, all of you, with your brothers. You do things in a hurry, don't waste time and also

don't forget what I'm going to preach to you. Your brothers are not dead yet. You do exactly as I tell you and you all'll pull through."

He told him: "This is a man-eater where we are getting to. Your brothers are already taken in by the man-eater. They're locked up."

"It's getting dusk, it's going to get night. We're going just a little ways and when we come in sight there'll be a house. That'll be the man-eater's, an old lady, and when we come in sight the dogs is going to bark at us, and the man-eater'll already know you're coming, these dogs are the man-eater's eyes and ears. And the old lady'll come out to meet you, she'll be tickled to see you, she'll claim you as a relative, that you're her grandson, and when you get off she'll pet you and pity you. And she'll never take her eyes off you, that man-eater, she's baiting you, she's going to kill you."

11. "She'll tell you: 'My poor grandson, you got here to me. Gee, you're traveling late, it's better that you camp. I think you're tired, you might get lost.'

"You'll tell her: 'Yes, yes, I got lost, and I didn't know where I was going, and I got scared to go on. I don't know the country and I never seen nobody to camp with, and then I seen your house, my grandmother. I don't want to travel at night in the dark. I'll camp with you and then in daytime I'll travel on.' And don't ask for your brothers, or she'll get suspicious this here man-eater."

"Then she'll give you the key, she'll point to the barn, and she'll tell you: 'See that building, the barn? I always keep it locked, because I'm afraid someone'll steal things, or they might set it afire, there's lots of horses in there, I got company, but there's room, there's one more stall that's empty. And I got feeds for horses in there, oats, hay, and there's water that you can water your horse. And when you're done fixing your horse you can come back and give me back the key. And I'll have everything cooked for you, and when you get back the table'll be set. When you get done eating and if you want to bathe you can bathe, and when you're done bathing, and I'll give you a bed. I'll tell you, you must be real tired.'"

12. And his horse told him: "Just take me to the barn, and as you open the door with this key, the birds'll start fussing, and the barn'll light up, just like the sun. When you see it, it'll blind your eyes, but you'll get used to it, and then you'll see that shining coming from the birds. When they fuss the light comes out. Them is the golden birds, that's owned by man-eaters only, and that's their

eyes and their ears, and they warn the man-eater."

13. The horse told him: "Don't pay attention to them, just put me in the barn where I'm supposed to stand. You'll see your brothers' horses, they're already in the barn, all in place, and there's one empty stall for your horse. Don't take the saddle off me. Don't take the bridle off. Leave everything as it is. Just tie me there, you're going to have quite a time getting away. That man-eater is quite fierce, and if you take the saddle off me, you won't be able to have time to put it back on me, and the bridle, and she'll be there. You're not able, but your brothers are grown, and they're smart, and they already took the saddles off. Just tie me there and don't feed me. I'll just nibble a little at the timothy hay. I want you to remember all of that."

14. "When you get back there the table is already set for you, she's got her grub on for you. She'll ask you: 'Grandchild, where's my key?' And you'll tell her: 'Well, grandma, I'm not giving it to you. Don't think anything of it. My horse was sweating too much, because I'm afraid to get too late or get lost, and I came fast, and he sweat a lot. I don't like to water him when he's sweating, and also feed him oats. It might harm him. And didn't even take the saddle off anyhow. I'll leave it on until he dries off, and then in the morning the sweat won't be dry on his body. It's hard to curry him then.'

That's what you have to tell the old lady. She'll believe you, she won't force you about the key. And if you give her the key, and how can you get away?"

15. "When you get done eating she'll say to you: 'I'll take you upstairs and I'll show you where you're going to sleep, I guess you're tired. And everything is already on, your pajamas,' she'll say. 'This is your bed and these are your pajamas.' And then the old lady'll come back down. She has her bait there, this man-eater has got four granddaughters, all virgins, and they're good looking. They all have night caps on, that's their mark, what they go by. She matches them together, the oldest one with your oldest brother, he'll get her to go to bed with; and the next one with the next woman, he'll sleep with her; and the middle one, he'll have the middle woman; and you two youngest, you'll go to bed with her. And your brothers will make lots of noise. The girls is playing with them, scratching them on their bellies, tickling them, and they're laughing, and the youngest one will play with you too."

16. Don't take your clothes off, maybe just your top clothes, pants, your top shirt, just your shoes. Go through the motions and just put your night shirt on top of your clothes. This man-eater won't know the difference. And don't make it too long."

"Just as soon as you crawl under the blanket the youngest one will take you in her arms, and she'll start kissing you, and then she'll tickle you and she'll roll around you, and she'll chew your face. She'll do everything. But it's not because she loves you, she's just faking you to put you to sleep in a hurry. And just when you fall asleep that's when the old lady comes over and kills all of you."

"You stop her, tell her: 'I'm not used to this kind of business. I've been traveling around, riding, I'm tired and I'm saddle weary, please leave me alone, I want to rest, I want to sleep.' She won't listen to you, she'll tickle your belly some more. Then you play sleep and snore, and she'll leave you alone. But do your best and don't fall asleep. If you sleep you're all goners, dead ducks, you'll all be dead. Because your brothers don't know ahead of time; but you, I pitied you, that's why I'm telling you this, and I brought you here. I am the old horse, I changed myself to back when I was young. I brought you to help them, because your brothers were all going to die, so they won't die. I know, I am acquainted with the man-eater, the old lady. I know all about it and don't dispute my word. If you dispute my word, and then you're all dead."

He got done preaching to him, and then he continued: "When she'll tickle you and she won't get no laugh out of you, then she'll be sleepy too. But watch her close."

17. "When you're sure that this woman's asleep, when she starts snoring and you push her and she won't even move, she'll keep on snoring, and all she'll do is groan, that's when you jump up easy and wake your brothers up. You tell them: 'Wake up, we're all going to die! This one is a man-eater. Change them caps, them women's caps, take them off and put them on yourselves. That might save you. And then change place with them, you lay next to the wall. You might stay alive. Don't go to sleep, pretend you're snoring, just pretend. Don't fall asleep. Because just as soon as you fall asleep you're dead. And from then on, if you're still alive I'll tell you what else to do. We might get away."

18. "And after you snore a little while, and then you'll hear the old lady come up. The lights are all out. Then the man-eater will come to the top of the steps. And then you'll see she'll be holding

a dangling lantern, it shines bright. And in the other hand she has a sword she's holding, and the first one she comes to is the oldest, because it's the first one, and she'll chop his head off, and his head'll come off its body and then the body will just quiver, jump up and down, and then it'll stop, and then the next one, the one closest to the first, that one too, she'll chop his head off. She'll do the same thing until the whole bunch is done, but it's her granchildren's she's cutting the heads off. That's why I told you what I told you, to put the caps on and to move next to the wall, and that's what the old lady goes by, the ones that's on this side, and she's been telling her grandchildren, 'Be sure and sleep next to the wall and keep the caps on, the ones that's on this side, them is the ones I kill.'"

"And then she'll go back downstairs."

19. "That's when you jump up, and tell your brothers: 'Run! All your clothes, your coats, and your hats, you know where they are, put all that on, and then run out. Don't forget anything.' You're the youngest one, and you're slow, and that's why I told you not to take your clothes off, just your shoes, then you'll just slip your shoes on, and they probably have boots on, that's got sharp heels, the ones with the high top, that's what we call in our language nusustíp‌xən, and in English *boots*. Then just as soon as you get down you'll do your best to get to the barn. Because you kept the key, you little one. Then you open the barn door, then them chickens will make noise, it'll shine, you'll be blinded, you'll tell them, 'Don't get puzzled, hurry up, put your saddles on, we might be saved yet.' And these here big boys they can go fast when they put the saddle on, but you're the youngest, you're helpless, if you had to put the saddle on you'd be slow."

"And just when you're coming out of the barn and you are on horses, that's when the old lady'll come out. Just after their heads was cut off, you'll run down and you'll be too noisy, and the old lady'll be right there, 'What's the matter, how is it, I had their heads cut off, and here they run down the stairs? There's something the matter.'"

That's what the horse told him, and that's what happened. The boys ran downstairs.

20. The old lady heard them run downstairs. And she got puzzled. And she thought: "What's the matter, since I come to my senses, since I become man-eater, nobody ever did that to me, and to my

grandchildren. I never did get ghosted like that before. There is something the matter."

She lit the lamp, she went downstairs. The boys are gone, the caps was lying around. Her grandchildren. "I sure did myself wrong. I killed my grandchilren by mistake. They can't go far, they'll be saddling their horses, I'll overtake them there, I'll clean them up."

She rushed over. Just when she was getting there, they were already on horses, coming out of the barn. They just waved good bye to the old lady, they're gone.

21. They started, and they didn't go far, it wasn't even a whole day, that they come in sight. They seen something like a town, they got close and they made it out, yes, it's a town. They went through the town. Gee, lots of people, it's a big town and it's white people that stays there, they said: "It must be white people."

Everybody was looking, they was puzzled with them, they look so much alike and they know they must be brothers, their father must be important people, the expensive clothes they had, and their horses, their saddles, their whole outfits.

Then the oldest one asked one of the white men, the one that he came close to, "Where's the king's house?" The oldest one put himself first to do the talking, and they answered him, "Over there, across the street, the big house, the high building. That's the king's house, it's written on the door."

They walked on the sidewalk, the oldest one took the lead and the rest of them followed, and the youngest one is way behind, trying to keep up. They got right to the door, sure enough there was a sign on the door of the boss's house. They knocked on the door.

22. Somebody came out to meet them, the king opened the door for them. They asked: "Are you the chief?" "Yes, I am the king," and he told them: "Come on in." And they came in. He put chairs on the floor for them to sit down. Then he said: "You must be important. Just by your clothes I can tell. Your father is important people." They told him, "Yes, that's right," and they named the place of their country, maybe Kewa, not Inchelium. They named a big place. "And our boss is truly a great king. We're all his children. And now we finished school, and we don't know anything about work. We learned all from the books, because we're the king's children, and that's why they never teached us work. And we told our father: 'Well, father, we're leaving you.' And our father asked

us, 'And where are you going and leave me? You don't know the country, you're going to hit it hard.' We told him: 'We don't know, we're just going to travel around the country.' And he said to us: 'I always respect your feelings, and now you feel that way. I always baby you around.' And we told him: 'That's why we're leaving you, we're not mad about anything. Now we've graduated, and all what you teached us at school, all we know is just reading. Work, they don't teach us that, because we're the king's sons. When we get aways from here we're going to look for a job, and we'll learn how to work.' And he told us: 'All right, you've got a good plan, I'm not trying to get rid of you.' And then we got here. And we want to work."

23. The oldest one was next to the king, and the king asked him: "You must be the oldest one." He said "Yes." "What is your business? Tell me, and I'll know about it, and I'll give you an answer. I'm just going to ask you, I'm not going to do your thinking, I'm just going to ask you what you want to do for a job." And the oldest one said: "Well, building houses is what I want to work at." The king said: "OK, I'll get you work." Then he took some paper and wrote. He wrote and then he signed his name and put it right in his hand. He told him: "Way over there across the street, that's where the boss of the carpenters is, it's got a sign on the door, that's the carpenter. You give him this letter, and he'll look at it, and he'll know that I sent you and he'll tell you: 'Yeah, you'll get the job.'" And the oldest one left.

24. And then he said to the other one, the next to the oldest one: "Now you. What is your business?" And he told the boss: "My business'll be just the same as my big brother. I just want a job. I don't know anything, but I'd like to teach myself." And the king said: "And what would you like to work at?" And he said: "Well, I wished I could do house-building, and you know, you're the boss, two persons can't do the same thing, it's just got to be just one to be the boss. So I'll take what's close to house-building, house painting. Because look, whenever you finish a new house, or a barn, then the painter has to go to work and paint it, it ain't the carpenter that does the painting. Only when they get hard-up for a painter will they paint."
The king said: "All right." Then he wrote a note and gave it to him. He said: "Way over there there's a house, there's a sign on the door, that's my boss for the painters. You just give it to him,

and when he looks at it he'll know that I sent you over there. And he'll give you your job. He'll tell you: 'You get the job. Report tomorrow, right now it's too late.' I suppose that's what he'll tell you, and then you'll go where they show you to camp." Then he went out and left.

25. Then he told the in-between one, he said: "Now you, what's your business?" He said: "Just the same as my brothers. I like to work. I don't know anything, but surely I'll learn, anybody shows me." The king said, "OK, tell me." He said: "Well, the oldest one took the house-building job, and the next one took the house-painting job, and I wish I had the carpenter job or the painting job. And it's a pity that I'm the youngest and then these oldest ones got first choice. They took them. And it can't be two of us working at the same job, because our father is a king, and when we get back he'll ask us, 'What did you learn?' and I'll tell him, after my brothers will tell their story first, then I come next, then he'll ask me, and if I tell him the painting or the carpenter work, then there'll be two on a job, and that won't be no good. It's better that we scatter what we learn. I'll take the blacksmith job. That's my job."

The king said "OK," he wrote, and gave it to him, and said: "Way to the other end of town there's an open place, and that's where he is. Because there's lots of room there, and the blacksmith's never clean. He's always having freight come in, and there's always hired people, and that's why he's at the other end. There's a wide place that there's nothing on. You give this to him, and when he sees it he'll know that I sent you, and he'll give you a job." And the in-between one left.

26. There's just the youngest one left, because as soon as they take the paper they go out, they go hunt their job, the king asked him, "You, the youngest one, are you the youngest one?" "Yes." "Well, what do you want for a job?" He told the king: "You see me, I'm not strong enough, I'm little and I got no sense, you said I was the youngest." The king said to him: "That's true, and like I told you, I'm going to ask you what job you'll be satisfied with, and whatever work you'll be satisfied with you're going to learn. That's why I asked your brothers first, and then you come next, and you've been listening all this time when I'm asking your brothers." The littlest one said: "Well, you can see that I'm very small, I'm the youngest one, and I don't come near to the heavy work, I'd like to

go to the cook house. I'll turn to that. And I can wash dishes, or set the table, or pack water, or get wood. A job in the kitchen, that's what I want for a job. Dishwashing."

The king said "All right." And he wrote, and gave it to him, and said: "Over there where I eat, that's where the boss of the cooks stays. You give him this paper, and he'll look at it, and he'll understand that I sent you over, and then he'll give you your job." And he went out.

27. Well, the boys gathered, they overtook one another. They just got one house, the four of them. And there's a bathroom there, a clothes-cupboard, they all had beds, each their own, all in one room for the four of them, they have a setting room, the beds are all by themselves. They got acquainted with where they're supposed to eat, they ate, they got done eating. Then their boss, the one they work for told them: "I'm the boss. How long are you going to stay if you're satisfied with your jobs?" And they told him: "One year. Not quite one year. Until the time comes close to the day when we got here. That's when we'll go back. Because we promised our father, and our father is a boss. We're the king's sons." And he named the country where they were from.

The boss said "OK, it will be so." And then he told the three oldest ones: "Don't work today, it's getting late. And I don't think you know how to work. Tomorrow. Now rest, tomorrow you go to work. Then go back to where you're supposed to stay, and you wait for the bell. Just when the bell rings that's when you'll eat. And then you go to the dining room. You go there and eat, get done eating, then you'll go back to your house. When you get sleepy go to bed. Tomorrow morning, just when it's time for the bell, it'll ring for eating time, and just as soon as you're done eating you'll go to your jobs. And then you work, don't take your time, don't take your time."

But this here the littlest one, the little boy, his boss told him, the cook: "You'll be the last one. When the working men get done eating, then you wash the dishes. And you got to take your time before you wash the dishes, but you can pack wood for tomorrow. I get up awful early, because I'm the cook. I make a fire and the stove gets warm, and then you don't have to pack wood, you've already packed wood in the evening, and you've already packed water, you've finished. And don't worry. Just when the bell rings you'll eat, you can follow them to go eat. But when you get done eating you start work. You'll be the last in the evening to get done. You won't be with these other workers. Now you know." And the little boy said "Yes."

28. Daylight comes, and they all scattered and went to their bosses. They told them: "You go ahead and work now." And when evening comes, when the day is ended, they get together again to their house. They washed their face, they took a bath, they changed, they waited for the bell. They're together. The bell rang. They went to the dining room, it's just the same, they ate at one table, gathered there, they got done eating. Then the oldest ones went back, but not the youngest one. He put his apron on, gathered the dishes and washed them. He washed, got done washing, he packed wood. Packed wood, packed water, got done packing water, his boss told him: "You're done for now, for today. Don't come early. You already got done with your work. Just wait for the bell, and when the bell rings I have everything set on the table, it's time to eat and you'll come. You'll eat with the rest of the working men, but when they get done eating, then it's time for you to go to work. You gather and wash dishes."

29. When the three oldest brothers get home after they get done eating, they go to their bunks, and then they rest. They tell what happened to them, what they learned. They say: "Now we're going to get used to what we're learning, our work. We're satisfied."

But this here little fellow he's still gone, because he's still washing dishes and packing wood. When he's done washing dishes in the evening, that's when his job is over.

Well, the oldest ones got envious of their little brother. The oldest one thought of something and he said: "He must be very powerful our little brother. He's very small, and the youngest one, and then he's smart. He saved our lives from the man-eater." They didn't even get pleased that he saved their lives, their little brother. And then they envied him.

The oldest one continued: "It's not for nothing, and he's just a young kid, and he brought us through that trouble, and the man-eater didn't kill us. And when we get back to our parents, and we tell them about our troubles, and then it's the youngest, our little brother that's the smartest. He'll be smarter than us. Our father is going to understand that the youngest one is the smartest at what we learned." The oldest one got jealous, he put himself lower. And he asked his brothers: "This is what I've been thinking, and what about you, what do you think?"

He repeated and his brothers said: "That's true, that's true, if he thinks that way, our father." And they never thought, they never appreciated if it wasn't for their little brother that saved them, they would be killed by the man-eater. They didn't see ahead of them. If their little brother hadn't caught up with them, they'd be dead. They just got jealous. And then they said to the oldest one: "Maybe you got something figured out. It's a pity you're the oldest one, whatever you think we'll stand behind you."

He said: "That's why I asked your opinion."

30. He continued: "It's better that we do away with him. We'll lie about him, and he'll be dead, and when we get back our parents'll miss him, and we'll tell them: 'Maybe he died, he never got to us. We've been together, and when our school [our ap-prenticeship] was out we come home. Our partner was gone, our little brother. We don't know.' That's the lie we're going to tell."

And then they started planning, and they got a plan. And the oldest one said: "We're going to send him back to that man-eater's, where we camped, at the old lady's. And I bet that the old lady is really mad at us because we killed her grandchildren. It's our fault that her grandchildren got killed, that she killed her grand-children by mistake. Oh boy. She sure must be mad at us. And just as soon as she finds out about this boy, because it's him, and she knows it, it's not for nothing she's a man-eater, she knows that it's that boy's smartness that we got saved, I bet she'll kill him. And then our minds will be settled, after we do away with our little brother."

And then their hearts got together, they agreed. "That's good thinking we done, that's what we'll do."

31. The oldest one took the paper and he started writing. He wrote, he got done writing and then he signed it with his little brother's name. And this is what he wrote to the king, he told the boss: "Dear King, I'm your working man, maybe you wish for this here man-eater's chickens, golden chickens. And if you want them I'll get them for you. That's why I'm writing this to you." And then he signed his name. And this here the little fellow he don't know nothing, he never heard nothing.

Then he read to his brothers what he wrote, and they told him: "What you wrote is good." They agreed. He put the letter in the envelope, and just when he got done sealing it their little brother come in. He had got done. The oldest brother gave it to him and told him: "We're tired, I'm tired. And I wrote a letter to the king and I'm too tired to deliver it to him. But you're the youngest, you deliver this letter to the chief." And the little boy went to deliver the letter to the chief.

32. The little boy went, and he got right up to the door of the king's house. He knocked on the door, they opened the door for him. "Come in." Then he went in. He said: "What is your business?" And he told him: "I'm delivering this letter to you," and he gave it to him, "because I am working, and I haven't got the time to deliver the mail in the morning. And now as soon as I got done, I delivered it to you."

Then he turned around to go out, but the boss told him: "Just a minute, til I get done looking at this letter, and then maybe you can go back." The boy stopped, the chief tore it open, he looked at it until he come to the end. And then the king told the little boy: "Is it true what you wrote in this letter? You wrote it to me, your name is down. You are asking me if I want the man-eater's (he named the place) power, the man-eater's golden birds. And then if I want it you're going to go after it." The boy never said nothing. But he thought: "My brothers is feeding me to him." And then the chief told him: "Yes, you're going to do a great deal for me, I've heard about the man-eater's birds. And I've always wanted it, I've never heard a bird being a-gold. You can go after it to-morrow."

The little boy went back. He went right to the barn.

33. He was still crying when he got to his horse. He was petting his horse, and crying at the same time, and then his horse asked him: "Well, my master, what are you feeling bad about? Did you hear from your folks, did any of your relatives die, or one of your parents?"

The little boy said: "No, no, I'm the one that's going to die." "And what happened to you, you are alive and you're dead?"

The little boy went on: "My brothers lied about me. I think it's the oldest one. They wrote to the king, and they signed my name. He told me to bring something to the king, a letter, and then I delivered it, and I just gave it to the king, and I was coming back, and I never thought it was my letter. Then the king stopped me, he told me: 'Wait a minute, when I see this letter and understand

-34-

it, I might answer it. And you'll deliver it back.' Then I waited
for him, and he opened it, and read it, and then told me: 'Yeah,
I always wished for them man-eater's birds, I didn't think I could
ever get them, because it isn't for nothing that they call him
man-eater. Now you tell me you'll go after them. Thank you, I'd
like them. Yeah, I like them. Go after them for me.' And that's
why I'm feeling bad."

"And even if I did tell on my brothers, there's three of them, I'm
alone, and besides I'm the youngest one. They're going to get the
best of me."

34. The horse told him: "Do you still got the key to the barn?"
"Yes, I got it." "That's just what I told you, to keep it and not
give it back to the old lady. That key is going to do you some good.
It's going to save your life."

The horse continued: "Those chickens are the man-eater's eyes,
and lets her know when there's danger. When they make lots of
noise and when they shine. When they see anything then the
man-eater goes after it. That's when she murders. But make your
feelings good, we'll go after them."

"But I'm going to tell you. You do what I tell you and that'll do
you good, it'll not harm you. But just as soon as you don't do what
I tell you, if you miss, then that'll harm you, death'll come to you."

The horse spoke on: "She's feeling pretty bad right now, for the
death, for the killing, that is, of her grandchildren. Because that's
her bait when she gets company from somebody. They play with
their visitor until he goes to sleep, and then the man-eater takes
her time killing the visitor."

"We'll go right straight to the barn. That's where the golden
chickens roost. You've seen it. I'll bring you over, don't guide me,
and don't fix your reins and bridle. Stay on the horse. Have the
key out. Stick the key in, and open the door. The birds'll start
squealing, but hurry, don't fool around, don't fuss with anything,
don't bother with me, I know what to do. You stand on my back
on the saddle, because you can't reach if you stay sitting on the
saddle. But if you stand you'll reach them just right. All you have
to do is grab them by their feet. Then get back on the saddle.
The minute you straddle it, you'll have them each in each hand.
Separate them, one bird on one side, and the other bird on the
other side of the horse. I'll turn around and go out. About that
time I'll be out. The birds'll be screaming and hollering. She'll hear

them and she'll run out, she'll hold her weapon, her sword. If you take your time we'll get caught, she'll stand right in the door and she'll kill us. But if we get out there's nothing she can do. She can't chase us, and even if she does chase us, she can't overtake us. And when we get out of sight I'll rise from the ground. You're used to it. And we'll go right next to the sky, between the clouds and the sky."

"That's what I preach to you. Now go on, go to bed. Be satisfied, don't feel bad any more about it. Have faith."

The little boy went back and went to bed.

35. The next morning the little boy went to get his horse. He saddled him up, got on. The barn man asked him: "What you gonna do?" And he said: "I'm just going for a ride, my horse is tired from doing nothing. I"ll be back after a while."

After they got out of sight the horse went up in the air. Right next to the sky. And they went.

Then the horse landed. Just a few steps and the horse got in sight of the barn. He got close to the door, the boy took the key out of his pocket, stuck it in and opened the door, put it back in his pocket, opened the door.

Gee, the birds started making lots of noise. The horse went right straight, stopped. He stood on his back, grabbed them by their legs, the hen in one hand and the rooster in the other. Got down on the saddle, twisted his horse around, they ran out. And the chickens were screaming and hollering.

Gee, the old lady heard and she ran out, she was holding a lamp and a sword. She ran out and she was half way when that horse run out of the barn. And the horse was shining and the birds squealing. The horse started running and then it got out of sight. The lady couldn't do a thing to run after them. The horse got out of sight and then he rose from the ground. He was flying. He went and got back to town.

36. He landed out of sight. The little boy went back to the barn, gave his horse back to the barn-man and told him: "Take care of my horse." Gee, the man that worked there saw what he was holding. Gee, it looks just like gold the way they shine, it's great, and he got puzzled. He thought: "He stole them. He must have stole them for the king, not for himself. Maybe the king sent him out. I'm not going to report on him."

The little boy went to the king. He went in, gave him the birds and told him: "This is what you've been wishing for, what you sent me for." Gee, the king was frightened to look at the chickens, they shine so even lamps don't come near it. They are truly golden birds.

The little boy turned around, went out. He went to the kitchen to lick plates again.

37. And that's fairy tales for you, it travels fast and it's got no feet, and his brothers already know over at the bunk house. "Our little brother already got those golden birds. And we lied about it." They sure got disgusted. They got more angry at him. "Well, we'll sure be ashamed when we tell the story about ourselves. Our little brother is way above us of being smart." And they never think, "Our little brother saved our lives."

Then the oldest one said: "We've got to think up something else. We just got to kill him. We just got to figure out how to kill him before we're satisfied." And his brothers said: "Yes, because he's going to embarrass us when we get home. He's the youngest and he's smarter than us older ones." And then they said: "Well, you're the oldest, you do the thinking. Maybe you already got something thought up, and we'll stand behind you."

The oldest one said: "Yes, I've got something thought up. Close to the shore of the big lake, the water that goes plum around the earth, the ocean, like they say in English, there's one place, only one place," and he named the place, "where the Golden Woman comes up. And it isn't very often that people sees the Golden Woman."

"I am going to write to the king again, I'm going to misinterpret our little brother, and I'm going to tell the king: 'If you like the Golden Woman, and if you wish to have her for your wife, I'll go after her for you.'" Because the king ain't got no wife, and even if he did have a wife, he's white man, and he can get a divorce. They told him, "Yes, yes, your thinking is good." They all agreed. And the oldest one started writing, he wrote, he addressed to the king.

In the evening when he finished washing dishes, the little boy got back. The oldest one gave him the letter and told him, "This is what I wrote to the king. You bring it to him for me. I'm too tired. You're the youngest, and you're not tired when you wash dishes."

And he never disputes his kind's, his big brother's word. He started packing mail, got to be a mail-carrier. He went over to the king, and gave him the letter. He was going to turn around and come back, but the king told him: "Wait a minute til I'm done reading this letter. I'm going to answer it." He tore it open and he looked. It's the little boy that signed it.

And the note said: "Maybe you've heard about this here big water, and about the Golden Woman. If you want her I'll go after it for you. It's a pity that I'm working for wages, and I'll go after anything you want." The king repeated what's in the letter: "That's what you said." No, he never said it. But he wouldn't tell on his brothers. And he wasn't sure that his brothers has written that. And the king said: "I've heard about the Golden Woman. Go ahead, go after her. Go get her for me." The boy went out.

38. The little boy cried and cried, and then he went to see his horse aagain. He got to his horse, and petted him, petted him. And he cried and sobbed. Then his horse asked him: "Now what are you feeling bad about, did you hear somebody from your parents died?" And the little boy told him: "No, I'm just feeling bad because my brothers misinterpreted me. They wrote to the king and then they told him that I said that I can go after the Golden Woman for him."

Then the horse told him: "Well, don't feel bad. People always takes a chance. We'll take a chance." And then he thought: "Now I'll preach to him."

He said: "There's one thing I'm going to tell you. Tomorrow you'll take four hankerchiefs. One blue, and one yellow, and one black, and another one red. And when you get there, right next to the ocean, you just look at the sky at night when the weather is fixing the day, and whatever color the weather in the sky is, take the handkerchief that's the same color and put it right on the shore, just a little ways from the water, where you think she'll get out of the water."

"That's what you've got to watch. When you're sure that she's complete out of the water (if her little toe or anything is even a little wet in the water you can't get her), when her whole body is out a little ways from the water, then you might by accident keep her. I'll give you the strength." And then he told him: "Easen your mind, go to bed. Tomorrow you'll rustle those handkerchiefs, and then we'll go." The little boy went, and he got back, and went to bed.

39. The next daylight he got the handkerchiefs. And then he went and got his horse. He put the saddle on, he got on. Towards the

evening the horse flew. Right next to the sky, that's where he went. That's when they made airplanes. They went, and it got evening, and then they struck the ground. Close to the ground he seen the water, the big water, water as far as you can see. And he doesn't see the other side. It's all water. "Well, I guess maybe that's the ocean."

Then the horse told the little boy: "Now we're here. Just do what I told you. Do your best. We might get her yet. This is out of sight, tie me here." Then the boy went, and just when he got to the shore the sun was going down. The weather fixed the sky. It was blue. The boy went and got the blue handkerchief. He put it right next to the shore. He put rocks on the corners to weigh it down, so the wind won't blow it away. And he sat down there.

In a little while something come out of the water, the woman. Gee, it shined, it shined all over the water. That was the Golden Woman. She's handsome. And her hair shines bright, just like money. She said: "Little boy, you sure got the prettiest handkerchief. Please pity me and give it to me." The boy told her: "I guess you're stuck on it. I like the handkerchief, but you can have it. You go after it, I'm not going to hand it to you, because if I get my feet wet I'll catch cold. I'm not going to wade in the water. I'm dead scared of the water. And maybe some of those little animals in the water might grab me."

The woman come closer, and she kept on a-begging: "Please bring it to me." "No, I told you no, if you like it, you come and get it. But I'm not going to give it to you. I don't like the water, I'm dead scared of the water."

Closer, closer, closer, closer, closer, to the shore. And she started walking. One foot is on the dry land and she started walking. She still keeps a-begging for it, and he still says no. Well, she's on dry land. And the boy thought: "She's all out of the water, nothing is touching in the water." But her little toe nail is, that's still in the water.

She got the handkerchief. He jumped and grabbed the woman. She jumped back, he dropped her. She got in the water, she's gone.

And that happed again with the yellow handkerchief, and it happened again with the black handkerchief. And the yellow hand-kerchief meant _____ weather, and the black handkerchief meant stormy weather. The Golden Woman slipped away.

40. And then the boy just hated his horse. "My horse didn't mean

it, he lied to me. Now I'm a goner, a dead duck. He lied to me."
He went to his horse, he took a stick and he beat his horse all over
his body, and even on the head. He sure must have had a quick
temper, this boy.

The horse tried to stop him: "I am pityful." And the boy told him:
"Why, I was going to die. You lied to me. Now I am going to die.
The Golden Woman got away from me again." And the horse told
him: "It isn't my fault, it's you. I told you to see that she's
completely out of the water, and then you can grab her. But her
little toe still had water on. And that's where her power comes
from, the water. Well, she drawed herself back, and you grabbed
your own hands, and she's gone." And the boy is still licking his
horse, hitting him on the head. And then the horse ran away.

When his horse got out of sight that's when the little boy come
to himself. "I'm disgusted with myself, it's all caused from my bad
temper that put me in bad. My horse left me because I licked him.
Now I'm disgusted of myself. What'll I do to get back? And even
if I get back I haven't got that woman. And my boss'll kill me, what
I promised him didn't come true." He cried, and cried, and he
started walking around.

41. He was walking around, and he got on a good track, and then
it started to rain. It rained and the wind blowed close to the shore,
and there were waves. It was on a good track, and he ran into
some baby eagles, just hatched, two of them. They didn't have a
feather on their body. They was just a-shivering from the cold.
He felt sorry for them. He started to gather pine needles, anything
to make a fire, and he started building a fire for the baby chicks,
the eagle babies. And they got warmed up.

42. All at once he heard something. It was the mother bird, a
woman. At first she got scared, then she come around. He got her
quieted down. Then they heard another one, and that's the father,
a man. He got more scared than her. He went around, finally he
got there, he landed. The eagles are tickled to get acquainted.
They told him: "Thank you for saving our children. We did our best
to get back from another country when the storm come, that's when
we tried our best to get back. And we didn't get here in time."

"And if it wasn't for you they'd have froze to death. You made
fire for them." And they asked him: "And what is your trouble?
There's no people here, there's just you that's people. You're the
only one that we see, and you saved our children. You must have

business here, there must be something you want for your business."

Then the boy told them: "They lied about me, my brothers lied to the king about what I said. That's my whole business. And the king sent me to get that Golden Woman. And my horse told me what to do. That's my power, my horse. And that's why I sat by the shore when the weather paints the sky, and I put the handkerchief on the ground, and I thought she was completely out of the water, that the whole body was out of the water, because that's what the horse told me. I jumped and grabbed her, but I didn't catch her. I just grabbed my own hands together. And she disappeared in the big water with the handkerchiefs. I'll never get another chance for her."

43. The eagles asked him: "Have you got another handkerchief?" And he said: "Yes, I've got another one." They said: "Well, we'll help you, because we was thankful. Don't put your whole hope in it, but just have a little hope. It's not for sure. She's invincible the Golden Woman. She's smart. She's a man-eater in the water. The water is her country.

They went on: "We're going to preach to you just like your horse did. You have to be sure that she's completely out of the water before you grab her. And then you can hold her. But if the water is touching a little bit in her body, because that's her power in the water, you can't do nothing. And this is what we're going to help you with, with your strength. If you can get her away from the water, we can stop her. But if you did like the first times, let on her toe nail just a little drop of water, that's her power, and you wouldn't have no show, and she's gone."

They got done telling him what to do. He agreed. The sun just went past noon. It quit raining.

The storm is over, and the sky is painted for a red hot weather. And that's red. And that's what's left, what he's keeping, the red handkerchief. The sky reported the weather signs, and it's red.

So he spread the red handkerchief close to the shore. In just a little while the Golden Woman came to the top of the water. She said: "Well, little boy, you've got a very pretty handkerchief. Give it to me." He told her: "I'm kind of stingy of it, but being you're stuck on it, come after it. I'm not going to hand it to you."

She came closer, and kept a-begging him to walk in the water. The boy told her: "For you it's easy to say, that's your country, and you're not scared of the water. You come after it."

Well, she got on dry land. This time he's sure she's complete out of the water, because he took it farther. Even if she stretched her leg she wouldn't reach. She's entirely away from the water before she can reach the handkerchief. She got to the handkerchief.

He jumped, he mocked the eagles, and he grabbed this woman. He caught hold of her. The woman tried to squirm around, but it's just like a vise. Because she's away from the water, from her power. She squirmed around but it didn't do no good. No. Because she's away from her power.

44. Then she started a-begging the boy. She said: "Please have pity on me and let me go." And he told her, "No, I'm not going to let you go. I came after you. I'm not going to let go of you unless we go a little ways off from the water, and then I'll let go of you." And then the Golden Woman went along. He had her hooked on the arm.

They went a little ways from the water and then they sat down. He said: "Now we're settled down, we'll talk things over." And then he played white man, and he was holding this woman's hands, hooked on the arms. And that's when the woman asked him: "And what for do I come in your business for you to take me?" And he told her: "I got a boss that sent me, a king. I didn't think I could make it, and it's a pity that I work for him, and that's why I had to come. I'm not qualified for nothing. I just took a chance and come after you. The king sent me, and I'm going to take you."

She said: "OK, I'll go back with you because you already got me. But since the world was made, there is no people or nothing ever that caught hold of me. And then you got me. Maybe it isn't for nothing. We just as well get married. You're the one that took me. You and I will get married." And this boy is good looking, I guess these eagles dolled him up.

But he said: "No, I'm working, I got a boss for my job." And she asked him: "And how old is the king?" He said: "He might be half, not too young, not too old." And she said: "Even if he is a king, he's getting too much old, he's already reached the old age, and you're just now commencing to grow, and I'm going to love you better. Let me think about if we can get married you and I."

And the Golden Woman thought: "He isn't for nothing, this little fellow is something to grow for, or he wouldn't have caught me. And these other people, they don't even touch my arm, but this here outstanding kid got me. He must be smart." She got stuck on that boy.

THE GOLDEN WOMAN

The boy's mind is settled. They went, and they got back.

45. They went over to the king's house. When they come in sight, they seen the boy coming, gee, the company he has was great, straight and great, shining, just like the sun, that must be the Golden Woman. All her body was shining, and her hair, just like gold. She's good looking.

They got right to the door of the king's house, he knocked on the door, the king opened the door for them, and it shined in his eyes. "That's the same boy, that must be the Golden Woman." The boy asked him: "Is this what you want, what you sent me for, this here Golden Woman?" Gee, but the king was surely glad, he said: "Well, well, thanks." And the little boy said: "Well, I'm done with my job. Now I'll go back to my house, I'm hungry and tired, it's a long trip where I've been traveling to get what I went after." Then he turned around and went to the kitchen to lick plates, because he was hungry.

46. The king was really surprised and glad because he got the Golden Woman. He gave her a place to stay. She got a beautiful room, her place to stay, it has a bed, and a bath, everything complete. Then the king told the Golden Woman: "I've heard about you, and that's why I sent for you, and now that I see you, I am a well-satisfied king. And now we'll get married. I'll invite people to come in, and then we'll get married. People are always gathering, my kind of people, kings, my children, everybody."

47. The Golden Woman said to him: "Yes, that's what we're going to do. But first I'm going to tell you one thing. Have you got any chickens, birds that are different?" "Yes. What kind of birds?" "A rooster and a hen. They got to be a pair, and they're different from other birds. Golden. Other chickens don't shine like gold." "Yes."

Then she told him: "You ask the people to come, kings from all tribes, and everybody, and when they gather together in one place, that's the time when you take those birds out, you set them on the table (there's a place for them to set on), and you tell all those people and all the kings, 'Now these chickens are going to tell the story.'"

And then she said: "And when they get done telling about themselves, and then I'll get married with the one I'm supposed to marry. And then we give a big dance. We'll take cigars, we'll smoke. Or we'll drink liquor."

That's what the Golden Woman told him, and how's the king going to refuse what she asks? His thoughts went high. He had everything he wanted, and he had the birds. The king agreed.

48. The evening when he put the date down, he told all the telephone operators: "You telephone operators, you telephone to all the kings like me here on earth, and the important people, they'll get here also. And you send an invitation to all those around here. There's no old or young. Everybody is going to gather here tonight."

Before evening the people started coming in from far away, maybe on airplanes, because this here boy's been flying around on his horse, his horse's been flying around. Well, the people gathered and gathered. A little after dark everybody was in.

49. And the cook thought of it, and then he told his dishwasher, this here boy: "This evening everybody is gathering, and they're asking us to the boss's house. The birds are going to tell stories, and just when the golden birds are done telling their story, then the king is going to get married, the Golden Woman is the one he'll have for his woman. And then they'll shake hands and then they'll give each of us a cigar, or else they'll give us liquor. And then we'll jump up and down, we'll dance. And he wants everybody, everybody beside kings, young people and elders, and you. And I guess the chiefs from all over the world are already gathered in, and you're just standing there. Get ready, quit working, let's get ready and go."

And the dishwasher told his boss, the cook: "Oh, no, I'm pityful, and look how dirty I am, I'm too ugly to go there." And his boss coaxed him, and told him: "Wash your face, doll up." And the dishwasher said: "And if I just wash my face, what good will I get out of it, I'm dirty in the body, and I ain't got no clothes. You go now, I just want to lick plates." That's the only work he likes, licking plates.

And then the cook went, he dolled up and went to watch the people and listen to the birds' story.

50. And it's way after dark, and the crowd quit coming in, and the house is packed full of people, kings and common people, the king's house is big. And then the king told them: "I asked you all people here, my kind, the kings, the rest of you people, everybody. Right now I'm going to get married, and this one is going to be my wife." They looked at her, she's nothing but shine, she's a true Golden Woman, even her hair is shining. And the king continued:

"But the one who's going to be my wife said for me to take these birds out, and now I'll set them down here, and they're going to tell a story about themselves."

They sure were puzzled the people, "And what's them birds going to talk about in front of the kings?" And then the king asked: "Now are you sure everybody is here? You kings, and then you my people around here, little boys or old men, old ladies or little girls, everybody. These birds are going to tell the story, and I want everybody to hear these here my golden birds." They said: "Yeah, yeah, we're all here."

51. Then the cook thought of it and said: "That's right, it was my worker, my plate licker that I coaxed for nothing. I got a worker, a boy, and I asked him to come, but no, he didn't want to leave his work, he got stingy of it and of his eatings, because he's licking plates. And he thinks it's too much to get ready, and he says his clothes is dirty, and he's too dirty, he hasn't taken a bath, he's not fresh. He said: 'No, it's not for me that the king asked people to come.'"

Then the king sent the sheriffs, two of them, and he told them: "You go get him, and if he refuses, grab him by both his arms, tie him up and bring him here. I said everybody, boys, old men, old ladies, girls."

Then the ones that tie up people run out; they got to where the boy is. They told him: "The king wants you. Why is it that you're not there?" He said: "Look, I'm too dirty." And they said: "That ain't nothing. The king said clothes don't count, even the age doesn't, no matter how young or old. Everybody is going to listen good, because he's going to get married. Look he's our chief. We got to be there."

The little boy just turned around away from them, he said: "No, it's not for me, I'm too ugly to be in front of the king or of the people, he'll get ashamed of me, I'm just his working boy. I'm not going." They grabbed him by the arms, he tried to squirm around, they walked off with him.

They brought him over, and they already got a chair there for him to sit down on, right close to the king, and the table was right there, right in the center, in between them. The Golden Woman and the king on one side, and the boy on the other side. And they'll set the birds right there, the rooster and the hen. They told the boy: "Sit down right there on that chair."

The king recognized him: "Oh, that's the boy that was the little brother of them workers. And then I asked him what he wants for a job and he said 'I'm too small, I'll go to the kitchen.' And he got the birds for me, and he's the one that got the Golden Woman too."

The Golden Woman recognized him too, "That's the boy that took me." And then she was satisfied, she likes the boy. And she thought: "I guess it isn't for nothing. He must be powerful, that's why he caught me. He must be powerful and smart even as young as he is. And this here chief is a king all right, but I won't get nothing out of him, he's too old. I'll go for this young boy."

Then they were all settled down. They said: "That's all of us."

52. Then the king opened the trunk and he set the birds down, the rooster on one end of the table, and the hen at the other. And they look exactly like this woman, they're gold, and the shine, they shine all over their body, they're golden chickens. Then the king said: "OK, you're going to tell a story about yourselves, that's why I called you."

The rooster was puzzled, and he asked his wife the hen, he told her: "Go ahead, you tell your story." And the woma told him: "No, you tell them about yourself, you speak, because you're a man. I'm just a woman, I'm not going to put myself ahead to tell the story." And the rooster said: "No, we're white people, I'll let you go first, you're woman. I'll put myself behind because I'm a man." And the woman told him: "No. The white man's way is that the man does the business, figgers out everything. The woman just does the house work. It's the man that does all the work for the eats, and for money to buy groceries. The woman never makes it their business, she just does the house work, cooks, washes, or cleans the house. That's all a woman does. They never put a woman boss. You go ahead, you're the leader, you're the head of the family, you do the talking and tell about yourself."

She talked him into it, and he said: "OK, OK, if that's what you think." And then he started to tell his story.

53. Then the rooster said: "OK, you told me to tell a story about myself. I'll tell you my story right from my country." Then he named the place from where he came, and where his parents live. He said: "That's where I was raised. And my elders, my father is a chief, big shot chief. My brothers are already big, and I'm the youngest one."

"When I came to my senses, got to thinking, and I seen my brothers, three of them, all boys, and my father and mother, and

I got to know them. And when I come to my senses I went to school, and they teached me, but I never did keep up with my brothers, I'm the youngest, and I couldn't keep up with the books to learn. But my brothers, they finished all the books, they learned them. Like they say in English they graduated, they finished school. And they went to see their father." And the rooster told the story with all the details.

54. *(2) They told their father: "Father, we've finished our school, and all we know is books. But if we travel around the country and look for a job, maybe we'll learn work. We're leaving you. We'll learn work, and then exactly one year from now, if we're still alive we'll come back." And their father consented...*

(3) He sent his working man to get the best horses and everything...

(4) And he gave them each plenty of money...

And the the rooster'd stop talking and ask the hen: "Am I telling it right?" And the hen said: "Yes, you're telling it right. That's just what you done." And then the rooster talked some more.

(5) The youngest boy wants to go along, but he's too young, and the king tells him no...

(6) But the chief's wife told her man: "Pity him, give him an old horse, and a few pennies, and he'll be happy. He'll ride around for a while, and get tired, and then come back..."

(7) And the chief thought that was good thinking, and he went along. He gave him an old horse, and a few pennies...

(8) And the boy got on his horse, that could hardly move, and slowly they walked away until they got out of sight...

And then the rooster asked the hen: "Is that what I've been doing, is that right?" And the hen told him: "Yeah, that's right, say some more. You're saying it right."

(8, cont'd) And then his horse lay down, and could go no farther. And the boy cried, and he whipped his horse, and he was angry. And the horse tried to stop him, that it wasn't his fault. But the boy kept beating him...

(9) All of a sudden a voice from above tells the boy to stop beating his horse. It's a beautiful horse that spoke, and it tells him to get on, and they'll catch up with his brothers, who're in danger. They have arrived at the man-eater's house. And the horse tells him that they'll fly through the air, he knows the way...

And then he asked the hen: "Is this what happened?" And the hen winked at him, and then she said: "Yeah, yeah, that's what happened. I know that you know the whole story, that's why I told you to talk first. I'm not going to tell your story, because I might not tell everything in your life." Then he'd go on with his story.

(10) At dusk the horse lands, and tells the boy that they are near the man-eater's house, and the man-eater is an old lady. The dogs will warn her of his arrival (they are his ears). She'll greet him as her grandson, and ask him to stay the night.

(11) She'll tell him to put the horse away in a barn that she keeps locked. But the horse insists that the little boy keep the key, to make his get-away, later that night.

(12) In the barn there will be golden birds, and they are the man-eater's eyes.

And at this point the rooster said: "And that's me and you, and that's why I'm telling the story." Right then the boy that washed dishes just like that he woke up. "That's my story what the rooster is telling about. That's me he's telling a story about." He remembered and understood what the rooster was saying. What he's been doing, he's been telling.

55. Well, the rooster was telling a story about himself with the hen, them is the golden birds. And the story the rooster is telling to all the people, that's what the boy did, he's telling about what he done. That boy, he kind of lost track of what happened to him. And this here Golden Woman is the one that figured it out because to this here boy that caught her, that's where her love is, that's who she wants to marry. This here king is too old. And that's why she thought this all out, when the rooster is telling the story maybe the boy might wake up and remember all what happened to him. And then they'll get married. That's what he told to the people. The rooster tells his hen: "Is that what I really done?" And then this here woman'll wink, the hen, she winks at her rooster, and she says "Yes, yes, yes, that's what you done. You know what you've been doing, and if I'd told the story I wouldn't know all of what you been doing." And then she said: "I always love you and I want you to marry me." Just like that that little boy woke up, that's him that's been doing that. "That's what I've been doing, he's telling

a story about me. He told it to all those people that's packed in there. And a bird never does talk to one another, or just talk, but this is the man-eater's birds, that's why they talk and tell about themselves." Well, this here boy just as soon as he knows that the rooster is repeating what he's done he disappeared. They didn't realize he was gone. They were just listening to the birds. They can hardly believe it. Then they missed the boy. He's gone. I guess he just slipped out. And then his brothers got the belly ache.

56. They're going to tell on them boys, them birds is going to tell on them. What they did to him, and the boys couldn't get out. The boss had told them: "Don't nobody go out." Then he told his working man: "Go and bring in the big tub. Put it right on the floor. Whoever gets the belly ache, he can use it. Don't nobody go out."
And then the king said: "Now we can get married." The preacher is already there, as soon as the birds quit talking they get married.

57. But the woman told him, the Golden Woman: "Don't you get in a hurry, we'll get married. But first I'm going to talk to you." They were walking up and down the room, they was holding arms he and the Golden Woman. They were walking up and down she told him: "There's very different in our age, you're old and I'm just a girl, and don't you think, if we get married, you'll be very sorry, you'll always be jealous, jealous hearted, because you're old?" The king said: "That's true enough, I am old, we're too unmatched, but we're going to get married."

58. He told the Golden Woman: "And you got good thinking. Do you know a good medicine to make me young again? Because I know about it, that's why I asked you." And she done like that and she pulled out of her clothes a bottle, a little bottle. She told him: "You drink this, drink it at once, and then you'll be back ten years younger, towards boy. And then we'll be even. Take it." She gave it to him, he took it down at once. Must be just a little spoonful, just one swallow, and it's gone. He did like that, the king has spasms, he let go and fell on his back, he just quivered. The people and the kings all rushed to him on both sides, there was a doctor there, but he didn't have no medicine. They rushed him to the hospital, but he never come to, he's dead. He's still dead.

59. All of a sudden the little boy come back in. The young guy, goodness he's handsome, he's a man now, he's got a good outfit, he's good looking. The Golden Woman runs towards him, she thought:

"Gee, his parents must be important people, and that's why he got good clothes. He's good looking. That's going to be my man." She went and met the man, and she shook hands, she said: "You got here too late at the meeting where the chickens told stories, and who are you? What's your name?" "Well, the birds, the rooster and the hen, that's what they're talking about when the rooster is telling the story, when he told about his life, that's me that the rooster is talking about." Gee, she throwed her arms around his neck and started chewing his face. She said: "Thank you, we'll get married now. Don't you find no excuse no more, the guy that you're always scared of is already dead, your king, then you'll take his place."

60. Then they called the preacher and he married them, he got done marrying them. The Golden Woman started giving them drinks, not from that little bottle, it's real liquor, everybody in the house, and the last she done they passed cigars. Everybody got a treat. Then they started jumping up and down, dancing, they danced until daylight, and then they said: "Now we'll scatter." They scattered.

61. These here boys got out of trouble, their boat come to the top. They said: "Well, our boss is dead. We're not going to be told on by our brother. Even if he did tell on us we're three, and all we've been scared of is the king. He won't tell on us, our little brother. If he was going to tell on us he'd have told on us the first thing what we did, when we lied in the letter."

Then they told the people: "We're leaving. We're leaving you what's left. Tomorrow is the date we put down that we'll be back, that's the date we give our father. And it's a long ways to go to his house, we have to camp on the way. We camped on the way here."

62. The Golden Woman wanted to go with their little brother, but they stopped her. The told her: "You took his place, and you better stay here. You just as well be the king here." They got no more king, and so the Golden Woman got to be the king. But she told them, the people that stay there: "The one that I come to see is dead, the one that was going to be my husband, and somebody took his place. And now I'm going to go with him. I'm not going to stay here with you. And what would I stay here for? You folks don't know me, anyway, and I'm no relation to you. Your king is dead, and you folks will think about getting a king, I'm not going to choose for you." They said: "OK, if that's what you want." And then she told the king's working men: "Go get me the very best horse, and a saddle and a bridle, the very best." The barn man

went, took the best horse, he saddled up, put the bridle on, then he brought it. Them others already had their horses out, they're ready to get on the horses.

63. She got on, and they all started out. They went, and they camped on the way. They took their time. They put the date down with their father, and that's when the oldest ones started to come away, and they come on the ground. And this one, their little brother with his horse came flying next to the sky. That's why he goes around fast, and when he falls back to the ground then he follows them.

When daylight comes, that's just the date that they left, and that's the day they come in sight. And the king and his wife have been looking all the time for them to come. Because they're lonesome for their children.

They missed the last one, and the king had sent people to look for the youngest child, but no, no tracks, just the three. When he got out of sight the horse lay down, and that's all they can see, where the horse lay down, and he got up, and no more tracks. That's when he flew under the sky. When the people that was looking for him got back, they said: "No." They can't figure it out. "What can we do? How can we fly if we want to track him? We can't track him up in the sky. If it was on the ground, we'd follow the tracks of the horse. From here there are tracks where the horse walked until he got out of sight, then he got tired, and then he rested, he lay down. That's where he lay down and stayed down. Then he got up and his tracks disappeared. Then he must have rose.

64. Daylight come and they've been looking. He seen his children, they come in sight. He kept a-looking. Gee, he was sure anxious. Before they got to the fence gate, they all run out with the women folks, with his wife. They are right to the door, they come in, they seen them. What kind of company do they got? In daytime and they have lamp? Gee, it shines this here... When they made out what it was, it was a woman. They got off the horse, and they started walking, and their youngest son is the one that's holding hands with the Golden Woman.

When they went and met them they kissed their oldest son, then the next one come and they kissed him too, they shook hands with him. And then the in-between one they done the same thing, they shook hands and kissed him. They're glad that they're alive. Then come the youngest one. They thought he's dead. That's what his parents thought because he was lost, they never found his body. He didn't have sense enough, they are grown up.

My, they were tickled to see their son, he's already a man. But they got backwards, because she's too good looking and she shines. Then his father asked him: "And who's your company? We're backwards, that's why we ask you. Give us introduction, get us acquainted."

He said: "This here is the Golden Woman. Maybe you've heard about her in a story, in some other country that I never seen where she popped out of the water. That's your daughter-in-law, that's the one I married. Right now we're married. I was the one that got her and then I brought her and then we got married and then we came back."

My, they just rushed to her, they shook hands with the woman. Her father-in-law and her mother-in-law hugged her around the neck and kissed her.

65. Now I'm going to walk away. The one I'm teaching, I'm teaching him, and then he wanted fairy tale stories, and then I told him: "All right, I'll tell you about the Golden Woman." And now it's two weeks and I'm talking all this time, and it's just now that I ended the story. Now I quit talking.

Analysis of the Tale

Just as the Australian aborigines have made English into an aboriginal language, according to Bruce Rigsby, of the University of Queensland, so Seymour has turned the western tale of "The Golden Woman" into a Colville narrative. That he told it in Colville, translating from English, is trivial compared to how he applied the requirements of Colville narrative strategy and in so doing transformed[1] the tale. And while he adapted some parts of the narrative to his white audience, I think that these can be shown to be minor departures from an otherwise distinctively Colville form, guided by an important underlying literary principle.

Seymour told me that he learned *The Golden Woman* from Lisette. I don't know how or when this happened, and beside the name I know nothing about this woman. I have found nobody in Inchelium who had heard of her, so I do not know the direct source of the tale. And while it probably isn't important for my purposes to trace the tale further back, it certainly is fun trying to discover the path it might have traveled.

The heart of the tale belongs to Aarne-Thompson (1961) type 531: "On the advice of a jealous courtier [brothers] the king assigns the hero difficult tasks, which he performs with the help of grateful animals. Bringing the beautiful bride for the king." Beyond this central type, a very large number of widespread motifs and several other common types can be identified. Of these other elements two are so richly elaborated in *The Golden Woman* as to make me suspect them of holding the key to the secret of the tale's source. The first

---

[1]The notion of "transformation" is not borrowed from linguistics. It refers to post-contact changes in narrative. Larry Evers, who is actively studying the "kinds of transformations that extended contact has occasioned," is attempting to "define these transformations by setting the contemporary material against the historical material."

is the switching of the caps, a caper upon which hinges the most dramatic episode of the tale, the decapitation of the man-eater's grandchildren (type 1119: "The ogre kills his own grandchildren. Places changed in bed (night-caps)"). I have found reference to this type in Weinhold's *Zeitschrift des Vereins für Volkskunde* where it is reported as "Caruseddu vertauscht die Kopfbedeckungen der Töchter des Menschenfressers mit denen seiner Brüder" (little boy exchanges the man-eater's daughter's cap with that of his brother). *Caruseddu* [karuséḍ·u] is Sicilian for "little boy," and while the type appears in one of the Sicilian tales collected by Laura Gonzenbach, it undoubtedly can be found in other parts of the world also. The other episode, which determines the outcome of the tale, is the strange performance of the golden birds. The episode involves a variant of motif D2006.1.3: "forgotten fiancée reawakens husband's memory by having magic doves converse." I searched extensively, and finally read in Sebillot that in France "quelques oiseaux domestiques jouent un rôle dans les cérémonies publiques ou privées. C'est ainsi qu'en plusieurs pays la poule est un accessoire pour ainsi dire obligé des mariages rustiques." (Some domestic birds play a role in private and public functions, just as in several countries the hen is a required accessory, so to speak, of rural weddings.) Like the little boy on his track to find the eaglets, I was on a good track. I followed it to the New Continent and discovered that, according to Dorrance, as reported in Carriere 1937, one tale stood out as a favorite among the French Missourians, "Les ouézeau de beauté pi les ouézeaux de verité" (pi = puis *then, and*). And there I lost my track,[2] because the text is not given by Dorrance. Who were the "Birds of Beauty and the Birds of Truth"?

In contrast with these easily identifiable elements of the tale, the sources of two other episodes, the second embedded in the first, remain mysterious to me. The first episode, fragmentary in Seymour's narrative, is that of the four handkerchiefs as bait for the Golden Woman. After three unsuccessful attempts at capturing the Golden Woman, the boy, behaving very much like an ingrate,

[2]One should not conclude that the tale is of French or Italian origin. Some of the details of *The Golden Woman* can be matched with remarkably similar counterparts elsewhere. For example, Degh 1965 reports a Hungarian tale of "a king, a prince, and a horse," in which the horse talks to the prince very much like the little boy's horse: "Listen, dear Master, you must not fasten me with the halter" (pp. 310ff). Some of the language in the Irish tale "The Black Horse" (as read on Spoken Arts Record AS1029 vol. 2) is also strikingly similar to that of *The Golden Woman* (I am indebted to T. Montler for this observation).

drives away his helper the horse. The second episode is embedded here and revolves around the eagles, who now fill the role previously played by the horse. With their help the boy catches the Golden Woman on his fourth try. I am unable to find clear analogs for both episodes, and I am at a loss to determine whether or to what extent these motifs are western or indigenous.[3]

[3]A good many motifs of the tale can be easily matched with identical or similar motifs listed in Thompson 1955, and studied by those who wish to do so. For example:

Z71.2.9	Four sons (1)
H1221	Quest for adventure (2)
H1229	Quest voluntarily undertaken (2)
P210	Husband and wife
L101	Unpromising hero. Usually ... also the youngest son (5)
P231	Mother and son (6)
B211.1.3	Speaking horse (8, 9)
B184.1	Magic horse (9)
A1233.6.1	Horse helper on quest (9, 34)
B540	Animal rescuer or retriever (9)
B540.2	Helpful horse rescues children (9)
G401	Children wander into ogre's house (9)
G11.6	Man-eating woman (9)
D657.2	Transformation to flying horse (9)
B563	Animals direct man on journey (9)
R155.1	Youngest brother rescues his elder brothers (10, 20)
B576.1	Animal as guard of person or house (10, 12, 34)
P292	Grandmother (10)
B102.1	Golden bird
K527	Escape by substituting another person in place of the intended victim (17)
K1611	Substituted caps cause ogre to kill his own children (18)
G270	Witch overcome or escaped (20)
G500	Ogre defeated (20)
P456	Carpenter (23)
P457	House-painter (24)
P447	Smith (25)
P442	Baker (26)
K2211.0.1	Treacherous elder brother(s) (29)
H918	Task assigned at suggestion contained in letter borne by the victim (31)
H1331.1.3	Quest for golden bird (31)
B542.2	Escape on flying horse (35)
H1241.1	Hero returning from successful quest
T11.1.1	Beauty of woman reported to king causes quest for her as bride (37)
F420.4.6	Water-man is rendered powerless if kept away from water (38)
B365.0.1	Bird grateful for rescue of its young (43)
B211.3	Speaking bird (47)
B122.6	Bird summarizes history (54)

But whatever veins the tale followed, its progress seems to have stopped at Seymour. That he retained in his memory so many details is most remarkable. And if he "made up" one or more of these details on the spot, the story is even more remarkable because its teller is also its maker.[4]

	P261	Father-in-law (64)
	P262	Mother-in-law (64)

Many other motifs of the tale can be matched with related motifs listed in Thompson 1955, such as the following:

	B81.0.2	Woman from water world
	B133.1	Horse warns hero of danger
	B186.1.6	Flight on magic horse
	B211.3.2	Speaking cock
	B364	Animals grateful for … rescue
	B393	Animals grateful for shelter
(?)	B655	Marriage to amphibia in human form
	D56	Magic change in person's age
(?)	D905	Magic storm
(?)	D1096.1	Magic handkerchief
(?)	D1338.1	Magic drink rejuvenates
	D1812.0.15	Weather signs
	F555.1	Gold hair
	F574	Luminous person
(?)	F790	Extraordinary sky and weather …
	F960	Extraordinary weather phenomena …
	H11.1	Recognition by telling life history
	H1154.7	Tasks: capturing bird
	H1242.1	Unpromising hero succeeds in quest
	H1381.1.2.3	Quest for dangerous maiden as bride
	J21.39	*"Do not travel without money"*
	J21.41	*"Be cautious before allowing yourself to fall asleep in a strange place"*
	J155.4	Wife as adviser
	L111.10	Unpromising fourth son succeeds
	P251.6.2	Four brothers
	R155.1	Youngest son rescues his …
	S111	Murder by poison

The following Aarne-Thompson types should also be consulted for similarities of themes and details: 301, 303, 314, 327, 400, 406, 408, 471, 502, 506, 516, 531, 532, 550, 551, 653, 655.

[4]Greenway is one of those scholars who pay tribute to the maker. In the chapter entitled "The Maker and the Gleeman" (Greenway 1964) he focuses on the maker "among the primitives" and on the relationship between the maker and his culture. He says: "In a practical sense the individual everywhere is the ultimate creator of literary material … but his identity is rarely preserved along with his creation. Quick oblivion is the fate of composers in societies without printing; their material is usurped by their listeners and becomes anonymous. Moreover … the material is further molded into the general cultural domain by what has been called the 'folk process'" (p. 150). For a wonderful example of how Waihusiwa transformed the tale of "the Cock and the Mouse" into an artistic Zuni story, see Greenway 1964 pp. 150ff. Greenway comments

If the story of *The Golden Woman* is so good, and if Seymour is such a good story-teller, then why did he not get to tell it often, and why did people not coax him to tell stories? Once Pete told me the Colville story of Coyote and Grizzly. When Madeline and I translated it several years later, I discovered that he had ended the story with these words: "I am taking a lot of time. I just now thought [it now occurs to me] that I am teaching, and my pupil is here sitting down by me. It isn't anybody that I am teaching, it's not my grandchildren. It's a white man that's getting himself teached. Now I have to go. It's the end of the story." The make-up of his audience was obviously a source of disappointment for Pete, or he wouldn't have focused on it at the end of his story. But if it was just an accident that Pete didn't get to tell stories to his grandchildren, then the roots of the accident are as deep as the roots of Pete's Indianness. How could it be that things had never been just right for Seymour to do the telling? I don't know the circumstances, but if John Greenway is right that "the entertainer is an individual apart from his society," then I might understand why one whose own society has already been drastically altered all around him, would not want to risk setting himself further apart from it.

THE FORM AND FUNCTION OF *THE GOLDEN WOMAN*

While Seymour tells his story, he prepares his audience deliberately and carefully for its outcome. He does so not by building up suspense, but by the opposite artifice, by giving advance clues of all the events to come. The tale is told as though its most im-portant functional principle were that of not surprising the audience. This principle takes several forms, all of which can be seen as narrative strategies or rhetorical devices; two of these are repe-tition and detail.

Repetition: Entire episodes of *The Golden Woman* are lavishly repeated. The golden birds repeat the story of the four boys, the little boy repeats to his horse the entire dialog he had had with the king, the job interviews are repeated, and so on. Repetition

that "Waihusiwa performed a feat of imaginative recomposition that in another time and another place might have made him a major author; it is hard to over-praise him. Yet how much credit should go to him, and how much to his culture?" (p. 158-9).

is probably a universal feature[5] of oral narrative. However, some of the specific forms repetition takes here are characteristically North American Indian. One such is Seymour's practice of punctuating the completion of an action with an explicit statement to that effect: "They got acquainted with where they're supposed to eat, they ate, they got done eating" (27); "go to the dining room. You go there and eat, get done eating" (27); "he gathered the dishes and washed them. He washed, got done washing" (28); "he started writing. He wrote, he got done writing" (31). This is a phenomenon very much like that reported by Hymes 1977: "a favorite device of Chinookan narrators is to make a verse of three lines, whose three verbs exhibit the pattern ... onset, ongoing, outcome" (p. 440).[6]

One of the more elegant forms of repetition found in North American Indian narrative is that of parallel constructions. In *The Golden Woman* (15) Seymour says:

> She matches them together
> the oldest one with your oldest brother
> She'll get her to go to bed with;
> and the next one with the next woman,
> he'll sleep with her;
> and the middle one,
> he'll have the middle woman;
> and you two youngest
> you'll go to bed with her.

This passage, which I have written with indentations to bring out the elements of the equation, is structurally very similar to Leslie Silko's (p. 164)

> all he could do
> was lock them up
> in four rooms of his house
> the clouds of the east in the east room
> the clouds of the south in the south room
> the clouds of the west in the west room
> the clouds of the north in the north room.
> . . .

[5]For example, Krohn 1971 lists 'repetition' along with 'skeletal presentation' and 'singleness of direction' as "characteristic for folk literature" (p. 108); Degh (in Dorson 1972) says that "repetition of certain passages, sequences, or the whole narrative adventure is essential to the tale structure itself" (p. 61).

[6]Note, however, that sometimes the Colville pattern disposes with the expression of one of the first two elements as in "And they started planning, and they got a plan" (30).

But one morning he went
first to the north top of the west mountain
then to the west top of the south mountain
and then to the south top of the east mountain;
and finally, it was on the east top of the north mountain
he realized they were gone.

Another special sort of parallel construction can be represented schematically ABA(B). Two terms of the construction are identical, and they are repeated with another interposed element which, in turn, may be accompanied by a parallel element. Seymour's narrative (with my indentations) goes (43):

the woman tried to squirm around, but it's just like a vise.
Because she's away from the water, from her power.
She squirmed around but it didn't do no good. No.
Because she's away from her power.

Another goes (43):

and the sky painted for a red hot weather. And that's red.
And that's what's left, what he's keeping, the red handkerchief.
The sky reported the weather signs, and it's red.

And Silko's narrative goes: (p. 112)

He struck the middle of the north wall
he took a piece of flint and
he struck the middle of the north wall.

These repetitive formulas, and probably several others, share the function of providing the audience with the means to understand and appreciate a Colville story, one of the aspects of the principle of no surprise.[7]

Detail. Good narrators know what, when and how to repeat. They also know when, and how to embroider their stories with detail. Details describe the qualities of the characters and the circumstances of the story. Their function is to remind the audience that if attention is paid to every detail, then the

----

[7]Other forms of repetition are equally functional, and Seymour applies the principle to suit the circumstances. For example, he elaborates: "He's got more than one son, four of them, all boys" (1); or "they have a big chief, and he's important" (1); he restates the obvious: "it's a big town, and it's white people that stays there, they said: 'It must be white people.' (21); or he spells out obvious deductions: "The oldest one was next to the king, and the king asked him: "You must be the oldest one."' (23). For a discussion of "stylized repetitions" in Clackamas Chinook cf. Jacobs 1959:244ff. where the author makes some inferences about historical developments. Jacob's exposition includes mention of several other "stylized devices and motifs."

outcome of the story cannot bring surprises. Why does the boy's father go into a lengthy explanation of his gift of cash and gold? Not to explain what money is used for, but to stress for them that it is best to be prepared. The man-eater has both dogs and birds to warn her in advance of visitors, but the dogs have no other function in the story, except to symbolize her preparedness. Timely attention to detail can make for dramatic effect in a precise narration. Thus when the horse asks the boy if he kept the key to the barn, both the audience and the boy must remain amazed at the relevance of that detail; similarly, when the eagles ask the boy if he has a fourth handkerchief. There WAS a good reason for not returning the key, and for rustling four handkerchiefs. Heeding the hidden message in these detail makes things work out. "Be prepared," Seymour seems to say; "check out every last detail."

One of the most dramatic of the rhetorical devices that serve the function just outlined is the formula of the contradicted reply. It consists of a yes/no question prematurely answered in the affirmative, and immediately corrected. It is regularly exemplified in the motif of the event in which all are to participate. In *The Golden Woman* (50-51) the dialog takes this shape:

> Question (the king): "I asked you all people here, my kind, the kings, the rest of you people, everybody... Now are you sure everybody is here? You kings, and then you my people around here, little boys or old men, old ladies or little girls, everybody."
> Reply (the crowd): "Yeah, yeah, we're all here."
> Correction (the cook): "That's right, it was my worker, my plate licker that I coaxed for nothing... I asked him to come, but no, he didn't want to leave his work."

The cook has just had a long discussion with the boy on the matter of attending the meeting--so that the device of the contradicted reply is strictly rhetorical. The formula recurs in at least half a dozen Colville stories that I have recorded, as well as elsewhere in the northwest, and almost certainly beyond. The Shuswap story of the Trout children and their grandparents reported by Kuipers 1974, contains an instance of the form: "Finally there was no one left, nobody had been able to hit the bird. They said to each other: 'there is no one left of us, who else is there yet?' Oh, they thought about it, and somebody said: 'our grandfather, let's drag our grandfather over here. He's the only one who hasn't tried yet" (p. 129).

THE VALIDATION OF CULTURE

It follows almost naturally that a story told methodically will explain more than the story itself. Very often a Colville story will contain an apparent explanation for a fact of nature quite separate from the story's core. This peripheral explanation is no more than a footnote to the story, and it is offered in a formula: "That's how/why..." Thus, for example, in the telling of a story about the demise of Owl from powerful monster to night predator, we incidentally learn how Chipmunk got stripes on his fur; and in similar fashion we learn how there happen to be wrinkles on Lynx's lip, and so on. To offer such explanatory remarks is to validate one's own world and culture.[8] In traditional Colville tales the narrator validates Colville culture; in the western story of *The Golden Woman* Seymour's use of the device is but an extension of the principle. And so Seymour explains the origin of airplanes with that formula: "Towards the evening the horse flew. Right next to the sky, that's where he went. That's when they made airplanes..." (39). Before evening the people started coming in from far away, maybe on airplanes, because this here boy's been flying around..." (48). The explanation is tentative, and half in jest. I would wager that Seymour didn't hear Lisette make it, nor the suggestion that mail carriers originated with the boy's deliveries, or telephone operators with the king's summons. Seymour, skillful narrator, can't resist applying the principle to validate a world which now includes airplanes, mail carriers and telephones.[9] Along with these strange ingredients come obscure laws that force a reexamination of values, and even the most basic of all human relationships, that between a man and a woman, becomes confused and unclear. Thus the exchanges between the rooster and the hen, and the attendant puzzlement of the audience, reflect

---

[8]Cf. Bascom's discussion of the notion in his article "Four Functions of Folklore." *Journal of American Folklore* 67:333-49 (1954).

[9]Seymour stopped short of applying the device to the episodes of the little boy who "started packing mail, got to be a mail carrier" (37), and that of the king telling the telephone operators: "You telephone operators, you telephone to all the kings..." (48) and gave the explanation for neither the mail carrier nor the telephone operator, the white counterparts of messengers and criers/announcers/translators.

Seymour's ambivalence toward the cultural changes brought about by the presence of the Whites.[10]

There is a way in which the narration of *The Golden Woman* is antithetical to the expectations of Western literature: it does not make use of suspense to keep the audience interested. There is no scene in *The Golden Woman* where a character is shown sneaking up on another. Rather, the narrative is performed like a musical piece, the score of which is known in advance, in the vein that satisfies Colville tastes. What is there in the collective Colville psyche that expects good stories to be told according to the principle of no surprise? Is it just a matter of taste, an accident, or is there some psychosocial correlate of these aesthetic values?

In their ancient world the Colville were at the mercy of outside forces: storms, droughts, and snowfall determined their living conditions. The survival of the Colville depended on successfully struggling against natural obstacles, and cleverly using natural resources to obtain tools, clothing, food, and shelter. The art of survival was to understand nature, to cope with the changes of the weather, to know the cycles of life, to interpret the clues given by the sky, to learn the habits of animals. The Colville elder Andy Joseph once explained to me that the Colville do not excuse themselves before walking In front of a person, as whites do, but warn persons behind whom they are about to walk, so as not to startle them. Are other instances of Colville social behavior similarly bent on avoiding anxiety of the unknown? Colville story telling is one such social activity, and it gives but a glimpse of the complex Colville psychosocial network.[11]

---

[10]In fact *The Golden Woman* is full of reminders to the audience, but also to the narrator, that there's White, and then there's Red, and the two are often in conflict. For example, the little boy "played white man, and he was holding this woman's hand, hooked on the arms" (44); the king "ain't got no wife, and even if he did have a wife, he's white man, and he can get a divorce" (37). While the narrative makes no exlicit reference to the ethnic identity of the four boys and their parents, Seymour talks of them as if they were non-White.

[11]The Colville psychosocial network includes the manifestations of what some would call the Colville worldview. Are there any linguistic categories that correlate with some of the Colville cultural norms? I think that the current controversy in Salish linguistics over the exact nature and function of "control" as a grammatical category bears on the problem. For the latest discussion of "control" in Salish cf. Thompson 1981; for a discussion of "control" in Navajo cf. Witherspoon 1980.

Time, weather, and other settings. Even though the boys' journey takes only two days and the events of the story take place in what seems like a short time, *The Golden Woman* is carefully framed in exactly one year's time (2, 27, 63). The time of day receives even more attention than the duration of the salient events of the story and must be considered one of the more significant formal devices of the narrative. Beginnings and ends of scenes are punctuated by observations of the markings of nature on the passing of time: "it was in the afternoon, going towards evening" (8); "and then the day started changing, the sun went down ... late in the evening the horse struck the ground ... It's getting dusk, it's going to get night" (9-10); "and it got evening,[12] and then they struck the ground... The weather fixed the sky" (39); "the sun just went past noon. It quit raining" (43); "and it's way after dark" (50); "when daylight comes, that's just the date that they left, and that's the day they come in sight" (63); "daylight come and they've been looking. He seen his children, they come in sight" (64). There are no salient descriptions of landscapes, but attention is always paid to the time of day, and everything magic, including the emergence of the Golden Woman from the water, seems to happen after dark, which is also the appropriate time for storytelling. One of the puzzling features of *The Golden Woman* is the lack of elaboration on the weather, on which the episode of the eagles hinges. Similarly the correlation of the weather with the color of the sky remains obscure in the fragmentary episode of the four handkerchiefs.[13]

While time and weather provide natural settings for some of the events of the narrative, social events provide the cultural setting for others. One of the most important Colville social events is the general gathering or feast. In *The Golden Woman* the gathering is one of Whites with chairs, liquor, cigars, handshakes, and up-and-down dancing, but is organized much like an Indian one. According

---

[12]Both this and the previous translation *evening* are probably infelicitous because the time is more likely late afternoon.

[13]Presumably blue is correlated with calm/cool weather; black with stormy; and red (the handkerchief with which the boy succeeds) with hot. The episode with the yellow handkerchief is missing. Reichard 1947 makes the following observation on Coeur d'Alene poetics: "conventionalizations [such as ... color and poetic allusions to natural phenomena like clouds, mists, mountains or stars ... are not used in Coeur d'Alene... Mole in her red dress is the only dash of color in the grayness of the Coeur d'Alene camas flat" (p. 34). One element of Colville cosmology that has remained intact in *The Golden Woman* is the sky: it still is the upper limit of the world (63), and the earth's cover above the clouds (34).

to Teit (in Boas 1930), the Chief among the Coeur d'Alene Salish would give a large scale feast once during the winter, and at that time "the people played games, made speeches, and told stories" (p. 163). Presents were given, a "joke often made with each present" (p. 163).[14] To invite the guests the chief would use "criers, who were generally elderly men and good speakers. When the chief wanted to assemble the people or talk with them on any matter he sent out the crier to inform the people that a general meeting would be held on the morrow. The crier went out in the middle of the camp circle and gave the information in a loud voice so that all might hear. If some of the lodges were too far away or were scattered, he went on foot or horseback, stopping in front of each lodge door, and gave the notice" (p. 154).[15]

Formulas. Among the formulas, two are preeminent, the opening and the closing formula. The closing formula is ņ–c̓əyxʷ–ʕápəlqs. I am not certain of the meaning of the root. In many of the stories Seymour told me later, he used, in addition to this formula, the expression ņxixay–ápəlqs,[16] which, according to him, was the Columbian Salish equivalent of ņ–c̓əyxʷ–ʕápəlqs. The ending formula is often accompanied by some comment about the circumstances of the story, such as the one of (65). Note further that Seymour makes reference to going or walking away, something that had also been noticed by Commons (p. 14).

The opening formula usually consists of a statement about the type of narrative about to be told. Seymour's announcement is both unobtrusive and almost incidental. On other occasions he began with the more formal "I'm going to tell the story of ..." The statement, nevertheless, is probably meant to help younger listeners discern between the various kinds of narratives.

---

[14]Teit also tells us that presents were not given at simple feasts that lasted one evening and at which only immediate neighbors were invited (p. 163). Cf. Silko's remarks on gifts for the storyteller quoted on page 13, footnote 6.

[15]In *The Golden Woman* Seymour has the people invited by phone. Reichard 1947 reports that Tom Miyal, a Coeur d'Alene story teller whose humor was "active and continuous" and who could be expected to give "a running stream of wisecracks," resorted to "the use of modern elements [to] attain his effects... He has the Land People 'phone' upriver to make a trap for Snake" (pp. 33-4).

[16]I am intrigued by the apparent similarity between this formula and the one quoted by Commons (p. 14).

Metaphors. Colville words are very often metaphorical extensions of the basic meaning of the root (plus the affixes, including lexical affixes). A morpheme-by-morpheme (etymological) translation would show this explicitly, but at the expense of intelligibility. For example t̓áq̓–əm–kst *six* is based on the root t̓aq̓ *cross*, plus the lexical affix –kst *hand*. *To cross one's hand* is the way to indicate the number *six*, an extension of, presumably, *five fingers plus one*. Normally interpreters translate forms with the post-derivational meaning, being unaware or marginally aware of the components of a given word. Cases where interpreters offer literal translations show these to be active metaphors, but these occurrences are fairly rare.

In *The Golden Woman* three metaphors as just defined, occur. The metaphor of trouble has a physical correlate in a mass of water, and to get out of a bad spot is to come afloat, to the top of the water: "these here boys got out of trouble, their boat came to the top" (61). The metaphor of envy/jealousy-pride has the physical correlate of vertical space (in mid-air), and to be proud of something is to go high, "his thoughts went high. He had everything he wanted" (47), while to be jealous/envious of somebody is to put oneself lower: "the oldest one got jealous, he put himself lower" (29). The metaphor of indebtedness/gratitude has as physical correlate a direction ahead or behind ego. Thus to be ungrateful is not to see ahead, "they never appreciated... They didn't see ahead of them" (29), and to be indebted or obligated is to stand behind someone: "you're the oldest one, whatever you think we'll stand behind you" (29).

An interesting related rhetorical device in narratives with bicultural content is the bilingual pun. An idiomatic expression in one language is borrowed and translated literally in the other. In *The Golden Woman* Seymour adapts literally to Colville, where it rings awkward, the English expression 'news travels fast'. So he adds the comment that 'it's got no feet' (37). Similarly, the literal Colville equivalent of 'bellyache' does not retain the notion of worrying and complaining'. When the boys get the "bellyache" at the golden birds' story, the king has a 'big tub' brought in, a sort of communal potty (56). As we were translating, Madeline DeSautel, who, I think missed the pun, commented that since the Golden Woman was a sea creature, the tub was meant for her to swim in.

Animals. In Colville cosmology the denizens of the world before the arrival of humans were ranked according to their powers. Eagle was highest among the birds, Grizzly was chief of those that walk on four feet, Chipmunk was innocuous and sexually inept, Magpie a kindly soul, and so on. But, except for the eagle, the animals of *The Golden Woman* postdate the arrival of Indian and White humans. The horse, which does not figure in Colville mythology, is instrumental in all of the little boy's feats, but disappears from the scene without leaving a trace. The golden birds are a sort of "generic" birds, with severely limited mobility and functions; and the dogs have but a cameo part in the narrative.

Special morpho-syntactic constructions. Two types of Colville constructions occur in *The Golden Woman* that are noteworthy because they have functional counterparts elsewhere in the Salish linguistic family.[17]

The root qʷə́n, "pity" occurs in a variety of constructions that are normally translated *it's a pity that* ... belying what must be much richer connotations. In *The Golden Woman* the expression is found several times (6, 7, 37, 43) and seems equivalent in function to the Coeur d'Alene cognate, to which Reichard (1947) refers as follows: "A common expression in life is, 'Poor thing, she is pitiable'" (p. 28); "a formal mealtime greeting is 'We are pitiable.' This is a common expression to gain sympathy for many causes, for instance, when begging for mercy, when pointing out a bad circumstance or offering sympathy, when announcing disaster" (p. 32).

The Colville root ʔx̣il *do like, act a certain way* occurs in *The Golden Woman* a total of 35 times, but only twice in a construction that accompanies a gesture or descriptive action: "and then she done like that and she pulled out of her clothes a bottle... He did like that, the king had spasms" (58). Such occurrences are very frequent in the texts of other narrators. Reichard 1947 has aptly labelled the Coeur d'Alene cognate the 'obscure simile', translating it 'he did like this' (p. 26). Its use seems attributable to either the narrator's wish to make use of visual effects, to shift the

---

[17]Only those who know the language very well can discuss with authority the special functions of particular forms and constructions in a narrative context. Work on these formal matters has been narrowly focused and, generally speaking, inaccessible and obscure. Only a few topics have received wide attention. For example, particles as signals of dramatic organization have been analyzed in detail in several languages: Wishram (Hymes 1977); Onondaga (H. Woodbury 1980); Pomo (McLendon 1980); etc. Work on other grammatical classes, syntactic constructions, etc. remains spotty.

audience's attention from the verbal to the visual, or, more likely in my opinion, it is attributable to the narrator's failure to come up with the precise term required by the narrative.[18]

[18] I may be overgeneralizing. Professor Richard Bauman has pointed out to me that whereas, for example, the word *lurk* has connotations of a dark setting and furtive doings, an accomplished performer may be able to convey all of the word's connotations by appropriate facial expression and body posture. I have speculated that there may be a sort of continuum that begins with mime, blends into drama, which in turn blends into narrative, with the importance of language virtuosity progressively increasing.

The Colville Text and Interlinear Translation

What follows is the verbatim transcript of Seymour's text up to
the point where, with the horse telling the boy that he and his
brothers will be able to escape from the man-eater's, Seymour
continues to talk as though the action had already taken place. At
this point, immediately following sentence 95, I add the
parenthetical remark that "it all happened just so, and the old
lady heard them" (p. 97). The narrative continues, and I continue
to give the verbatim transcript until Seymour gets caught in the
"round" that begins at sentence 436, when the rooster starts
telling the story over. I do not transcribe the entire sequence of
rounds or repetitions, but take up with Seymour's concluding
segment. The repetitions are irregular because he started
splicing his story where he remembered to have left it off, and he
was interrupted unpredictably by the end of the tape. However,
the fragments repeat many of the passages of the story in
interesting variants. I add the richest of these in the form of
appendices. In each case I indicate to what stretches of the
transcribed text these correspond, and anyone who wishes to study
what sorts of differences obtain in the various tellings can do so
with ease.

I have organized the text as follows. Every Colville word is
aligned directly above its English counterpart, the free translation
spontaneously given by Madeline DeSautel.[1] The English inter-

---

[1]The translations are transparent. Are they also accurate? Strictly speaking
l?iw-s-əlx should be glossed *man's father-3rd possessive-pl.* Similarly,
a form like cu-nt-m-əlx consists of the morphemes
say-transitive-indefinite-plural. The analysis of the first form is no more
illuminating than the straight-forward *their father*; the analysis of the second
cannot clarify without further explanation that *indefinite* is the subject and *pl*
the object. The problem here is with *subject* and *object*. —əlx can
pluralize the subject or the object, depending on the construction. The form
cu-ņt-əm (the singular of cu-nt-m-əlx) is equivalent to cu-s (singular
of cu-s-əlx) and informants translate both with *he told him.* The difference

linear translation is remarkably intelligible, showing that the word order of Colville is to some extent compatible with that of English.

The Colville language has a predilection for sentences with an initial predicate[2] followed by only one (unmarked) major relation (the subject, the direct object, the indirect object), as follows:

(a) if the predicate is intransitive then the (unmarked) subject follows;

(b) if the predicate is transitive then the (unmarked) direct object follows;

(c) if the predicate is ditransitive then either the (unmarked) direct or the (unmarked) indirect object follows, depending on which of two ditransitive suffixes occurs.

Intransitive predicates (case a) may be recognized by the pronoun that accompanies them, one of the following four proclitics and one suffix:[3] kən *I*; kʷ *you sg*; ɵ *third person*; kʷu *we*; p *you pl*; or the suffix −əlx *third pl*. In a simple intransitive sentence the predicate may be followed by a nominal (non-pronominal) subject as in: *he went the chief.* Examples of intransitive sentences in the text can be found in 1, 3, 5, etc.

Transitive predicates may be recognized by one of two transitivizing suffixes (−nt or −st) that are added to the stem, followed by object pronoun, and subject pronoun. Schematically a transitive predicate form takes the desinences shown in tables I and II.

In a simple transitive sentence the predicate may be followed by a nominal (non-pronominal) subject[4] as in: *he told the man.* Examp-

---

is that the expansion of cú−nt−əm is the logical agent (preceded by the agentive particle t): cù−nt−əm i? t l?íw−s *he was told by his father*, while the expansion of cú−s is the logical goal (which remains unmarked--in both constructions i? is the article): cú−s i? sqʷsí?−s *he told his son*. While −əlx pluralizes the object in the indefinite (−m) construction: cu−nt−m−əlx *they were told [by...]*, it pluralizes the subject in the third person (−s) construction: cu−s−əlx *they told* ... Having considered this and other problems, I concluded that the returns to be expected from a morpheme-by-morpheme translation would not be worth the space it would take.

[2]This statement glosses over the question of whether or not the distinction between nouns and verbs is a meaningful one in Salishan (and other Northwest) languages. For recent discussions of the issue, cf. Kuipers 1968, Kinkade 1983, Jacobson 1976, and others.

[3]Intransitive predicates may also be accompanied (in some of their forms) by the possessive affixes: i(n)− *my*; a(n)− *your sg*; −s *third person*; −mt *our*; −mp *your pl*; −s−əlx *their*.

[4]Readers are reminded of the expansions of indefinite transitive forms with adjuncts introduced by t, as discussed in footnote 1, page 69.

les of simple transitive sentences in the text can be found in 1, 3, 5, etc.

Ditransitive predicates consist of a stem, a ditransitivizer (−ɫt or −x(í)t), object pronoun and subject pronoun. Schematically a ditransitive verb form takes the desinences shown in tables III and IV.

In a simple ditransitive sentence the predicate may be followed by[5] a nominal (non-pronominal) object as in: *he gave her the money* (−ɫt); *he gave it to the woman* (−x(í)t). Other adjuncts may accompany any type of sentence, and they are usually marked by particles. Examples of ditransitive sentences in the text can be found in 4, 49, 60, etc. (−ɫt); and in 7, 151, 235, etc (−x(í)t). Examples of ditransitive predicates followed by marked adjuncts (preceded by a particle) can be found in sentences 28, 30, 43, etc.

For the details of Colville grammar I am forced to refer the reader to my *Colville Grammatical Structure*, and to a few articles on various grammatical topics[6] (Mattina 1979, 1980 etc.)[7]

The orthography I use is that most commonly used[8] for Salish languages. Aside from problems of phonetic indeterminacy[9] that remain concealed when a text is committed to print, I have

---

[5]The nominal adjunct is often preceded by the article i?, as already pointed out in footnote 1, p. 69, but is not preceded by other particles.

[6]I have done no analysis of discourse-level phenomena, but the language data promise to yield interesting information. Note for example, that the language has the following pairs of deictic elements:

ixí? — axá̰?
ití? — atá̰?
ilí? — alá?
iɫlí? — aɫlá̰?
ikli? — akla?.

What rules govern the use of each pair's members?

[7]Other works on Colville and/or Okanagan are available (Watkins 1970, Hebert 1982).

[8]Other scholars use only slightly different systems (for example, Kuipers whose x̌ = x); others claiming to be using "practical" orthographies avoid the use of most diacritic marks, but clutter their lines with digraphs (for example Bouchard whose hl = ɫ, kW = kʷ etc.)

[9]These are of two types: (a) uncertainty of the phonetic reality of some lexical items. For example, is the w of tətwít always glottalized? (b) uncertainty of the status of certain phones. For example, are there more/fewer than four pharyngeals in the language? Bouchard and Watkins report only one in Northern Okanagan; Kinkade (p. c.) informs me that at least some Colville speakers distinguish between unrounded voiced, rounded voiced, and (unrounded) voiceless, and that each of these occurs plain or glottalized.

-nt paradigm *

Subj	1sp	2s	3s	2p	3p Obj
1s		-nt-s-(í)n	-(nt-í)n	-ł(úl)m-ən	-(nt-í)n-əlx
2s	kʷu -nt-(í)xʷ		-nt-(í)xʷ		-nt-(í)xʷ-əlx
3s	kʷu -(nt-í)s	-nt-s-(ís)	-(nt-í)s	-ł(úl)əm-s	-(nt-í)s-əlx
1p		-nt-s-(í)t	-nt-(í)m	-ł(úl)əm-t	-nt-(í)m-əlx
2p	kʷu -nt-(í)p		-nt-(í)p		-nt-(íp)-əlx
3p	kʷu -(nt-í)s-əlx	-nt-s-(í)s-əlx	-(nt-í)s-əlx	-ł(úl)əm-s-əlx	-(nt-í)s-əlx
Indef			-nt-(í)m		-nt-(í)m-əlx

TABLE I

-st paradigm

Subj	1sp	2sp	3s	3p Obj
1s		-st-(ú)m-ən	-st-(í)n	-st-(í)n-əlx
2s	kʷu -st-(í)xʷ		-st-(í)xʷ	-st-(í)xʷ-əlx
3s	kʷu -st-(í)s	-st-(ú)m-s	-st-(í)s	-st-(í)s-əlx
1p		-st-(ú)m-t	-st-(í)m	-st-(í)m-əlx
2p	kʷu -st-(í)p		-st-(í)p	-st-(í)s-əlx
3p	kʷu -st-(í)s-əlx	-st-(ú)m-s-əlx	-st-(í)s-əlx	-st-(í)s-əlx
Indef			-st-(í)m	-st-(í)m-əlx

TABLE II

-łt paradigm

Subj	1sp	2sp	3s	3p Obj
1s		-łt-s-(í)n	-łt-(í)n	-łt-(í)n-əlx
2s	kʷu -łt-(í)xʷ		-łt-(í)xʷ	-łt-(í)xʷ-əlx
3s	kʷu -łt-í)s	-łt-s-(ís)	-łt-(í)s	-łt-(í)s-əlx
1p		-łt-s-(í)t	-łt-(í)m	-łt-(í)m-əlx
2p	kʷu -łt-(í)p		-łt-(í)p	-łt-(íp)-əlx
3p	kʷu -łt-(í)s-əlx	-łt-s-(ís-)əlx	-łt-(í)s-əlx	-łt-(í)s-əlx
Indef			-łt-(í)m	-łt-(í)m-əlx

TABLE III

-x(í)t paradigm

Subj	1sp	2sp	3s	3p Obj
1s		-x(í)t-m-ən	-x(í)t-ən	-x(í)t-n-əlx
2s	kʷu -x(í)t-xʷ		-x(í)t-xʷ	-x(í)t-xʷ-əlx
3s	kʷu -x(í)t-s	-x(í)t-əm-s	-x(í)t-s	-x(í)t-s-əlx
1p		-x(í)t-əm-t	-x(í)t-əm	-x(í)t-m-əlx
2p	kʷu -x(í)t-p		-x(í)t-p	-x(í)t-p-əlx
3p	kʷu -x(í)t-s-əlx	-x(í)t-əm-s-əlx	-x(í)t-s-əlx	-x(í)t-s-əlx
Indef			-x(í)t-əm	-x(í)t-m-əlx

TABLE IV

*In these tables the parentheses are notational devices that abbreviate stressed and unstressed allomorphs. These suffixes retain their stressed vowels when occurring in forms with weak roots, and lose it in forms with strong roots. In addition to losing the suffix vowels, root-stressed forms lose —nt— in the first singular, third singular, and third plural subject with third singular object, as well as —1— in all subject persons with second plural objects. kʷu is the proclitic first person object, the only particle in the otherwise all-suffix set.

adopted some practices that should be pointed out.

I indicate syllabic nasals and [l] with a subscript dot.[10] Perhaps inconsistently,[11] neither do I follow the same practice for the syllabic [y, w], nor do I write [i, u]. I avoid the subscript dot because it would be unsightly with the [y], and I do not write [i, u] because I want to preserve the integrity of the underlying forms. I write predictable schwas[12] because I feel that their inclusion facilitates reading.

Aside from these idiosyncrasies, my practice of including the hyphens of morphological analysis, conceals the following morphophonemic behavior of the language: a stop plus ʔ coalesce into a glottalized stop only at morpheme boundary, and not root-internally. Thus c-ʔiɬən is [ċiɬən], but tkʷút is [tkʷʔút].

---

[10]I don't find the syllabicity of resonants entirely predictable. For example, why nəxʷənxʷ-iws (but not nxʷ-ənxʷiws), and why n̩stils (but not nəstils)? Is the first ə of nəxʷənxʷiws a trace of the underlying a (cf. náxʷnəxʷ ~ náxʷənxʷ)?

[11]I have followed my instincts in trying to set up a maximally readable orthography. My decisions, I realize, may not be consistent or systematic. Once the orthography will have a chance to be tested (by Colville and Okanagan readers--there are plans to hold public hearings on the matter), I will be able to judge better the extent to which it should be morphophonemic, and the extent to which it should include phonetic redundancy.

[12]Colville (left-linear) rules of epenthesis require a schwa before a resonant, after a glottalized obstruent, and between identical obstruents.

The Golden Woman

1.   kʷl-ìwt   yə?   ṇ̓kʷ-c-wíx-tn
1.   They were sitting around   one tribe of people,

    ƚəxʷ   axà? táwn,   sílxʷa? tàwn, uƚ aƚì?
    it's a town,   a big   town:

    naχəmƚ lut   ƚə c-my-st-ìn   i?
    but   (I) don't   know   the

    skʷist-úla?xʷ-s,   swìt   captíkʷƚ.
    name of the place, it's nothing but a fairy tale.

2.   uƚ   axà? kƚ-ylmíxʷm-əlx   ixì? ḷ táwn,
2.   And   they have a chief   in that town,

    sìlxʷa? ylmíxʷəm-s, s-my-s-qílxʷ uƚ k-ƚəƚ-s-qʷsí?,
    a big   chief,   he's important and he has sons,

    k-mús-əms,   yə-yˁà-t tu?-twít.
    four of them, all   boys.

3.   ixì? uƚ   ṇ-pƛ̓-m-ùs   i?   s-c-ma?-máya?, way̓
3.   And it was over the   school,   it's

    ƚəxʷ   s-qípc,   way̓ ta?m-úla?xʷ;   uƚ
    early spring,   the snow is all gone; and

    ixì? t-xʷùy-m-s-əlx   axà? i?   s-xa?-x?ìt-x i?
    they went to see   the   oldest

1. They were sitting around one tribe of people, it's a town, a big town: but (I) don't know the name of the place, it's nothing but a fairy tale.
2. And they have a chief in that town, a big chief, he's important and he has sons, four of them, all boys.
3. And school was over, it's early spring, the snow is all gone; and the oldest

t-ka?-ka?ɬis   yə?   ḷ?íw-s-əlx.
three   their father.

4. cù-s-əlx: "waẏ ḷ?íw,   kʷ ylmíxʷəm,   uɬ
4. They said: "Father,   you are the chief, and

   k-s-màya?-ɬt-s-t   i?   s-c-k̇əɬ-pá?x̣-tət.
   we are going to tell you what we are thinking.

5. uɬ ʕapnà? waẏ uɬ kʷu ?àc-əcqa? i? təl
5.   Now   we are out   of

   s-ən-ma?-máya?-tṇ   uɬ   cə̇m   pən-?kìn   mi
   school,   and it will be some time before

   kʷu ɬ-ma?-máya?-m;   ƛ̇əxʷ waẏ pùƛ-əm-st-əm
   we   get back to school;   we are done with

   axà? i? s-ən-ma?-máya?-tṇ, uɬ axà? kʷu
   this   school,   and this we

   k-s-təkʷ-təkʷ?-ùt-a?x i?   t təmxʷ-úla?xʷ.
   are going to travel   the   country over.

6. kʷu k-s-mi?-mya?-ncùt-a?x   i?
6. We   are going to have our own experience, whatever

   t k-s-c-my-p-nwiɬən-tət.
      we learn.

7. uɬ waẏ axà?   i?   k-s-c̣əxʷ-xìt-əm-t,
7. And   this is what we are going to tell you,

   ḷ?íw,   ninwi?   put   ṇk̇ʷ-əs-pìn-tk kʷu
   father, it will be exactly one year that   we

three went to see their father.

4. They said: "Father, you are the chief, and we are going to tell you what
   we are thinking.
5. Now we are out of school, and it will be some time before we get back
   to school; we are done with this school, and we are going to travel the
   country over.
6. We are going to have our own experience, whatever we learn.
7. And this is what we are going to tell you, father, it will be exactly one
   year that we will be gone; if we're still alive, (we) will come back.

kʷu ɬ-c-yáʕ-p.
come back.

8. ixìʔ   s-x̣əl-x̣ʕàl-t   iʔ   t   x̣ʷúy-tən-tət,   məɬ
8. The   day   we leave,

   ixìʔ   s-x̣əl-x̣ʕàl-t   kʷu   ɬ-c-yáʕ-p."
   that is   the day   we   come back."

9. cù-nt-m-əlx   iʔ   t   ɬʔíw-s: "way̓   mət
9. He said   their father: "OK,   if

   s-pu?-ús-əmp.
   that's what's going to please you.

10. lut   p   tə   s-c-yaʕ-p-cín-x,   c-my-st-ìp
10. (You're) not   hard up,   you know

    kən   ylmíx̣ʷəm,   yə-yʕà-t   stìm   x̣m-ìnk-ənt-p   uɬ
    I   am the boss,   any   thing you want

    x̣ʷíc-ɬm-ən,   uɬ   kʷu   a-s-c-ən-pət?-íls-əm.
    I give to you   because   you respect my feelings.

11. uɬ   axàʔ   x̣m-ínk-ənt-p   uɬ   s-pu?-ùs-əmp
11. And   this is   what you want,   and   it's your wish to

    p   k-s-təkʷ-təkʷʔ-út-aʔx,   uɬ   way̓   p   x̣ʷúy."
       travel around,   OK,   go on."

12. ixìʔ   cù-s   iʔ   səx̣ʷ-k̓ʷùɬ-əm-s   yəʔ   ylmíx̣ʷəm:
12.   He told   his working man   the   chief:

    "x̣ʷùy-x   iʔ   s-x?ìm-ɬ-x̣às-t   yəʔ   n̦-k-?əmt-íw̓s-tn̦,
    "Go (get)   the   very best   saddle horses,

    ixìʔ   mi   c-ʕac-ʕac-ənt-ìxʷ   ka?ɬís;   uɬ   ixìʔ
           tie them,   three of them;   and

8. The day we leave, that is the day we come back."
9. Their father said: "OK, if that's what's going to please you.
10. You're not hard up, you know I am the boss, anything you want I give
    to you because you respect my feelings.
11. And this is what you want, and it's your wish to travel around, OK, go
    on."
12. The chief told his working man: "Go (get) the very best saddle horses,
    tie them, three of them; and

nixʷ s-x?im-ɫ-x̣as-t yə? ṇ-tək̓ʷ-ki?-sqáx̣a?-tṇ, uɫ
also the best   saddles,   and

ixì? ṇ-tək̓ʷ-tk̓ʷ-íkən̓-(n)t-xʷ, məɫ ixì? laprít, kəm̓
       put a saddle on each,   and the bridle, and

i? kɫ-c̓əl-c̓l-íp̓ɫxən, kəm̓ k-s-k-əwp-wp-áqst-xən, kəm̓
     get spurs,   fur chaps,   or

s-k-cəw-cəw-ʕáqst-xən.
fringed wing chaps.

13. ixì? kʷ i-k-s-cún-əm."
13. These   are my orders to you."

14. waẏ ixì? s-?ácqa?-s i? səxʷ-k̓ʷúl-əm-s; waẏ
14. So   he went out   the working man;

ixì? s-xʷùy-s i? k̓əl s-ən-qlàw̓-tṇ yə? ylmíxʷəm;
       he went   to   the bank   the chief;

ixì? c-?ácqa?-st-s i? s-qláw̓-s uɫ ixì?
       he took out   his money and

c̓ək-xìt-s   i? t k-s-qláw̓-s   axà? i?
he started counting   his money (for)   the

t-ka?-ka?ɫís.
three of them.

15. ka?ɫəl-lùp i? s-c-wtán-s axà? i? k-nàqs
15. Three piles   he counted,   one (for)

i? s-x?ít-x, ixì?   uɫ tk̓ʷ-ənt-ís; məɫ axà? i?
the oldest,   and this   he put down; and

qə?-ìw̓s   ilì? tk̓ʷ-ənt-ís;   məɫ
(for) the one in between there he put it down; and

also the best saddles, and put a saddle on each, and the bridle, and get
spurs, fur chaps, or fringed wing chaps.

13. These are my orders to you."

14. So the working man went out; the chief went to the bank; he took out
his money and he started counting his money for the three of them.

15. Three piles he counted, one for the oldest, and this he put down; and
for the one in between there he put it down; and

akià? i? s-t?íw-t-x ilì? tk̓ʷ-ənt-ís,   məɬ
to   the last one   there he put it down, and then

cx̣ʷá-p.
more.

16. uɬ   lut   c-my-st-ìn k̓ʷinx-ɬ-?ùpən-kst kəm̓
16. And (I) don't know   how many tens   or

k̓ʷin(x)-x̣əc-c-íkst, naxəmɬ ixì? i?
how many hundreds,   and   that

k-s-qláw̓-s-əlx.
is going to be their money.

17. c-x?ìt cù-nt-m-əlx   i? t ɬ?íw-s-əlx:
17. First   he told them   their father:

"ixì?   tík̓l-ənt-s-ən; aɬì? cəm̓   kʷm̓iɬ
"This is for your grub;   I doubt that soon

atlà? p kəɬ-k̓làxʷ   mi   p
after you get out of sight (you) will

ta?xʷ-s-c-k̓ʷúɬ, məɬ way̓ p x̓̌xʷù-p i? t
get jobs,   and then you will get   some

s-qláw̓; lut, p təkʷ-təkʷ?-út,   lut   p
money;   no, you will be traveling, (you) don't

tə c-my-n-úla?xʷ-əm; p təkʷ-təkʷ?-ùt p
   know the country; you will travel, you

x̓̌a?-x̓̌a?-ùs-əm   la ?kìn mi
will look for a place to settle   where (you) will

xs-t-mì-nt-p i? k-s-c-k̓ʷúɬ-əmp.
be satisfied to work.

to the last one there he put it down, and then more.
16. And I don't know how many tens or how many hundreds, and that is going
    to be their money.
17. First their father told them: "This is for your grub; I doubt that right
    away after you get out of sight you will get jobs, and then you will get
    some money; no, you will be traveling, you don't know the country; you
    will travel, you will look for a place to settle where you will be satisfied
    to work.

18. uɫ   waẏ   p   k-s-ək-s-qlàw-aʔx
18. And   you   have got to have money

kɫ-k-ʔíɫən-tn-əmp,   kəm   p   k-təmxʷ-íca?,
for you to eat,   or   you   will wear your clothes out,

uɫ   ixì?   p   k-təw-ċa?-ncút."
and then you   will have to buy some."

19. uɫ   ixì?   waẏ   wi?-s-xc-əm-st-ím-əlx;   waẏ
19.   Well,   he's got them all fixed up;

axà?   i?   s-tə-t?ìw-t-a?x   pùt-i?
       the youngest one   is still

xʷúp-t,   ixì?   s-ən-kxn-íls-c.
unable to do anything, (but) he wanted to go along.

20. cù-s-əlx   i?   t   ƛəx-əx-ƛxá-p-s: "waẏ   lut,
20. They told him   his elders: "No,

waẏ   cəm   ṇ-qa?-ìls-ənt-xʷ   a-s-k̓ʷíƛ-t-əm,   waẏ
     (you) will   bother   your brothers,

myàɫ   kʷ   k̓ʷə-k̓ʷy-úma?,   waẏ   kim   kʷ   s-mút-x,
too much you are small,   you   stay home,

kʷu   a-s-k-?am·ùt-əm   i?   kʷu   an-ƛəx-əx-ƛxá-p."
stay with us   elders."

21. lut   axà?   i?   s-t?ìw-t-x   ixì?   ti
21. He wouldn't   the youngest one,   and

s-ċqʷ-áqʷ-s.
he started to cry.

22. cù-nt-əm   axà?   i?   t   s-k̓ʷúy-s,   təxʷ   axà?   i?
22. She said   his mother,   the

18. And you have got to have money for you to eat, or you will wear your
    clothes out, and then you will have to buy some."
19. Well, he's got them all fixed up; the youngest one is still unable to do
    anything, (but) he wanted to go along.
20. His elders told him: "No, you will bother your brothers, you are too small,
    you stay home, stay with us elders."
21. The youngest one wouldn't, and he started to cry.
22. His mother, the

s-ənk̓ʷ-əɬ-mr·ìm-s   axà?   yə?   ylmíxʷəm,   cù-s   i?
one married to   the   chief,   she told

s-qəl-tmíxʷ-s: "wa̓y uyá?,   ṇ-qʷən̓-mì-nt i?
her husband: "Listen   have pity on

s-qʷsí?-tət;   cəm̓   ṇ-k̓əs-t-mì-s,   cəm̓
our son;   that might   do him harm,   he might

ṇ-q̓əl-t-ùs-əs,   wa̓y   ṇ-ɬm̓-íls-ənt.
get sick,   respect his feelings.

23. wa̓y   nixʷ   t   k̓ʷə-k̓ʷy-ìna?   i?   t   s-qlàw̓
23.   Also   a little   money

   xʷíc-əxt-xʷ,   məɬ   cù-nt-xʷ   y   a-səxʷ-k̓ʷùl-əm
   give him,   and   tell   your working man (to get)

   i?   t   x̱ʷùp-t   i?   s-ən-kɬ-ca?-sqàxa?-tṇ   i?   t   k̓ìw-lx,
   a   lazy   horse,   an   old one,

   ilì?   mi   k-?əmt-íw̓s.
   there   put him on it.

24. nìn̓wi?   cəm̓   t̓i   alà?   k-?əm-?əmt-íw̓s,
24.   Maybe   just   around here   he'll ride,

   mi   ṇ-t̓a?l-ìls   mi
   (that) will   settle his feelings   and he will

   ɬ-c-kíc-x;"   ṇ-st-ìls   axà?   yə?   ylmíxʷəm,   "wa̓y
   come back;"   he thought   the   chief,   "Yes,

   wníxʷ."
   that's true."

25. wa̓y   cù-s   i?   səxʷ-k̓ʷúl-əm-s: "xʷúy-x
25.   He told   his working man: "Go

one married to the chief, she told her husband: "Listen, have pity on our son; that might do him harm, he might get sick, respect his feelings.

23. Also give him a little money, and tell your working man (to get) a lazy horse, an old one, put him on it.

24. Maybe he'll ride just around here, (that) will settle his feelings and he will come back;" the chief thought, "Yes, that's true."

25. He told his working man: "Go

c-ʔaw-s-ˤacà-nt ixì? i? s-ən-kɬ-ċa?-sqàx̣a? i? t
tie up the horse that's

s-c-hú··y-x ixì? i? t s-k̓iw-ḷx waẏ uɬ
finished up so old

x̣ʷp-t-wílx.
it's worthless.

26. ixì? mi c-ˤac-ənt-íxʷ, ṇ-t̓kʷ-ìki?-ɬt-xʷ
26. That one you will tie up, saddle it up for

i-s-t?əw-t-ílt; ixì? kɬ-ən-k-?əmt-íws-tṇ-s,
my youngest boy; he's going to ride it,

alà? k-s-k-?əm-?əmt-íws-a?x."
around here he's going to ride it."

27. waẏ ixì? s-?àcqa?-s uɬ s-x̌ʷúy-s, waẏ
27. He went out and went, and

ɬ-c-kíc-x-ɬt-əm.
he came back with it.

28. waẏ ixì? wt-xìt-əm t k-s-qláw̓-s, t̓i mət
28. He gave him some money, maybe

kʷə-kʷə̓r-kʷr̓-ísxən, nìkxna? lìm-t axà? i?
pennies, gee he was tickled the

tə-tw̓ít.
little boy.

29. waẏ ṇ-pkʷ-ɬ-ƛ̓àq-na?-m i? t s-qláw̓-s.
29. He put it in his pocket his money.

30. waẏ kən-xìt-əm i? t ḷ?ìw-s
30. He helped him his father

tie up the horse that's finished up so old it's worthless.
26. You will tie up that one, saddle it up for my youngest boy; he's going to ride it, around here he's going to ride it."
27. He went out and went, and he came back with it.
28. He gave him some money, maybe pennies, gee the little boy was tickled.
29. He put his money in his pocket.
30. His father helped him get on the horse.

k–t̓k̓ʷ–íẃs–ənt–əm.
get on the horse.

31. ixì? s–xʷəs–cqáx̣a?–s   uɬ   aɬì?
31.   He started his horse,   and

k̓ɬ–c̓əl–c̓l–íp̓ɬxən,   kɬ–qəxʷ–sqáx̣a?–tn̩.
he had spurs,   (and) a whip.

32. waẏ lut   s–ək–s–c–xʷùy–s axà? i?   tə–twít,
32.   He didn't go far   the boy,

t̓əxʷ mət   k̓əɬ–k̓làxʷ,   ixì? uɬ
       maybe he got out of sight,   and

tiɬ–x   axà? i? kəwáp–s,   aɬì?   waẏ
he stood still   his horse,   because

s–c–hùy–x i? t   s–k̓íw–ḻx.
he's done   from old age.

33. t̓i   c–xʷíst–s,   uɬ   iwà? k–sp̓–ìca?–s   uɬ
33. He just walks,   and   he whipped him and

iwa? t–xm–ìca?–s; waẏ uɬ ɬq–ìlx   axà? i?
      spurred him;   he just lay down   the

s–ən–kɬ–c̓a?–sqáx̣a?.
horse.

34. uɬ   iwà? səp̓–ənt–ìs   i? t   qəxʷ–sqáx̣a?–tn̩,
34. And   he clubbed him   with the ship,

waẏ uɬ k–ɬəc̓–qí–s.
      and he was going to whip him on the head.

35. uɬ   t̓i kʷmìɬ   ixì? qʷəl–qʷìl–st–əm i? t
35. And all at once   he talked to him

31. He started his horse, and he had spurs, (and) a whip.
32. The boy didn't go far, maybe he got out of sight, and his horse stood
    still, because he's done from old age.
33. He just walks, and he whipped him and spurred him; the horse just lay
    down.
34. And he clubbed him with the whip, and he was going to whip him on the
    head.
35. All at once his horse talked to him.

kəwáp—s.
his horse.

36. t—x̣ʔən—cən—míst—m—ənt—əm; cù—nt—əm: "wa̓y
36. He stopped him;   he said:

ta—tw̓ìt   kʷu n̩—qʷən̓—mí—nt, wa̓y lùt   nàx̣əmɬ kʷu
"Little boy   pity me,   don't

a—k—s—k—ɬəc̓—qín—əm,   wa̓y cəm̓   kʷu
whip me on the head,   you might

n̩—tk̓ʷ—ús—ənt—xʷ.
blind me.

37. aɬì? wa̓y qʷən̓—cìn   kən s—əc—hùy—x   i?
37.   It's a pity I   am so finished

t   s—kíw̓—l̩x, uɬ aɬì? wa̓y kən
with old age,   and It's a pity I

x̣ʷp—t—wílx   uɬ ixì? kən
can't do anything any more   I

s—c—x?ím—scút—x.
am right to the limit.

38. alà? kən tìɬ—x, ùɬi?   kən tk̓ʷ—əncút; humà?
38. Here I   stood, and then I   lay down;

ʕácəx̣ aklà? i? kəl a—k—s—ən—wís—t—əm."
look   above you."

39. taʔx̣ìl—əm kát̓—qn—əm,   nìkxna? alà?
39.   He raised his head, goodness

ʔəks—wìx i? s—ən—kɬ—c̓aʔ—sqáx̣aʔ, qʷàm—qʷəm—t i?
stood   a   horse,   a beautiful

36. He stopped him; he said: "Little boy pity me, don't whip me on the head, you might blind me.
37. It's a pity I am so finished with old age, I can't do anything any more I am right to the limit.
38. Here I stood, and then I lay down; look above you."
39. He raised his head, goodness, there stood a horse, a beautiful

s-ən-kɬ-ċaʔ-sqáx̣aʔ,   uɬ   ņ-ɬəkʷ-kiʔ-sqàx̣aʔ-tņ,   uɬ   iʔ
horse,   and a saddle,   and   the

laprìt,   ɬəxʷ   x̣ƛá-p.
bridle,   complete.

40.   cù-nt-əm   axàʔ   iʔ   t   x̣às-t   iʔ   t
40.   He said to him   the   beautiful

s-ən-kɬ-ċaʔ-sqáx̣aʔ: "xʷùs-t-x   c-k-ʔəmt-íws-x,   uɬ
horse: "Hurry,   get on,

aɬìʔ   waẏ   ḱláxʷ.
because   it's already   late.

41.   a-s-ḱʷiƛ-t-əm,   waẏ   ḱaʔìt-t-əlx   iʔ   ḱə
41.   Your brothers   are just getting   to

ņ-ʔəɬn-aʔ-s-qílxʷ-tņ,   waẏ   ti
the man-eater's,

ƛ̣xʷ-ənt-ìm-əlx."
they're all going to get killed."

42.   waẏ   ixìʔ   taʔx̣ìl-əm,   ixìʔ   c-k-ʔəmt-íws.
42.   Then   he did like that,   and   he got on.

43.   uɬ   aɬìʔ   captìkʷɬ   ƛəm   axàʔ
43.   And   because   it's fairy tale,   first

kən-xìt-əm   iʔ   t   ḷʔíw-s   kiʔ   k-ʔəmt-íws;
he helped him   his father   when   he first got on;

t-qəl-wit-əm   k-ʔəmt-íws.
now he put his foot in the stirrup (and)   got on.

44.   cù-nt-əm: "kʷ   ņ-cìp-ċəp-s-əm   məɬ   lut
44.   He told him: "Shut your eyes   and   don't

horse, and a saddle, and the bridle, complete.

40. The beautiful horse said to him: "Hurry, get on, because it's already late.
41. Your brothers are just getting to the man-eater's, they're all going to
    get killed."
42. Then he did like that, and he got on.
43. And because it's fairy tale, first his father helped him when he first got
    on; now he put his foot in the stirrup (and) got on.
44. He told him: "Shut your eyes and don't

a–k–s–ən–x̣íɬ;   ńíńwiʔ kʷ   ṇ–x̣íɬ,   məɬ   waẏ
get scared;   if   you   get scared

ƛ̓àxʷ–t   y a–s–k̓ʷíƛ–t–əm."
they'll die   your brothers."

45. ti axàʔ ʔax̣l–ìkst–əm–s   uɬ   ṇ–wìs–əlx   iʔ
45.   He did like that and he rose   the

s–ən–kɬ–ċaʔ–sqáx̣aʔ,   c–ʔx̣íɬ t ṇ–waʔ–waʔs–xán.
horse,   like   the feet left the ground.

46. waẏ k–s–ən–x̣íl–aʔx   uɬ   ixìʔ
46.   He was going to get scared and so

s–ən–ċíp–ċəp–s–əm–s.
he shut his eyes.

47. waẏ uɬ ti s–nìw̓–t   kmix kiʔ c–ʔanwì–st–s   iʔ
47.   The wind   only   he could feel

t   s–kʷƛ̓–ús–c.
on his face.

48. xʷú··y,   məɬ   k–cp–s–ʕám;   waẏ
48. They'll go,   and then   he'll bat his eye;

lut   tə c–wìk–st–s iʔ təmxʷ–úlaʔxʷ, kmix iʔ
he doesn't   see   the country,   only the

s–t–k̓m–ásqət yəʔ c–wík–st–s; nak̓ʷəm s–əc–tùxʷt–x
sky   he sees;   he's flying

axàʔ yəʔ ṇ–k–ʔəmt–íw̓s–tṇ–s.
          his horse.

49. ixìʔ k̓làxʷ   kiʔ təkʷ–k̓ʷ–ùlaʔxʷ
49.   Late in the evening   he struck the ground

get scared; if you get scared your brothers will die."
45. He did like that and the horse rose, like the feet left the ground.
46. He was going to get scared and so he shut his eyes.
47. Only the wind he could feel on his face.
48. They'll go, and then he'll bat his eye; he doesn't see the country, only
the sky he sees; his horse is flying.
49. Late in the evening the horse struck the ground;

axà? i? s-ən-kɫ-ċa?-sqáx̣a?; cù-nt-əm: "waẏ kʷu
the horse; he said:

kəɫ-q̇əẏ-ɫt-ìxʷ axà? i? qʷəl-qʷíl-st-m-ən,
"Put it down in writing what I'm telling you,

lut a-k-s-ən-ɫíp-t-əm.
don't you forget it.

50. uɫ ńińwi? sic mi kʷ sláp-əp,
50. And if you will make a mistake,

ņ-ɫìp-t-m-ənt-xʷ axà? i? cú-nt-s-ən, waẏ ƛi
if you forget what I told you,

p ƛ̣àxʷ-t, i? la?ɫ a-s-k̇ʷíƛ̣-t-əm.
all of you will die, (you) and your brothers.

51. axà? ņ-?əɫn-a?-s-qìlxʷ-tņ i? kíc-ənt-əm.
51. This is a man-eater where we are going.

52. a-s-k̇ʷìƛ̣-t-əm waẏ ņ-p-pìlx-st-m-əlx i? tə
52. Your brothers already are taken in by

ņ-?əɫn-a?-s-qílxʷ-tņ, waẏ laklí-nt-m-əlx.
the man-eater, they are locked up.

53. axà? kʷu yàʕ-p, ɬ t-k̇əm-kṅ-íɫxʷ mi kʷu
53. When we get there, on the outside

ʕac-ənt-íxʷ ɬ kɫ-ən-k̇m-íp.
you'll tie me to the door.

54. uɫ ńińwi? cəṁ ixì? wah-ənt-s-ìs i? t
54. And then they'll bark at you the

k-kəw?áp-a?; mi c-k-?àcqa?-m-ənt-s axà? i?
dogs; she'll come out to meet you the

he said: "Put down in writing what I'm telling you, don't you forget it.
50. And if you will make a mistake, if you forget what I told you, all of you
will die, (you) and your brothers.
51. This is a man-eater where we are going.
52. Your brothers already are taken by the man-eater, they are locked up.
53. When we get there, you'll tie me to the door outside.
54. And then the dogs will bark at you; the man-eater will come out to meet

tə n̓-ʔəɬn-aʔ-s-qílxʷ-tn̩, ixìʔ cə́m lìm-t-m-ənt-s
man-eater,   she'll be tickled

pə-ptwínaxʷ.
the old lady.

55. cə́m ixìʔ məɬ k-ʔəm-plaʔ-ncùt-m-ənt-s
55.   She'll claim you as a relative,

kʷ   s-ən-ʔím-aʔ-t-s.
that you are her grandson.

56. cù-nt-s,   'wa̓y kʷ   k̓əlxʷ-núxʷ, wa̓y t̓i
56. She'll say to you,   'You are late,

kʷ púlx.'
    camp here.'

57. məɬ cù-nt-xʷ: 'wa̓y aɬìʔ   lut   kən
57. And you tell her: 'Yes, because (I) don't

t̓ə c-my-n-úlaʔxʷ-əm, uɬ   lut   in-χm-ìnk ɬ
know the country,   and   (I) don't like

s-ən-kʷə-kʷʔàc i-k-s-xʷy-lwís;   wa̓y kən   púlx.'
late   to travel around; I'll camp.'

58. uɬ n̓in̓wi̓ʔ xʷìc̓-əɬt-s   iʔ laklí.
58. And then   she'll give you the key.

59. cù-nt-s,   'n̓in̓wi̓ʔ kʷ xʷúy iʔ k̓əl
59. She'll tell you, 'When   you go   to

s-ən-t̓əws-cqàχaʔ-tn̩, k̓ɬ-ən-k̓ahk̓ʷ-íp-ənt-xʷ, məɬ wa̓y
the barn,   you'll open the door,   and

ilìʔ a-s-k̓ʷíƛ-t-əm, t̓əxʷ ilìʔ   tuʔ-twít,
there are your kind,   there are boys,

you, the old lady will be tickled.
55. She'll claim you as a relative, that you are her grandson.
56. She'll say to you, 'You are late, camp here.'
57. And you tell her: 'Yes, because I don't know the country, and I don't like
    to travel around late; I'll camp.'
58. And then she'll give you the key.
59. She'll tell you, 'When you go to the barn, you'll open the door, and there
    are your kind, there are boys,

ilì?   way k-s-ən-kɫ-ċa?-sqáχa?;   way alà?   kən
there are   horses;   there I

k-s-ən-p-púlx.
have company.

60. kəm c-ən-χáq   ilí?;   ilì?   ṇ-tíɫ-x-st-x^w;
60. But   there's room   there;   there set your things;

wi?-s-k̓^wùɫ-ənt-x^w   an-kəwáp,
and when you're done fixing your horse,

wi?-s-?am-t-íx^w,   k^w ɫ-c-kíc-x məɫ nìṅwi? k^wu
after you feed it you come back and

x^wìc̓-əɫt-x^w   i? laklí.
give me back the key.

61. uɫ   way alà? nìṅwi?
61. And

wi?-s-k̓^wúɫ-cən-(n)t-s-ən,   way uɫ
I'll have everything cooked for you,   and

kɫ-səl-xìt-m-ən   mi   k^w ɫ-c-kíc-x.
the table will be set when you come back.

62. ixì? k^w wi?-cìn   uɫ nìṅwi? ɫ
62. When you get done eating   if

a-s-pu?-ùs ɫ a-k-s-cˁaw-ḷx, k^w cˁáw-ḷx;   k^w
you want   to bathe,   you can bathe;

wi?-s-cˁàw-ḷx   mi   x^wìc̓-əxt-m-ən t
when you're done bathing (I) will give you

a-k-s-ən-ɫq̓^w-út-(t)ṇ, máya?-ɫt-s-ən.
a bed,   I'll show it to you.

there are horses; there I have company.

60. But there's room there; set your things there; and when you're done
fixing your horse, after you feed it come back and give me back the key.

61. And I'll have everything cooked for you, and the table will be set when
you come back.

62. When you get done eating if you want to bathe, you can bathe; when
you're done bathing I will give you a bed, I'll show it to you.

63. wa**y** mət taʔlìʔ kʷ ʔáyx̣ʷ–t.'"
63. (You) must be very tired.'"

64. cù–nt–əm: "wa**y** yə–yʕà–t ixìʔ
64. He went on: "All of that

    c–ən–ɫə**k**ʷ–ɫə**k**ʷ–t–mí–st–xʷ, uɫ nínwiʔ ixiʔ kʷu
    I want you to remember, and when

    wiʔ–s–**k**ʷùɫ–ənt–xʷ, lut kʷu
    you get done taking care of me, don't

    a–k–s–ən–**k**ʷíxʷ–k**n**–əm; ilìʔ kən
    take the saddle off me;

    c–ən–ɬ**k**ʷ–íkə**n** ilìʔ kən
    leave the saddle on me,

    c–laprít, ilìʔ kən kɫ–yə–yʕ–ílxʷ; mi
    leave the bridle on me, and everything; then

    ilìʔ kʷu ʕac–ənt–íxʷ.
    there tie mi up.

65. mi kʷ xʷùy kəl cítxʷ, uɫ lut
65. Then you go to the house, but don't

    a–kɫ–xʷìc–əɫt–əm iʔ laklí.
    give her the key.

66. uɫ nínwiʔ iwàʔ x̣lìt–ɫt–s, mi
66. And if even she asks for it, (you) will

    cù–nt–xʷ, 'uɫ alìʔ s–k–s–kʷəɫ–t–míx in–kəwáp uɫ
    tell her, 'He's sweating my horse and

    lut ṫ in–x̣m–ìnk ɫ i–k–síwst–əm–st–əm.
    (I) don't want to water him.

63. You must be very tired.'"
64. He went on: "All of that I want you to remember, and when you get done taking care of me, don't take the saddle off me; leave the saddle on me, leave the bridle on me, and everything; then tie mi up there.
65. Then you go to the house, but don't give her the key.
66. And if even she asks for it, you will tell her, 'My horse is sweating and I don't want to water him.

67. nìnwi? ?ayxáxa?   k-sa?x-ìca?   mi
67. When   in a little while he cools off (I) will

   k-síwst-əm-st-ən,   məł ?am-t-ìn   t   lawán.
   water him,   and I'll feed him some oats.

68. ixì? mi sic ł-xʷìc-əłt-s-ən an-laklí,
68.   Then I'll give you   your key,

   s-c-?x̣il-x uł lut   ſapnà? kʷ
   that's why (I) don't   now

   i-k-s-xʷíc-əłt-əm.'
   give it to you.'

69. məł cəm   cù-nt-əm,   'wáy.'
69. And she'll say,   'OK.'

70. ixì? uł way kł-c-səl-xìt-əm-s,   uł   kʷ
70. Then   she'll have set the table, and you

   ?íłən,   uł cù-nt-əm,   'way təxʷ kʷ
   will eat and she'll say,

   i-k-s-màya?-łt-əm   y a-k-s-ən-łq̓ʷ-út-(t)ņ.'
   'I'm going to show you   where you're going to sleep.'

71. axà? ņ-cəq̓-əmn-ìls-ənt-xʷ   axà? i?
71.   You'll have given a false hope to   the

   pə-ptwínaxʷ, ņ-łip-t-əm-s   i? laklí; uł nìnwi?
   old lady,   she forgot about the key;   and when

   màya?-łt-s   a-k-s-ən-łq̓ʷ-út-tņ, uł way   ilì?
   she shows you your bed,   already there

   a-s-k̓ʷíƛ-t-əm;   way k-s-ənk̓ʷ-ł-(ł)əq̓ʷ-łəq̓ʷ-lùt-əlx,
   are your brothers;   they each have a bed partner,

67. When in a little while he cools off I'll water him, and I'll feed him oats.
68. Then I'll give you your key, that's why I don't give it to you now.'
69. And she'll say, 'OK.'
70. Then she'll have set the table, and you will eat and she'll say, 'I'm going
    to show you where you're going to sleep.'
71. You'll have given a false hope to the old lady, she forgot about the key;
    and when she shows you your bed, already there are your brothers; they

t   s–ma?–m?ím.
women.

72. yə–yʕà–t c–qʷəc–qʷác–qn–əlx, c–s–ən–qáp–qən,
72. They all have caps on,   night caps,

c–s–ɬq́–əlx–áya?–qən, uɬ aɬì? ixì?   i?
caps,   that's what

k–tə́k–mín–s, uɬ axà? cə́m ?íck–st–əm–s;   cə́m
they go by, and   they play with them;

axà? anwì?   waẏ ilì? nixʷ
(with) you   also

a–s–ənk̇ʷ–əs–t?íw–t–x.
(will play) the youngest one.

73. yə–yʕà–t   ca?ps–íẇs ixi? i? pə–ptwínaxʷ i?
73. They're all sisters,   the old lady's

s–ən–?əm–?ím–a?–t–s.
grandchildren.

74. waẏ ilì? s–ənk̇ʷ–əs–t?ìw–t–x ilì?
74.   The youngest one

c–k̇əɬ–?ìm–st–əm–s 1 a–k–s–ən–ɬq́ʷ–út–(t)ṇ.
is waiting for you in your bed.

75. cə́m waẏ ti   kʷ kìc–x ilì?, cə́m
75.   Just when you get   there, she will

ṇ–kəlx–ús–ənt–s,   məɬ ixì?
throw her arms around your neck, and

k̇əɬ–tə̇m–ʕás–ənt–s.
she'll suck your face.

each have a bed partner, women.
72. They all have caps on, night caps, caps, that's what they go by, and they
    play with them; the youngest one will play with you.
73. They're all sisters, the old lady's grandchildren.
74. The youngest one is waiting for you in your bed.
75. Just when you get there, she will throw her arms around your neck, and
    she'll suck your face.

76. hú·∙y məł ƚi   kʷ łq̓-ilx   məł ixi?
76.   And as soon as you go to bed

ʕay-ʕay-ínk-ənt-s,   ilì··?   məł   kʷ
she'll start tickling you, she'll keep it up until you

k̓əł-ʔət-ətx-númt, ƚəxʷ lut a-k-s-ʔítx, ixi?
fall asleep,   but don't fall asleep, that's what

kʷ i-k-s-cún-əm,   lut a-k-s-ʔítx.
I'm telling you, don't fall asleep.

77. nàx̌əmł kʷ ʔət-ʔətx-áya?, kʷ x̌ʷáq̓ʷ-əlqs-əm.
77. But   play sleep,   snore.

78. cəm̓ ʔayx̌áx̌a?   təl a-k-s-x̌ʷàq̓ʷ-əlqs-əm
78.   A little while after you snore

mi   c-k̓əł-nixəł-m-ənt-xʷ i? pə-ptwínaxʷ; ixi? cəm̓
you'll hear   the old lady;   she

mi   c-t-k̓íw-ļx;   uł ałi? c-ƛ̓əw̓-ƛ̓áw̓   i?
will be climbing up; and because they're all out the

c̓íkʷ-əsxən, c-t-k̓íw-ļx   kł-c̓íkʷ-əsxən,   uł
lights,   when she comes up she'll have a lamp and

ixi? kł-ən-sp̓-ús-tņ;   uł ax̌à?
     she'll have a sword; and she

c-k̓ìc-s   i? s-x?ít-x.
will come directly to the oldest.

79. nàx̌əmł   kʷ ʔət-ʔətx-áya? uł ixi? kʷ
79. But (when) you play sleep

k̓-ka?l-í?st; uł way̓ ʔìtx
go easy;   and when she's asleep

---

76. As soon as you go to bed she'll tickle you, she'll do it til you fall asleep,
    but don't fall asleep, that's what I'm telling you, don't fall asleep.

77. But play sleep, snore.

78. A little while after you snore you'll hear the old lady; she will be climbing
    up; and because the lights are all out, when she comes up she'll have
    a lamp and she'll have a sword; and she will come directly to the oldest.

79. But (when) you play sleep go easy; and when your bed partner

a-s-ənk̓ʷ-ł-łəq̓ʷ-łəq̓ʷ-lút,   ixì? k̓ʷəƛ̓-ł̓t-ìxʷ i?
your bed partner,   then take off

qʷác-qən-s, məł anwì? kʷ kł-əł-qʷác-qn-a?x.
her bonnet, and you   put it on.

80. məł itlì? t-xʷùy-m-ənt-xʷ i? k-náqs, ixì?
80. And then you go to   the next,   then

nixʷ k̓ʷəƛ̓-qìn-(n)t-xʷ i? tkłm-ílxʷ, məł
also take the cap off the woman,   and

a-ł-qà-qc-a?   ixì? ł-qʷác-qən-(n)t-xʷ.
(on) your oldest brother   put it on.

81. uł ixì? waẏ   kəł-qł-əł-t-nùmt
81. And he's already been awakened

a-ł-qá-qc-a?,   cù-nt-xʷ,   'waẏ kʷ
your oldest brother, you tell him,   'You

t-xƛ̓-míst,   waẏ kʷu k-s-ƛ̓əxʷ-t-míx-a?x,
watch for yourself,   we   are going to die,

ṇ-?əłn-a?-s-qìlxʷ-tṇ axá?.
she's a man-eater   this one.

82. uł ixì? a-s-x̣c-m-əncút.'
82.   Get ready.'

83. uł ałì? ?ətx-ìlx   i? s-ma?-m?ím, uł
83.   They are asleep the women,   and

kəl sk̓ʷùt   i? p łq̓-ílx.
to   one side   you sleep.

84. k̓ ən-ła?-m-ìnk   mi   kʷ łq̓-ílx məł
84. Next to the wall (you) will   sleep, and

is asleep, then take off her bonnet, and you put it on.

80. And then you go to the next, then also take the cap off the woman, and
    put it on on your oldest brother.

81. Your oldest brother has already been awakened, tell him, 'You've got to
    look out for yourself, we're going to die, she's a man-eater.

82. Get ready.'

83. The women are asleep, and you sleep to one side.

axà? c-k-cah-əm-st-ìp   axà? i?
    where they can easily be reached   the

tkɨm-ílxʷ, p k̓əɫ-?əys-əncút.
women,   change place with them.

85. uɬ axà? cəm̓ put t-x̌ƛà-p-əlx
85. And   when they are all told

wi?-s-qʷəc-qʷác-qən-m-əlx,   ixì? uɬ kʷ ɬq̓-ílx,
(and) they have their caps on,   then   you   go to bed,

ixì? uɬ kʷ ɬ-x̌ʷáq̓ʷ-əlqs-əm.
and   start snoring again.

86. wa̓y c-k̓əɬ-?anwì-s-əlx i? pə-ptwìnaxʷ
86.   They'll hear   the old lady

c-t-k̓íw-ḷx.
climb up.

87. wa̓y c-kɬ-qíl-t,   wa̓y
87.   She'll get to the top,

kɬ-c̓íkʷ-əsxən,   uɬ k̓əl s-k-sək̓ʷt-ìkst
she'll hold a light,   and   in   the other hand

kɬ-ən-sp̓-ús-tṇ.
she'll have a sword.

88. wa̓y ixì? wìk-ɬt-s i? ṇ-sp̓-ùs-tṇ yə?
88.   He'll see the sword   which

c-kʷís-kʷs-(s)t-s,   wa̓y ɬəxʷ k̓əl s-k-cəh-ìkst-s,
side is holding it,   yes,   it's   in   her right hand,

k̓əl s-k-c̓íkʷ-a? i? c̓íkʷ-əsxən.
in   the left   the   lamp.

84. Sleep next to the wall to reach the women, change with them.
85. And when they are all told (and) they have their caps on, then you go
to bed, and start snoring again.
86. They'll hear the old lady climb up.
87. She'll reach the top, she'll hold a light, and in the other hand a sword.
88. He'll see the sword which side is holding it, yes, it's in her right hand,
in the left the lamp.

89. way̓ c̓ik̓ʷ-ənt-əm   axà? i?
89.   She'll put the light over   the

s-x?ít-x,   way̓ ixì? ṇ-sp̓-ús-ənt-əm;
oldest one,   and then she'll hit him with the sword;

 uɬ itlì? k̓əl k-náqs,   hùy   uɬ t-xƛ̓à-p i?
and then to   the next, until   all

k-mús-əms.
four.

90. ixì? ɬəɬ-sáx̣ʷ-t-s;   ixìxi? təl
90. Then she'll go back downstairs; a while after

ɬəɬ-sàx̣ʷ-t-s ṇ-tíkɬ-c, ixì? uɬ way̓ k̓əɬ-?anwì-s way̓
she goes down below,   he'll hear

ɬq̓-ìlx   axà? i? pə-ptwínax̣ʷ.
she's gone to bed   the old lady.

91. ixì? uɬ kʷ xʷt̓-t̓-əp-nùmt ixì?   məɬ
91. That's when you jump up,   that's when

p   xi̓?t-mist i? k̓əl s-ən-ɬəws-cqáx̣a?-tṇ; uɬ aɬì?
you   run   to   the barn;   and

anwì? kʷ s-x̣ʷùp-t-x   kʷ s-t?íw-t-x,   aɬì?
you   are helpless, you are the youngest,

cakʷ niṇwi? kʷ ṇ-təkʷ-ki?-sqàx̣a?-ṃ   məɬ kʷ
if   you had to put the saddle on   you

míl-mət.
would be slow.

92. uɬ axà?-m aɬì? i? xƛ̓-àƛ̓   xʷùs-xʷs-t   ɬa?
92. And these   big boys can go fast when

89. She'll put the light over the oldest one, and then she'll hit him with the sword; and then to the next, until all four.
90. Then she'll go back downstairs; a while after she goes down below, he'll hear the old lady has gone to bed.
91. Then jump up, that's when you run to the barn; you are helpless, you are the youngest, if you had to put the saddle on you would be slow.
92. And these big boys can go fast when they put saddles on.

ṇ–taǩw–kiʔ–sqáx̣aʔ–m–əlx.
they put saddles on.

93. ixìʔ cəm̓ put   p   c–ʔàc–əcqaʔ   iʔ tәl
93.   Just when you are coming out   of

s–ən–tәws–cqáx̣aʔ–tṇ, cəm̓ mi   c–łx̣ʷp̓à–m   axàʔ
the barn,   she'll come running out

iʔ pә–ptwínax̣ʷ.
the old lady.

94. wa`y uł atìʔ p   wiʔ–s–t–kʷəl·–íẉs,   uł
94.   And   you are already on the horses,

wa`y p   súx̣ʷ–əx̣ʷ.
      you are gone.

95. ixìʔ wiʔ–s–ən–kәt–kt–ús–əs,   uł atìʔ p
95.   After their heads are cut off,   you

c–ʔuc–kì–áp–əm, uł cəm̓ taʔlìʔ   p ṇ–łәx̣–cín,
run downstairs, and   (you'll be) too   noisy,

uł cəm̓ axàʔ iʔ pә–ptwìnax̣ʷ wa`y ilíʔ."
and   the old lady   will be there."

[It all happened just so, and the old lady heard them.]

96. "uł háʔ s–c–ʔkìn–x   hàʔ,
96. "And   what's the matter

ṇ–kәt–kt–ús–n–əlx,   uł háʔ ł–c–t–qʷa`y–ḷx iʔ
I had their heads cut off, and   they come down the

t s–ən–t–ǩìw–ḷx–tṇ, puw–ṇ–cˤát–əlx?
   stairs,   they make noise running down?

97. mәt wa`y la ʔkìn   s–c–ʔkín–x."
97.   Something is the matter."

93. Just when you come out of the barn, the old lady will come running out.
94. And you are already on the horses, you are gone.
95. After their heads are cut off, you run downstairs, and you'll be too noisy,
    and the old lady will be there."
96. "And what's the matter I had their heads cut off, and they come down
    the stairs, they make noise running down?

98. waẏ ixì? s-t-k̓ìw-ḻx-s,   ik̓lì?
98.   She went upstairs,

    k̓ł-qíl-t.
    she got to the top.

99. "há? s-c-?k̀in-x?
99. "What is this?

100. waẏ ixì? i-s-ən-?əm-?ìm-a?-t   yə?
100.   It's my grandchildren whose

    ṇ-kət̓-kt̓-ús-əs,   k̓əł-?aw-?aw-cn-í?st-əm-s.
    heads are cut off, all by mistake yet.

101. uł lut   t̓ə c-qʷəc-qʷàc-qən   axà?
101. And they didn't   have their hats on those

    yə?   c-ən-kət̓-kt̓-ús-c.
    whose heads are cut off.

102. uł axà?   ilì? i? qʷəc-qʷàc-qən
102.   The others   the caps

    ?ísk̓ʷ1-əm-s.
    threw down.

103. waẏ   kən k̓əł-ḻəp̓-m-əncút, waẏ
103. Certainly I   did myself wrong,

    k̓əł-?aw··-cn-ì?st-m-ən i-s-ən-?əm-?ím-a?-t.
    I killed by mistake   my grandchildren.

104. ṇta? cəm̓   alà?
104.   (They) will

    c-ən-t̓ək̓ʷ-ki?-sqáx̣a?-m-əlx, mi   ṇ-kcn-ík̓ṇ-(n)-əlx."
    be saddling their horses,   (I)'ll overtake them."

97. Something is the matter."
98. She went upstairs, she got to the top.
99. "What is this?
100. It's my grandchildren whose heads are cut off, all by mistake yet.
101. And those whose heads are cut off didn't have their hats on.
102. The others threw down the caps.
103. Certainly I did myself wrong, I killed by mistake my grandchildren.
104. They will be saddling their horses, I'll overtake them."

105. uɬ ixì? ɬx̣ʷpá-m,   uɬ put wìk-s   waỳ
105.   Then she ran out, and   she saw that

      wi?-s-t-kʷəl·-íẃs-əlx   uɬ c-?àc-əcqa?-ɬx i? təl
      they were already on horses   coming out   of

      s-ən-ṫəws-cqáx̣a?-tṇ.
      the barn.

106. waỳ ṫi   tàq-s-əlx axà? i?
106.   (They) just waved to   the

      pə-ptwínaxʷ, kutpày-s-əlx   uɬ súxʷ-əxʷ.
      old lady,   they said good bye, and they were gone.

107. waỳ itlì?   xʷúy?-ɬx;   xʷùy?-ɬx,
107.   From there they went; they went,

      yàʕ-p-əlx   k̉əl   s-k̉láxʷ,   yàʕ-p-əlx k̉əl sìlxʷa?
      they arrived towards evening, they got   to   a big

      ṫáwn.
      town.

108. uɬ ixì? k̉əɬ-sìw-s-əlx   i? s-yləmxʷ-íɬxʷ,
108. And   they inquired about the chief's house,

      yə? ylmíxʷəm; waỳ cù-nt-m-əlx   i? t tàwn, "waỳ
      the chief;   they told them, the   town,

      ik̉lì?   ki? c-wíx."
      "Over there he lives."

109. waỳ xʷúy?-ɬx,   yàʕ-p-əlx   uɬ k̉ɬ-ən-ɬa?-ìp-əlx
109.   They went, they got to   the door

      k̉əl s-yləmxʷ-íɬxʷ.
      to   the chief's house.

105. Then she ran out, and she saw that they were already on horses coming
     out of the barn.
106. They just waved to the old lady, said good bye, they were gone.
107. They went; they went, and towards evening arrived at a big town.
108. And they inquired about the chief's house; they told them, the town,
     "Over there he lives."
109. They went, they got to the door to the chief's house.

110. way̓ k̓ɬ-ən-ca?-íp-m-əlx,
110.   They knocked on the door,

k̓ɬ-ən-k̓ahk̓ʷ-ìp-ɬt-m-əlx   uɬ   cù-nt-m-əlx,   "way̓
they opened the door for them   and   they said,

c-ən-p-pílx-wi?."
"Come right in."

111. way̓ c-ən-p-pìlx-əlx k-mús-əms-əlx.
111.   They went in   the four of them.

112. "way̓ təl   ḷkʷ-ùt   p   s-qílxʷ,
112.   "(You come) from   far away   you   people,

lut   t̓ə c-wík-ɬm-ən,   sìc
(I) haven't   seen you before,   this is the first time

p ɬ   i-k-s-wík--əm.
that   I see you.

113. huy stìm̓   i? s-c-ən-q̓a?-íls-əmp?"
113.   What is   your business?"

114. cùt   axà? i? s-x?ít-x: "way̓ t̓əxʷ kʷu
114. He said   the oldest one: "We

s-əc-ƛ̓a?-ƛ̓a?-mìx-a?x i? t k-s-c-k̓ʷúl-tət."
are looking for   a   job."

115. "stím̓ an-x̣m-ìnk   a-k-s-c-k̓ʷùl?"
115. "What do you want for a job?"

116. cùt,   "səxʷ-k̓ʷúl-ɬxʷ-əm."
116. He said, "Carpenter."

117. way̓ ixì? kʷì-s i? q̓əy̓-mín,   way̓
117. So   he took   some paper,

110. They knocked, they opened the door for them and said, "Come in."
111. The four of them went right in.
112. "You people come from far away, I haven't seen you before, this is the
     first time that I see you.
113. What is your business?"
114. The oldest one said: "We are looking for a job."
115. "What do you want for a job?"
116. He said, "Carpenter."

q̓əy̓–ɬt–ím–əlx.
he wrote a note.

118. cù–nt–əm: "way̓ axa? xʷìc̓–əɬt–s–ən   axà? i?
118. He said: "I'll give you   this

q̓əy̓–mín, ixì? k̓əl səxʷ–k̓ùɬ–ɬxʷ–əm mi xʷíc̓–əɬt–xʷ;
note,   to the carpenter   take it;

uɬ ʕác̓–əs,   məɬ way̓ aɬì? i–s–cún–əm 'way̓
    he'll look at it,   and   I told him

a–k–s–xʷìc̓–əɬt–əm t k–s–k̓ʷúl–s, a–k–s–ma?–máya?–m̓.'
'Give him   a job,   teach him.

119. ixì? kʷ k̓əl·–ì?st,   uɬ màya?ɬt–m–əlx
119. Then you get to working, and they'll tell you

i? kɬ–c–cítxʷ–s–əlx."
where to find bunks."

120. way̓ uɬ itlì? k–nàqs   uɬ cú–nt–əm:
120.   And then to the other one   he said:

"hu–hùy uɬ anwí?, stìm̓ uɬ a–s–c–ən–q̓a?–íls?"
"Now   you,   what is   your business?"

121. cù–s   yə? ylmíxʷəm: "way̓ put nìxʷ ti
121. He said to the chief: "Just

c–?x̣ìɬ axà? i? t i–ɬ–qà–qc–a?   i–s–c–ən–q̓a?–íls,
like   my oldest brother my business is,

way̓ ti k–s–c–k̓ʷúl.
     a job.

122. lut   tə c–my–st–ìn   uɬ kən
122. (I) don't   know anything, but I

117. So he took some paper, he wrote a note.
118. He said: "I'll give you this note, take it to the carpenter; he'll look at
    it, and I told him 'Give him a job, teach him.
119. Then you get to working, and they'll tell you where to find bunks."
120. And then he said to the other one: "Now you, what is your business?"
121. He said to the chief: "My business is ust like my oldest brother, a job.
122. I don't know anything, but I would like to teach myself."

k-s-mi?-mya?-ncút-a?x."
would like to teach myself."

123. "wa̓y stìm u₺ a-k-s-c-k̓ʷúi?"
123. "What would you like to work at?"

124. "wa̓y t̓əxʷ s-mí₭-ə₺xʷ-əm."
124. "A house painting job."

125. ixì? c-kʷi-s i? q̓əy̓-mín u₺ q̓əy̓-nt-ís.
125. So he took some paper and he wrote.

126. wa̓y ixì? xʷ ̓ic-ə₺t-əm u₺ cú-nt-əm: "kʷ
126. He gave it to him and he said: "You

xʷúy, ik̓li? c-k̓₺-ən-q̓ə?-íp; ixì? i?
go, there will be a sign on the door; that's the

s-yləmxʷ-i₺xʷ-s i? səxʷ-mí₭-ə₺xʷ-əm.
house of the boss of the painters.

127. ixì? xʷ ̓ic-ə₺t-xʷ u₺ nínwi? ʕàc-əs
127. This you give to him, and when he looks at it

u₺ my-p-nù-s t incà? kʷ i-s-kʷúlst-əm, u₺ mi
he'll know I sent you, and he'll

cú-nt-s 'x̣là-p mi kʷ c-xʷúy, wa̓y kʷ
tell you 'Tomorrow you report, you

k̓ʷúi-əm; ʕapnà? wa̓y u₺ k̓láxʷ.'
get the job; right now it's late.'

128. kʷ xʷùy ik̓li? i? k̓əl a-s-ən-púlx-tṇ,
128. You go there to where you'll camp,

mət wa̓y cù-nt-s yə? ylmíxʷəm."
I suppose he'll tell you the chief."

123. "What would you like to work at?"
124. "A house painting job."
125. So he took some paper and he wrote.
126. He gave it to him and he said: "You go, there will be a sign on the door; that's the house of the boss of the painters.
127. Give him this, and when he looks at it he'll know I sent you, and he'll tell you 'Report tomorrow, you get the job; right now it's late.'
128. You go there to where you'll camp, I suppose the chief will tell you."

129. ixìʔ s-ʔàcqaʔ-s uɬ xʷúy.
129. Then he went out and he left.

130. alàʔ iʔ q̓əʔ-íws; cù-nt-əm, "uɬ anwíʔ,
130. Then the middle one; he asked him, "And you,

    stím uɬ a-s-c-ən-q̓aʔ-íls?"
    what is your business?"

131. "waẏ nìxʷ ɫi put c-ʔx̣ìɬ t axàʔ
131.   "Just like

    i-ɬəɬ-q̓á-qc-aʔ, waẏ in-x̣m-ìnk iʔ s-k̓ʷúl-əm.
    my brothers, I'd like a job.

132. ɫəxʷ iwàʔ lut tə c-my-st-ín uɬ
132.   (I) don't know anything, but

    aɬiʔ waẏ nìn̓wiʔ kən my-p-nwíɬən, t swìt kʷ
              I will learn, anybody

    máyaʔ-ɬt-s, uɬ waẏ mət nìn̓wiʔ my-p-nú-n."
    shows me, and   I'll learn."

133. cú-nt-əm, "ɫəxʷ màyaʔ-nt stím."
133. He said,   "Tell me what."

134. "waẏ s-taʔ-ɬ-wl-wlím."
134.   "A blacksmith."

135. "a·· , waẏ."
135. "Ah, OK."

136. ixìʔ q̓əẏ-ɬt-í··s, ixìʔ xʷìc̓-əɬt-əm,
136.   He wrote,   gave it to him,

    cú-nt-əm: "iklìʔ kiʔ səxʷ-taʔ-ɬ-wl-wlím iʔ cítxʷ-s.
    said: "There is the blacksmith's house.

129. Then he went out and he left.
130. Then the middle one; he asked him, "And you, what is your business?"
131. "Just like my brothers, I'd like a job.
132. I don't know anything, but I'll learn, anybody shows me, I'll learn."
133. He said, "Tell me what."
134. "A blacksmith."
135. "Ah, OK."
136. He wrote, gave it to him, said: "There is the blacksmith's house.

137. ixȉʔ xʷic̓-əɬt-xʷ   uɬ   ninwiʔ   ʕac̓-əs,   uɬ
137. This give to him, and   he'll   look at it, and

way c-my-st-ìs i-s-kʷúlst-əm,   məɬ way
he'll know I sent you over,   and

xʷic̓-əxt-əm-s   t a-k-s-c-k̓ʷúɬ."
he'll give you   a job."

138. cù-nt-əm axàʔ iʔ s-t?íw-t-x,   "uɬ   anwìʔ
138. He asked   the youngest one, "And   you

stȉm?"
what?"

139. cùt: "way ɬəxʷ kʷu qʷən-cin-m-ənt-xʷ uɬ
139. He said: "It's a pity that

aɬìʔ kən s-t?íw-t-x,   uɬ   pùt-iʔ kən
I   am the youngest one,   and   still I

k̓ʷə-k̓ʷy-úmaʔ, kən s-psʕáy-aʔ.
am too small, I   got no sense.

140. way ɬəxʷ s-ən-c̓iw-m, kəm s-k-slip̓-əm,
140.   Dishwashing, or   packing wood,

ka?m-ísəlp̓-əm; ɬ s-ən-k̓ʷəɬ-cən-(n)cùt-tn̩
packing wook in; in the cook house

in-xm-ínk."
is what I like."

141. way q̓əy-xí··t-əm, uɬ cù-nt-əm: "way kʷ xʷuy
141.   He wrote, and he said: "you go   there

ik̓líʔ k̓əl s-ən-k̓ʷəɬ-cən-(n)cút-(t)n̩; ilìʔ xʷic̓-əɬt-xʷ
to   the cook house;   give it to

137. Give this to him, he'll look at it, and he'll know I sent you, and he'll
give you a job."
138. He asked the youngest one, "And you what?"
139. He said: "It's a pity that I am the youngest one, and I am still too small,
I got no sense.
140. Dishwashing, or packing wood, packing wood in; in the cook house is
what I like."
141. He wrote, and he said: "you go there to the cook house; give it to

iʔ   səxʷ–k̓ʷəl̓–cən–(n)cút,   ul   ixìʔ   ʕàc̓–əs
the   cook,   and   he   will look at it

ul   waỷ   my–p–nù–s   t   incàʔ   k̓ʷúlst–m–ən.
and   he'll know   I   sent you.

142.   waỷ   k–s–xʷìc̓–əxt–əm–s   iʔ   t   a–k–s–c–k̓ʷúl̓."
142.   He'll give you   a   job."

143.   waỷ   ʔácqaʔ.
143.   He went out.

144.   húy,   axàʔ   yáʕ̓–lx,   yaʕ̓–m–ìlx–əlx
144.   Well,   they gathered,   they got together,

n̥–kəc–kən̓–wíxʷ–əlx.
they overtook one another.

145.   waỷ   ti   nəqs–ìlxʷ–əlx   k–mús–əms–əlx.
145.   They have one house   the four of them.

146.   x̣lìt–ənt–m–əlx   k–s–ʔíl̓n–aʔx–əlx;   waỷ   k̓liʔ
146.   They asked them   to come and eat;

my–p–úlaʔxʷ–əlx   iʔ   k̓əl
they got acquainted with   where

k–s–ən–ʔíl̓ən–tn̥–s.
they're supposed to eat.

147.   waỷ   ʔíl̓ən–əlx,   wiʔ–wiʔ–cín–əlx;   c–xʷùyʔ–lx
147.   They ate,   they got done eating;   they went

k̓əl   s–ən–púlx–tn̥–s.
to   their sleeping place.

148.   waỷ   kl–x̣l̓á–p–əlx,   ilìʔ
148.   They have everything,   there

the cook, and he will look at it and he'll know I sent you.
142. He'll give you a job."
143. He went out.
144. Well, they gathered, they got together, they overtook one another.
145. The four of them have one house.
146. They asked them to come and eat; they got acquainted with where
they're supposed to eat.
147. They ate, they got done eating; they went to their sleeping place.

k-s-ən-ʔácqaʔ-tn̥,   k-s-ən-cˤáw-l̩x-tn̥,   uɬ
they have an outhouse,   they have a bath tub   and

k--s-ən-ɬq̓ʷ-út-(t)n̥-əlx.
they have beds.

149. cù-nt-m-əlx   iʔ   tə ylmíxʷəm   iʔ
149. He told them the   boss,   the

s-ən-k̓ʷúl-mən-s-əlx: "aɬiʔ kən ylmíxʷəm;   taʔkìn
one they work for: "I   am the boss; how

iʔ k-s-q̓sà-p-iʔ-s iʔ k-s-c-alàʔ-m̩p   ɬ
long   are you going to stay if

x̩s-t-mì-nt-p iʔ s-c-k̓ʷúl-əmp?"
you like   your jobs?"

150. cùt-əlx: "waẏ təxʷ ti n̥kʷ-əs-pín-tk, təxʷ
150. They said: "One year,

iʔ lùt-iʔ   k-s-ənkʷ-əs-pín-tk.
not quite one year.

151. nàx̩əmɬ waẏ ixìʔ k̓aʔt-àsqət   ɬ
151. But   when the time comes close to

s-x̩əl-x̩ˤàl-t ˤapnàʔ təxʷ ɬ   c-k-yaˤ-p-tán-tət,
the day   when we got here,

ixìʔ   uɬ kʷu ɬ-xʷúy;   uɬ aɬiʔ
that's when   we will go back;   because

ćəxʷ-xìt-əm yəʔ l̩ʔíw-tət,   aɬiʔ ylmíxʷəm,   kʷu
we promised   our father,   he's a boss, we

qaʔɬ-ylmíxʷəm."
are the boss's sons."

148. They have everything, they have an outhouse, they have a bath tub and they have beds.

149. The boss told them, the one they work for: "I am the boss; how long are you going to stay if you like your jobs?"

150. They said: "One year, not quite one year.

151. But when the time comes close to the day when we got here, that's when we will go back; because we promised our father, he's a boss, we are the boss's sons."

152. ixì? ?úm‑la?xʷ‑s   i?   s‑ən‑ilí?‑tn‑s.
152. And   he named the country   where   they came from.

153. waẏ x̣là‑p   ixì?   s‑xʷúy?‑s‑əlx,
153.   In the morning   they went,

   px̣ʷ‑m‑əncút‑əlx; xʷùy?‑lx, i? k̓əl kɫ‑ylmíxʷəm‑s‑əlx,
   they scattered;   they went   to   their bosses,

   iklì? yáˤ‑p‑əlx, waẏ cù‑nt‑m‑əlx: "waẏ uɫ p
   there they got,   they told them: "You

   k‑s‑k̓ʷúl‑əm‑s."
   go ahead and work."

154. huy k̓làxʷ   n‑px̣̓‑m‑ùs i?   s‑x̣əl‑x̣ˤál‑t,
154. When evening comes it's ended   the   day,

   məɫ ɫ‑yáˤ‑m‑ìlx‑əlx k̓əl cítxʷ‑s‑əlx; uɫ ax̣à?
   and   they get together to   their house;

   nàx̣əmɫ i? sìnca?‑s‑əlx   uɫ n‑yˤìp k̓áw,
   but   their little brother   still is gone,

   aɫì?   s‑c‑ən‑cìw̓‑x   uɫ
   because he's still washing dishes   and

   s‑əc‑ka?m‑ísəlp̓‑a?x.
   packing wood.

155. nìn̓wi? wi?‑s‑ən‑cìw̓‑m   ɫ s‑k̓làxʷ,
155. When   he's done washing dishes   in the evening,

   ixì?   mi   w?‑íkst;   uɫ ax̣à? c‑x?ìt i?
   that's when his job is over; and when

   s‑k̓ʷìx̣‑t‑əm ɫ‑c‑yàˤ‑p‑əlx, ti wi?‑wi?‑cín‑əlx,
   his brothers get back,   they get done eating,

152. And he named the country where they came from.
153. In the morning they went, they scattered; they went to their bosses, they got there, they told them: "You go ahead and work."
154. When evening comes the day has ended, and they get together at their house; but their little brother is still gone, because he's still washing dishes and packing wood.
155. When he's done washing dishes in the evening, that's when his job is over; and when his brothers get back, they get done eating,

ɬ–xʷùy–s–əlx   ḱəl   cítxʷ–s–əlx,   məɬ   ixì?
they go back   to   their bunks,   then

ɬá?xʷ–sḱit–m–əlx.
they rest.

156.   məɬ   ixì?   máy?–ncùt–əlx   ṫəxʷ   ɬ
156.   And   they tell each other

s–c–my–p–nwíɬən–s–əlx;   waẏ   uɬ   cút–əlx,
what they learned;   and   they say,

"k–s–qʷa?m–ìkst–m–ənt–əm   i?
"We're going to get used to   what

s–c–mí?–mya?–ncút–(t)ət,   i?   s–c–ḱúɬ–tət,   waẏ   ṫi
we're learning,   our work,

x̣s–t–mí–nt–əm."
we are satisfied."

157.   ixì?   ḱəɬ–kʷìs–əst–əm–s–əlx   ɬ
157.   They got envious   of

sí–sənca?–s–əlx.
their little brother.

158.   cùt–əlx,   "waẏ   mət   waẏ   yəˤʷ–p–yàw–t
158.   They said: "He must be   powerful

axà?   i–ɬ–sí–sənca?;   lut   x̣əl   tanmùs
our little brother;   it's not   for   nothing,

s–tə–t?ìw–t–a?x   ùɬi?   kʷu
he's just a young kid   and

xʷəl–xʷəl–t–st–ím,   lut   kʷu
he brought us through that trouble,   she didn't

they go back to their bunks, then they rest.
156. And they tell each other what they learned; and they say, "We're going
     to get used to what we're learning, our work, we are satisfied."
157. They got envious of their little brother.
158. They said: "our little brother must be powerful; it's not for nothing,
     he's just a young kid and he brought us through that trouble, the
     man-eater didn't kill us."

ƛ̓x̌ʷ-ənt-ìm   iʔ   t   ṇ-ʔəɫn-aʔ-s-qílxʷ-tṇ."
kill us   the   man-eater."

159.   ṇtaʔ uɫ lut   s-ləm-lìm-t-s-əlx   təl
159.   They didn't even get pleased   that

xʷəl-xʷəl-t-st-ìm-əlx   t   ɫ-sí-səncaʔ-s-əlx,   uɫ
he saved their lives   their little brother,   and

k̓əɫ-k̓ʷís-əst-əm-s-əlx.
they envied him.

160.   cùt-əlx: "cə̀m   k̓ʷu   ɫ-yaʕ-p   iʔ   k̓əl
160.   They said: "When we   get back   to

ƛ̓əx̌-əx̌-ƛ̓x̌à-p-tət cə̀m   k̓ʷu   ɫ-mi̓ʔ-ncút,   uɫ
our parents,   when we   tell of our trouble,   and

axà? iʔ s-t?ìw-t-x̌-tət   iʔ ɫ-sì-səncaʔ-tət
          it's the youngest of us   our little brother

cə̀m ixìʔ ɫaʔ k-s-my-s-px̌-páx̌-t,   iʔ
           that's the smartest,   who

k-s-c-my-p-nwiɫən-s; uɫ aɫ̓iʔ k̓ʷu xʷəl-xʷəl-t-st-ím.
learned more;   and   he saved our lives.

161.   uɫ minà háʔ   tanmùs,   wa̓y̓ t̓i
161.   And maybe it's not for nothing

x̌às-t   ɫ   k̓əɫ-x̌ʷíl-st-əm.
it's better that we do away with him.

162.   t̓əxʷ k-məlx̌aʔ-íplaʔ-nt-əm, mi   ƛ̓l-ál,
162.   We'll lie about him,   he will be dead,

uɫ nìn̓wi̓ʔ k̓ʷu ɫ-yà̓ʕ-p, uɫ nìn̓wi̓ʔ xs-nù-s-əlx   iʔ
and when   we   get back, and when   they'll miss him

159. They didn't even get pleased that their little brother saved their lives, and they envied him.

160. They said: "When we get back to our parents, when we tell of our trouble, and it's the youngest of us our little brother that's the smartest, who learned more; and he saved our lives.

161. And maybe it's not for nothing it's better that we do away with him.

162. We'll lie about him, he will be dead, and when we get back his parents

t ƛ́əx̣-əx̣-ƛx̣á-p-s, məɫ cù-nt-əm-əlx, 'mət aɫí?
his parents, then we'll tell them, 'Maybe

s-ƛ́l-əl-míx, lut kʷu t́ə ɫ-kíc-ənt-əm, ixì?
he died, he never got to us,

ilì? kʷu c-yaʕ-m-ílx.
we have been all together.

163. ùɫi? ṇ-pƛ́-m-ùs i? s-ən-ma?-máya?-tṇ,
163. And when was finished our training,

  uɫ-i? kʷu əɫ-c-xʷúy, uɫ k̓aw axà? i?
  we came home, and he was gone

s-ɫáx̣-t-(t)ət.'
our partner.'

164. ixì? k-s-c-málx̣a?-tət."
164. That's the lie we're going to tell."

165. wa̓y̓ k̓əɫ-pa?x̣á··-m-əlx, huy
165.   They planned, well,

  k̓əɫ-pa?x̣-x̣-í?st-əlx.
  they got a plan.

166. cùt-əlx: "wa̓y̓ t́i ɫ-kʷùlst-əm
166. They said: "We're going to send him back

  ixì? i? k̓ə ṇ-?əɫn-a?-s-qìlxʷ-tṇ ɫ
   to the man-eater where

s-c-ən-púlx-tən-tət, i? k̓əl pə-ptwínaxʷ.
we camped, to the old lady.

167. uɫ kʷa mət ta?lì? ʕìm-t ixì? i?
167. And I bet she's very angry the

will miss him, then we'll tell them, 'Maybe he died, he never got to us,
we have been all together.

163. And when our training was finished, we came home, and our partner
was gone.'

164. That's the lie we're going to tell."

165. They planned, well, they got a plan.

166. They said: "We're going to send him back to the man-eater where we
camped, to the old lady.

pə-ptwínaxʷ,   kʷa   k-ƛ̓aʔ-ìplaʔ-nt-əm   ƛ̓əxʷ-ɫt-ìm
old lady,   because it's our fault that   she killed

iʔ s-ən-ʔəm-ʔìm-aʔ-t-s, uɫiʔ ƛ̓əxʷ-ənt-ìs iʔ
    her grandchildren,   she killed

s-ən-ʔəm-ʔìm-aʔ-t-s k̓əɫ-ʔaw-cn-íʔst-əm-s.
her grandchildren   by mistake.

168.   mət   taʔlìʔ   kʷu   ʕìm-t-m-ənt-əm.
168.   She must be very   angry at us.

169.   uɫ   cəm ti   sic   axàʔ
169.   And   just as soon as

my-p-nù-nt-əm   axàʔ iʔ tə-twít, nak̓ʷ-aʔ
she finds out about this   boy,   because it's not

təl tanmùs kiʔ   ṇ-ʔəɫn-aʔ-s-qílxʷ-tṇ, way̓
for nothing that she's a man-eater,

c-my-st-ìs cniɫc   ɫaʔ k-sy-sy-ùs kiʔ   kʷu
she knows it's for him   who is smart that   we

xʷəl-xʷál-t.
got saved.

170.   cəm   way̓ ti púl-st-əm.
170.   I bet   she kills him.

171.   ixìʔ məɫ kʷu ṇ-qəm-p-íls,
171.   Then   our minds will be settled,

ƛ̓l-əl-nù-nt-əm   iʔ ɫ-sí-səncaʔ-tət."
we'll do away with   our little brother."

172.   way̓ yaʕ-s-puʔ-ús-m-əlx,   uɫ cùt-əlx,
172.   Their hearts got together, and they said,

167. And I bet the old lady is very angry, because it's our fault that she killed her grandchildren, she killed her grandchildren by mistake.

168. She must be very angry at us.

169. And just as soon as she finds out about this boy, because it's not for nothing that she's a man-eater, she knows it's for him who is smart that we got saved.

170. I bet she kills him.

171. Then our minds will be settled, we'll do away with our little brother."

"waẏ,   waẏ x̣às–t   i? s–c–k̓əɬ–páx̣–tət.
"Yes,   that's good   thinking we've done.

173. waẏ n̓in̓wi? ili?   k̓ʷu ?x̣íl–əm."
173.   That's what we   will do."

174. waẏ ixì? s–kɬ–mùt–s   axà? i?   s–x?ít–x,
174.   So   he sat down   the   oldest one,

      ixì? s–q̓ẏá–m–s;   q̓ẏà·∙–m i? k̓əl ylmíxʷəm.
      he started writing;   he wrote to   the chief.

175. q̓ẏà·∙–m, wi?–s–q̓ẏ–ənt–ìs i?   s–c–q̓áẏ–s,
175. He wrote, got done writing what he was writing,

      uɬ   ixì? pa?–pín–i?–s, n̓–ləʕʷ–ənt–ís,
      and   he folded it, he put it in an envelope,

      k̓ɬ–ən–tɬ–íp–s, uɬ   ixì? q̓əẏ–ɬt–ìs–əlx axà? i?
      sealed it,   and then they signed

      ɬ–si–sənca?–s   i? skʷíst–s.
      their little brother's   name.

176. uɬ   axà?   i?   s–c–cùt–s–əlx ḷ
176. And that's what they said   in

      s–c–q̓áẏ–s–əlx: "waẏ kʷ ylmíxʷəm,   uɬ pnà? ḷ
      their letter: "Dear boss,   maybe

      stìm   kʷ c–yaʕ–p–cín.
      something you want.

177. uc   kʷa yaʕ–p–cìn–m–ənt–xʷ ixì? yə?
177. Do you ever   get hard up for   the

      n̓–?əɬn–a?–s–qìlxʷ–tn̩ sumíx–s.
      man–eater's   spirit?

172. Their hearts got together, they said, "Yes, we've done good thinking.
173. That's what we will do."
174. So the oldest one sat down, started writing; he wrote to the chief.
175. He wrote, got done writing what he was writing, he folded it, put it
     in an envelope, sealed it, and signed their little brother's name.
176. And that's what they said in their letter: "Dear boss, maybe you want
     something.
177. Do you ever get hard up for the man-eater's spirit?

178. mˁan   ɬ   s-xaʔ-xàʔ-s   iʔ s-kəkˁákaʔ-s uɬ ƛi
178. Look   how   powerful are   her birds   and

kmix   kʷə-kʷɾí-t.
they're nothing but gold.

179. uɬ   nìnwiʔ ɬ an-xm-ìnk,   uɬ waẏ
179. And   if   you want it,

ƛaʔ-ɬt-s-ín."
I'll go after it for you."

180. ixìʔ   iʔ   s-c-q̇áẏ-s.
180. That's what he wrote.

181. waẏ ɬ-c-kìc-x   iʔ   ɬ-sí-səncaʔ-s-əlx,
181.   He came back home   their little brother,

uɬ   xʷìc-əɬt-s-əlx axàʔ iʔ q̇əẏ-mín; cù-s-əlx,
and they gave him   that   letter;   the told him,

"waẏ axàʔ ʔùkʷ-ɬt-xʷ   yəʔ ylmíxʷəm; axàʔ iʔ
      "Give this to   the king;   that's the

q̇əẏ-mìn iʔ s-c-q̇áẏ-tət."
letter   we wrote."

182. uɬ   aɬìʔ waẏ c-my-st-ìs   iʔ
182. And since   he knows where

s-yləmxʷ-íɬxʷ,   waẏ s-xʷúy-s.
the king's house is,   he went.

183. xʷúy,   k̇ɬ-ən-caʔ-íp-əm   iʔ   kəl
183. He went, he knocked at the door of the

ylmíxʷəm; huy   k̇ɬ-ən-k̇ahk̇ʷ-íp-ɬt-əm, waẏ ṇ-ʔúɬxʷ.
chief;   then they opened the door,   he went in.

178. Look how powerful her birds are and they're nothing but gold.
179. And if you want it, I'll go after it for you."
180. That's what he wrote.
181. Their little brother came back home, and they gave him that letter; they
     told him, "Give this to the king; that's the letter we wrote."
182. And since he knows where the king's house is, he went.
183. He went, he knocked at the door of the chief; then they opened the
     door, he went in.

184. cù-nt-əm: "wáy   tə-twit,   stìm
184. They asked him: "Well, little boy, what is it

a-s-pu?-ús?"
you want?"

185. cù-nt-əm,   "axà? q̓əy̓-mìn kʷ
185. He told them: "This letter

i-s-c-?úkʷ-ɫt-əm."
I'm bringing you."

186. ixì? uɫ   k-s-k̓ɫ-ən-t̓l-íp-i?-s;   uɫ   ixì?
186.   And he was going to open it; and he

k-s-p̓əlk̓-m-əncùt-a?x   kɫ-əɫ-c-xʷúy-a?x,
was about to turn around and go back,

cù-nt-əm   i? tə ylmíxʷəm: "ma? ilí?-x-əx,
when he said the   king: "Just a minute,

nìn̓wi? k̓ʷa? i-s-wi?-s-ʕàc-əm   axà? i? q̓əy̓-mín.
until   I get done looking at this   letter.

187. mi sic   kʷ   ɫ-xʷúy, pná?."
187.   Then you can go, maybe."

188. wáy ixì? s-ƛ̓là-p-s axà? i? tə-twít; wáy
188.   Then he stopped   the boy;

k̓ɫ-ən-t̓l-ìp-s axà? yə? ylmíxʷəm; ʕà··c-əs uɫ
he tore it open   the chief;   he looked until

púƛ̓-əm.
he came to the end.

189. cù-nt-əm axà? i? tə ylmíxʷəm axà? i?
189. He told   the chief   to the

---

184. They asked him: "Well, little boy, what is it you want?"
185. He told them: "I'm bringing you this letter."
186. And he was going to open it; and he was about to turn around and go back, when the king said to him: "Just a minute, until I get done looking at this letter.
187. Then you can go, maybe."
188. Then the boy stopped; the chief tore it open; he looked until he came to the end.

tə-twít: "há? wníxʷ nakʷəm anwì? kʷ ła?
boy: "Is it true indeed you

k-s-c-q̇ay̓ axá?, anwì? kʷu q̇əy̓-xít-xʷ?
wrote this, you wrote it to me?

190. a-skʷìst yə? c-q̇ay̓; uł há? wníxʷ
190. Your name is written down; and is it true

há? ixì? a-s-c-qʷəl-qʷìl-t l a-s-c-q̇áy̓?
what you said in your letter?

191. kʷu a-s-əc-sìw-m ninwi? ł in-x̣m-ìnk yə?
191. You are asking me if I want the

ņ-?əłn-a?-s-qìlxʷ-tņ," ?úm-la?xʷ-s, "yə?
man-eater's," he named the place, "the

ņ-?əłn-a?-s-qìlxʷ-tņ yə? kł-kʷ-kʷrì k-s-kəkʕáka?.
man-eater that owns golden birds.

192. ninwi? ł in-x̣m-ìnk uł ixì?
192. If I want it

a-k-s-λ̓?á-m."
you're going after it."

193. way̓ lut s-cìnt-s axà? i? tə-twít.
193. He never said anything the boy.

194. ņ-st-ìls, "way̓ nakʷəm kʷu
194. He thought,

?əłn-əm-sqàx̣a?-m-s-əlx axà? i? t
"They are feeding me to her

i-łəł-qá-qc-a?."
my brothers."

189. The chief told the boy: "Is it true indeed you wrote this, you wrote
it to me?
190. Your name is written down; and is what you said in your letter true?
191. You are asking me if I want the man-eater's," he named the place, "the
man-eater that owns golden birds.
192. If I want it you're going after it."
193. The boy never said anything.
194. He thought, "My brothers are feeding me to her."

195. ul   ixì? cù-nt-əm   i? tə ylmíxʷəm: "waẏ
195. And   he told him the   king: "Well,

     s-c-?kìn-x   há??
     is that so?

196. kʷu a-k-s-kʷúkʷ-əm;   waẏ nìnwi?
196.   You'll do a great deal for me;

     λa?-nt-íxʷ;   ixì? c-k̓əl-nìxì-əm-st-ən ixì?
     you can go after it;   I've heard about

     yə? n̓-?əln-a?-s-qílxʷ-tn̩ i? s-kək̓sáka?.
     the man eater's   birds.

197. ul   ta?lì? x̣m-ínk-ən,   ali?   swit
197. And always I've wanted them, because not any

     s-kək̓sàka? yə? l kʷə-kʷr̓í-t; waẏ
     bird   is gold;

     λa?-nt-ìxʷ   x̣lá-p."
     you can go after them tomorrow."

198. ixì? ləl-xʷúy-s.
198. Then he went back.

199. waẏ ti axà? yàs-p-əlx   ùli?
199.   When they had got there and

     xʷìc-əxt-m-əlx   i? t k-s-c-k̓úl-s-əlx, uli? t
     they had given them a   job,   and

     kl-cítxʷ-s-əlx, ul kəm-lt-ìm   i?
     a place to stay,   they took away from them

     kəw?áp-s-əlx i? tə ylmìxʷəm i? səxʷ-k̓úl-əm-s.
     their horses the   chief's   working men.

195. And the king told him: "Well, is that so?
196. You'll do a great deal for me; you can go after it; I've heard about the man-eater's birds.
197. And always I've wanted them, because not any bird is gold; you can go after them tomorrow."
198. Then he went back.
199. When they had got there and they had given them a job, and a place to stay, the chief's working men took away from them their horses.

200. uɬ   ixìʔ   cú-nt-m-əlx,   "uɬ   lut
200. And   they told them,   "Don't

k-s-ən-q̇aʔ-ìls-əmp axàʔ ḷ   kəwʔáp-əmp;   s-xiʔ-mìx
bother your mind   about your horses;   anytime

p   wʔ-íkst,   p   k-s-xʷùy-aʔx   kəm p
you are done working, (if) you want to go away   or

k-ɬəɬ-xʷúy-aʔx,   ixìʔ uɬ ɬ-km-ənt-ìp
back to where you came from,   you can pick up

iʔ kəwʔáp-əmp.
your horses.

201. axàʔ iʔ t i-səxʷ-k̇ʷùl-əm nìṅwiʔ
201.   My working man   will

c-k̇ʷúl-ɬəm-s,   c-ʔam-ɬùləm-s   ḷ   s-ən-təws-cqáx̣aʔ-tn̩
care for them, he'll feed them in the barn

kəm̀ təxʷ ḷ pǽsčər,
or   in the pasture,

c-k̇ʷúl-ɬəm-s,   lut
he'll take care of them for you, don't

k-s-ən-q̇aʔ-ìls-əmp."
bother your head about it."

202. waẏ ixìʔ s-paʔ-paʔs-ìnk-s   axàʔ iʔ
202.   He started to feel bad   the

tə-twìt iʔ   s-tʔíw-t-x.
boy,   the youngest one.

203. waẏ ixìʔ t-xʷùy-əm-s   iʔ kəwáp-s,   waẏ
203.   He went to see   his horse,

200. And they told them, "Don't bother your mind about your horses; anytime
you are done working, (if) you want to go away or back to where you
came from, you can pick up your horses.

201. My working man will take care of them, he'll feed them in the barn
or in the pasture, he'll take care of them for you, don't bother your head
about it."

202. The boy started to feel bad, the youngest one.

    xʷùy   kíc.
    he went (and) got there.

204. ixì? ɬá··c-q-s   uɬ   tx-ənt-ìs   uɬ
204.   He patted and combed him and

    la?ɬ   s-əc-ċqʷ-áqʷ-s.
    at the same time he was crying.

205. c-ən-ɬìk̓-ɬìktá-m,   uɬ kʷmiɬ   uɬ ixì?
205. He was sobbing,   and all at once   and

    qʷəl-qʷìl-st-əm i? t kəwáp-s: "uɬ stìm
    he spoke to him   his horse: "And what

    a-s-c-nìxəl,   mət   kʷ   nìxəl i? təl
    did you hear, maybe you heard   from

    an-ɬəx̣-əx̣-ɬx̣á-p; há?   s-k̓l-əl-mìx-əlx, há?
    your folks;   are they dead,   is there

    s-əx-?kìn-x-əlx?
    something wrong?

206. uɬ   waẏ kʷ pa?-pa?s-ínk."
206. And   you are awful sorry."

207. cùt,   "waẏ kʷu s-ən-məlx̣a?-cìn-əm-s-əlx
207. He said, "Yes,   they told a lie about me

    i-ɬəɬ-qá-qc-a?, kʷu ?am-ən-sqàx̣a?-m-s-əlx i? k̓ə
    my brothers,   they fed me   to

    ylmíxʷəm; uɬ waẏ   mi kən k-s-k̓l-ál.
    the king; and for sure I'll   be dead.

208. s-c-?x̣ìl-x ki? kən əc-pa?-pa?s-ínk, s-c-?x̣ìl-x
208. That's why   I   feel bad,   that's why

203. He went to see his horse, he went (and) got there.

204. He patted and combed him and at the same time he was crying.

205. He was sobbing, and all at once his horse spoke to him: "And what did you hear, maybe you heard from your folks; are they dead, is there something wrong?

206. And you are awful sorry."

207. He said, "Yes, my brothers told a lie about me, they fed me to the king; and for sure I'll be dead.

úɬi? kʷ i-s-c-ʔaw-s-ʔúkʷ-maʔ-m,   úɬi?

I came over to bid you good bye, and

c-t-xʷúy-m-ənt-s-ən."

I came to you."

209. cù-nt-əm: "huy kʷu c-máyaʔ-nt
209. He said: "Tell me

a-kɬ-ən-ƛ̓l-əl-tán?"
what's going to kill you."

210. cùt: "wa̓y̓ kʷu ņ-məlxaʔ-cì-s-əlx   axà?
210. He said: "They lied about my talk

i-s-k̓ʷíƛ-t-əm; nak̓ʷəm qy̓à-m-əlx uɬ incà? kʷu
my kind;   they wrote and

qə̓y̓-ɬt-ìs-əlx i-skʷíst, i-k-s-c-qʷəl-qʷíl-t, kʷa
they signed   my name,   like I was speaking,   that

i-s-cùn-əm yə? ylmìxʷəm n̓in̓wi? ɬ xm-ìnk-s,
I told   the king   if   he wanted,

ņ-qəm-s-cìn-əm-s yə?   ņ-ʔəɬn-aʔ-s-qìlxʷ-tņ i?
if he wished for   that   man-eater's

s-kəkʕákaʔ-s, i?   kʷə-kʷrì-t i? s-kəkʕákaʔ.
birds,   the golden   birds.

211. uɬ ixì? i-k-s-ƛ̓aʔ-ɬt-ím.
211. And then I'm supposed to go after them.

212. kʷa ilì?   kʷu c-t-k̓ʷƛ̓-qən-(n)cùt ilì?
212.   That's where we   made a narrow escape   where

ḷ s-ən-púlx-tən-tət."
we camped."

208. That's why I feel bad, I came over to bid you good bye, and I came to you."

209. He said: "Tell me what's going to kill you."

210. He said: "My kind lied about my talk; they wrote and they signed my name, like I was speaking, that I told the king if he wanted, if he wished for that man-eater's birds, the golden birds.

211. And then I'm supposed to go after them.

212. That's where we made a narrow escape where we camped."

213. uɬ   aɬìʔ pùt-iʔ   əc-t-xƛ̓-əst-ìs iʔ laklí,
213. And   he still has   the key,

lut   tə ɬ-xʷìc̓-əɬt-s   iʔ pə-ptwínaxʷ.
he didn't   give it back to   the old lady.

214. c̓ù-nt-əm: "uɬ c-t-xƛ̓-əst-ìxʷ   iʔ laklí;
214. He told him: "You still hold the key;

waẏ nìṅwiʔ ƛ̓aʔ-nt-ím.
                we'll go after them.

215. nìṅwiʔ kʷu xʷùy, kʷu yáˤ-p,   uɬ lut
215. When   we   go,   we   get there,   don't

naxəmɬ a-k-s-yxʷ-m-əncút; nìṅwiʔ kən sy-m-scút,
       get off;   I   will do my best,

lut   kʷu k-s-k̓əɬ-ʔanwí-nt-əm, taʔlìʔ
they won't   hear us,   very

k-yw-yw-ína?-ɬx.
good hearing they have.

216. uɬ k-yw-yw-ús-əlx,   uɬ kʷa l ən-k̓ìm̓,
216. And they have good eyes, and   in the dark

uɬ aɬìʔ put s-c-ʔx̣ìɬ t c̓ík̓ʷ-əsxn-əlx; iʔ
        just as well as in the light;

s-kʷə-kʷr̓ì-t-s ṇ-p̓ʔáxʷ-əlx; ɬ s-ən-ɬəws-cqàx̣aʔ-tṇ
their gold   shines;   in the barn

ṇ-p̓ʔáxʷ-əlx.
there will be light.

217. uɬ nìṅwiʔ ilìʔ kʷ k-ʔəmt-íws,
217. And   there you will stay on the horse,

213. And he still has the key, he didn't give it back to the old lady.
214. He told him: "You still hold the key; we'll go after them.
215. When we go, we get there, don't get off; I will do my best, they won't hear us, they have very good hearing.
216. And they have good eyes, and in the dark just as well as in the light; their gold shines; in the barn there will be light.
217. And there you will stay on the horse, you'll grab the whole thing.

mi   c-k-yí-m-íws-ənt-xʷ.
you'll   grab the whole thing.

218. nəxʷ-ənxʷ-íws i? s-kəkʕáka? yə?
218. A pair   of birds,   the

ņ-?əɬn-a?-s-qílxʷ-tņ, lipúl uɬ likúk.
man-eater's,   a hen and a rooster.

219. ixì? uɬ   way kʷ kʷən-ɬ-ƛ̣áq-na?-m, ḷ
219.   And   you take a sack,   in

ƛ̣aq-na? ņ-qmí-nt-xʷ-əlx.
the sack put them.

220. uɬ ninwi? iwà? ɬ c-kɬ-wk-cùt axà? i? t
220. And when   she sees   the

pə-ptwínaxʷ, uɬ way ninwi? kʷu ɬ
old lady,   we

c-?ác-əcqa?,   uɬ lut kʷu ƛ̣ə
will be out of there, and never

k-s-ən-kcn-ìkən-(n)t-əm ƛ̣əxʷ iwà?   sy-sy-ús.
will she overtake us   with all her smartness.

221. ixì?   a-kɬ-cáw-t;   nàxəmɬ kʷ ɬa?
221. That's what you've got to do; but   if

yxʷ-m-əncùt way c-ən-kcn-íkən-(n)t-s, ƛ̣1-əl-nú-nt-s.
you get off   she'll overtake you, she'll kill you.

222. naxəmɬ ilì? kʷ k-?əmt-ìws,   way ixì?
222. But   you stay on the horse, and

a-ɬəɬ-c-xʷúy.
you'll come back alive.

218. A pair of birds, the man-eater's, a hen and a rooster.
219. And you take a sack, put them in the sack.
220. And when the old lady sees, we will be out of there, and never will
she overtake us with all her smartness.
221. That's what you've got to do; but if you get off she'll overtake you, she'll
kill you.
222. But you stay on the horse, and you'll come back alive.

223. waẏ ti iwà?   kɬ-wk-cùt,   kəɬ-my-p-nùmt,
223.   For nothing she'll see, find out,

    axà? i? pə-ptwínaxʷ; uɬ waẏ c-?àcqa?   axà?
    the old lady;   and   she'll come out and

    kʷ k-?əmt-íws,   lut   kʷu tə
    you are on the horse, never

    k-s-c-ən-kcn-íkən-(n)t-əm.
    will she overtake us.

224. iwà?   kʷu n̦-?ùc-xən-(n)t-əm kʷu
224. Even if   she follows us

    sɫ-ùs-m-ənt-əm   i? t s-k-təm-tám-t; tə
    she's going to lose us   in the clouds;

    n-yxʷ-t-ìnk i? t s-t-k̇m-àsq̇ət mi kʷu c-xʷúy.
    below   the sky   we will travel.

225. kʷ n̦-qm-íls-əm,   lut   a-k-s-pa?-pa?s-ínk.
225.   Ease your mind, don't feel bad.

226. ninwi? c-kìc-x-st-xʷ i? s-kəkʕáka?, mi
226. When   you bring back the birds,

    ?ùkʷ-ɬt-xʷ   yə? ylmíxʷəm; cù-nt-xʷ, 'waẏ axà?
    bring them to the king;   tell him,   'This is

    y   a-s-c-ən-q̇əm-s-cín,   waẏ axà?
    what you've been wishing for,

    c-kíc-x-ɬt-s-ən.'
    I got it here for you.'

227. waẏ n-st-ìls   yə? ylmíxʷəm, 'n̦ta? wáẏ,
227.   He'll think the king,   'My,

223. For nothing the old lady'll see, find out; and she'll come out and you are on the horse, never will she overtake us.
224. Even if she follows us she's going to lose us in the clouds; below the sky we will travel.
225. Ease your mind, don't feel bad.
226. When you bring back the birds, bring them to the king; tell him, 'This is what you've been wishing for, I got it here for you.'
227. The king'll think, 'My,

way   xaʔ-xáʔ;   aɬiʔ   yə-yˤà-t swìt
(he's) really important; because every   body

c-ən-x̣ìl-əm-st-s axàʔ ɬ təmxʷ-ùlaʔxʷ ixìʔ
is scared of   on this earth   this

ṇ-ʔəɬn-aʔ-s-qílxʷ-tṇ.
man-eater.

228. lut   tə kɬ-t-k̇ə-k̇ət-m-əncùt-(t)ṇ, uɬ yəʔ ɬ
228. Nobody   goes near it,   and

c-nàq̇ʷ-əm-ɬt-s iʔ s-kəkˤáka?-s.
he stole   her birds.

229. wáy̆ way̆ mət   yəˤw-p-yàw-t axàʔ iʔ
229. Yes,   he must be really powerful this

tə-twít.'"
little boy.'"

230. way̆ púlx-əlx.
230.   They went to bed.

231. uɬ aɬiʔ way̆ my-p-nù-s-əlx iʔ t
231. And   they found out

s-k̇ʷiƛ̇-t-əm-s.
his brothers.

232. way̆ itlìʔ   mi s-k̇ɬ-yíxʷ-əls-əm-s-əlx.
232.   From that   they envied him worse.

233. itlìʔ ɬ-k̇əɬ-paʔxá-m-əlx,   way̆
233. Then   they figured out another way,

ɬ-k̇əɬ-paʔx̣-x̣-íʔst-əlx.
they planned some more.

he's really important; because everybody on this earth is scared of this
man-eater.
228. Nobody goes near it, and he stole her birds.
229. Yes, he must be really powerful this little boy.'"
230. They went to bed.
231. And his brothers found out.
232. From that they envied him worse.
233. Then they figured out another way, they planned some more.

234. cùt-əlx: "waẏ k̓əl   ɫʔ-əm-cn-ìtkʷ axà?
234. They said: "Close to   the shore of

    iʔ   sìlxʷaʔ iʔ síwɫkʷ, iʔ t̓íkʷət, kʷa iʔ sìwɫkʷ
    the big   water,   the lake,   the water

    uɫ   xl·àk-ək   axà? ɫ   təmxʷ-úlaʔxʷ," uɫ
    that goes plum around   the earth,"   and

    ixì? ʔúm-laʔxʷ-s,   "ilì? ki?   c-t̓ʔàk̓ʷ i?
          he named the place,   "that's where is   the

    kʷə-kʷr̀ì-t iʔ tkɫm-ílxʷ.
    Golden   Woman.

235. waẏ ixì? k-s-ən-məlxaʔ-cín-(n)t-əm; ixì?
235.   We'll misrepresent him;   that's what

    i-k-s-q̓əẏ-xìt-əm   yə? ylmíxʷəm."
    I am going to write to   the king."

236. yaʕ-s-puʔ-ùs-m-əlx, "waẏ, waẏ xàs-t
236. They all agreed,   "Yes,   it's good

    a-s-c-k̓əɫ-páʔx̣;" waẏ s-q̓ẏà-m-s   i?
    your thinking;"   he started writing   the

    s-x?ít-x.
    oldest one.

237. q̓ẏà··-m, waẏ kɫ-ən-t̓ɫ-íp-s, waẏ
237. He wrote,   he sealed it,

    t-q̓ẏ-ìcaʔ-s   i? k̓ə ylmíxʷəm.
    he addressed it   to the king.

238. waẏ k̓làxʷ
238.   In the evening

234. They said: "Close to the shore of the big water, the lake, the water
    that goes plum around the earth," and he named the place, "that's where
    the Golden Woman is.
235. We'll misrepresent him; that's what I am going to write to the king."
236. They all agreed, "Yes, your thinking is good;" the oldest one started
    writing.
237. He wrote, he sealed it, he addressed it to the king.

wi?-s-ən-ciw̓-m̓   ɬ-c-kic-x   axà? i?
when he finished washing dishes he came back   the

tə-twít.
little boy.

239. way̓ x^wic-əɬt-əm   i? t s-x?ít-x;
239.   He gave it to him the   oldest one;

cù-nt-əm: "way̓ axà?   i-s-c-q̓ày̓ i? k̓la
he told him: "This is what I wrote   to

ylmíx^wəm.
the king.

240. way̓ k^wu ?úk^w-ɬt-x^w,   way̓ incà? myàɬ
240.   You take it for me,   I   too much

kən c-?áyx̣^w-t.
am tired.

241. anwi?-m t̓əx^w-əm k^w s-tə-t?íw-t-a?x,   lut   k^w
241. You   are the youngest, don't

t̓ə ?áyx̣^w-t   k^w ɬa? c-ən-ciw̓-m̓."
get tired   when you wash dishes."

242. uɬ aɬi? lut   t̓ə c-ən-x̣^wil-c-st-s   i?
242. And   he never   disputes the word of

s-k̓^wíx̣-t-əm-s.
his brothers.

243. way̓ ixì? s-?ək^w-ɬ-q̓əy̓-mín-əm-s;   way̓
243.   So   he got to be a mail carrier;

kic-x-st-s i? q̓əy̓-mín, way̓ ixì? x^wic-əɬt-s
he delivered the   letter,   he gave it to

238. In the evening when he finished washing dishes the little boy came back.
239. The oldest one gave it to him; he told him: "This is what I wrote to the king.
240. You take it for me, I am too tired.
241. You are the youngest, you don't get tired when you wash dishes."
242. And he never disputes the word of his brothers.
243. So he got to be a mail carrier; he delivered the letter, he gave it to

yə? ylmíxʷəm,   waẏ kɬ-əɬ-c-xʷúy-a?x,   uɬ
the king,   he was going to come back,   and

cù-nt-əm   i?   tə ylmíxʷəm: "ma? ilí?-x-əx
he told him   the   chief: "Wait a minute

k̓ʷa? axà? i-s-wi?-s-ʕàc-əm i?   q̓əẏ-mín;
until   I'm done reading the letter;

i-kɬ-əɬ-k̓əɬ-kʷínxʷ-cn-əm."
I'm going to answer it."

244. waẏ kɬ-ən-t̓.1-íp-s,   waẏ ʕác-əs;   waẏ ixì?
244.   He tore it open,   he looked;

      axà? i? tə-twìt   ɬa? k-s-c-q̓áẏ,   i?
                it's the boy that writes them,   the

s-t?íw-t-x.
youngest one.

245. nak̓ʷəm cnìɬc   ɬa? k-s-c-q̓àẏ   uɬ
245.   It's he   that writes them and

c-?úkʷ-st-s.
brings them.

246. cù-s   yə? ylmíxʷəm: "waẏ axà? i?
246. It said to the king:

q̓əẏ-xìt-m-ən   i?   kʷ ylmíxʷəm, aɬì?
"I'm writing this to you the   king,   because

qʷən-cìn   ɬəxʷ kən s-əc-kʷúl̓-x, uɬ   pna? kʷ
it's a pity I   am working,   and maybe you

c-k̓əɬ-q̓má-m.
are wishing for something.

the king, he was going to come back, and the chief told him: "Wait a
minute until I'm done reading the letter; I'm going to answer it."
244. He tore it open, he looked; it's the boy that writes them, the youngest
one.
245. It's he that writes them and brings them.
246. It said to the king: "I'm writing this to you the king, because it's a pity
I am working, and maybe you are wishing for something.

247. ixì? ik̓lì? mət   c-k̓əɬ-nìxɬ-əm-st-xʷ   i? k̓əl
247.   Maybe you've heard about   to

   sìlxʷa? i? k̓əl sìwɬkʷ i? kʷə-kʷrì-t i? tkɬm-ílxʷ.
   the big   water the Golden   Woman.

248. nìn̓wi? ixì? ɬ x̣m-ìnk-ənt-xʷ uɬ way̓
248. If   you want her,

   ƛ̓a?-ɬt-s-ín.
   I'll go after her for you.

249. aɬì? qʷən̓-cìn   kən s-əc-k̓ʷúɬ-x,   uɬ
249.   It's a pity I   am working for wages, or

   way̓ kʷ i-k-s-ƛ̓a?-ɬt-ìm y   an-x̣m-ínk.
       I'd go after   anything you want.

250. way̓ ixì? n̓-cəw̓-cì-s axà?   i? q̓əy̓-mìn
250.   He repeated what's in the letter

   yə? ylmíxʷəm.
   the king.

251. "way̓ ixì? axà?   a-s-c-qʷəl-qʷíl-t."
251.   "That's what you said."

252. way̓ lút, lut   t̓ə s-c-qʷəl-qʷíl-t-s, uɬ
252.   No, he never   said it,

   nax̣əmɬ tìlxʷ-s   ɬə k-s-ən-ma?-ìpi?-s i?
   but   he couldn't   tell on

   s-k̓ʷiƛ̓-t-əm-s, aɬì?   lut   t̓ə mìy-st-s i?
   his brothers, because he wasn't   sure

   s-k̓ʷiƛ̓-t-əm-s ɬa? k-s-c-q̓áy̓-əlx.
   his brothers   had written that.

247. Maybe you've heard about the Golden Woman at the big water.
248. If you want her, I'll go after her for you.
249. It's a pity I am working for wages, or I'd go after anything you want.
250. The king repeated what's in the letter.
251. "That's what you said."
252. No, he never said it, but he couldn't tell on his brothers, because he
     wasn't sure his brothers had written that.

253. uɫ ixì? cù-nt-əm i? tə ylmíxʷəm, "waẏ
253. And he told him the king, "Yes,

c-k̇əɫ-nìxɫ-əm-st-əm ixì? i? kʷə-kʷṙì-t i? tkɫm-ílxʷ,
I've heard about this Golden Woman,

waẏ kʷu ƛa?-ɫt-íxʷ."
go get it for me."

254. waẏ uɫ pa?-pa?s-ìnk axà? i? tə-twít; waẏ
254. He felt sad the little boy;

ċqʷ-á··qʷ, waẏ ɫ-t-xʷùy-əm-s i? kəwáp-s.
he cried, he went to see his horse.

255. waẏ ɫ-kìc-s i? kəwáp-s, uɫ ixì?
255. He got to his horse, and

ɫəc-ənt-ìs i? kəwáp-s; kɫ-ṫìc-əlxʷ-s uɫ ċqʷ-àqʷ
he patted his horse; he stroked it and he cried

ṇ-ɫik̇-ɫik̇tá-m.
sobbing.

256. cù-nt-əm i? t kəwáp-s: "stìṁ yə?
256. He asked him his horse: "What

c-k-pa?-pa?s-ínk-əm-st-xʷ?
are you feeling bad about?

257. há? kʷ s-nìxəɫ há? s-ƛl-əl-mìx i? təl
257. Did you hear somebody died from

an-ƛəx̣-əx̣-ƛx̣á-p?"
your parents?"

258. cùt: "lút, waẏ wnìxʷ kən
258. He said: "No, I'm sure

253. And the king told him, "Yes, I've heard about this Golden Woman, go
get it for me."
254. The little boy felt sad; he cried, he went to see his horse.
255. He got to his horse, and he patted his horse; he stroked it and he cried
sobbing.
256. His horse asked him: "What are you feeling bad about?
257. Did you hear somebody from your parents died?"
258. He said: "No, I'm sure

s-c-paʔ-paʔs-ínk   waẏ   kʷu s-ən-məlx̣aʔ-cìn-əm-s
feeling bad   because   they misrepresent me

i-s-k̓ʷíx̣-t-əm.
my brothers.

259. q̓ẏà-m-əlx   iʔ k̓ə ylmíxʷəm, kʷu
259. They wrote   to the king,

q̓əẏ-x̣t-ìs-əlx   incà? i-s-c-qʷəl-qʷíl-t
they wrote for me that   I   said

i-k-s-x̣̓aʔ-x̣t-ìm   yəʔ ylmìxʷəm iʔ   kʷə-kʷx̣ì-t iʔ
I can go after for   the king   the Golden

tkx̣m-ílxʷ."
Woman."

260. cù-nt-əm   axà? iʔ t kəwáp-s,   "waẏ
260. He said to him   his horse,   "Well,

lut   a-k-s-paʔ-paʔs-ínk.
don't feel bad.

261. càw-t-s iʔ s-qìlxʷ iʔ c-mús-kst-əm, waẏ
261. Always   people   take chances,

nìn̓wi? kʷu mús-kst-əm.
we will   take a chance.

262. ux̣   naqs   iʔ kʷ i-k-s-cùn-əm
262. But one thing   I'm going to tell you,

náx̣əmx̣ waẏ nìn̓wi? x̣là-p   kʷ   km̀à-m   t   mus
                       tomorrow you will take   four

s-q̓l-íps.
handkerchiefs.

feeling bad because my brothers misrepresent me.
259. They wrote to the king, they wrote for me that I said I can go after
the Golden Woman for the king."
260. His horse said to him, "Well, don't feel bad.
261. People always take chances, we will take a chance.
262. But one thing I'm going to tell you, tomorrow you will take four
handkerchiefs.

263. axà? i? naqs qʷʕáy,   uɬ   axà? i? naqs
263.   One   blue,   and   one

kʷrí–lxʷ, uɬ axà? i? naqs kʷíl–ḷxʷ, uɬ axà? i?
yellow,   and   one   red,   and

naqs ɬəxʷ q̓ʷʕáy.
one   black.

264. ṅiṅwi? iḱlì? kʷu ɬ–yáʕ–p, kʷu
264. When   there we   get,

ɬa?–cn–ítkʷ,   uɬ   ɬi ʕàc–ənt–xʷ i?   s–x̣əl–x̣ʕál–t,
near the water,   and   you look at the day,

ɬəxʷ ḷ s–ḱlàxʷ   məɬ
      in the evening when

ṇ–ḱʷúɬ–cn–əm,   uɬ ċa?kn–ìlxʷ   c–?kìn
the weather fixes the day,   whatever color

i?   s–ən–ḱʷúɬ–cn–əm   uɬ ixì?   kʷìn–(n)t–xʷ
the weather in the sky is,   the same take

i?   s–q̓l–íps,   məɬ xʷp–cn–ítkʷ–ənt–xʷ.
the handkerchief,   and put it right on the shore.

265. put i? k–s–l–əlkʷ–ùt–s i? təl yaʕ–cìn
265. Just   a little ways   from the water line

put   kʷ ṇ–st–ìls waẏ
just where you think

ɬíx–əlx.
she'll get out of the water.

266. uɬ ixì?   a–k–s–t–xɬá–m,   ṅiṅwi? put
266.   That's what you've got to watch,   when

263. One blue, and one yellow, and one red, and one black.
264. When we get there, right next to the water, and you look at the day,
     in the evening when the weather is fixing the day, whatever color the
     weather in the sky is, the same (color) take the handkerchief, and put
     it right on the shore.
265. Just a little ways from the water line just where you think she'll get
     out of the water.
266. That's what you've got to watch, when

miy-st-x^w   t́ix-əlx;   cak^w
you're sure   she's completely out of the water; if

iwà? i? s-tawn-qìna?-xən-s kəm stìm   ki?
even   her little toe   or   anything

ɬə-ɬ^ʕàt   ɬ sìwɫk^w,   uɫ lut   ť
is a little wet in the water,   you can't

a-k-s-k^wən-nún-əm.
catch her.

267. naxəmɫ yə-y^ʕà-t i? s-qìl-tk-s k-əlk^w-àk^w
267. But   her whole   body   is a little ways

i? təl síwɫk^w,   uɫ wa̗y pna?   cmay
    from the water,   you might

k^wən-nú-nt-x^w.
catch her.

268. ṅiṅwi? x^wìc-əɫt-s-ən a-k-s-yu?-yá^{ʕw}-t, wa̗y k^w
268. I will give you   your strength,

ṇ-qm-íls-əm,   wa̗y k^w púlx.
ease your mind,   go to bed.

269. ṅiṅwi? s-xlà-p mi   ṇ-q́a?-ìls-m-ənt-x^w i?
269.   Tomorrow you'll rustle   those

s-q́l-íps,   ixì? məɫ k^wu tək^w?-út."
handkerchiefs,   then   we   will go."

270. wa̗y ɫ-x^wùy, ɫ-kíc-x, wa̗y púlx.
270.   He went, got back,   went to bed.

271. wa̗y k-s-xəl-p-ìna?   wa̗y s-ta?x^w-s-q́l-íps-əm-s,
271.   The next daylight   he got handkerchiefs,

you're sure she's completely out of the water; if even her little toe or
anything is a little wet in the water, you can't catch her.

267. But her whole body is a little ways from the water, you might catch
her.

268. I will give you your strength, ease your mind, go to bed.

269. Tomorrow you'll rustle those handkerchiefs, then we will go."

270. He went, got back, went to bed.

271. The next daylight he got handkerchiefs,

way̓ t–xʷùy–m–s   i? kəwáp–s.
he went to get   his horse.

272. ṇ–tk̓ʷ–íki?–s,   way̓ k–?əmt–íws; way̓
272. He put the saddle on,   he got on;

kəl   k–s–k̓làxʷ uɫ t̓ùxʷt   i? kəwáp–s.
towards evening   he flew   his horse.

273. tə n–ɫa?–m–ìnk   i? t s–t–k̓m–ásqət ki?
273.   Right next to the   sky

xʷúy;   nak̓ʷəm ixì? i? k̓ʷùl–s–əlx i? t̓əxʷt–lwís.
he went;   they made   airplane.

274. xʷúy?–ḻx,   uɫ way̓ mət k̓làxʷ   ki?
274. They went, and   it was evening when

t̓əkʷ–k̓ʷ–úla?xʷ;   t̓əxʷ wìk–s   k̓a?t–úla?xʷ,
they struck ground;   he saw   close to the ground,

uɫ wík–s i? síwɫkʷ, sìlxʷa? i? síwɫkʷ, sìwɫkʷ
he saw the water,   big   water,   water

uɫ nís,   sìwɫkʷ uɫ
as far as you can see, water

nís.
as far as you can see.

275. uɫ lut   tə c–wìk–s k̓əl na–ɫá?,
275. And he doesn't   see   to   the other side,

way̓ kmìx   síwɫkʷ.
it's all   water.

276. way̓ ixì? mət   i? sìlxʷa? síwɫkʷ.
276.   That must be the big   ocean.

he went to get his horse.
272. He put the saddle on, he got on; towards evening his horse flew.
273. Right next to the sky he went; they made airplane.
274. They went, and it was evening when they struck ground; he saw close to the ground, he saw the water, big water, water as far as you can see, water as far as you can see.
275. And he doesn't see to the other side, it's all water.
276. That must be the big ocean.

277. way̓ ilì? t̓əkʷ-k̓ʷ-ùla?xʷ   ɬ təmxʷ-úla?xʷ;
277.   He hit the ground;

    cù-nt-əm "way̓ axà? kʷu yáʕ-p,   ixì? c̓x̣ʷ-ənt-s-ìn
    he said,   "We are here, what I tell you

    uɬ ixì? kʷu ņ-ləxʷ-úɬt-xʷ.
              you follow.

278. ta?lì? kʷ k-swít-mist,   pna? cmay ni̓ni̓wi?
278.   Do your very best,

    kʷən-nú-nt-əm.
    we might catch her.

279. alà?   c-k̓əɬ-k̓làxʷ   məɬ alà? kʷu
279. This place is out of sight,   here

    ʕac-ənt-íxʷ."
    tie me."

280. way̓ ixì? s-xʷúy-s; xʷùy
280.   He went; he went (and)

    put   iklì? ɬa?-cn-ítkʷ, uɬ way̓
    just when (he got) to   the shore,

    kɬ-xn̓-ùs-əs   i? x̣yáɬnəx̣ʷ, way̓
    it was going down the sun,

    ņ-k̓ʷúl-cn-əm.
    the weather fixed the sky.

281. axà? ɬ s-k̓s-àsqət   i? s-ən-k̓ʷúl-cn-əm, ixì?
281.   It was stormy   weather,

    q̓ʷʕáy.
    black.

277. He hit the ground; he said, "We are here, what I tell you you follow.
278. Do your very best, we might catch her.
279. This place is out of sight, tie me here."
280. He went; he went (and) just when (he got) to the shore, the sun was
    going down, the weather fixed the sky.
281. It was stormy weather, black.

282. waẏ ixì? c-kʷì-s i? q̇ʷ⹁ày-ḻxʷ i?
282.   He took the black

s-q̇l-íps;   ixì? xʷp-cn-ítkʷ-s.
handkerchief;   he spread it next to the shore.

283. waẏ i? t xʌ́ut mìy-s   s-ən-ṫəp-ṫp-áqs-əs
283.   Rocks he put on the corners

lut   i? t s-nìẇ-t k-s-níẇ-ənt-əm; waẏ
(so) it won't the wind   blow it away;

ixì? ilì? s-mút-s.
     there he sat down.

284. waẏ ṫi ixìxi?   c-ṫ?àk̇ʷ   axà? i?
284.   In a little while she came out   the

tk⹁m-ílxʷ.
woman.

285. ixì? i? s-ṗ?àxʷ-s u⹁ k⹁-ṗa?xʷ-ítkʷ."
285.   She shone   all over the water;

ixì?   nak̇ʷəm i? kʷə-kʷr̀ì-t i? tk⹁m-ílxʷ.
that was   the Golden   Woman.

286. ṇta? waẏ s-wi?-númt-x,   u⹁ axà? i?
286.   She's handsome, and

qp-qín-tən-s put c-?x̣ì⹁ t s-qlàẇ c-ṗ?áxʷ.
her hair   just like   money   shines.

287. cù-nt-əm: "waẏ tə-twít,   waẏ x̣às-t
287. She said: "Little boy,   it's pretty

a-s-q̇l-íps,   waẏ kʷu ṇ-qʷəṅ-mì-nt kʷu
your handkerchief,   pity me (and)

282. He took the black handkerchief; he spread it next to the shore.
283. He put rocks on the corners (so) the wind won't blow it away; there
he sat down.
284. In a little while the woman came out.
285. She shone all over the water; that was the Golden Woman.
286. She's handsome, and her hair shines just like money.
287. She said: "Little boy, your handkerchief is pretty, pity me (and)

xʷíc̣-ə⁊t."
give it to me."

288. cú-s: "a··, wa̓y̓ mət
288. He said to her: "Ah,   I guess

a-s-ən-q̓əm-s-cín-əm, wa̓y̓ t̓əxʷ iwà?   in-χm-ìnk,
you're stuck on it,   even though I like it,

u⁊ wa̓y̓ kʷín-(n)t-xʷ.
       you can have it.

289. t̓əxʷ naχəm⁊ t anwì? ⁊a?-nt-íxʷ, lut   kʷ
289. But   you   go after it, I'm not

t̓ i-k-s-xʷíc̣-ə⁊t-əm,   cəm   kən ⁊a?-⁊a?t̓-xˁan
   going to hand it to you, should I   get my feet wet

mi   kən hə-hú?,   lut   t̓
I'll   catch cold, I'm not

i-k-s-ən-xʷst-ítkʷ.
going to wade in the water.

290. cəm   itì? kʷu c-ən-kʷín-kst-s-əlx i? t
290. They might   grab me

ŋ-sa?p-m-átkʷ."
those little animals."

291. wa̓y̓ c-k̓ìt-əlx   i? tk⁊m-ílxʷ, wa̓y̓ u⁊
291.   She came closer the woman,

n-yˁìp c-ən-qʷən̓-qʷn̓a-míst-m-ənt-əm, "wa̓y̓ kʷu
she kept a-begging,

c-?úkʷ-⁊t-xʷ."
"Bring it to me."

give it to me."
288. He said to her: "Ah, I guess you're stuck on it, even though I like it,
     you can have it.
289. But you go after it, I'm not going to hand it to you, should I get my
     feet wet I'll catch cold, I'm not going to wade in the water.
290. Those little animals might grab me."
291. The woman came closer, she kept a-begging, "Bring it to me."

292. cù-s: "lút, waẏ cù-nt-s-ən lút.
292. He said: "No, I told you no.

293. ṅiṅwi? ɬ an-x̣m-ìnk uɬ kʷín-(n)t-x̣ʷ, t
293. If you like it you come and get it,

anwi? ƛ̓a?-nt-íx̣ʷ; nax̣əmɬ lut kʷ t̓
you get it; I'm not

i-k-s-x̣ʷíc-əɬt-əm.
going to hand it to you.

294. lut t̓ in-x̣m-ìnk i? síwɬkʷ,
294. I don't like the water,

i-s-ən-x̣əl-x̣əl-s-núx̣ʷ."
I'm dead scared of it."

295. húy, húy, huy, huy,
295. She kept coming

c-ƛ̓a?-cn-itkʷ; waẏ t̓əx̣ʷ c-ən-x̣ʷst-ítkʷ,
closer to the water; she started walking,

s-ql-wt-ùla?x̣ʷ uɬ ixì? s-c-ən-x̣ʷst-ítkʷ-s.
she stepped on dry land and she started walking.

296. uɬ t n-yʕip iwà?
296. And she keeps to no avail

c-qʷəṅ-qʷəṅ-s-cín-m-ənt-əm; n-yʕip lút-st-s.
a-begging for it; he keeps saying no.

297. huy c-t̓íx-əlx, uɬ ṇ-st-ìls ax̣à? i?
297. She's on dry land, and he thought the

tə-twít, "waẏ waẏ c-t̓íx-əlx, lut
little boy, "She's all out of the water, no

292. He said: "No, I told you no.
293. If you like it you come and get it, you get it; I'm not going to hand it to you.
294. I don't like the water, I'm dead scared of it."
295. She kept coming closer to the water; she started walking, she stepped on dry land and she started walking.
296. And she keeps a-begging for it to no avail; he keeps saying no.
297. She's on dry land, and the little boy thought, "She's all out of the water,

stìm-s ɬ sìwɬkʷ ťə c-tká-nxʷ.
thing in the water is touching.

298. naǩʷəm axà? i? s-tawn-qína?-xən-s i?
298. But her little toe,

qʷəx-qìn-xən-s, naǩʷəm ixi? pùt-i? ɬ síwɬkʷ
her toenail, that still in the water

c-wtán.
is.

299. ṇ-wìs-əlx kʷni-ùtya?-st-s axà? i?
299. He jumped up (and) grabbed the

tkɬm-ílxʷ, uɬ aɬi? waẏ kʷì-s axà? i?
woman, and already she has the

s-q̇l-íps.
handkerchief.

300. ṇ-wìs-əlx axà? i? kʷə-kʷrì-t i? tkɬm-ílxʷ,
300. She jumped the Golden Woman,

ǩʷəɫ-ǩʷəɫ-p-íkst-əm-s, waẏ ṇ-?əɫxʷ-ítkʷ
he dropped her, she got in the water,

nís.
she was gone.

301. uɬ aɬi? mət s-ən-xʷt-xʷt-ìls-x
301. And because he must have had a quick temper

axà? i? tə-twít, ixì? uɬ kəs-t-mì-s i?
the little boy, he blamed

kəwáp-s; "lut c-?xìɬ t s-k-ċaxʷ-s, kʷu
his horse; "He didn't mean it,

nothing is touching the water.
298. But her little toe, her toenail, that is still in the water.
299. He jumped up (and) grabbed the woman, and already she has the handkerchief.
300. The Golden Woman jumped, he dropped her, she got in the water, she was gone.
301. And because the little boy must have had a quick temper, he blamed his horse; "He didn't mean it,

màlxa?-s   i? t in-kəwáp.
he lied to me   my horse.

302. waẏ, waẏ kən kɫ-ƛ̓l-ál,   kʷu ɫ
302. Yes,   I   am a goner,

málxa?-s."
he lied to me."

303. ixì? ɫ-t-xʷùy-m-s i? kəwáp-s,   ixì?
303.   He went to   his horse,

s-kʷnì-m-s i? t s-xə-x̣c̓í?, k-sp̓-ìc̓a?-s   i?
he took   a   stick,   he hit him on the body

kəwáp-s,   la?ɫ k-səp̓-qí-s.
his horse, even hit him on the head.

304. iwà?   t-x̣?ən-cən-mìst-m-ənt-əm i? t
304. He tried to stop him

kəwáp-s: "waẏ kʷu c-qʷn̓-íkst-əm-st-xʷ."
his horse: "Have pity on me."

305. cù-s: "uɫ s-c-?kìn-x kən k-s-ƛ̓l-əl-mìx-a?x
305. He said: "Why,   I   am going to die

ùɫi?   kʷu ɫ málxa?-nt-xʷ.
and then   you lied to me.

306. ɫx̣ʷp-nù-n   i? kʷə-kʷrì-t i? tkɫm-ílxʷ."
306. She got away the Golden   Woman."

307. iwà? cù-nt-əm   i? t kəwáp-s: "waẏ
307.   He told him   his horse:

km̓a?   incà? i-s-k-c̓áx̣ʷ, anwí?,   waẏ
"It's not   my fault,   it's yours,

my horse lied to me.
302. Yes, I am a goner, he lied to me."
303. He went to his horse, he took a stick, he hit his horse on the body,
     even hit him on the head.
304. His horse tried to stop him: "Have pity on me."
305. He said: "Why, I am going to die and then you lied to me.
306. The Golden Woman got away."
307. His horse told him: "It's not my fault, it's yours,

```
cù-nt-s-ən,   'mìy-st-xʷ  k-əlkʷ-àkʷ  c-màlkʷ      i?
I told you,   'make sure  it's out    completely

s-qíl-tk-s,   k-əlkʷ-àkʷ  i?  təl   síwɫkʷ,     mi
her body,     far             from  the water,  and then

kʷni-útya?-st-xʷ.'
you can grab her.'
```

308. uɫ aɫì? ƙəm i? s-tawn-qìna?-xən-s i?
308.   But   her little toe's

```
q̓ʷəx̣-qín-xən-s  yə?  c-k-ɫˤac-p         t   síwɫkʷ.
nail                 still had a drop  of  water.
```

309. ixì?   aɫì? i? k-sy-sy-ùs-tən-s i?   síwɫkʷ.
309. That's   her power,   the water.

310. wa̓y wi?-s-kʷì-s   i? s-q̓l-íps,   ili?
310.   She already had the handkerchief,

```
qc-p-m-əncút,  iwà?              kʷ  kʷən-s-qìlxʷ  uɫ  ƛi
she drew back, (you) tried to       grab her        and

kʷ  ṇ-kʷən-ks-əncùt          yə?  ?x̣i?  uɫ
you grabbed your own hands,        and

nís."
she's gone."
```

311. lut, n-yˤìp   pùl-st-s i? kəwáp-s   uɫ
311. No,   he's still licking   his horse and

```
k-səp̓-qí-s.
hitting him on the head.
```

312. ɫx̣ʷp-nù-s   axà? i? kəwáp-s, wa̓y
312. He got away   the horse,

I told you, 'make sure her body is completely out, far from the water,
and then you can grab her.'
308. But her little toe's nail still had a drop of water.
309. That's her power, the water.
310. She already had the handkerchief, she drew back, you tried to grab her
     and you grabbed your own hands, and she's gone."
311. No, he's still licking his horse and hitting him on the head.
312. The horse got away, his horse got out of sight.

kəw-p-ùs-əm-s   i? kəwáp-s.
he got out of sight   his horse.

313. waẏ   ki?   c-?x̣ìɫ t ṇ-t́a?l-íls.
313. That's   when   he came to himself.

314. "ṇta?, waẏ waẏ kən k-ɫəṕ-əm-scút,
314. "Gee,   I   am disgusted with myself,

     waẏ uɫ t́i i-s-ən-xʷt-xʷt-ìls   uɫ
         and   it's all from my bad temper   that

     ṇ-k̇əs-t-mí-n.
     put me in bad.

315. waẏ kʷu x̣ʷìl-st-s   in-kəwáp təl
315.   He left me   my horse   because

     púl-st-ən,   waẏ ixì? uɫ sìc kən
     I beat him,   and now I

     k-ɫəṕ-m-əncút.
     am disgusted with myself.

316. kən əx-?kn-əm-scùt mi kən ɫ-k̇əɫ-kíc-x?
316.   What can I do   to   get back?

317. cəm̀ iwà?   kən ɫa? ɫ-k̇əɫ-kìc-x, uɫ
317. And even if I   get back,

     k̇aw   axà? i? tkɫm-ílxʷ, uɫ waẏ kʷu
     she's gone   that   woman,   and

     pùl-st-s   in-ylmíxʷəm.
     he'll kill me my boss.

318. uɫ aɫì? lut   t́ə c-ən-ləՙw-ùs i?
318.   It didn't   come true   what

313. That's when he came to himself.
314. "Gee, I am disgusted with myself, and it's all from my bad temper that
     put me in bad.
315. My horse left me because I beat him, and now I am disgusted with
     myself.
316. What can I do to get back?
317. And even if I get back, that woman is gone, and my boss'll kill me.
318. It didn't come true what I promised him.

ċəx̌ʷ–xít–ən."
I promised him."

319. waẏ ċqʷ–à··qʷ   uɫ   ťi   x̌ʷst–lwís;   waẏ
319.   He cried   and   he walked around;

cəh–xən–mì–s   uɫ   aɫì?   k–sá–sq̇t–əm;
he was on a good track   and   it started to rain;

k–sà–sq̇t–əm   uɫ   nìw̓–t   axà?   i?   ɫ?–əm–cn–ítkʷ
it rained   and   the wind blew   close to shore

uɫ   ŋ–?íwl–əm.
and   there were waves.

320. waẏ cəh–xən–mì–s   nakʷəm ixì?   ɫ
320.   He was on a good track

məl–qn–ùps   yə?   s–qʷs–qʷa?síya?–s   sic   mət
there were eagle   babies   just

s–k–ťí–ɫəqʷ–s–a?x,   ?asíl.
hatched,   two of them.

321. waẏ ťi k–cqʷ–cʕìqʷ–ċa?   lut   ťə
321.   Their bodies   didn't

k–spúm–t.
have any feathers.

322. ŋťa? waẏ uɫ ťi x̌ʷár,   x̌ʷár,
322.

x̌ʷàr–əlx   i?   t   s–ċáɫ–t.
They were shivering   from   the cold.

323. waẏ ŋ–qʷəṅ–mí–s,   waẏ ixì?
323.   He felt sorry for them,

319. He cried and he walked around; he was on a good track and it started
    to rain; it rained and the wind blew close to shore and there were
    waves.
320. He was on a good track, there were eagle babies just hatched, two of
    them.
321. Their bodies didn't have any feathers.
322. They were shivering from the cold.
323. He felt sorry for them,

a-ʔù··lus-əm   iʔ t k̓áماʔ,   iʔ t
he started to gather   pine needles,

stím;   ixìʔ k-wr̓-ìcaʔ-s   axàʔ iʔ
anything;   he started building a fire for   the

pə-pˤás-pəs, iʔ qaʔɬ-məl-qn-úps, ilìʔ uɬ
baby chicks, the eagle babies,   and

kʷaʔ-kʷʔáɬ.
they warmed up.

324. ti kʷmiɬ   kiʔ c-k̓əɬ-nìxɬ-əm-s ti
324.   All at once   he heard

x̓ám·;   way̓ alàʔ c-kíc-ənt-əm, way̓ ixìʔ nak̓ʷəm
something;   there she got,

iʔ túm-təm̓, iʔ tkɬm-ílxʷ.
the mother, a woman.

325. way̓ ṇ-x̓il-m-ənt-əm la c-xʔít-iʔ, huy
325.   She was scared at first,   then

kíc-ənt-əm,   way̓ qəm-p-nú-s.
she came around,   she quieted down.

326. way̓ nixʷ c-k̓əɬ-nìxɬ-əm-s-əlx iʔ náqs,
326.   They heard   another one,

ixìʔ   nak̓ʷəm iʔ s-qəl-tmíxʷ.
that's   the man.

327. way̓ ixìʔ nax̓əmɬ my-s-ən-x̓il-m-ənt-əm;
327.   He   was more scared;

t-xəlk-mì··-nt-əm, way̓   kíc-ənt-əm,
he went around,   finally he got there,

      he started to gather pine needles, anything; he started building a fire
      for the baby chicks, the eagle babies, and they warmed up.
    324. All at once he heard something; she got there, the mother, a woman.
    325. She was scared at first, then she came around, she quieted down.
    326. They heard another one, that's the man.
    327. He was more scared; he went around, finally he got there, landed.

ɫəkʷ–k̓ʷ–úla?xʷ.
landed.

328. way̓ ixì? lìm–t–m–ənt–m–əlx axà? i? t
328.   They are tickled   the

  məl–qn–úps; cù–nt–m–əlx: "way̓ lìm–ləm–t   kʷu
  eagles;   They said to him: "Thank you for

  xʷəl–xʷəl–ɫt–ìxʷ i? s–qʷs–qʷa?síya?–tət.
  saving   our children.

329. way̓ ixì? iwà?   ki? kʷu ɫ c–k–swìt–mist
329.   For nothing we   did our best

  yə? ?x̣i? təl   nàqs təmxʷ–úla?xʷ
              (to come back) from another country

  ki? k–sá–sq̓t–əm,   itlì? ki? kʷu ɫ
  when the storm came, that's when we

  c–tkʷú–p–xən   iwà?; uɫ way̓
  tried to get back in vain; and

  c–k̓əɫ–twín̓–nt–əm;   cakʷ lut   anwì?
  we didn't get here in time; if it weren't for you,

  uɫ ƛ̓axʷ–t–əlx   i? t s–c̓áɫ–t,
     they would have died   frozen,

  way̓ k–wɪ̓–íca?–nt–xʷ–əlx.
  and you made a fire for them.

330. way̓ uɫ stìm̓ y a–s–yaʕ–p–cín?
330.   And what is   your trouble?

331. lut   alà? ɫə k–s–ɫəl–s–qílxʷ, k–anwì?
331. There aren't here any earth people, only you

328. The eagles are tickled; They said to him: "Thank you for saving our
    children.
329. For nothing we did our best (to come back) from another country when
    the storm came, that's when we tried to get back in vain; and we didn't
    get here in time; if it weren't for you, they would have died frozen,
    and you made a fire for them.
330. And what is your trouble?
331. There aren't any earth people here, only you

alà? kʷ s-t̓əl-s-qìlxʷ alà? ɬ wìk-ənt-s-t i? kʷu
here are people that we see

əɬ xʷəl-xʷəl-ɬt-ìxʷ i? s-qʷs-qʷa?síya?-tət; uɬ
and you saved our children; and

mət kʷ s-ək-s-c-ən-q̓a?-íls-s, mət
you must have business here, there must be

stìm̓ kʷ yaˤ-p-cín, a-s-c-ən-q̓a?-íls."
something you want, your business."

332. waẏ ixì? s-m̓ay?-ncùt-s axà? i? tə-twít,
332.   Then he told them   the boy,

cùt, "waẏ ixì? axà? i-s-c-ən-q̓a?-íls.
he said, "Here's my business.

333. ixì? kʷu s-k-məlxa?-ípla?-m-s-əlx, kʷu
333.   They lied about me,

s-məlxa?-cìn-əm-s i-s-k̓ʷíɬ-t-əm i? kə
they lied about my words my brothers to

ylmíxʷəm; itlì? kʷu c-kʷùlst-s yə? ylmìxʷəm
the boss; then he sent me the chief

i-s-ƛ̓?à-m i? kʷə-kʷrì-t i? tkɬm-ílxʷ.
to get the Golden Woman.

334. ixì? uɬ axà? i? kʷu c̓əxʷ-c̓xʷ-ənt-ìs
334.   And   he told me what to do

in-kəwáp iwà?, ixì? aɬì?
my horse but it didn't work, that's

in-k-sy-sy-ús-tn̩.
my power.

here are people that we see and you saved our children; and you must
have business here, there must be something you want, your business."
332. Then the boy told them, he said, "Here's my business.
333. They lied about me, my brothers lied about my words to the boss; then
the chief sent me to get the Golden Woman.
334. And my horse told me what to do but it didn't work, that's my power.

335. ul   ixì?   alà?   kən   k̓ə�-?əm-cn-ìtkʷ   ixì?
335. And   there I   sat by the shore where

  ṇ-k̓ʷúl-cn-əm,   ul   ixì?
  the weather paints the sky,   and

  xʷip-la?xʷ-ən   i?   t   s-q̓l-íps,   ul   kən
  I spread on the ground   the   handkerchief, and   I

  ṇ-st-ìls   way̓   t̓íx-əlx,   way̓   yə-yʕà-t
  thought   she was out of the water,   her whole

  i?   s-qìl-tk-s   t̓íx-əlx,   ul   a�ì?
       body   was out of the water, and

  ixì?   kʷu   cù-s   in-kəwáp.
  that's what   he told me   my horse.

336. way̓   kən   ṇ-wìs-əlx   ul   ixì?   kən
336.   I   jumped up   and   I

  kʷən-kʷən-(n)t-wíxʷ,   way̓   ul   lut   t̓
  grabbed her,   but   I didn't

  i-s-kʷən·-í?st.
  catch her.

337. way̓   t̓i   kən   c-kʷən-kʷən-ks-əncút.
337.   I   just grabbed my own hands.

338. yə?   ?x̣i?   t̓i   �ip   i?   t   silxʷa?   i?
338.   She disappeared   in   the big

  t   síw�kʷ,   kʷì-s   i?   s-q̓l-íps.
  water,   with   the handkerchief.

339. way̓   ul   lut   t̓
339.   And I'll never

335. And there I sat by the shore where the weather paints the sky, and
  I spread the handkerchief on the ground, and I thought she was out of
  the water, her whole body was out of the water, and that's what my
  horse told me.
336. I jumped up and I grabbed her, but I didn't catch her.
337. I just grabbed my own hands.
338. She disappeared in the big water, with the handkerchief.
339. And I'll never

i-kł-əł-təq-q-nún-əm."
get another chance to fool her."

340. cù-nt-əm: "há?   k̇im   k^w
340. They asked him: "Do you have another

k-s-q̇l-íps?
handkerchief?

341. wȧy̓ t̓əx^w ṅiṅwi? kən-xìt-əm-t   ałi?   k^wu
341.   We'll help you because we

s-lím-t-x;   t̓əx^w k^w c-mú-ṁs-əlx,   lùt-əm
are grateful;   have a little hope, it's not

k-s-míy-s, nak̇wà?   tù··1   ixì? i? k^wə-k^wṙł-t
for sure, she's not beatable   the Golden

i? tkłm-ílx^w i? t   sy-sy-ús-c.
Woman   because she's smart.

342. ṇ-?əłn-a?-s-qìlx^w-tṇ ł síwłk^w,   ixì?   i?
342. She's a man-eater   in the water, that's

təmx^w-úla?x^w-s.
her country.

343. put   c-?x̣ìł i? t an-kəwàp   i?
343. Just like   your horse

k-s-c̓x̣^w-ənt-s-ít;   ṅiṅwi?   put
we're going to preach to you; (you) will just

miy̓-st-x^w   wȧy̓ k-əlk^w-àk^w təl sìwłk^w
have to be sure that   she's away from the water

mi   k^w k^wən-k^wən-twíx^w, wȧy̓ k^wən-nú-nt-x^w.
before you grab her,   then you can hold her.

get another chance to fool her."
340. They asked him: "Do you have another handkerchief?
341. We'll help you because we are grateful; have a little hope, it's not for
     sure, the Golden Woman is not beatable because she's smart.
342. She's a man-eater in the water, that's her country.
343. Just like your horse we're going to preach to you; (you) will just have
     to be sure that she's away from the water before you grab her, then
     you can hold her.

344. uɬ naxəmɬ ixìʔ c-tka-nxʷ   iʔ s-qíl-tk-s,
344.   But   if it's touching   her body,

   uɬ aɬiʔ   ixìʔ   k-sy-sy-ús-tṇ-s, ixìʔ ɬ   sìlxʷaʔ
      because that's her power,   in the big

   ɬ síwɬkʷ, uɬ waỳ lut   a-k-s-əkɬ-cáw-t.
      water,   you can't do anything.

345. uɬ waỳ nìnwiʔ iʔ k-s-kən-xìt-əm-t   iʔ
345.   We're going to help you

   ɬ   a-k-s-kʷəc-kʷác-t; ixìʔ nìnwiʔ k-əlkʷ-akʷ-st-ìxʷ
   with your strength;   when   you get her away

   iʔ təl sìwɬkʷ,   uɬ waỳ nìnwiʔ ƛl-əl-p-nú-nt-əm.
      from the water,   then   we can stop her.

346. naxəmɬ kʷ ʔxìl-əm la c-xʔìt-iʔ   pùt-iʔ
346. But if you do like   the first time when

   kəm iʔ q̇ʷəx-qìn-xən-s c-ɬə-ɬc-ʕáp, uɬ aɬiʔ ixìʔ
      her toenail   had water on,   that's

   k-sy-sy-ús-tṇ-s, lut   a-k-s-əkɬ-càw-t, uɬ
   her power,   you won't have any show, and

   nís."
   she'd be gone."

347. waỳ wiʔ-s-c̣xʷ-ənt-ìs-əlx,   waỳ
347.   They got done telling him what to do,

   k̇əɬ-ʔəm-cín.
   he agreed.

348. ixìʔ uɬ waỳ ṃʔán,   waỳ təxʷ
348.   It was past noon,

344. But if her body is touching, because that's her power, in the big water,
     you can't do anything.
345. We're going to help you with your strength; when you get her away from
     the water, then we can stop her.
346. But if you do like the first time when her toenail had water on, that's
     her power, you won't have any show, and she'd be gone."
347. They got done telling him what to do, he agreed.
348. It was past noon,

wi?-ásqət,   uɫ   ixì?   ɫ s-ən-ca?x̣-ùla?x^w   yə? ɫ
it quit raining, and   a red hot weather

ṇ-k̓^wúɫ-cn-əm,   uɫ   ixì?   k̓wíl.
the sky painted, and that's red.

349. uɫ ixì? k̓im   i? k̓wìl-ḷx^w i?
349. And that's what's left,   the   red

s-q̇l-íps,   yə? c-t-x̣ɫ-əst-ís.
handkerchief, what he's keeping.

350. ixì? x^wp-cn-ìtk^w-s i? s-q̇l-íps.
350. So   he spread   the handkerchief.

351. wa̓y ti ixìxi?   uɫ c-t̓?àk̓^w
351.   In a little while   she came to the top

axà? i? k^wə-k^wrì-t i? tkɫm-ílx^w.
    the Golden   Woman.

352. cù-nt-əm: "wa̓y   tə-tw̓ít,   wa̓y x̣às-t
352. She said: "Well little boy,   it's pretty

a-s-q̇l-íps,   wa̓y k^wu x^wíc-əɫt."
your handkerchief,   give it to me."

353. cù-s: "a··, wa̓y t̓əx^w iwà? i-s-q̇íx̣-q̇əx̣-t,
353. He said: "Ah,   I'm stingy of it,

t̓əx^w aɫi? a-s-ən-q̇əm-s-cìn-əm, wa̓y c-ƛ̓a?-nt-íx^w,
but since you're stuck on it,   come after it,

lut   nax̣əmɫ k^w t i-k-s-?úk^w-ɫt-əm."
I'm not   going to hand it to you."

354. wa̓y uɫ c-k̓ít-əlx-m-ənt-əm,   uɫ iwà?
354.   She came a little closer,

    it quit raining, and the sky painted a red hot weather, and that's red.
349. And that's what's left, the red handkerchief, what he's keeping.
350. So he spread the handkerchief.
351. In a little while the Golden Woman came to the top.
352. She said: "Well little boy, your handkerchief is pretty, give it to me."
353. He said: "Ah, I'm stingy of it, but since you're stuck on it, come after
    it, I'm not going to hand it to you."
354. She came a little closer,

k̓əɬ-ʔəxʷ-ʔəxʷ-kʷu̓-kst-əm   k-s-ən-xʷst-i̓tkʷ-aʔx.
a-begging him   to walk in the water.

355. cu̓-s: "lut, wa̓y cu̓-nt-s-ən
355. He said: "No,   I told you

i-s-ən-x̌əi̓-x̌əi̓-s-nu̓xʷ iʔ si̓wɬkʷ; uɬ ixi̓ʔ-m̓ anwi̓ʔ
I'm dead scared of   the water;   and that's your

an-təmxʷ-u̓laʔxʷ,   uɬ   lut   c-ən-x̌i̓l-əm-st-xʷ;
country,   and you're not   afraid;

wa̓y ƛ̓aʔ-nt-i̓xʷ."
     you come after it."

356. hu̓··y c-ti̓x-əlx;   wa̓y mi̓y-st-s
356. Well, she got on dry land;   he was sure

k-əlkʷ-àkʷ iʔ təl si̓wɬkʷ   uɬ aɬi̓ʔ
she's out   of   the water   because

k-l-əlkʷ-i̓lx-st-s.
he took it farther.

357. put wa̓y ni̓ṅwi̓ʔ cakʷ iwàʔ ɬ k-ƛ̓áq̓-əxn-əm,   uɬ
357.   If   even   she stretched,

lut   ɬə k-s-k̓əɬ-ki̓c-x-s; uɬ wa̓y put
she can't   reach it;   and   she's entirely

k-əlkʷ-àkʷ iʔ təl si̓wɬkʷ   mi   k̓əɬ-ki̓c-s
out   of   the water before she can reach

iʔ s-q̓l-i̓ps.
the handkerchief.

358. wa̓y k̓əɬ-ki̓c-s axàʔ iʔ s-q̓l-i̓ps,
358.   She got to   the handkerchief,

a-begging him to walk in the water.
355. He said: "No, I told you I'm dead scared of the water; and that's your country, and you're not afraid; you come after it."
356. Well, she got on dry land; he was sure she's out of the water because he took it farther.
357. If even she stretched, she can't reach it; and she's entirely out of the water before she can reach the handkerchief.
358. She got to the handkerchief,

ṇ-wìs-əlx,   ṇ-cəẃ-cəẃ-cì-s i? məl-qn-úps,
he jumped up, he mocked   the eagles,

kʷni-ùtya?-st-s axà? i? tkɫm-ílxʷ, waý kʷən-nú-s.
he grabbed   the woman,   he held her.

359. axà? iwà?   t-qəl-p-m-əncùt axà? i?
359.   She tried to squirm around   the

tkɫm-ílxʷ, waý ƛi qˁáy,   uɫ aɫi?
woman,   it's like a vise,   because

k-əlkʷ-àkʷ i? təl síwɫkʷ, i? təl s-k̓ʷəc-k̓ʷác-t-s.
she's away   from water,   from her power.

360. waý wì·ˑm   s-ən-cəq̓-cəq̓-mìst-s i?
360.   To no avail she squirmed around the

kʷə-kʷṙì-t i? tkɫm-ílxʷ.
Golden   Woman.

361. ixì? ṇ-qʷəṅ-qʷṅa-mìst-əm-s axà? i? tə-twít:
361. Then she started begging   the boy:

"waý kʷu ṇ-qʷəṅ-mì-nt   kʷu ɫwn-íkst-m-ənt."
     "Have pity on me,   let me go."

362. cù-s: "lut aɫi? kʷ ƛ
362. He said: "No,

i-k-s-ɫwn-íkst-əm,   waý kʷ i-s-c-k̓?á-m."
I'm (not) going to let you go,   I came for you."

363. uɫ aɫi? s-wi?-nùmt-x axà? i? tə-twít, uɫ
363. And   he's handsome   the boy,

aɫi? miṅà   lut k̓ʷùl-kst-əm-s-əlx t
     probably   they dolled him up

he jumped up, he mocked the eagles, he grabbed the woman, he held her.

359. The woman tried to squirm around, it's like a vise, because she's away from water, from her power.

360. To no avail the Golden Woman squirmed around.

361. Then she started begging the boy: "Have pity on me, let me go."

362. He said: "No, I'm (not) going to let you go, I came to get you."

363. And the boy is handsome, probably the eagles dolled him up.

həɬ-məl-qn-úps.
the eagles.

364. waẏ ixì? cù-s: "ɫəxʷ lut kʷ ṫ
364.   He said to her: "I'm not

i-k-s-ɬwn-ìkst-əm put ṅiṅwi? ḱla? ɫəxʷ kʷu
going to let you go until   we

k-əlkʷ-ìlx   i? təl síwɬkʷ; ixì? ilì?
are a little ways off from the water;

mi sic ɬwn-íkst-m-ənt-s-ən."
  then I'll let you go."

365. waẏ ixì? s-t-kxən-m-əncùt-s axà? i?
365. Then she went along   the

kʷə-kʷrì-t i? tkɬm-ílxʷ.
Golden   Woman.

366. uɬ alì? c-ən-q̇əl-q̇əlxʷ-áx̣n-əm-st-s, waẏ
366.   He had her hooked under the arm,

iḱlì? k-əlkʷ-àkʷ-əlx   i? təl síwɬkʷ, waẏ
  they went a little ways from the water,

ixì? s-kʷíl·-s-əlx.
  they sat down.

367. ixì? cù-s: "hu-húy put kʷu
367.   He said: "Now   we

c-kʷìl-lx,   ixì? sic kʷu may?-xt-wíxʷ."
are settled down, now we can talk things over."

368. waẏ nàx̣əmɬ alì? wəypáy-əm,   uɬ
368.   Then he played white man, and

364. He said to her: "I'm not going to let you go until we are a little ways
off from the water; then I'll let you go."
365. Then the Golden Woman went along.
366. He had her hooked under the arm, they went a little ways from the
water, they sat down.
367. He said: "Now we are settled down, now we can talk things over."
368. Then he played white man, and

c–kʷən–kʷìn–ks–(s)t–s   axà? i? tkɬm–ílxʷ,
he was holding hands with   the woman,

c–ən–q̇əl–q̇əlxʷ–áx̣n–əm–st–s, uɬ kʷíl–lx.
he hooked her in the arm,   and they sat down.

369. ixì? uɬ–i? cù–nt–əm   i? t tkɬm–ílxʷ: "uɬ
369.   Then   she asked him the   woman:

kʷa x̣əl stìm ki? kʷu əc–ən–q̇a?–íls–əm–st–xʷ
  "For what that   it's your business with me

kʷu ɬ a–k–s–kʷnì–m, ṫəxʷ aɬì? kʷu
  to take me,

c–ƛ̣a?–nt–íxʷ?"
(and) you got me?"

370. cù–s,   "waẏ aɬì? kən s–əc–k̇ʷùl–x   i?
370. He said: "Well,   I   have been working

l   ylmíxʷəm; uɬ waẏ iwà? kən
for the chief; and   I

k̇əɬ–twǹ–əls–míst;   kən c–mùs–kst–əm uɬ–i?
didn't think I could do it; I   took a chance and

c–ƛ̣a?–nt–s–ín;   waẏ ṫəxʷ iwà? lut
I came after you;   I'm not

i–s–yəʕʷ–p–yáw–t."
qualified for anything."

371. cù–nt–əm: "wáẏ, waẏ ǹiǹwi? ɬ–kxən–(n)t–s–ìn
371. She said: "Well,   (I) will go back with you

uɬ aɬì?   waẏ kʷu kʷən–nú–nt–xʷ, waẏ kʷu
  because   you got me,   we

he was holding hands with the woman, he hooked her in the arm, and
they sat down.

369. Then the woman asked him: "Why is it your business with me to take
me, (and) you got me?"

370. He said: "Well, I have been working for the chief; and I didn't think
I could do it; I took a chance and I came after you; I'm not qualified
for anything."

371. She said: "Well, I will go back with you because you got me, we

ł-xʷùy   kxən-(n)t-s-ín.
will go back,   I'll follow you.

372. uł ałì? təl   s-c-k̓ʷùl-s   i?   təmxʷ-úla?xʷ,
372.   Since   it was made   the   world,

    lut   i?   t   s-qílxʷ   kəm   t   stìm̓   kʷu   tə
    there is no   person   or   anything

    c-kʷən-nú-st-s.
    that can catch me.

373. t anwì? ki? kʷu kʷən-nú-nt-xʷ.
373.   You   got me.

374. uł minà   tanm̓ús,   uł waẏ ťi
374. And maybe it's not   for nothing,

    la?ł anwì? mi   kʷu   c-mr·ím.
    with you   (I) will   get married.

375. cakʷ iwà? há? ylmìxʷəm,   uł ałì? mət waẏ
375. If   even   he's a king,

    i? k̓əl s-ƛ̓əx̣-əx̣-ƛ̓x̣à-p-s,   waẏ mət n̓-k̓əw-ḷx-ílx;
    he has reached old age,   he's old;

    uł axà? anwì? sic   kʷ s-c-k̓ʷùl-ḷx uł
    and   you   are beginning   to grow,   and

    anwì? kʷ   i-kł-my-ł-x̣m-ínk."
    you   I'm going to love better."

376. uł ałì? n̓-st-ils   kʷə-kʷr̓ì-t i? tkłm-ílxʷ,
376. And   she thought   the Golden   Woman,

    "min̓à   tanm̓ús axà? i? tə-twít; mət waẏ
    "It's not for nothing this   boy;

will go back, I'll follow you.
372. Since the world was made, there is no person or anything that can catch me.
373. You got me.
374. And maybe it's not for nothing, I will get married with you.
375. Even if he's a king, he has reached old age, he's old; and you are beginning to grow, and I'm going to love you better."
376. And the Golden Woman thought, "This boy is not for nothing;

k-s-c-k̓x̣à-p̣   ki?   kʷu
he'll grow into something,   that's why

kʷən-nú-s.
he caught me.

377. uł   axà? i?   k̓ʷìƛ-ət i?   s-qílxʷ   lut
377. And   the rest of the   people   can't even

     kʷu t̓ə c-kəlq̓ʷ-íkst-s-əlx, uł   axà? s-my-ł-tə-twìt
           touch my arm,   and this outstanding boy

     kʷən-nú-s; way̓ mət   s-yəʕʷ-p-yáw-t-x."
     caught me; he must be   smart."

378. s-c-?x̣ìl-x uł axà? x̣m-ìnk-s   axà? i?
378. That's how   she got stuck on that

     tə-twìt.
     boy.

379. way̓ uł xʷúy?-ɬx,   c-ən-q̓əl-q̓əlxʷ-àx̣n-əm-st-s
379.   They went, he hooked his arm on

     axà? i?   tkłm-ílxʷ,   aɬì?   way̓ uł k-əlkʷ-àkʷ,
         the woman's,   because   they're far,

     uł   way̓ ṇ-qm-ìls-əm   axà? i?   tə-twìt, uł
     and   his mind is settled,   the boy's,   and

     t̓əxʷ nax̣əmł ilì? c-t-kʷən-ks-ənwáxʷ-əlx,
                    they're holding hands,

     wəypáy-m-əlx.
     they're playing white people.

380. way̓ ł-xʷùy?-ɬx   ł-yáʕ-p-əlx;   way̓
380.   They went back, they got back;

he'll grow into something, that's why he caught me.

377. And the rest of the people can't even touch my arm, and this
outstanding boy caught me; he must be smart."

378. That's how she got stuck on that boy.

379. They went, he hooked his arm on the woman's, because they're far, and
his mind is settled, the boy's, and they're holding hands, they're playing
white people.

380. They went back, they got back; they went to the king's house.

xʷùyʔ-ḷx   iʔ   k̓əl   s-yləmxʷ-iɬxʷ.
they went   to   the king's house.

381. níkxnaʔ   ɬ   c-k̓əɬ-k̓ʷiɬ-əp-t-əlx,   n̓taʔ
381. Gee,   when   they come in sight,

wik-s-əlx   iʔ   tə-twit   ɬə   c-xʷúy,   n̓taʔ   iʔ
they saw   the boy   coming,   gee

səx-cùt-s   s-k-p̓aʔxʷ-icaʔ-s,   n̓taʔ   tàɬ-t   uɬ
his company   is shiny,   straight   and

kɬ-càw-t   iʔ   s-p̓ʔáxʷ-s;   put   c-ʔx̣iɬ   iʔ   t
great   her shining;   just   like   the

x̣yáɬnəx̣ʷ,   iʔ   təl   x̣yàɬnəx̣ʷ   iʔ   s-p̓ʔáxʷ-s.
sun,   from   the sun   the   shining.

382. waẙ   ixiʔ   mət   kʷə-k̓ʷri-t   iʔ   tkɬm-ilxʷ.
382.   That must be   the Golden   Woman.

383. n̓taʔ   s-wiʔ-númt-x,   uɬ   yə-yʕà-t   iʔ
383. My,   she's good looking,   and all   the

s-qil-tk-s   s-əc-p̓ʔáxʷ-s,   uɬ   iʔ   qp-qin-tn̩-s   put
body   shines,   and   her hair   just

c-ʔx̣iɬ   t   kʷə-k̓ʷri-t   iʔ   s-ʕác-əc.
like   gold   looks.

384. waẙ   k̓ɬ-ən-caʔ-íp-əm,   waẙ
384.   They got close to the door,

k̓ɬ-ən-k̓ahk̓ʷ-ip-ɬt-əm   iʔ   tə   ylmíxʷəm.
they opened the door,   the   king.

385. n̓taʔ   n̩-p̓aʔ-p̓aʔxʷ-ùs   axàʔ   yəʔ   ylmíxʷəm.
385.   It shone in his eyes   the   king.

381. Gee, when they come in sight, they saw the boy coming, gee his company
     is shiny, her shining straight and great; just like the sun, the shining
     from the sun.
382. That must be the Golden Woman.
383. My, she's good looking, and all the body shines, and her hair looks just
     like gold.
384. They got close to the door, the king opened the door.
385. It shone in the king's eyes.

386. waẏ ixì? axà? i? tə-twít, waẏ ixì?
386.   That's the boy,   that

    mət   i?   kʷə-kʷrì-t   i?   tkɫm-ílxʷ.
    must be   the   Golden   Woman.

387. cù-nt-əm axà? i? tə-twít: "uc ixì? axà?
387. He said   the boy: "Is this

    i?   an-χm-ínk,   axà?   i?   kʷə-kʷrì-t   i?   tkɫm-ílxʷ,
    what you wanted,   the   Golden   Woman,

    ixì?   i?   kʷu   k-s-kʷəlst-úɫt-xʷ."
    what   you sent me for."

388. níkxna?   i?   s-c-lìm-t-s axà? yə? ylmíxʷəm,
388. Goodness,   he was glad   the king,

    cùt,   "waẏ, waẏ, waẏ waẏ lím-ləm-t-x."
    he said,   "Thanks."

389. "waẏ ɫəxʷ ixì? kən ɫ w?-íkst,   waẏ kən
389. "Now   I   have finished,   I

    ɫ-xʷùy   kəl in-cìtxʷ   kəl i-s-k̓ʷíx̣-t-əm.
    will go back   to   my house,   to   my brothers.

390. kən ɫa?xʷ-skìt,   waẏ ta?lì?   i-s-?áyx̣ʷ-t,
390. I   will take a rest,   I'm very tired,

    ta?lì? ḻkʷ-ùt i-s-c-xʷy-lwìs, ki? c-kʷən-nú-n."
    very   far   I've traveled   to   get what I got."

391. waẏ níkxna? axà? yə? ylmíxʷəm; n̥-?ùɫxʷ-st-s
391.   Goodness   the king;   he took her

    i?   kəl s-yləmxʷ-íɫxʷ   i?   kəl cítxʷ-s,   uɫ
    to   the king's house,   to   his house,   and

386. That's the boy, that must be the Golden Woman.
387. The boy said: "Is this what you wanted, the Golden Woman, what you sent me for."
388. Goodness, the king was glad, he said, "Thanks."
389. "Now I have finished, I will go back to my house, to my brothers.
390. I will take a rest, I'm very tired, I've traveled very far to get what I got."
391. Goodness the king; he took her to the king's house, to his house, and

cu‑s   axà? i? tkɬm‑ílxʷ: "kʷə‑kʷrì‑t
he said to   the woman: "Golden

tkɬm‑ílxʷ, wáẏ, waẏ aɬi? c‑k̓əɬ‑nìxɬ‑əm‑st‑m‑ən,
Woman,   I've heard about you,

s‑c‑?x̣ìl‑x ki? t‑kʷəlst‑ípla?‑nt‑s‑ən; uɬ   waẏ
that's why   I sent for you;   and

ʕapnà? wìk‑ənt‑s‑ən uɬ waẏ ta?lì?   kən
now   that I see you   I'm a well

ṇ‑pùt‑əls kən ylmíxʷəm.
satisfied   king.

392. waẏ uɬ ixì? kʷu s‑c‑mrím‑s."
392. Now   we   will get married."

393. cù‑nt‑əm   axà? i? t kʷə‑kʷrì‑t i?
393. She said to him   the   Golden

tkɬm‑ílxʷ: "waẏ uc kʷa kʷ k‑s‑kəkʕáka??"
Woman: "Do   you have birds?"

394. cùt   axà? yə? ylmíxʷəm, "wáẏ."
394. He said   the king,   "Yes."

395. "uɬ kʷ kɬ‑lipùl uɬ   kʷ kɬ‑likúk?
395.   "A hen   and   a rooster?

396. nəx̣ʷ‑ənx̣ʷ‑ìws y a‑k‑s‑kəkʕáka?."
396. A pair of   birds."

397. "wáẏ."
397. "Yes."

398. "kʷə‑kʷrí‑t?"
398. "Gold?"

he said to the woman: "Golden Woman, I've heard about you, that's why
I sent for you; and now that I see you I'm a well satisfied king.
392. Now we will get married."
393. The Golden Woman said to him: "Do you have birds?"
394. The king said, "Yes."
395. "A hen and a rooster?
396. A pair of birds."
397. "Yes."

399. "a·· , kíw."
399. "Ah, yes."

400. cù-nt-əm: "waỳ nínwi? ixì? x̣lìt-ənt-xʷ i?
400. She said: "You'll   ask   the

    s-qílxʷ, uɬ nínwi? n̦-yà··ʕ-ɬx ɬ cítxʷ; nínwi?
    people, and they'll gather in a house; they'll

    t-x̣ƛ̣à-p i? s-qílxʷ, yə-yʕà-t swít, yə?
    all come the people, every body, the

    s-ənkʷ-ɬ-yl-ylmìxʷəm təl yʕa-ɬ-cw-ílxʷ-tn̦, iwà?
    kings   from all the tribes,   even

    s-wi?-nùmt   kəm̓ iwà? la?ɬ ks-ús,   kəm̓ iwà?
    the good looking   and   the ugly,

    i? la?ɬ ƛ̣əx̣-ƛ̣x̣à-p kəm̓ iwà? la?ɬ tə-twít,
    and the old men   and   the boys,

    yə-yʕà-t swít.
    every body.

401. nínwi? n̦-yàʕ-ɬx ɬ cítxʷ, t-x̣ƛ̣á-p,
401. When they gather in the house, everybody,

    ixì?   mi   ?àc-əcqa?-st-xʷ axà? a-s-kəkʕáka?, uɬ
    that's when you take out those birds,   and

    aɬì? k-s-ən-ilì?-tn̦-s   k-s-kʷl-íwt-(t)n-əlx.
    there will be a place to set them down.

402. ixì? məɬ kɬ-kʷìl·-st-xʷ ɬ latáp, məɬ
402. Then you'll place them on the table, and

    cù-nt-xʷ-əlx axà? i? a-s-ənkʷ-əs-qílxʷ,
    you'll tell the people,

398. "Gold?"
399. "Ah, yes."
400. She said: "You'll ask the people, and they'll gather in a house; the
    people'll all come, everybody, the kings from all the tribes, even the good
    looking and the ugly, and the old men and the boys, everybody.
401. When they gather in the house, everybody, that's when you take out
    those birds, and there will be a place to set them down.
402. Then you'll place them on the table, and you'll tell the people,

a-s-ənk̓ʷ-ɬ-yl-ylmíxʷəm,   cù-nt-xʷ-əlx: 'waẏ axà?
the chiefs,   you'll tell them:

i?   s-kəkʕàka? k-s-máy?-ncút-a?x-əlx.'
'The   chickens   are going to tell a story.'

403. nìnẉi? wi?-s-máy?-ncút-əlx,
403. When   they're done telling about themselves,

ixì? məɬ kʷu c-mrìm,   la?ɬ
      then we   will get married, (I) with

i-k-s-ənk̓ʷ-əɬ-mr·ím.
the one I'm supposed to marry.

404. ixì? məɬ kʷu s-q̓ʷəy-m-əncút-s,   kʷu
404. Then   we   will give a big dance,   we

s-ən-ɬs-ìpna?-m   uɬ kʷu mánxʷ,   kəm̓ kʷu
will have cigars and we   will smoke,   or   we

sìwst   t   n̩-qʷʕáw-tn̩."
will drink   liquor."

405. ixì?   i?   cù-nt-əm   axà? i?   t
405. That's what she told him   the

kʷə-kʷrì-t i? tkɬm-ílxʷ,   uɬ aɬì? lut
Golden   Woman,   and   how can he

k-s-ən-x̣ʷəl-cən-ɬtìɬn-a?x axà? yə? ylmíxʷəm.
refuse what she asks   the   king.

406. waẏ tə n̩-wìs-t   i? s-pu?-ús-c,   uɬ
406.   They went high   his thoughts,

aɬì? waẏ xƛ̓à-p   xƛ̓-p-əls-cút ixì?
      he had everything   he wanted,

the chiefs, you'll tell them: 'The chickens are going to tell a story.'
403. When they're done telling about themselves, then we will get married,
    (I) with the one I'm supposed to marry.
404. Then we will give a big dance, we will have cigars and we will smoke,
    or we will drink liquor."
405. That's what the Golden Woman told him, and how can the king refuse
    what she asks.
406. His thoughts went high, he had everything he wanted,

k-s-kək˥áka?.
he had the birds.

407. u˥ axà? way̌ x̌əlt-s-qílxʷ
407. And   they started calling the people

axà? mət ḷ t-qʷəl-qʷəl-t-íw̌s, ḷ rétyo, u˥
maybe on the telephone, on the radio,

way̌ c-məlǩʷ-m-úla?xʷ ḷ təmxʷ-úla?xʷ.
all over the land in the world.

408. nìxə˥ i? t s-qílxʷ, way̌ ťi lùt-i?
408. They heard the people, before

s-ǩlàxʷ-s, lùt-i? s-kip-úla?xʷ-s u˥
it got late, before it got dark,

y?à˥ i? s-qílxʷ; y?á··˥? u˥ way̌
they gathered the people; they gathered and

ta?lì? q̌sà-p-i? i? s-qà-qs-c ixì? u˥ c-?x̌i˥
it's long after dark that

ƛ̌là-p i? s-c-ya˥-p-míx.
they quit coming in.

409. ṇťa? u˥ s-ťsà-qən i? cítxʷ.
409.   It's packed the house.

410. way̌ cu-nt-m-əlx: "há? way̌ p s-x̌ƛ̌à-p i?
410.   He asked them: "Are you all

p s-qílxʷ alà?, kəm̌ i? p yl-ylmíxʷəm, kəm̌ axà?
people here,   you kings,   or

i? p i-s-nəqs-ìlxʷ alà?, cakʷ iwà? tə-twìt kəm̌
you my people,   boys and

he had the birds.

407. And they started calling the people maybe on the telephone, on the radio, all over the land in the world.

408. The people heard, before it got late, before it got dark, the people started to gather; they gathered and it's long after dark that they quit coming in.

409. The house is packed.

410. He asked them: "Are you all you people here, you kings, or you my

iwà? ƛəx̣-ƛx̣à-p, kəm̓ iwà? pə-ptwínax̌ʷ kəm̓ iwà?
old men, and old women and

xì-xw-t-əm, yə-yˤà-t swít.
little girls, every body.

411. alà? p k-s-kə-k̓nìya?-x̣,
411. You will listen,

k-s-m̓ay?-ncùt-a?x̣-əlx axà? i? kʷə-kʷr̓ì-t
they're going to tell a story these Golden

i-s-kəkˤáka?."
birds of mine."

412. nìxì-əm-s axà? i? kʷəl̓-cən-(n)cút-(t)ņ, uƚ
412. He heard it the cook, and

aƚì? way̓ x̣lìt-s i? səxʷ-ən-c̓íw̓-əm-s,
he asked the dish washer,

səxʷ-ən-t̓áqʷ-əm-s, cù-s: "way̓ kʷu
the one who licks plates, he said: "We

s-c-x̣lìt-əm i? kəl s-yləmxʷ-íƚxʷ; way̓
have been asked to the boss's house; way̓

k-s-yaˤ-míx-a?x̣, way̓
they're gathering,

k-s-m̓ay?-ncùt-a?x̣ i? s-kəkˤáka?.
they're going to tell their story the birds.

413. ixì? n̓ìn̓wi? wi?-s-m̓ay?-ncùt
413. When they're done telling their story

axà? i? kʷə-kʷr̓ì-t i? s-kəkˤáka?, ixì? məƚ
the golden birds, that's when

people, boys and old men, and old women and little girls, everybody.
411. You will listen, these Golden birds of mine are going to tell a story."
412. The cook heard it, and he asked the dish washer, the one who licks plates, he said: "We have been asked to the boss's house; they're gathering, the birds are going to tell their story.
413. When the golden birds are done telling their story, that's when

c-mrím-əlx.
they'll get married.

414. kʷən-ks-ənwíxʷ-əlx,   məɫ ixì? uɫ sic kʷu
414. They'll shake hands, and   then

ņ-xλ̣-ìks-ənt-əm   i? t s-ən-ɫs-ípna?, kəṁ   axà?
they'll give us all   cigars,   or else

kʷu síwst-əm-st-əm;   ixì? məɫ kʷu
     they'll give us liquor; and   then we

tŕ-əŕ-q-q-áq,   kʷu q̓ʷəy-m-əncút.
will jump up and down, we   will dance.

415. hùy xc-m-əncút, λ̣là-p i? t a-s-c-k̓ʷúl."
415. Now get ready,   quit   your work."

416. "stá?, lút, xa?s-àqs-m-ən i? s-c-ən-ɫáqʷ."
416. "Oh,   no,   I'd rather   lick plates."

417. aɫì?   i? s-c-ən-ɫáqʷ   kmix   i?
417. Because   licking plates is the only

s-c-k̓ʷúl-st-s.
work he likes.

418. wi·˙ṁ   k-?əxʷ-kʷùn-m-ənt-xʷ i? tə
418. For nothing he coaxed him   the

ylmíxʷəm-s i? t səxʷ-k̓ʷəl-cən-(n)cút; wa̓y ixì?
chief's   cook;   so

xʷùy   səxʷ-k̓ʷəl-cən-(n)cút, ?aw-s-yə-yáxa?-ṃ,
he went the cook,   he went to watch (and)

?aw-s-kə-k̓nìya? i? k̓əl s-kəkˤàka? i?
listen   to   the birds'

they'll get married.

414. They'll shake hands, and then they'll give us all cigars, or else they'll give us liquor; and then we will jump up and down, we will dance.
415. Now get ready, quit your work."
416. "Oh, no, I'd rather lick plates."
417. Because licking plates is the only work he likes.
418. For nothing the chief's cook coaxed him; so the cook went, he went to watch (and) listen to the birds' story.

k-s-may?-ncút-a?x.
story.

419. way ixì? n-ɬəkʷ-əkʷ-mì-s   i?
419.   Then he thought of it   the

kʷəɬ-cən-(n)cút-(t)n̩.
cook.

420. "na?ɬc-cá-m,   i-səxʷ-kʷùl-əm, i-səxʷ-ən-ṫàqʷ-əm
420. "That's right,   my worker,   my plate licker

wim̀   c-x̣lít-əm."
for nothing   I coaxed him."

421. cù-s   yə? ylmíxʷəm: "waỳ   n-ɬəkʷ-əkʷ-mí-n,
421. He told   the chief: "Yes, I remember,

na?ɬcá-m,   kən k-səxʷ-kʷúl-əm i? t tə-twít,
I thought of it,   I   have a worker   a   boy,

uɬ iwà? c-x̣lìt-əm   uɬ lút,
and   I asked him (to come) but no,

q̇ix̣-x̣-əm-s   i? s-c-kʷúl-s uɬ ṫəxʷ i?
he didn't want to leave   his work   and

s-c-?íɬən-s; kʷa   s-c-ən-ṫáqʷ-x.
his eatings; because   he's licking plates.

422. cùt,   'waỳ stá? pùt-əm kma?   x̣əl incà?
422. He said,   'It's not   for   me

ki? x̣əlt-s-qílxʷ.'"
that he asked people to come.'"

423. cùt   yə? ylmíxʷəm: "lút,"
423. He said   the king: "No,"

419. Then the cook thought of it.
420. "That's right, my worker, my plate licker for nothing I coaxed him."
421. He told the chief: "Yes, I remember, I thought of it, I have a worker
   a boy, and I asked him (to come) but no, he didn't want to leave his
   work and his eatings; because he's licking plates.
422. He said, 'It's not for me that he asked people to come.'"
423. The king said: "No,"

kʷəlst-íɫən,   "xʷúy-wiʔ, mi c-əlk̓-ənt-íp,
(and) he sent somebody, "You go,   tie him up,

c-kəm̓-km̓-àxən-(n)t-p   c-xʷúy-st-p.
grab him by both arms (and) bring him here.

424. waẏ kən cùt yə-yʕà-t swít: cakʷ iwà?
424.   I   said every   body:

tə-twít, kəm̓ pə-ptwìnaxʷ, kəm̓ xí-xw-t-əm,   yə-yʕà-t
boys,   old ladies,   little girls,   every

swít."
body."

425. waẏ lixʷp̓-ət   axàʔ iʔ   sxʷ-əlká-m,
425.   They ran out   those who tie up people,

waẏ ik̓lìʔ kìc-s-əlx axàʔ iʔ tə-twít.
     there they got to   the boy.

426. waẏ c-ən-ɫáqʷ-əm;   cù-s-əlx:
426.   He was licking plates; they said to him:

"waẏ kʷ s-c-xlìt-əm-s   yəʔ ylmíxʷəm."
      "He sent for you   the king."

427. waẏ k̓laʔ ʔax̣l-ús-əm,   cùt: "staʔ
427.   He just turned away, he said:

kʷu c-qʷən-cín-əm-st-xʷ, kma?   incá?, lut
    "I am pitiful,   it's not for me,   I'm not

ɫ i-k-s-xʷúy."
   going."

428. c-kəm̓-km̓-áx̣-s-əlx,   wì··m̓
428. They grabbed him by the arms, he tried to

(and) he sent somebody, "You go, tie him up, grab him by both arms
(and) bring him here.
424. I said everybody: boys, old ladies, little girls, everybody."
425. Those who tie up people ran out, they got to the boy.
426. He was licking plates; they said to him: "The king sent for you."
427. He just turned away, he said: "I am pitiful, it's not for me, I'm not
going."
428. They grabbed him by the arms, he tried to

s–c–ən–cəq̓–la?xʷ–míst–s,　way̓　xʷst–ús–əlx.
squirm around,　　　　　　they walked off with him.

429.　xʷùy–st–s–əlx　ṇ–?ùɫxʷ–st–s–əlx　ilí?,　uɫ
429.　They took him,　they brought him in　there,　and

way̓　　　c–kɫ–c̓àlxʷ　　　i?　k–s–ən–kɫ–mút–(t)ṇ–s;
already　there was a chair　　for him to sit down;

way̓　ilì?　kɫ–mút–st–s–əlx.
　　there　they sat him down.

430.　way̓　wìk–ənt–əm　i?　t　kʷə–kʷrì–t　i?　tkɫm–ílxʷ
430.　　She saw him　the　　Golden　　　Woman

axà?　i?　tə–twít;　way̓　súxʷ–ənt–əm,　　　way̓　ixì?
　　the　boy;　　　she recognized him,

axà?　　i?　　tə–twìt　i?　　kʷu　kʷí–s."
that's　the　boy　　who　　took me."

431.　ixì?　cùt–əlx:　　"way̓　ixì?　kʷu
431.　　　They said:

t–xʎá–p;"　　　　way̓　yə?　ylmìxʷəm　k̓ahk̓ʷ–qì–s　axà?
"That's all of us;"　　the　chief　　opened

yə?　ḷkasát;　way̓　ḷ　latàp　　kɫ–mút–st–s,　ak̓là?
the　trunk;　　on　the table　he set them,

k̓əl　skʷùt　i?　lipúl,　uɫ　k̓əl　skʷùt　　i?
to　one side　the　hen,　and　to　the other　the

likúk.
rooster.

432.　cù–nt–m–əlx:　　"hu–húy,　may̓?–ncùt–wi?
432.　He told them:　"OK,　　tell about yourselves,

squirm around, they walked off with him.

429. They took him, they brought him in there, and already there was a chair for him to sit down; there they sat him down.

430. The Golden Woman saw the boy; she recognized him, "that's the boy who took me."

431. They said: "That's all of us;" the chief opened the trunk; he set them on the table, to one side the hen, and to the other the rooster.

432. He told them: "OK, tell about yourselves,

i? cáw-t-əmp."
the story."

433. wáy ti kɬ-kʷl-iwt-əlx   wáy ti
433.   They just sat there,

sił-ḷx   axà? likùk   la?ɬ lipúl;   wáy
they were puzzled   the rooster and   the hen;

iti? ɬ-cù-nt-m-əlx.
      he repeated it.

434. wáy cùt   axà? i? s-qəl-tmíxʷ, cù-s   i?
434.   He said   the man,   he told the

tkɬm-ílxʷ,   təxʷ axà? i? lipúl: "wáy anwí? mi kʷ
woman,   the hen: "You

qʷəl-qʷíl-t,   kʷ   máy?-ncút-x."
do the talking, you tell the story."

435. cù-nt-əm, "lút, anwì? kʷ likúk,   uɬ
435. She said, "No, you   are the rooster, and

anwì? kʷ ylmíxʷəm;   incà? kən tkɬm-ílxʷ,
you   are the boss;   I   am a woman,

lut   t əc-ylmìxʷəm-st-s-əlx i? tkɬm-ílxʷ, wáy
they never   put as boss   a   woman,

anwí?."
you do it."

436. wáy ixì? s-c-máy?-ncùt-s   i?
436.   Then he started telling his story the

likúk;   yə? ?x̣ì? itlì?   i? c-xʷùy
rooster;   from where   he came

the story."
433. They just sat there, the rooster and the hen were puzzled; he repeated it.
434. The man said, he told the woman, the hen: "You do the talking, you tell the story."
435. She said, "No, you are the rooster, and you are the boss; I am a woman, they never put as boss a woman, you do it."
436. Then the rooster started telling his story; from where he came

c-ʔùm-la?xʷ-s   i? təl táwn, uɬ aɬi?
he named the place, the   town, and

ylmíxʷəm   i? ɬəx̣-əx̣-ƛ̣x̣à-p-s.
they're kings   his parents.

437. waẏ ixì? pùƛ-əm-st-s-əlx i? q̇əẏ-mìn ax̣à? i?
437.   When they finished   school

s-k̇ʷíƛ-t-əm-s, ixì? ùɬi? k-sw-pla?-mìst-əlx   i?
his brothers,   they asked permission

təl ḷ?íw-s-əlx: "waẏ uɬ ixì? ɬwìn-(n)t-s-t
of   their father: "We are leaving you

i? kʷ ɬəx̣-ƛ̣x̣á-p."
        father."

438. cù-nt-m-əlx: "uɬ s-c-?kín-x,   há?
438. He asked them: "And what's the matter, is

ḷ   stìm-m̀   há? p s-ən-k̇a?s-ìls-x, uɬi? kʷu
there something   you are angry about,   that

k-s-ɬwín-(n)t-p?
you're leaving me?

439. ta?lì? uɬ c-x̣s-ìkst-əm-ɬm-ən   p
439. Very   well I have treated you

s-qʷs-qʷa?síya?, c-ən-pət?-íl-ɬəm-t."
children,   we respect your feelings."

440. cùt-əlx: "lút, uɬ alà? t-kʷl-ìwt-m-ənt-s-t
440. They said: "No,   here we've been with

anwí? uɬ lut   stìm   tə k-s-my-p-nú-nt-əm;
you   and we won't anything   learn;

he named the place, the town, and his parents are kings.
437. When his brothers finished school, they asked permission of their father:
     "We are leaving you father."
438. He asked them: "And what's the matter, is there something you are angry
     about, that you're leaving me?
439. I have treated you children very well, we respect your feelings."
440. They said: "No, we've been here with you and we won't learn anything;

way puƛ-st-əm   i? q̓əy̓-mín, uɬ axà? pna? kʷu
     we've finished   school,   and   maybe we

təkʷ-təkʷ?-ùt   i? t təmxʷ-úla?xʷ, kʷu
will travel around   the   country,   we

ƛa?-ƛ̓?à-m   i? t k-s-k̓ʷúɬ-tət, uɬ ixì? nínwi?
will look for   a   job,   and   we'll

my-p-nù-nt-əm i? k-s-c-k̓ʷúɬ-tət, uɬ ixì? nínwi?
find   work,   and   we'll

kʷu qʷa?-qʷa?m-əncút, uɬ ixì? xʷùy nàx̣əmɬ
     practice,   and then come

ƛ̣xiw-t-wílx put ʕapnà? s-x̣əl-x̣ʕàl-t i? kʷu
next year   just the same day   we

təkʷ?-ùt,   uɬ ixì?   s-x̣əl-x̣ʕàl-t mi   kʷu
walked away,   that same day   we'll

ɬ-c-yáʕ-p.
come back.

441. nínwi? kʷu ɬ s-əc-xʷəl-xʷál-t-s, təxʷ k-nàqs
441. If   we   are alive,   one

káw,   uɬ ixì? way̓ s-ƛl-əl-míx, ixì? mi
might be gone,   if   he's dead,   we'll

kʷu ɬ-yaʕ-m-ílx."
     get together."

442. uɬ cù-nt-m-əlx i? t l̓?íw-s-əlx: "uɬ ka
442. And he asked them   their father: "And

?kìn p k-s-xʷúy-a?x?"
where   will you be going?"

we've finished school, and maybe we will travel around the country, we
will look for a job, and we'll find work, and we'll practice, and then come
next year just the same day we walked away, that same day we'll come
back.
441. If we are alive, one might be gone, if he's dead, we'll get together."
442. And their father asked them: "And where will you be going?"

443. cù-s-əlx   yə?   ⅃?íw-s-əlx: "k-waẏ
443. They told   their father:

c-my-st-ìxʷ   lut   kʷu   ƚə   c-k̓ə⅃-kəlxʷ-ùs-əm-st-xʷ
"You know   never   we   get out of your sight

kʷu   təl   s-k̓ʷú⅃-s;   u⅃   lut   kʷu   ƚə
      since we were born;   and we don't

c-my-n-ùla?xʷ-əm   i?   t   təmxʷ-úla?xʷ;   waẏ   ƚi
know anything about   the   country;

tanm̓ùs   itì?   kʷu   k-s-təkʷ?-ùt-a?x   i?   t
for nothing   we   will go in   the

s-píl-əm.
open country.

444. kʷu   yàʕ-p   k̓a   ?kin   kʷu   ņ-cah-əh-qín,
444. We   will get where ever   we   are facing,

ik̓li?   kʷu   ⅃   k-s-tx̣ʷ-m-əncút-a?x."
that's where   we   are going."

445. u⅃   waẏ   ƚi   k̓ʷìnx-cən   i?
445. And   every few words

k-s-qʷəl-qʷìl-t-s   axà?   i?   likúk,   mə⅃   ⅃-sìw-s
he spoke   the rooster,   he asked

axà?   i?   lipúl: "uc   ixì?   in-cáw-t?"
       the hen: "Is   this   what I've been doing?"

446. mə⅃   axà?   cut   ixì?   i?   lipúl,   "waẏ,
446. And   she'd say that's   the hen,   "Yes,

ixì?   an-cáw-t;   qʷəl-qʷìl-t-x   itlí?,   waẏ   pùt
that's   right;   talk   more,   right

443. They told their father: "You know that we never get out of your sight
since we were born; and we don't know anything about the country; for
nothing we will go in the open country.
444. We will get wherever we are facing, that's where we are going."
445. And every few words the rooster spoke, he asked the hen: "Is this what
I've been doing?"
446. And the hen'd say, "Yes, that's right; talk more, right

a–s–c–qʷəl–qʷíl–t."
you're saying it."

447.   wáy̓   ixì?   m̓àya?–ɫt–s   i?   cáw–t–s.
447.   Well,   he went on telling   his story.

448.   uɫ   ixì?   cù–s   i?   səxʷ–k̓ʷúl–əm–s: "wáy̓
448.   And   then   he told   the   working man:

c–kəm̓–xìt–xʷ   i?   t   s–x?im–ɫ–x̣às–t   i?   t
"Go get   the   very best

n̩–k–?əmt–íw̓s–tn̩;   ʕác̓–ənt   qa?ɫ–ylmíxʷm–əlx,   kən
saddle horses;   look,   they are the king's sons,   I

s–my–ɫ–ylmíxʷəm,   uɫ   s–c–?x̣ìl–x
am an important king,   and   that's the reason for

i–s–x̣s–əlscùt,   i?   s–x?im–ɫ–x̣às–t   i?
my very best clothes,   the   very best

kɫ–k̓ʷúl–mən–s–əlx,   i?   k–s–cəq–p–əncút–s–əlx,
they're going to use,   what   they are taking with them,

axà?   n̩–ƛ̓əkʷ–ki?–sqáx̣a?–tn̩,   i?   laprít,   i?
the   saddles,   the   bridle,   the

s–k–əwp–wp–áqst–xən,   kəm   s–k–cəw–cəw–ʕáqst–xən,
fur chaps,   or   fringed leather wing chaps,

kəm̓   axà?   i?   qə?–xán,   i?   s–t–təm̓–tím̓,   yə–yʕà–t
or   shoes,   clothes,   everything

s–x?im–ɫ–x̣ás–t.
the very best.

449.   uɫ   axà?–m̩   itlì?   in–wèrhaws   mi
449.   And   from   my warehouse   they'll

you're saying it."
447. Well, he went on telling his story.
448. And then he told the working man: "Go get the very best saddle horses;
   look, they are the king's sons, I am an important king, and that's the
   reason for my very best clothes, the very best they're going to use, what
   they are taking with them, the saddles, the bridles, the fur chaps, or
   fringed leather wing chaps, or shoes, clothes, everything the very best.
449. And from my warehouse they'll

km̓-ənt-ís-əlx,　 uł　náx̣əmł　i?　s-qláw̓　təl
take things,　　but　　the　money　from

i-s-ən-qláw̓-tṇ,　t　incà?　　mi　x̌ʷíc̓-əłt-n-əlx."
my bank,　　　　I myself　will　give to them."

450.　way̓　ixì?　łx̌ʷp̓à-m　　axà?　i?　səxʷ-k̓ʷúl-əm;
450.　　Then　he ran out　　the　working man;

?ayx̣àxa?　　　　　c-yaʕ-p-st-ís,　　way̓
in a little while　he got everything,

c-wi?-s-ən-t̓ək̓ʷ-ki?-sqáx̣a?-tṇ.
they're all saddled up.

451.　uł　axà?　x̌ʷùy-st-s　i?　s-qʷs-qʷa?sìya?-s　k̓əl
451.　And　then　he took　　his children　　　　to

s-ən-t-təm̓-tím̓-tṇ;　way̓　k-s-tə-təm̓-tím̓-s-əlx;
get clothes;　　　　they got clothes;

yə-yʕà-t　　ṇ-səlxʷa?-áqs-əm,　i?　kł-q̓ə?-xàn-s-əlx,
they're all　expensive,　　　　　their shoes,

kł-qʷàc-qən　ṇ-səlxʷa?-áqs-əm.
their hats　are all expensive.

452.　way̓　ł-yaʕ-p-st-ìs　　　　uł　axà?
452.　　He brought them back　and

c-yàʕ-p　　　　i?　kł-kəw?áp-s.
they got there　　their horses.

453.　way̓　s-ən-qláw̓-tṇ　kł-ən-k̓ahk̓ʷ-íp-s;　way̓　ixì?
453.　　The bank　　　　he opened;　　　　　　way̓　ixì?

c-wt-ənt-ìs　i?　s-qláw̓-s,　way̓　ixì?　kʷə-kʷrí-t.
he took out　the　money,　　　　　　　　it's gold.

take things, but the money from my bank, I myself will give to them."
450. Then the working man ran out; in a little while he got everything,
they're all saddled up.
451. And then he took his children to get clothes; they got clothes; they're
all expensive, their shoes, their hats are all expensive.
452. He brought them back and they got there their horses.
453. He opened the bank; he took out the money, it's gold.

454. waý k̓əɬ-t̓k̓ʷ-ənt-ìs   ka?ɬəl-lúp,   náqs,   uɬ
454.   He put it there in   three piles,   one,   and

itlì? náqs,   uɬ   itli?   náqs.
then   another, and then   another.

455. hú··y, uɬ ta?lì? uɬ   xʷ?ìt   axà?   i?
455.   Lots and   lots of

c-?əs-?əsəl-?ùpən-kst i? kʷə-kʷr̓ì-t, ta?lì? uɬ
twenty dollar   gold pieces, quite

cx̣ʷá-p.
a lot.

456. "nak̓ʷà?   cəm   atlà?   kʷ
456. "You won't   maybe as soon as   you

k̓əɬ-k̓láxʷ   məɬ kʷ ta?xʷ-s-c-k̓ʷúl̓, lut   t̓ə
get out of sight   get a job,   you don't

c-my-st-ìp k̓a ?kìn p   kɬ-ək-s-xʷúy-a?x.
know   where you are going.

457. pna? cmay   p kìc-x la ?kìn ḷ táwn   uɬ
457.   You might   get   to town, and

lut xʷùs   p ta?xʷ-s-c-k̓ʷúl̓; ixì?
not in a hurry   get a job;   this is

kɬ-k-?ìɬən-tn-əmp uɬ   kɬ-k-?ítx-tn-əmp."
for your eats   and for your sleeps."

458. waý ixì? s-ən-pkʷ-s-qlàw̓-m-s-əlx
458.   They put the money in their pockets

axà? i? tu?-tw̓ít.
      the boys.

---

454. He put it there in three piles, one, and then another, and then another.
455. Lots and lots of twenty dollar gold pieces, quite a lot.
456. "Maybe you won't get a job as soon as you get out of sight, you don't know where you are going.
457. You might get to town, and not get a job in a hurry; this is for your eats and for your sleeps."
458. The boys put the money in their pockets.

459. cù-s-əlx   yə? ḷ?íw-s: "waẏ axà?
459. They told   their father: "This

k-s-c̓əx̣ʷ-xít-əm-t,   ṅiṅwi?   put
is what we want to tell you, it'll be exactly

ṇ̓k̓ʷ-əs-pìn-tk put ʕapnà? s-x̣əl-x̣ʕàl-t mi   kʷu
one year   to day   when   we

ɫ-c-yáʕ-p,   kʷu ɫ s-c-x̣ʷəl-x̣ʷál-t-s, uɫ ṅiṅwi?
will come back,   if we're alive,   and if

k-naqs lút,   uɫ waẏ ixì?   s-ƛ̓l-əl-míx.
one   doesn't,   that's the sign he's dead.

460. uɫ aɫi? nak̓ʷà? c-my-st-ìm ṅiṅwi? kʷu
460.   We don't know   if   we

c-?úlus.
will be together.

461. pna? axà? kʷu px̣ʷ-x̣ʷá-m,   kəm̓ kʷu
461. Maybe   we   will scatter, or   (if) we

t-x̣s-əs-m-ìkst uɫ ƛ̓i ḷ nəqs-lùp kʷu ilí?,   kʷu
are lucky   in one place we   will be,   we

c-wk-t-wìxʷ   ḷ s-k̓láxʷ."
will see each other   in the evening."

462. waẏ ixì? t-kʷəl·-ìẉs-əlx   uɫ
462.   They got on their horses and

təkʷ?-út-əlx.
left.

463. waẏ ixì? uɫ s-ən-kxn-ìls-c   axà? i?
463.   And he wanted to go along   the

459. They told their father: "This is what we want to tell you, it'll be exactly one year today when we will come back, if we're alive, and if one doesn't, that's the sign he's dead.
460. We don't know if we will be together.
461. Maybe we will scatter, or (if) we are lucky we will be in one place, we will see each other in the evening."
462. They got on their horses and left.
463. And the youngest one wanted to go along,

s-t?íw-t-x,   uɫ   aɫì?   k̓ʷə-k̓ʷy-úma?.
youngest one,   but   he's small.

464. cu-nt-əm   i? t ḽ?íw-s: "lút, way̓ k̓im
464. He told him   his father: "No,

    kʷ   s-mút-x,   way̓ myàɫ   kʷ   k̓ʷə-k̓ʷy-úma?;
    you stay home,   too much you are small;

    cəm̓   ṇ-q̓a?-ìls-ən-t-xʷ axà? a-s-k̓ʷíɫ-t-əm.
    you might give worries to   your brothers.

465. məɫ kʷ   c-pə-psˁáy-a?   cəm̓
465.   You have got no sense, you might

    k-ƛ̓a?-ípla?-nt-xʷ-əlx, pna?   kʷ
    cause them problems,   you might

    qʷˁáw-mist;   way̓ alà? k̓im s-mút-x,
    do something silly;   here   stay,

    t-xtà-nt   i? kʷu an-ɫəx-əx-ƛ̓x̣á-p, kʷu
    take care of   us   old people,   with us

    k-?am·út-m-ənt-xʷ."
    stay."

466. ṇta? uɫ lút, aɫì?   swit əc-psˁày-a?   i?
466. But   no,   because   has no sense a

    tə-tw̓ít;   ṇta? uɫ ixì? s-ćqʷ-áqʷ-s.
    little boy;   gee, but he   cried.

467. wim̓ uɫ   ṇ-qʷən̓-mì-nt-əm i? t s-k̓ʷúy̓-s,   uɫ
467.   Then she pitied him   his mother,   and

    ixì? cù-s   i? s-qəl-tmíxʷ-s: "way̓
         she told   her husband:

but he's small.
464. His father told him: "No, you stay home, you are too small; you might
    give worries to your brothers.
465. You have got no sense, you might cause them problems, you might do
    something silly; stay here, take care of us old people, stay with us."
466. But no, because a little boy has no sense; gee, but he cried.
467. Then his mother pitied him, and she told her husband:

ņ-ɬm-ìls-ənt   i? s-qʷs-qʷsí?-tət; waẏ təxʷ iwà?
"Pity his feelings,   our boy's;

kəm s-k-nəqs-əlt-íla?t-(t)ət,   uɬ   qʷəṅ-cìn
     he's the only child we got left, and it's a pity

?u-?əxt-íla?t.
he's just a baby.

468. axà? kʷ
468.

     i-k-s-kəɬ-pa?x-xít-əm: kʷ xʷuy
     I'm going to give you something to think about: go

     t-kʷəlst-ìpla?-nt-xʷ mi c-ʕac-xìt-s-əlx axà? i? t
     send somebody   to tie for him   the

     kìw-ḷx i? t s-ən-kɬ-ċa?-sqáxa?.
     old   horse.

469. ixì? təxʷ iwà? xàs-t   uɬ   waẏ kíw-ḷx,
469.   He's good, but   he's old,

     uɬ   lut   qɬ-nù-s ka   ?kin ɬə k-s-xʷúy-s, ɬə
     and he isn't able   any where to travel,   to

     k-s-xʷɬ-p-əncút-s.
     run.

470. waẏ ti kmix   kim ti c-xʷist-s,
470.   All he does   is walk,

     ixì?   mi   c-ʕac-ɬt-ís-əlx,
     that's the one they'll tie up for him,

     ņ-tkʷ-íki?-ɬt-s-əlx.
     saddle up for him.

"Pity our boy's feelings; he's the only child we got left, and it's a pity
he's just a baby.
468. I'm going to give you something to think about: go send somebody to
tie for him the old horse.
469. He's good, but he's old, and he isn't able to travel anywhere, to run.
470. All he does is walk, that's the one they'll tie up for him, saddle up for
him.

471. waẏ nìnẃi? alà?   k-?əm-?əmt-íẃs,
471.   He'll   around here ride,

wiṁ   k-səp-ənt-ís, uɬ   cəṁ   ixì?
it won't do any good to whip him,   but he might

ṇ-x̣s-əls-wìlx   mi ɬ-c-kíc-x.
get in a good humor,   and come back home.

472. ixì? uɬ lut   k-s-ən-k̓əs-t-mí-s,   lut
472.   And he won't get to feeling bad,   he won't

k-s-ən-q̓əl-t-ús-i?-s; nax̣əmɬ t̓i n-yȼìp
get sick over it;   but if   you keep saying

tx̣ʷ-m-ùt lút-st-xʷ, uɬ pna? cmay   ṇ-q̓əl-t-ús-əs,
straight no,   he might get sick,

ṇ-ƛ̓l-əl-mí-s axà? i?   tə-twít, ṇ-k̓əw-p-ìls
he might die   the boy,   get lonesome (and)

pa?-pa?s-ínk."
feel bad."

473. cùt   axà? yə? ylmíxʷəm: "a··, waẏ
473. He said   the chief: "Ah,

x̣às-t   i?   kʷu k̓əɬ-pa?x̣-xít-xʷ," ixì? kʷùlst-s
it's good   the   idea you gave me,"   so   he sent

i? səxʷ-k̓ʷúl̓-əm-s.
his working man.

474. cù-s: "waẏ ixì? c-ȼac-ənt-ìxʷ i?
474. He said: "Go tie   the

s-əc-hùy-x i? t   s-k̓íw-ɬx,   lut   k̓əm
finished   from old age (horse),   that's not

471. He'll ride around here, it won't do him any good to whip him, but he
    might get in a good humor, and come back home.
472. And he won't get to feeling bad, he won't get sick over it; but if you
    keep saying straight no, he might get sick, the boy might die, get
    lonesome (and) feel bad."
473. The chief said: "Ah, the idea you gave me is good," so he sent his
    working man.
474. He said: "Go tie the horse that's finished from old age, that's not

ṇ-k̓ʷu̓l-mən ḷ stím,   uɬ aɬiʔ s-k̓íw-ḷx."
good   for anything,   the old one."

475. uɬ ti kmix   təl x̀as-t
475. And   only (because it comes) from a good

s-ən-kɬ-c̓aʔ-sqáx̣aʔ uɬ ṇìṇwiʔ   t
horse   (they keep it) until from

ṇ-x̣l-əl-tàn mi   x̣l-ál, uɬ kmix
death   he'll die,   they only

c-ʔam-st-ìs-əlx, lut   tə c-k̓ʷu̓l-əm-st-s-əlx.
feed him,   they don't   use him.

476. "ixì?   mi   c-ʕac-ɬt-ìp
476. "That's the one you'll tie up

ṇ-t̓k̓ʷ-íkiʔ-ɬt-p."
(and) saddle up."

477. wa̓y ixì? x̣̓aʔ-nt-ìs   c-k̓íc-x-st-s;
477.   He went got it (and) brought it there;

wa̓y x̣ʷìc-əxt-s iʔ s-qʷsìʔ-s t   k-s-qláw-s, ixì?
     he gave   his son   some money,

mət   k̓ʷə-k̓ʷy-ìnaʔ píq-sxən ti
maybe a little   silver   just

k-s-ən-x̣s-t-əls-míst-aʔx; uɬ lut   tə ṇ-st-ìls
to satisfy him;   and he never   thought

ṇìṇwiʔ ɬx̣ʷp-nù-s   təx̣ʷ ṇ-ʔúc-xən.
he would get away (and)   follow them.

478. aɬiʔ wa̓y   yəʔ ʔx̣ì? kəɬ-k̓íl·x̣ʷ-t,
478.   Already   they're out of sight,

good for anything, the old one."
475. And only (because it comes) from a good horse (they keep it) until he'll
     die from death, they only feed him, they don't use him.
476. "That's the one you'll tie up (and) saddle up."
477. He went got it (and) brought it there; he gave his son some money,
     maybe a little silver just to satisfy him; and he never thought he would
     get away (and) follow them.
478. Already they're out of sight,

uɫ lut   nixʷ tə k-s-ən-kìl-kiʔ-s iʔ
and he couldn't   follow

s-k̓ʷíƛ-t-əm-s kəm k-s-ən-kcn-íkiʔ-s;   uɫ axàʔ ti
his brothers   or   catch up with them;

c-xʷst-ùtyaʔ   iʔ kəwáp-s.
he can only walk   his horse.

479. wa̓y k-ʔəmt-íws-st-s, wa̓y qʷàm-qʷəm-t iʔ
479.   He put him on,   it's happy

s-puʔ-ùs-c axàʔ iʔ tə-twít.
his heart   the boy's.

480. n̓taʔ uɫ iwàʔ k-sp̓-ícaʔ-s uɫ k-sp̓-ícaʔ-s,
480.   And   he whipped   and whipped him,

n̓taʔ lút, wa̓y ti xʷst-út-əm,   wa̓y lut
but   no,   he just walks,   he couldn't

qɫ-nù-s ɫə k-s-qà-qc-əlx-s axàʔ iʔ
even   trot   this

s-ən-kɫ-c̓aʔ-sqáx̣aʔ.
horse.

481. huy   uɫ k̓əɫ-k̓láxʷ,
481. Finally   he got out of sight,

k̓əɫ-k̓làxʷ   uɫ wa̓y tìɫ-x   iʔ
he got out of sight and   he stood there

kəwáp-s,   uɫ ɫq̓-ílx.
his horse, and he lay down.

482. wa̓y ixìʔ wi··m̓ səp̓-ənt-ís,   uɫ ixìʔ
482.   He clubbed him,   and

and he couldn't follow his brothers or catch up with them; his horse can only walk.

479. He put him on, the boy's heart is happy.

480. And he whipped and whipped him, but no, he just walks, this horse couldn't even trot.

481. Finally he got out of sight, he got out of sight and his horse stood there, and he lay down.

482. He clubbed him, and

pùl-st-s   i? kəwáp-s,   k-səp-qí-s.
he licked   his horse, hit him on the head.

483. huy   t-x̣?ən-cən-mìst-m-ənt-əm i? t
483. Finally he stopped him

kəwáp-s; cù-nt-əm "way̌ uyà?   kʷu
his horse; he said,   "Listen,

ṇ-qʷəṅ-mì-nt   tə-twít;   way̌ nakʷà?
have pity on me little boy;   I'm not

i-s-k-c̓áx̣ʷ.
doing it on purpose.

484. way̌ aɬi? kən s-way̌-x i? t   s-kíw-ḷx, uɬ
484.   I   am done from old age, and

lut   qɬ-nù-n itlì? nixʷ   ti i-k-s-xʷíst,
I can't even   farther   go,

ùɬi?   kən ɬq-ílx, uɬ kən təlxʷ-mìst ɬ
and that's why I lay down, and I can't

i-k-s-xʷt̓-ílx."
lift myself up."

485. uɬ   lut   axà? i?   tə-twít; uɬ
485. But he wouldn't (stop)   the boy;   and

aɬì? la?ɬ   s-c̓qʷ-àqʷ-s ùɬi?
    at the same time he was crying

c-k-?x̣íl-əm-st-s.
he kept beating him.

486. ti kʷmìɬ   axà?   i? təl
486.   All at once something   from

he licked his horse, hit him on the head.

483. Finally his horse stopped him; he said, "Listen, have pity on me little
boy; I'm not doing it on purpose.

484. I am done from old age, and I can't go any farther, and that's why I
lay down, and I can't lift myself up."

485. But he boy wouldn't (stop); and at the same time he was crying he kept
beating him.

486. All at once something from

s-k-ən-wìs-t-əm-s   qʷəl-qʷíl-st-əm: "waẏ uyá?
above   spoke to him: "Come now

c-qʷṅ-ìkst-əm-st-xʷ ixì? an-kəwáp;   waẏ t incà?
have pity on   your horse; and   I

ṇ-qʷəṅ-mí-nt-s-ən."
will pity you."

487. c-?əks-wìx   nìkxna?   qʷàm-qʷəm-t i?
487. There was standing goodness a beautiful

s-ən-kɬ-ċa?-sqáx̣a?;   ṇta? qʷàm-qʷəm-t yə?
horse;   a beautiful

ṇ-ṫəkʷ-ki?-sqáx̣a?-tṇ-s, i? laprít-s.
saddle,   (and) a bridle.

488. cù-nt-əm: "waẏ xʷs-xʷús-əlx, waẏ
488. He said: "Hurry,

c-k-?əmt-íws-x, waẏ cəm   ƛ̓m-ìp-st-xʷ   y
get on,   you'll be too late for

a-ɬəɬ-qá-qc-a?.
your brothers.

489. waẏ uɬ ixì? s-ƛ̓áxʷ-t-s-əlx, waẏ t
489.   And   they are dead,

ṇ-?əɬn-a?-s-qìlxʷ-tṇ k-s-ƛ̓xʷ-ənt-ím-əlx;   cəm ṫi
the man-eater   is going to kill them; if

kʷ   məl-mìl-ḷx   mi   ƛ̓m-ìp-st-əm.
you   fool around you'll be late.

490. uɬ lùt   a-k-s-ən-x̣íɬ; uɬ aɬì?
490. And don't be scared;   because

above spoke to him: "Come now have pity on your horse; and I will pity you."

487. Goodness, there was standing a beautiful horse; a beautiful saddle, (and) a bridle.

488. He said: "Hurry, get on, you'll be too late for your brothers.

489. And they are dead, the man-eater is going to kill them; if you fool around you'll be late.

490. And don't be scared; because

a–k–s–xʷəl–xʷəl–t–st–ìm   a–s–k̓ʷíƛ–t–əm.
you're going to save   your brothers(' lives).

491. axà? cəm̓ ƛi   kʷ   k–ʔəmt–ìws,   məɬ
491.   As soon as you get on the horse,

   kən n̓–wís–əlx;   axà? nìn̓wi? i? t
   I   will go in the air;   if

   s–k–ɬa?–m–àsqət   mi   kʷu xʷúy, mi uc
   right next to the sky we'll   go,   we might

   ɬə k–s–pənh–íws–ənt–əm.
       get there on time.

492. naxəmɬ axà? i? t   təmxʷ–ùla?xʷ kʷu ɬ xʷúy,
492. But   by ground   if we go,

   uɬ way̓ ƛi ƛm–íp–st–əm.
              we'll be late.

493. uɬ nìn̓wi? kʷ n̓–xíɬ,   təxʷ kʷ
493. And if   you get scared, just

   t–kʷən–kʷní–m, uɬ lut   kʷu t̓
   hold on,   you don't

   a–k–s–ʔaxl–íkst–əm, t incà? way̓ c–my–st–ìn k̓a ʔkin
   have to guide me,   I   I know   where

   kʷu ɬə k–s–xʷúy–s.
   we   are going.

494. way̓ ƛi ilì? kʷu ʕàw–m–ɬt–xʷ yə?
494.   Just   let loose   the

   ʕac–sqáxa?–tn̓; way̓ ƛi kʷ t–kʷən–kʷní–m, uɬ
   reins;   just   hang on,   and

you're going to save your brothers(' lives).

491. As soon as you get on the horse, I will go in the air; if we go right
    next to the sky, we might get there on time.

492. But if we go by ground, we'll be late.

493. And if you get scared, just hold on, you don't have to guide me, I know
    where we are going.

494. Just let loose the reins; just hang on, and

nìnwi? kʷ ɬa? ņ-səl-səl-p-ús,   təxʷ kʷ ɬa?
if   you   get dizzy in the eyes, or

ņ-səl-p-qín, uɬ kʷ ņ-cìp-cəp-s-əm, kəm kʷ
in the head, then   shut your eyes, or   you

kín-t;   kʷ ņ-cìp-cəp-s-əm."
will get scared; you   shut your eyes."

495. waỳ k-?əmt-ìws axà? i? tə-twít;   uɬ waỳ
495.   He got on   the little boy; and

c-?x̣ìɬ t ņ-wa?-wa?s-x̣án, c-?x̣ìɬ t
           he rose,   like

s-ən-wa?s-míx;   ixì? s-ƛa?-ƛa?-ús-əm-s.
he rose in the air;   then he opened his eyes.

496. waỳ wnìxʷ   ņ-w?às-əlx   i? təl
496.   Sure enough they were high   off

təmxʷ-úla?xʷ.
the ground.

497. waỳ uɬ ti k-s-ən-səl-səl-p-ús-a?x; ixì? uɬ
497.   And   his eyes started to turn; then

s-ən-cìp-cəp-s-əm-s uɬ axà? c-t-kʷən-kʷní-m.
he shut his eyes   and   he hung on.

498. waỳ məɬ k-cí-cəx̣ʷ-s-əm,   waỳ lut
498.   He'll peek now and then,   he can't

tə c-wìk-st-s i? təmxʷ-úla?xʷ, waỳ ti kmix i?
    see   the ground,   only the

s-t-k̇m-ásqət.
sky.

if you get dizzy in the eyes, or in the head, then shut your eyes, or you
will get scared; you shut your eyes."
495. The little boy got on; and he rose, like he rose in the air; then he
opened his eyes.
496. Sure enough they were high off the ground.
497. And his eyes started to turn; then he shut his eyes and he hung on.
498. He'll peek now and then, he can't see the ground, only the sky.

499. way̓ xʷúy?-ḻx;   kʷmiḻ
499.   They went;   all of a sudden

ḻ-təkʷ-kʷ-úla?xʷ;   cù-nt-əm: "way̓ pənh-ip-ənt-əm
they hit the ground; he said: "We're in time for

y a-s-k̓wíḻ-t-əm, uḻ way̓ púlx-əlx.
   your brothers,   they're in bed.

500. uḻ axà? anwi? kʷ xʷùy k̓əl cítxʷ;   nin̓wi?
500.   You   go   to the house;

cə̓m i? t k-kəw?àp-a? wah-ənt-s-ís,   uḻ   way̓
      the   dogs   will bark at you, and

my-p-nù-nt-s   i? t n̓-?əḻn-a?-s-qílxʷ-tn̩.
you'll know (you're at)   the   man-eater's.

501. uḻ aḻi?   ixi? s-t-kʷəḻ-kʷḻ-ùs-tn̩-s uḻ
501.   Because that's her eyes   and

tən-ṭina?-s axà? i? k-kəw?àp-a?.
her ears   these   dogs.

502. uḻ cə̓m   ixi? c-k-?ácqa?-m-ənt-s,   uḻ
502. And she'll   come out to meet you, and

ixi? pə-ptwínaxʷ,   uḻ ixi? lìm-t-m-ənt-s
she's an old woman, and   she'll be tickled that

kʷ ḻ yxʷ-m-əncút,   uḻ ḻác-qən-nt-s,   uḻ
you   came down,   and she'll pat you and

cxʷ-ənt-s-ís.
make over you.

503. ixi? uḻ kʷ s-ən-ʕac-ùs-əm-s k-s-púl-st-əm-s;
503.   But   she's baiting you to kill you;

499. They went; all of a sudden they hit the ground; he said: "We're in time
    for your brothers, they're in bed.
500. You go to the house; the dogs will bark at you, and you'll know (you're
    at) the man-eater's.
501. Because those dogs are her eyes and her ears.
502. And she'll come out to meet you, and she's an old woman, and she'll
    be tickled that you came down, and she'll pat you and make over you.
503. But she's baiting you to kill you;

cə́m k-ʔəm-plaʔ-ncùt-m-ənt-s   kʷ s-ən-ʔímaʔt.
      she'll call you a relative,   a grandson.

504. cə́m   cù-nt-s: 'wa̓y kʷ
504. She'll   say to you: 'You

k̓əlxʷ-núxʷ,   wa̓y t̓i x̣às-t   kʷ   ɫ
are traveling late,   it's good that you

púlx, cə́m   kʷ n̩-sɫí-p.'
camp, you might   get lost.'

505. mi   cù-nt-xʷ: 'wa̓y nak̓ʷà? kən
505. You'll say to her: 'Yes, I don't

c-my-n-úla?xʷ-əm uɫ   lut   t̓ in-x̣m-ìnk ɭ
know the country and I don't   like   in

s-ən-kʷə-kʷʔàc ɫ   i-k-s-xʷy-lwís; wa̓y kən
the dark   to travel;   yes, I

púlx.'
will camp.'

506. mi   cə́m xʷìc-əɫt-s i? laklí, cù-nt-əm:
506. She'll   give you   the key,   she'll say:

'aɫì?   c-laklì-st-ən i? s-ən-t̓əws-cqáx̣a?-tn̩.
'Because I lock   the barn.

507. kʷ xʷùy iklí?, kɫ-ən-kahkʷ-íp-ənt-xʷ,   uɫ
507. You go   there, open the door,   and

ilì? wa̓y k-s-ən-ʔəks-wìx-tn-a?x an-kəwáp,   uɫ
there   there's a place for   your horse,   and

ilì? kən k-s-ʔam-ən-sqáx̣a?   t lawán, t
there I   have feed for horses,   oats,

she'll call you a relative, a grandson.
504. She'll say to you: 'You are traveling late, it's good that you camp, you
     might get lost.'
505. You'll say to her: 'Yes, I don't know the country and I don't like to travel
     in the dark; yes, I will camp.'
506. She'll give you the key, she'll say: 'Because I lock the barn.
507. You go there, open the door, and there there's a place for your horse,
     and there I have feed for horses, oats,

s-wp-úla?xʷ,   uɬ   ilì?   k-sìwɬkʷ   kʷ
hay,   and   there is water for you

sə?st-əm-sqáx̣a?.'
to water your horse.'

508. k̓ɬ-ən-k̓ahkʷ-ìp-ənt-xʷ   uɬ   cə̓m   sy-m-əncʕàt
508. When you open the door   they'll   make noise

i?   s-kəkʕáka?,   uɬ   aɬì?   ṇ-p̓?àxʷ   i?
the birds,   and   it'll be lit up   the

s-ən-t̓əws-cqáx̣a?-tṇ uɬ   ixì?   cə̓m   wìk-ənt-xʷ   i?
barn   and you'll see   the

s-kəkʕáka?.
birds.

509. uɬ   nak̓ʷəm i? təl   s-kəkʕàka? ùɬi?
509. And   from the birds

əc-p̓?áxʷ;   ixì?   sy-m-əncʕàt uɬ ax̣à?
it's shining; when   they fuss

ṇ-p̓?áxʷ.
the light shines.

510. ixì?   aɬì?   kʷə-kʷr̓ì-t s-kəkʕáka?.
510. They're   the golden birds.

511. ixì?   ṇ-?əɬn-a?-s-qìlxʷ-tṇ   ɬa?   k-s-kəkʕáka?;
511. They're the man-eater's   birds;

uɬ   ixì?   s-t-kʷə̓ɬ-kʷ̓ɬ-ús-tṇ-s t̓ən-t̓ìna?-s níxʷ.
and they're her eyes (and)   her ears   also.

512. uɬ   lut   ixì? a-k-s-t-q̓a?-íls-əm;   kʷu
512. And don't   pay any attention to them;

hay, and there is water for you to water your horse.'
508. When you open the door the birds will make noise, and the barn'll be
lit up and you'll see the birds.
509. And from the birds it shines; when they fuss the light shines.
510. They're the golden birds.
511. They're the man-eater's birds; and they're her eyes (and) her ears also.
512. And don't pay any attention to them;

n̩-tiⱡ-x-st-x^w   iliʔ   i-k-s-ən-ʔəks-wíx-tn̩,   lut
put me in the barn   where   I'm supposed to stand,   don't

k^wu a-k-s-ən-k̓^wíx^w-kn̩-əm,   iliʔ kən
     take the saddle off me,

c-ən-tk̓^w-íkən̩,   kən c-kⱡ-yə-yˤ-ílx^w.
leave the saddle on me,   (and) everything else.

513. kmix iliʔ k^wu ˤac-ənt-íx^w, uⱡ lut   k^wu
513. Just there   tie me,   and   don't

a-k-s-ʔam-na-m.
feed me.

514. uⱡ n̓in̓wiʔ k^w ⱡ-kìc-x ikliʔ, uⱡ way̓
514. And when   you   get back there,

wiʔ-s-kⱡ-səl-xít-əm-s   iʔ t pə-ptwínax^w iʔ
the table has already been set   by the old lady

t   a-k-s-c-ʔíⱡən; way̓   wiʔ-s-kⱡ-əwt-ⱡt-s-ìs iʔ
for   you to eat;   already she's put

s-tⱡkəl-s a-k-s-c-ʔíⱡən.
her grub   for you to eat.

515. uⱡ cəm̓   cù-nt-s, 'ʔkín   in-lakliʔ?'
515. And she'll ask you, 'Where's my key?'

516. mi   cù-nt-x^w, 'way̓, way̓ lut   k^w t̓
516. You'll tell her, 'Yes,   I'm not

i-kⱡ-əⱡ-x^wìc-əⱡt-əm   uⱡ aⱡiʔ   s-k-s-k^wəⱡ-t-mìx
going to give it to you   because he was sweating

in-kəwáp, uⱡ aⱡiʔ kən s-k̓ìn-t   ⱡ
my horse, and   I   was afraid that

put me in the barn where I'm supposed to stand, don't take the saddle
off me, leave the saddle on me, (and) everything else.
513. Just tie me there, and don't feed me.
514. And when you get back there, the table has already been set by the
    old lady for you to eat; already she's put her grub for you to eat.
515. And she'll ask you, 'Where's my key?'
516. You'll tell her, 'Yes, I'm not going to give it to you because my horse
    was sweating, and I was afraid that

i-k-s-ən-kʷaʔc-núxʷ   kəm   ɫ   i-k-s-ən-slí-p,   ùi?
I'd be late   or   that I'd get lost,   and then

kən   c-əwʕi-mist   uɫi?   k-s-kʷáɫ-t.
I   came fast   and   he got warm.

517.   uɫ   aɫì?   lut   ṫ   i-k-síwst-əm-st-əm,   ṫ
517.   And   I wouldn't   water him,   or

i-k-s-ʔam-nà-m   t   lawán,   cəm   ṇ-kəs-t-mí-s.
feed him   oats,   that might   harm him.

518.   uɫ   nixʷ   lut   ṫ   ṇ-kʷìxʷ-kən-ṇ,   uɫ
518.   And   even I didn't   take the saddle off,

aɫì?   cəm   ṇ-skʷ-íkəṇ;   uɫ
because it might swell his back;

ilì?   ṅiṅwi?   kʷa?   s-k-saʔt-íca?-x,   mi
(I'll leave it) there   until   he dries off,

sic   ʔaw-s-kʷúɫ-ən.
then I'll go tend to him.

519.   ʔaw-s-síwst-əm-st-ən,   məɫ   ṅiṅwi?
519.   I'll go water him,   and   then

ṇ-kʷíxʷ-kən-ṇ,   ʔam-t-ìn   t   lawán,   məɫ
take off the saddle,   I'll feed him   oats,   and

kɫ-tx-ílxʷ-ən;   ixì?   məɫ   x̣là-p   lut
I'll curry him;   then in the morning   it won't

k-s-x̣ʷ-àw-s   i?   s-k-s-kʷàɫ-t-s   ɬ   s-qíl-tk-s;   mi
be dry   his sweat   on his body;   it'll

s-tìl-təlxʷ-t   ɫ   i-k-s-c-kɫ-tx-ílxʷ-s.'
be hard   to curry him.'

I'd be late or that I'd get lost, and then I came fast and he got warm.
517. And I wouldn't water him, or feed him oats, that might harm him.
518. And I didn't even take the saddle off, because his back might swell; (I'll
leave it) there until he dries off, and then I'll go tend to him.
519. I'll go water him, and then take off the saddle, I'll feed him oats, and
I'll curry him; then in the morning his sweat won't be dry on his body;
it'll be hard to curry him.'

520. ixì? a-k-s-cùn-əm i? pə-ptwínaxʷ; waẏ
520. That's what you'll tell the old lady;

cə́m n-wnxʷ-ína?-m-ənt-s, lut
she'll believe you, she won't

k-s-əlk̇-əm-st-ùm-s i? x̣əl laklí-s.
force you about her key.

521. uɫ nínwi? kʷ wi?-cín məɫ cə́m
521. And when you are done eating she'll

ixì? t-k̇ìw-ḷx-st-əm-s k̇a ṇwís-t.
take you up to the upstairs.

522. cù-nt-əm, 'waẏ ixì? kʷ i-k-s-màya?-ɫt-əm y
522. She'll say, 'Now I'll show you

a-k-s-ən-ɫq̇ʷ-út-(t)ṇ, mət waẏ kʷ ?áyx̣ʷ-t.
where you'll sleep, you must be tired.

523. uɫ ixì? ilì? c-kɫ-wtàn waẏ
523. And everything is ready,

a-k-s-ɫq̇-əlx-álqs; axà? a-k-s-ən-ɫq̇ʷ-ùt-(t)ṇ uɫ
your pajamas; this is your bed and

ixì? a-k-s-ɫq̇-əlx-álqs.'
these are your pajamas.'

524. uɫ ixì? uɫ cə́m ɫ-sàx̣ʷ-t i?
524. Then she'll come back down the

pə-ptwínaxʷ; uɫ ixì? ilì? kɫ-míla?, ixì? aɫì?
old lady; and there she has bait,

k-mùs-əms i? s-ən-?əm-?íma?t, i? s-ta?-ta?k̇míx,
four granddaughters, young virgins,

520. That's what you'll tell the old lady; she'll believe you, she won't force
you about her key.

521. And when you are done eating she'll take you up to the upstairs.

522. She'll say, 'Now I'll show you where you'll sleep, you must be tired.

523. And everything is ready, your pajamas; this is your bed and these are
your pajamas.'

524. Then the old lady'll come back down; and there she has bait, four
granddaughters, young virgins,

s-wi?-wi?-númt-x.
handsome.

525. axà? i? s-ma?-m?ìm yə-yſà-t c-qʷác-qn-əlx,
525. These   women   all   have hats on,

t̓əxʷ i? k-s-ɬq̓-əlx-áya?-qən.
      night caps.

526. uɬ ixì? yə-yſà-t q̓ɬ-íẃs-ənt-əm   axà?
526. And   she puts them together

i? s-x?ìt-x uɬ axà? i? s-x?ìt-x l
the oldest and   the oldest of

a-ɬ-qá-qc-a?, ixì?   ùɬi? k-s-ənk̓ʷ-ɬq̓ʷ-lút-s.
your brothers, that one   he'll go to bed with.

527. uɬ axà? itlì? i? t kí-k̓a?t, uɬ   axà?
527. And   the   next one, with

i? t k̓ì-k̓a?t i? tkɬm-ílxʷ, uɬ ixì?
the   next   woman,

k-s-ənk̓ʷ-ɬq̓ʷ-lút-s; uɬ axà? i? q̓ə?-íẃs,   uɬ
he'll sleep with her; and   the middle one, with

ixì? q̓ə?-ìẃs   i? tkɬm-ílxʷ; uɬ axà? i? p
     the middle   woman;   and   you

s-ta?-t?íw-t-x   uɬ ixì? axà?
two youngest ones,   that

a-k-s-ənk̓ʷ-ɬq̓ʷ-lút.
will be your bed partner.

528. cəm̀   axà? t̓i sy-sy-ſàlx
528. They'll   make a lot of noise

handsome.
525. These women all have hats on, night caps.
526. And she puts them together the oldest and the oldest of your brothers,
    that one he'll go to bed with.
527. And the next one, with the next woman, he'll sleep with her; and the
    middle one, with the middle woman; and you two youngest ones, that
    will be your bed partner.
528. They'll make a lot of noise

a-s-k̓ʷíƛ-t-əm; ʔick-st-əm   iʔ t   s-maʔ-m?ím,
your brothers;   they're playing   with   the women,

c-qs-qs-ìnk-st-m-əlx,   c-háht-əlx.
they're tickling them,   they're laughing.

529. cə̇m axàʔ nixʷ ti
529.   As soon as

kəɫ-ʔəɫxʷ-ìcaʔ-nt-xʷ   axàʔ iʔ   s-tʔìw-t-x   məɫ
you crawl under the blanket   the   youngest one

cə̇m   ixì? nixʷ kʷín-(n)t-s, məɫ ixì?
she'll   also take you,   and

kəɫ-tə̇m-ʕás-ənt-s, qs-qs-ìnk-ənt-s k-mílk̓ʷ-əst-m-ənt-s.
kiss you,   tickle you,   she'll rub on you.

530. uɫ   lut   ixì? kʷ s-c-χm-ínk-əm-s, ti
530. But it's not that   she loves you,

kmix   kʷ   k-s-kə̇ɫ-ʔət-ətx-númt-aʔx; ixì? nìnẁi? kʷ
just so you fall asleep;   when   you

kəɫ-ʔət-ətx-nùmt ixì? mə̇ɫ c-ʔaw-s-ƛ̓əxʷ-ɫùləm-s
fall asleep   then she'll come and kill you

iʔ   t pə-ptwínaxʷ.
the   old woman.

531. uɫ   ixì? nìnẁi? wim̓   axàʔ
531. And   in vain

a-k-s-t-χ?ən-cən-mìst-əm axàʔ y a-s-ənk̓ʷ-ɫq̓ʷ-lút,
you'll try to stop   your bed partner,

lut   k-s-ƛ̓l-əl-p-st-ùm-s ɫaʔ
she won't stop

your brothers; they're playing with the women, they're tickling them,
they're laughing.

529. As soon as you crawl under the blanket the youngest one she'll also take
you, and kiss you, and she'll tickle you, she'll rub on you.

530. But it's not that she loves you, just so you fall asleep; when you fall
asleep then the old woman will come and kill you.

531. And in vain you'll try to stop your bed partner, she won't stop

c-qs-qs-ínk-st-əm-s.
tickling you on the belly.

532. məɫ cù-nt-xʷ: 'waẏ taʔlì?   uɫ kən
532. And you tell her: 'Too much   I

s-ʔáyx̣ʷ-t uɫ waẏ kən k-s-ʔítx.'
am tired, and   I   am going to sleep.'

533. uɫ   cə̀m yəʔ ʔx̣iʔ iʔ tkɫm-ìlxʷ lut
533. And   that   woman   won't

k-s-níxəl-m-ənt-s; waẏ məɫ ixì? tanmù s
listen to you;   pretend

a-s-x̣ʷáqʷ-əlqs-əm, waẏ cə̀m məɫ ixì?
you're snoring,   and

cíʔ-st-əm-s.
she'll leave you alone.

534. waẏ məɫ nixʷ cniɫc ʔìtx   axà? iʔ
534.   And too she will sleep   the

tkɫm-ílxʷ, nìxəl-m-ənt-xʷ x̣ʷáqʷ-əlqs-əm.
woman,   you'll hear her snore.

535. uɫ   lut   a-k-s-ʔítx,   lut
535. But   don't fall asleep, don't

a-k-s-kə̀ɫ-ʔət-ətx-númt; ixì? kʷ kə̀ɫ-ʔət-ətx-nù mt,
fall asleep;   if   you fall asleep,

ixì? uɫ p   ṇ-ćəs-p-úlaʔxʷ, ɫəxʷ-ɫúləm-s.
then   you all will be killed, dead.

536. uɫ waẏ miy-st-xʷ   ʔìtx   axà? iʔ
536.   When you're sure she's asleep   the

tickling you on the belly.
532. And you tell her: 'I am too tired, and I am going to sleep.'
533. And that woman won't listen to you; pretend you're snoring, and she'll
     leave you alone.
534. And the woman will sleep too, you'll hear her snore.
535. But don't fall asleep, don't fall asleep; if you fall asleep, then you all
     will be killed, dead.
536. When you're sure the woman is asleep

tkɬm-ílxʷ,   iwà?   ?ic-ìkst-m-ənt-xʷ   uɬ   kmix
woman,   even if you shake her up   all she does

ṇ-ckʷ-ckʷ-ìskit-əm,   uɬi?   kʷ   k̉-ka?ɬ-í?st,   uɬ   kʷ
is groan,   then   you   go easy,

xʷt-ílx,   k̉ʷəƛ-qìn-(n)t-xʷ   i?   t   qʷác-qən-s,   uɬ
get up,   take off   her cap,   and

anwí?   mi   kʷ   ɬ-qʷác-qən.
                     put it on your head.

537. uɬ   yə?   ?x̣i?   i?   k̉ə   n-ɬa?-m-ìnk   mi   kʷ
537. And   next to the wall   you

ɬq̉-ílx;   uɬ   ixì?-m   n̉ìn̉wi?   ɬ
go lie down; but   that's   after

wi?-s-k̉əɬ-ləxʷ-ənt-ìxʷ   a-s-k̉ʷíƛ-t-əm.
you've told what to do to   your brothers.

538. ti̓   ixì?   kʷ   xʷt-ílx,   qiɬ-ənt-xʷ   uɬ
538. As soon as   you   get up,   wake him up   and

ixì?   cù-nt-xʷ   axà?   i?   t   kì-ka?t   a-ɬ-qá-qc-a?,
        tell   the   nearest of   your brothers,

k̉əɬ-ləxʷ-ənt-íxʷ: 'qíɬ-t-x,   wa̓y   kʷu
you tell him: 'Wake up,   we

k-s-ƛəxʷ-t-míx-a?x.'
are going to die.'

539. uɬ   k̉ʷəƛ-qì-s   axà?   i?
539. And   he should take off the cap of

s-ənk̉ʷ-ɬq̉ʷ-lút-s;   ixì?   cniɬc
his bed partner;   he

even if you shake her up all she does is groan, then you go easy, get
up, take off her cap, and put it on your head.

537. And go lie down next to the wall; but that's after you've told your
brothers what to do.

538. As soon as you get up, wake him up and tell the nearest of your
brothers, you tell him: 'Wake up, we are going to die.'

539. And he should take off the cap of his bed partner; he

ł-qʷác-qn-əm-s.
should put it on his head.

540. 't-k̓ʷìt-x-əlx-m-ənt-xʷ   an-tkłm-ílxʷ,   axà?
540. 'Step over   the woman

a-s-ənk̓ʷ-łq̓ʷ-lút,   uł   anwì? kʷ ł
you're sleeping with,   and you

ṇ-ła?-m-ínk.'"
get next to the wall.'"

541. waẏ   wi?-s-kəł-?íys-əs   axà? i?
541. After he got done changing

ł-qá-qc-a?-s,   itlì? xʷuy   k̓əl k-náqs,
his oldest brother,   then   he went to   another,

ixì?   nixʷ qìł-t-s   xʷús-t-cn-əm-s;
that one also he woke up (and) hurried him up;

qìł-t-s   ixì? nixʷ ?x̣íl-st-s;   k̓ə
he woke him up   too   did the same;   next to

n-ła?-m-ìnk łq̓-ílx.
the wall   he lay.

542. hùy uł t-x̣ƛ̓á-p-əlx;   cù-s   axà?-m
542.   He got them all fixed up; he told

i? s-k̓ʷíƛ̓-t-əm-s: "ixì? məł məlx̣a?-s-x̣ʷáq̓ʷ-əlqs-əm,
    his brothers: "Pretend to be snoring,

uł   naxəmł lut   k-s-?ətx-ílx-əmp, itlì? waẏ kʷu
but   don't go to sleep,   else   we

k-s-ƛ̓əxʷ-t-míx-a?x."
are all going to die."

should put it on his head.

540. 'Step over the woman you're sleeping with, and you get next to the
wall.'"

541. After he got done changing his oldest brother, then he went to another,
he woke that one too (and) hurried him up; he woke him up too, did
the same; he lay next to the wall.

542. He got them all fixed up; he told his brothers: "Pretend to be snoring,
but don't go to sleep, else we are all going to die."

543. ixỉʔ sic c–kȉc–x iʔ k̓əl s–ənk̓ʷ–łq̓ʷ–lút–s
543.   Then he got back to his bed partner

uł cniłc iʔ qʷác–qn–əm, uł k̓ə
and he put the cap on, and

n–ła?–m–ȉnk łq̓–ílx, ixỉʔ uł
got close to the wall, lay down, and

məlx̣aʔ–s–x̣ʷáq̓ʷ–əlqs–əm.
pretended to snore.

544. wa̓y kʷmȉł uł c–k̓əł–níxəl̓.
544.   At once he heard a noise.

545. uł ałỉʔ c–ƛ̓a̓w iʔ c̓ȉk̓ʷ–əsxən, n̓–k̓ím.
545.   They're out the lights, it's dark.

546. wa̓y c–k̓əł–nȉxəl̓ tla yx̣ʷ–út.
546.   He heard something from below.

547. wa̓y c–t–k̓ȉw–lx wa̓y c–xək–xk–ílx; huy
547.   She was coming up, there's a noise;

uł c–kł–qíl–t.
she got to the top.

548. wa̓y ixỉʔ k–c̓í–cəx̣ʷ–s–əm, uł ałỉʔ ti mət ḷ
548.   He peeked,

nəqs–íłcaʔ, wa̓y c–kʷən–ł–c̓ȉk̓ʷ–əsxən ixỉʔ
they were in one room, she was holding a lamp

iʔ pə–ptwínaxʷ, yəʔ n̓–ʔəłn–aʔ–s–qílxʷ–tn̩.
the old woman, the man-eater.

549. uł k̓əl s–k–sək̓ʷt–ȉkst–s n̓–sp̓–ús–tn̩.
549. And in one hand she has a sword.

543. Then he got back to his bed partner and he put the cap on, and got
     close to the wall, lay down, and pretended to snore.
544. At once he heard a noise.
545. The lights are out, it's dark.
546. He heard something from below.
547. She was coming up, there's a noise; she got to the top.
548. He peeked in the room, the old woman held a lamp, the man-eater.
549. And in one hand she has a sword.

550. waẏ číkʷ-ənt-m-əlx;   uɬ   aɬì?
550.   She shone the light on them; and

    c-k-čí-čəx̣ʷ-s-əm, waẏ uɬ
    he was peeking,

    c-məlx̣a?-s-x̣ʷáq̓ʷ-əlqs-əm.
    he was pretending to be snoring.

551. uɬ waẏ ixì? s-c-x̌ʷùy-s   axà? i?
551.   She came closer   the

    pə-ptwínax̌ʷ.
    old woman.

552. yə? ?x̣i? təl   s-x̣?ìt-x   ixì?
552.   (She started) from the oldest one

    ņ-xl-ús-əs;   ɬtàp   i? ča?sì-qən-s uɬ
    (and) cut his head off; it came off   his head

    axà? i? s-qíl-tk-s,   itlì? c-x̌ʷùy   axà? i?
        (from) his body, then   she went on   the

    pə-ptwínax̌ʷ, ņ-xl-ú·ˑs-ənt-əm   uɬ
    old lady,   she chopped off their heads

    t-x̌ƛ̓à-p-əlx k-mús-əms.
    all of them, four of them.

553. waẏ ixì? ɬəɬ-sàx̌ʷ-t-s   ņ-tíkɬ;   uɬ
553.   Then she went back down downstairs and

    ixi? sic xʷt-əlscút-s   axà? i?
    then she took her clothes off   the

    pə-ptwínax̌ʷ, ixì? sic púlx-s.
    old lady,   and went to bed.

550. She shone the light on them; and he was peeking, he was pretending to be snoring.

551. The old woman came closer.

552. (She started) from the oldest one (and) cut his head off; his head came off (from) his body, then the old lady went on, she chopped off their heads all of them, four of them.

553. Then she went back down downstairs and then the old lady took her clothes off, and went to bed.

554. ṇ-qəm-p-íls.
554. She was satisfied.

555. waẏ x̣w-ənt-is   i?   cík̓w-əsxən.
555.   She put out   the   lights.

556. waẏ axà? i?   s-k̓wix̣-t-əm-s   qx̣-qíx̣-t-s,   cù-s:
556.   His brothers   he woke up,   he said:

   "xwús-t-wi?,   waẏ   xwt̓-lílx-wi?,   x̣c-m-əncút-wi?.
   "Hurry up,   get up,   get ready.

557. waẏ   kwu   k-s-x̣ix̣wṗ-t-a?x   ninwi?   uc   kwu   x̣
557.   We   are going to get away   if   we

   k-s-x̣íx̣wṗ-ət-s."
   can."

558. waẏ ixì? xwt̓-t-əp-númt,   ux̣ ax̣ì? waẏ
558.   They jumped up,

   c-my-st-is   axà? i? x̣əx̣-qá-qc-a?-s, ux̣ ax̣ì?
   they know   his brothers,   because

   c-ʕac̓-əst-s-əlx   axà? i? s-ənk̓w-x̣əq̓w-lút-s-əlx yə?
   they saw   their bed partners

   ṇ-xəl-xl-ús-ənt-m-əlx.
   get beheaded.

559. waẏ wi?-s-x̣c-m-əncút-əlx,   waẏ ux̣
559.   They got ready   and

   k̓wəx̣-qín-m-əlx,   ilì? t̓əq-m-ís-əlx   i?
   they took their caps off,   they threw down

   qwác-qən-s-əlx,   s-t-qwaẏ-s-əlx i?   t
   their hats,   they ran down   the

554. She was satisfied.
555. She put out the lights.
556. He woke his brothers, he said: "Hurry up, get up, get ready.
557. We are going to get away if we can."
558. They jumped up, his brothers know, because they saw their bed partners get beheaded.
559. They got ready and they took their caps off, they threw down their hats, they ran down the

s-ən-t-k̇íw-əlx-tṇ,   ixì?   uɬ   k̇əl
stairs,   and (went) straight to

s-ən-ṫəws-cqáx̣a?-tṇ.
the barn.

560. cù-nt-m-əlx   i? t ɬ-sí-sənca?-s-əlx: "ta?lì?
560. He told them   their little brother:

p   k-swít-mist;   uc nìṅ̇wi? kʷu ɬ
"You do your very best; if   we

k-s-?ac-əcqa?-ì?st i? təl s-ən-ṫəws-cqáx̣a?-tṇ, nìṅ̇wi?
can get out   of   the barn,

ixì? kʷu c-ən-?ùc-xən-(n)t-əm i?   t
            she'll follow us   the

ṇ-?əɬn-a?-s-qílxʷ-tṇ, i?   t pə-ptwínaxʷ.
man-eater,   the   old lady.

561. wa̧y nax̣əmɬ kʷu k-?əmt-ìws ḻ kəwáp-tət,   kʷu
561.   But if we   can get   on our horses, we

c-?ác-əcqa?, ixì? uɬ pna? cmay kʷu xʷəl-xʷál-t."
get out,   then   maybe   we   will be safe."

562. uɬ   aɬì? ixì? nixʷ i?
562. And

səxʷ-t-x̣tá-m-s,   i?   s-kəkʕáka? ilì? la
those who take care of her, the birds,

n-yxʷ-ùt   kʷə-kʷrì-t i? s-kəkʕáka?.
they are there the golden   birds.

563. ixì?   yə? t s-ən-ṗ?àxʷ uɬ ixì? yə? t
563. Whenever   they light up or

stairs, and (went) straight to the barn.
560. Their little brother told them: "You do your very best; if we can get
out of the barn, the man-eater will follow us, the old lady.
561. But if we can get on our horses, we get out, then maybe we will be
safe."
562. And those who take care of her, the birds, the golden birds are there.
563. Whenever they light up or

sy-m-ənc⸱át   yə?   c-my-p-numt   way̓
they make noise   she finds out

s-qílxʷ;   ixì? məł ik̓lì? łx̣ʷpà-m   axà?
there are people;   then   she runs out

i? tkłm-ílxʷ, i? pə-ptwínaxʷ.
the woman,   the old lady.

564. way̓ cù-nt-m-əlx: "axà? incà? uł lut   kən t̓
564.   He told them: "I   never

ṇ-k̓ʷəxʷ-ki?-sqáx̣a?-ṃ, uł ałì?   kən s-x̣ʷúp-t-x;
took the saddle off,   because I   am helpless;

axà? mnìmł-əmp p q̓ʷíł-q̓ʷəł-t, uł   way̓ ti p
     you folks   are smart,   and   you

sy-m-scùt   i? k-s-xʷs-xʷús-əlx-əmp."
do your best   (and) hurry."

565. uł ałì? way̓ n-wnxʷ-ìna?-m-s-əlx   axà?
565. And   they started believing

ł-sí-sənca?-s-əlx.
their little brother.

566. way̓ ixì? s-tkʷú-p-xn-əm-s-əlx,
566.   They ran,

ṇ-t̓əkʷ-ki?-sqáx̣a?-m-əlx,   laprít-m-əlx;
they threw the saddles on, put the bridles on;

?àc-əcqa?-st-s-əlx i? kəw?áp-s-əlx.
they took out   their horses.

567. uł ałì? axà? t̓əxʷ   k̓ł-ən-k̓ahk̓ʷ-ip-s i?
567.   Just when they opened   the

they make noise she finds out that there are people; then the woman
runs out, the old lady.

564. He told them: "I never took the saddle off, because I am helpless; you
folks are smart, and you do your best (and) hurry."

565. And they started believing their little brother.

566. They ran, they threw the saddles on, put the bridles on; they took out
their horses.

567. Just when they opened the

s-ən-t̓əws-cqáx̣aʔ-tņ,   ut   sy-m-əncˤàt
barn door,   they started to make noise

ax̣àʔ iʔ s-kəkˤáka?, ut   p̓ʔáxʷ,   ax̣àʔ
      the birds,   and they shone,

ņ-p̓ʔáxʷ,   c-ʔx̣ìt t s-x̣əl-x̣ˤál-t.
it was bright then   like   daylight.

568. s-c-ʔx̣ìl-x ut ixìʔ iʔ c̓íkʷ-əsxən-s-əlx utiʔ
568. That's why   it's bright   and

x̣ʷús-x̣ʷs-t-əlx,   utiʔ miʔ-máy?-t-əlx,
they could hurry,   and   they got things right,

lùt   s-k-pàx̣-əm-s-əlx iʔ t s-wr̓-ìsəlp̓
they didn't   have to light   matches

s-c̓íkʷ-əm-s-əlx.
to look around.

569. waỳ wiʔ-s-t-kʷəl·-ìws-əlx   ixìʔ   kiʔ
569.   After they were on their horses that's   when

łx̣ʷp̓à-m   ax̣àʔ iʔ   pə-ptwínaxʷ.
she ran out   the   old lady.

570. ut atìʔ waỳ ņ-waʔl-ìls-əm-s ax̣àʔ iʔ
570.   She got puzzled   the

pə-ptwínaxʷ; kʷm̓it s-c-kət-nìxəl̓-s təl
old lady;   at once she heard

s-t-qʷàỳ-s-əlx iʔ təl s-ən-t-k̓íw-əlx-tņ, ut ax̣àʔ
them run   downstairs,   and

ņ-st-ìls,   "ut háʔ s-c-ʔkìn-x   háʔ?
she thought,   "What's the matter?

barn door, the birds started to make noise, and they shone, it was bright
then like daylight.

568. That's why it's bright and they could hurry, and they got things right,
they didn't have to light matches to look around.

569. After they were on their horses that's when the old lady ran out.

570. The old lady got puzzled; at once she heard them run downstairs, and
she thought, "What's the matter?

571. way̓ təl   i-s-c-px̣-px̣-t-wilx,   təl
571.   Since I came to my senses,   since

      i-s-ən-ʔəɬn-aʔ-s-qílxʷ-tṇ,   lut   xʷuy̓   ilíʔ kʷu
      I became a man-eater,   nobody came who

      c-ʔx̣íl-st-s.
      did that to me.

572. lut   stim̓ kən tə c-kəw-kəwik   x̣əl
572. I never   have been ghosted by

      stím̓.
      anything.

573. way̓ mət   la ʔkin
573.   There must

      s-c-ʔkín-x."
      something be the matter."

574. way̓ ixíʔ s-x̣c-m-əncut-s,   k-c̓ik̓-s-əs iʔ
574.   She got ready,   she lit   the

      c̓ik̓ʷ-əsxən, ixíʔ s-t-k̓íw-ḷx-s.
      lamp,   she went upstairs.

575. way̓ kɬ-qíl-t,   way̓ k̓aw   iʔ
575.   She got upstairs,   they're gone the

      tuʔ-twít.
      boys.

576. way̓ iʔ s-ən-ʔəm-ʔìmaʔt-s   nak̓ʷəm
576.   Her grandchildren's

      ṇ-x̣əl-xl-ús-əs;   ilíʔ   c-k̓əɬ-t̓aq   axàʔ iʔ
      heads she cut off; there they were laying   the

571. Since I came to my senses, since I became a man-eater, nobody came
     who did that to me.
572. I never have been ghosted by anything.
573. There must something be the matter."
574. She got ready, she lit the lamp, she went upstairs.
575. She got upstairs, the boys are gone.
576. Her grandchildren's heads she cut off; the caps were laying there.

qʷəc-qʷác-qən-s.
caps.

577. uɬ ixì? nak̓ʷəm ixì? c-k-cah-m-əncùt
577.   They were on the wrong side

i? s-ən-ʔəm-ʔíma?t-s; uɬ aɬì? ixì? kʷə-kʷìm-m-t
     her grandchildren;   she went too far

yə? ɬ ən-xəl-xl-ùs-əs   i?
          (and) she cut off the heads of

s-ən-ʔəm-ʔíma?t-s.
her grandchildren.

578. waẏ ixì? i? pə-ptwínaxʷ ṇta? ixì? ki?
578. Well,   the old lady   that's when

c-ɬx̌ʷpá-m,   t-x̌ʷt̓-p-əm-s-qílxʷ i? k̓əl
she rushed out, she rushed   to

s-ən-t̓əws-cqáx̌a?-tṇ; ṇ-st-ìls: "k-waẏ nìnẇi?
the barn;   she thought: "They'll

ilì? məl-míl-ḷx, mi k̓ɬ-ən-ʔəɬxʷ-íp-n-əlx, ixì?
there lose time, I'll get them in there,   that's

mi ṇ-k̓áw-la?xʷ-st-n-əlx."
when I'll clean them up."

579. waẏ ixì? t-x̌ʷt̓-p-əm-s-qílxʷ, waẏ put
579.   She rushed over,   just when

c-kìc-x   t-kʷəl·-ìws-əlx   i? tu?-tẇít;
she got there they were on their horses the boys;

waẏ t̓i kutpáy-s-əlx,   táq-s-əlx, súxʷ-xʷ-əlx.
        they said goodbye, they waved, they're gone.

577. Her grandchildren were on the wrong side; she went too far (and) she
    cut off the heads of her grandchildren.
578. Well, that's when the old lady rushed out, she rushed to the barn; she
    thought: "They'll lose time there, I'll get them in there, that's when I'll
    clean them up."
579. She rushed over, just when she got there the boys were on their horses;
    they said goodbye, they waved, they're gone.

580. waẏ itlì? xʷúy?-ḻx,   lut
580.   They went, they didn't

    s-ək-s-c-xʷúy-s-əlx, lut   ťəxʷ
    go far,   it wasn't even

    s-k̇əlxʷ-núxʷ-s-əlx, waẏ k̇əɫ-k̇ʷƛ̇á-p-əlx,   waẏ ťi
    a whole day,   they came in sight,

    c-?x̣iɫ   t tàwn   i? s-c-wík-s-əlx.
    it's like a town what they saw.

581. waẏ ka?ít-t-əlx   uɫ k-my-p-ùs-əm-s-əlx waẏ
581.   They got closer and they made out that

    táwn.
    it was a town.

582. waẏ ṇ-p-pəlx-ìws-əlx k̇əl táwn.
582.   They went through   town.

583. ṇťa? ťi c-əwxʷ-ùs-əm-st-s-əlx i?   t
583.   They were all staring   the

    s-wyápix.
    white people.

584. cùt: "waẏ mət   s-wyápix."
584. They said: "They must be white people."

585. waẏ x̣s-əlscút-əlx,
585.   What they have is beautiful,

    x̣às-t   i? kəw?áp-s-əlx, uɫ waẏ
    they're beautiful   their horse,   and

    ṇ-wa?l-ìls-m-ənt-m-əlx axà? i? t s-tàwn i? t
    they got puzzled   the   town's

580. They went, they didn't go far, it wasn't even a whole day, they came
    in sight, it's like a town what they saw.
581. They got closer and they made out that it was a town.
582. They went through town.
583. The white people were all staring.
584. They said: "They must be white people."
585. What they have is beautiful, their horses are beautiful, and the town's
    people got puzzled;

s-wyápix;   ṇ-st-ils-əlx: "waẏ   mət
people;   they thought: "They must be

s-my-s-qílxʷ   axà?   yə?   ṇ-k̓ʷúl-tṇ-s   axà?   i?
important people   the   parents of   these

tu?-twít."
boys."

586.   uɫ   aɫi?   waẏ   miẏ-st-m-əlx
586.   They have an idea

tu?-twít.
they're young boys.

587.   waẏ   saʕ-m-əncút-əlx,   uɫ   ixì?
587.   They got off their horses,   and

sw-ɫtíɫn-əlx.
they started asking.

588.   ixì?   ùɫi?   k-sìw-pla?-s-əlx   yə?
588.   Then   they started asking (where)   the

ylmíxʷəm,   k̓a   ?k̓ìn   i?   s-ylmxʷ-íɫxʷ;   ixì?
king is,   where   the   king's house is;

cù-nt-m-əlx: "ixì?   ik̓lì?   əc-wíx,   ixì?
they told them: "That   there   building,   that's

s-ylmxʷ-íɫxʷ."
the king's house."

589.   cù-s-əlx: "waẏ   lím-ləm-t-x,"   waẏ   ik̓lì?
589.   They said: "Thanks,"   and

s-kɫ-təkʷ?-út-s-əlx.
they walked on.

they thought: "The parents of these boys must be important people."
586. They have an idea they're young boys.
587. They got off their horses, and they started asking.
588. Then they started asking (where) the king is, where the king's house
     is; they told them: "That there building, that's the king's house."
589. They said: "Thanks," and they walked on.

590. ṭi xʷúˑˑyʔ-lx,   uɬ   kɬ-ən-ɬaʔ-ìp-əlx   iʔ k̓əl
590.   They went,   and they got to the door   to

     s-yləmxʷ-íɬxʷ;   wa̓y ixì? s-k̓ɬ-ən-caʔ-íp-əm-s-əlx,
     the king's house;   they knocked on the door,

     wa̓y c-k̓ɬ-ən-k̓ahk̓ʷ-ìp-ɬt-m-əlx   iʔ tə ylmíxʷəm.
          he opened the door for them   the   king.

591. wa̓y s-ən-p-pílx-s-əlx; wa̓y wt-xìt-m-əlx   iʔ
591.   They went in;   they got for them

     t   k-s-ən-kɬ-mút-(t)n̥-s-əlx.
     some chairs.

592. wa̓y n̥-st-ìls   axà? yə? ylmíxʷəm: "n̥taʔ wa̓y
592.   He thought   the king:

     mət   s-my-s-qìlxʷ   iʔ ɬəx-əx-ɬx̣á-p-s;
     "they must be important people   their parents;

     axà? ṭəxʷ tuʔ-twìt-əlx axà? iʔ s-ʕác-s-əlx,   uɬ
           young boys   they look like,   and

     t x̣s-ícaʔ-lx,   yə?
        they have expensive clothes,

     x̣s-əlscút-əlx.
     (and) everything else.

593. wa̓y mət   s-my-s-qìlxʷ   iʔ
593.   They must be important people

     ɬəx-əx-ɬx̣á-p-s; uɬ aɬì? iʔ kʷu
     their parents;   and

     c-k-təɬ-m-əncút-əm-s-əlx."
     they come straight to me."

590. They went, and they got to the door of the king's house; they knocked
     on the door, the king opened the door for them.
591. They went in; they got some chairs for them.
592. The king thought: "Their parents must be important people; they look
     like young boys, and they have expensive clothes, (and) everything else.
593. Their parents must be important people; and they come straight to me."
594. He asked them: "And what is your business, that you come to me, into
     my house?

594. cù-nt-m-əlx: " uɬ   stìm i? s-c-ən-q̓a?-ìlx-əmp,
594. He asked them: "And   what   is your business,

   ki?   kʷu c-t-xʷúy-m-ənt-p, kʷu c-ən-p-pílx-m-ənt-p?
   that   you come to me,   into my house?

595. kʷu máya?-ɬt-p."
595.   Tell me."

596. "waẏ ḻ?íw-tət   yə? ylmíxʷəm; lut   kʷu
596.   "Our father   is a king; he didn't

   ṫə s-c-kʷúlst-əm."
     send us."

597. ?ùm-la?xʷ-s-əlx tla ?kín.
597. They named   from where (they came).

598. ṫi mnìmɬ-tət s-pu?-ús-tət."
598.   "We   made up our own minds."

599. uɬ aɬi? waẏ xəⱦ-p-nù-nt-əm i? q̓əẏ-mín; swit
599.   We've finished   school;

   aɬi? ylmìxʷəm   ḻ?íw-tət, uɬ ṫi kmix   kʷu
   since   he's a chief our father,   he just

   s-tu?-tíwa?-st-əm, lut stìm   ṫə c-my-st-ím; uɬ
   babied us,   not anything   we know;   and

   axà? təl s-ən-ṁa?-máya?-tṇ, uɬ nixʷ lut   kʷu
       from school,   they don't

   ṫə c-ṁa?-ṁáya?-ɬt-əm stìm   ḻ   s-k̓ʷúɬ-əm.
     teach us   anything about work.

600. uɬ s-c-?x̣ìl-x ki? kʷu ṇ-st-ìls, 'waẏ kʷu
600. And that's why   we   thought,   'We

595. Tell me."
596. "Our father is a king; he didn't send us."
597. They named from where (they came).
598. "We made up our own minds."
599. We've finished school; since our father is a chief, he just babied us, we don't know anything; and from school, they don't teach us anything about work.
600. And that's why we thought, 'We are going to travel around the country,

k-s-təkʷ-təkʷʔ-ùt-aʔx   iʔ   t təmxʷ-úlaʔxʷ,   kʷu
are going to travel around   the   country,   we

k-s-ƛaʔ-ƛaʔ-s-c-kʷúl-aʔx,   k-s-my-p-nù-nt-əm
are going to look for a job, we're going to learn how

iʔ s-kʷúl-əm.'"
   to work.'"

601. cù-nt-əm: "a··, wáy̓, wày̓ anwíʔ   háʔ kʷ
601. He said: "Ah,   are you

s-xʔìt-x?"
the oldest one?"

602. "wáy̓;" "way̓ anwì? mi   xaʔt-əm-st-úm-ən;
602. "Yes;"   "You   I will take care of first;

stìm an-xm-ìnk a-k-s-c-kʷúl a-k-s-c-my-p-nwíłən?"
what do you like to work at   to learn?"

603. cùt   axàʔ iʔ   tə-twít: "way̓, way̓
603. He said   the   boy:

səxʷ-kʷùl-łxʷ-əm in-xm-ìnk i-k-s-c-kʷúl; ixìʔ
"Carpentry   I'd like to do;   that's

i-k-s-c-mi̓ʔ-m̓yaʔ-ncút."
what I want to go to school for."

604. cù-nt-əm, "wáy̓," way̓ qəy̓-xí··t-əm,   cù-nt-əm:
604. He said, "OK,"   he wrote a note, he said:

"axàʔ kʷ   xʷuy ik̓líʔ,   ik̓lìʔ
    "You go   over there, there is

c-k̓ł-ən-q̓əʔ-íp: ixìʔ   iʔ səxʷ-kʷúl-łxʷ-əm; ixìʔ
a sign on the door; that's the carpenter's;

   we are going to look for a job, we're going to learn how to work.'"
601. He said: "Ah, are you the oldest one?"
602. "Yes;" "I will take care of you first; what do you like to work at to
    learn?"
603. The boy said: "Carpentry I'd like to do; that's what I want to go to school
    for."
604. He said, "OK," he wrote a note, he said: "You go over there, there is
    a sign on the door; that's the carpenter's;

kʷ   n̩–ʔúɫxʷ,   uɫ ixì? aɫì? yə? ylmíxʷəm
you go there,   he   is the boss

ḷ s–c–k̓ʷúl–x,   səxʷ–ma̓?–ma̓ya?–m̩.
of the workers, the teacher.

605. ixì? xʷìc–əɫt–xʷ i? q̓əy̓–mín; ńìńwi?
605.   Give him this paper;

    ʕác̓–əs,   uɫ way̓ my–p–nù–s t incà? kʷ
    he'll look at it, and   he'll know   I

    i–s–k̓ʷúlst–əm; uɫ way̓ xʷìc̓–əxt–əm–s t
    sent you;   and   he'll give you a

    a–k–s–c–k̓ʷúl."
    job."

606. cù–nt–əm   axà? ilì? i? t–k̓í–k̓a?t: "hu–húy
606. He said to   the next one: "Now

    anwì? stìm̓ an–xm–ìnk a–k–s–c–k̓ʷúl?"
    you, what do you want for a job?"

607. cù–s: "way̓   axà? i–ɫ–qà–qc–a? kʷì–s ixì?
607. He said: "Well,   my brother   took

    i? səxʷ–k̓ʷúl–ɫxʷ–əm; uɫ ixì? c–t–kɫà–m ixì? i?
    the job of carpentry; and that's another

    s–k̓ʷúl–ɫxʷ–əm; uɫ axà? c–t–kɫà–m i?
    job carpentry; and that's another

    s–míʎ–əɫxʷ–əm.
    job house painting.

608. uɫ incà? i? s–míʎ–əɫxʷ–əm, ixì?
608. And I   the house painting, that's what

you go there, he is the boss of the workers, the teacher.

605. Give him this paper; he'll look at it, and he'll know I sent you; and he'll
    give you a job."

606. He said to the next one: "Now you, what do you want for a job?"

607. He said: "Well, my brother took the job of carpentry; and that's another
    job carpentry; and that's another job house painting.

608. House painting, that's what

in-xm-ìnk   i-k-s-my-p-nún-əm."
I want   to learn."

609. cù-nt-əm: "a··, wáy;" q̓ỳà··-m, ixì?
609. He said: "Ah, OK; he wrote,

x̌ʷíc-əłt-əm.
he gave it to him.

610. cù-nt-əm: "iǩlì? c-wìx i? səxʷ-miλ-əłxʷ-əm
610. He said: "There lives the house painters'

yə? ylmíxʷəm; iǩlì? kʷ x̌ʷúy, kʷ kíc-x   məł
     boss;   there you go,   you get there and

ixì? x̌ʷíc-əłt-xʷ axà? in-q̓əy̓-mín;   way̓ ti
      give him   what I wrote;

ʕác-əs,   uł way̓ mìy-st-s   t incà? kʷ
he'll look at it and   he'll know that   I

i-s-kʷúlst-əm; way̓ n̓in̓wi? x̌ʷíc-əłt-əm-s t
sent you;   he'll   give you   a

a-k-s-c-ǩʷúl."
job."

611. way̓   cakʷ   cù-s   in-(n)-qʷəl-qʷíl-tn̩,
611. Well, as   they say in my language,

n̩-x̌ʷ?-íłp-cən, way̓ itlì? kən c̓əpq-s-ìws-əm   i?
in Colville   I   am going to splice

t in-captíkʷł,   axà? i? t kʷə-kʷr̓ì-t i?
   my fairy tale,   the   Golden

tkłm-ílxʷ.
Woman.

I want to learn.
609. He said: "Ah, OK; he wrote, he gave it to him.
610. He said: "There lives the house painters' boss; go there, you get there
     and give him what I wrote; he'll look at it and he'll know that I sent
     you; he'll give you a job."
611. Well, as they say in my language, in Colville I am going to splice my
     fairy tale, the Golden Woman.

612. ixì?   kʷa   ilì?   kən   ƛà-p   i?   t
612. That's   where   I   stopped

    i-s-c-captíkʷɬ;   axà?   s-c-máy?-ncùt-a?x   i?
    telling my story;   he was telling his story   the

    likúk   i?   na?ɬ   lipúl,   axà?   həɬ-kʷə-kʷr̀ì-t
    rooster   with   the hen,   the golden

    s-kəkˤáka?.
    birds.

613. uɬ   axà?   i?   likúk   c-máy?-ncút,   axà?
613. And   the   rooster   is telling a story,

    i?   k̓əl   xʷ?ìt   i?   k̓əl   s-qílxʷ,   uɬ   nak̓ʷəm
    to   all   the   people,   and   indeed

    ixì?   i?   tə-twìt   i?   cáw-t-s,   ixì?
    that's what   the   boy   did,   that's what

    əc-máy?-st-ís.
    he's telling.

614. ixì?   əc-máya?-ɬt-s   i?   cáw-t-s;   uɬ   aɬì?   kʷa
614.   He's telling   what   he did;   and

    axà?   i?   tə-twìt   c-?x̣iɬ   t   n̩-ɬìp-t-əm-s   i?
    the   boy   like   he forgot   what

    cáw-t-s.
    happened to him.

615. uɬ   ixì?   k̓əɬ-pa?x̣-ənt-ìs   i?   kʷə-kʷr̀ì-t
615. And   she thought of a plan   the   Golden

    i?   tkɬm-ílxʷ,   uɬ   aɬì?   axà?   i?   k̓əl   tə-twìt   itì?
    Woman,   because   to   the boy   that

612. That's where I stopped telling my story; the rooster was telling his story
with the hen, the golden birds.

613. And the rooster is telling a story, to all the people, and indeed that's
what the boy did, that's what he's telling.

614. He's telling what he did; and the boy like he forgot what happened to
him.

615. And the Golden Woman thought of a plan, because to the boy that

iʔ kʷín-(n)t-əm, ixíʔ iklíʔ yəʔ k-s-puʔ-ús,
caught her, that's where her heart is,

iklíʔ xm-ìnk-s k-s-c-mrím-aʔx.
that's who she wants to marry.

616. uɬ axàʔ yəʔ ylmìxʷəm uɬ waẏ myàɬ
616. And the king is too

ɬəx-ɬxá-p; uɬ s-c-ʔxìl-x ixíʔ
old; and that's why all of this

kəɬ-paʔx-ənt-ís.
she thought out.

617. nìnẁiʔ axàʔ maẏʔ-ncùt iʔ likúk,
617. When he's telling his story the rooster,

uɬ pnaʔ cmay ɬ-qiɬ-t ṇ-ɬəkʷ-kʷ-mì-s axàʔ iʔ
maybe he'll wake up (and) remember the

tə-twìt iʔ cáw-t-s, uɬ ixíʔ nìnẁiʔ
boy what happened to him, and then

mi sic c-mrím-əlx.
they'll get married.

618. ixíʔ iʔ cəxʷ-xìt-s-əlx iʔ s-qílxʷ, ixíʔ
618. That's what is told to the people,

uɬ cù-s iʔ likùk iʔ lipúl-s, "háʔ
and he tells the rooster (to) the hen, "Is it

wnìxʷ ixíʔ in-cáw-t?"
true what I've done?"

619. ixíʔ məɬ ṇ-ɬəkʷ-s-əncùt axàʔ iʔ tkɬm-ílxʷ,
619. Then she winks at him the woman,

caught her, that's where her heart is, that's who she wants to marry.
616. And the king is too old; and that's why she thought out all of this.
617. When the rooster is telling his story, maybe the boy'll wake up (and)
remember what happened to him, and then they'll get married.
618. That's what is told to the people, and the rooster tells the hen, "Is
it true what I've done?"
619. Then the woman winks at him,

i? lipúl, ņ-tək^w-s-əncùt-xt-s i? likúk-s, mə+
the hen, she winks at him the hen, and

cù-s, "wáy̓, wáy̓, wáy̓, ixì? an-cáw-t.
she says, "Yes, yes, yes, that's what you've done.

620. kmàtəm k^w i-s-c-my-+t-ìm ixì? way̓ ixì?
620. Certainly I know this is what

an--cáw-t, u+ cak^w t incà? + ņ-cəw̓-cí-+t-s-ən
you've done, and if I had told the story,

u+ lut yə-yˤà-t k^w i-k-s-c-my-+t-ìm
I I wouldn't have everything known

an-cáw-t.
that you've done.

621. u+ a+ì? way̓ ti n-yˤip k^w in-x̣m-ínk, way̓
621. And always I love you,

k^w t i-k-s-c-mrím-a?x."
I want you to marry me."

622. way̓ ixì? tə-twìt c-?x̣ì+ t s-qí+-t-x.
622. The boy like he woke up.

623. "way̓ incà? kən +a? k+-cáw-t, i? k^wu
623. "I have done that, what

c-may̓?-+t-ís."
he's been telling about me."

624. u+ ixì? way̓ qì+-t, u+ ņ-+ək^w-k̓^w-mì-s
624. He woke up, and he thought

ixì? cní+c i? càw-t-s ixì? cù-nt-m-əlx
that's he whose deeds they're telling to

the hen winks at him, and she says, "Yes, yes, yes, that's what you've
done.
620. Certainly I know this is what you've done, and if I had told the story,
I wouldn't have known everything that you've done.
621. And always I love you, I want you to marry me."
622. The boy like he woke up.
623. "I have done that, what he's been telling about me."
624. He woke up, and he thought that's he whose deeds they're telling

yə? ṇ-yàt̓ i? s-qílxʷ.
all the people.

625. kʷa lut pən-?kìn i? s-kəkˤàka? t̓ə
625. Not ever do birds

c-m̓ay?-xt-wíxʷ-əlx, t̓ə c-qʷa?-qʷ?ál-x; uɫ aɫi?
talk to one another, or just talk; but

axà? ṇ-?əɫn-a?-s-qìlxʷ-tṇ ɫə k-s-kəkˤáka?,
these are the man-eater's birds,

s-c-?x̣il-x ki? əc-qʷa?-qʷ?àl-x yə?
that's why they talk

c-m̓ay?-ncút-əlx.
(and) tell about themselves.

626. wa̓y axà? i? tə-twìt t̓i ixì?
626. Well, this boy as soon as

my-p-nù-s wa̓y cniɫc yə?
he realized that it's his

c-ən-caw-c-í?st-əm i? t likúk, wa̓y
deeds (being talked about) by the rooster,

c-k-sɫ-ípla?.
he disappeared.

627. lùt c-?x̣iɫ t c-my-st-ís, uɫ t̓i kəl
627. They didn't realize it, and just to

s-kəkˤàka? i? s-c-ən-x̣a?s-ína?-s-əlx.
the birds they were listening.

628. wa̓y uɫ axà? i? sx-nù-s-əlx axà? i?
628. Then they missed the

all the people.

625. Not ever do birds talk to one another, or just talk; but these are the
man-eater's birds, that's why they talk (and) tell about themselves.
626. Well, as soon as this boy realized that it's his deeds (being talked about)
by the rooster, he disappeared.
627. They didn't realize it, they were just listening to the birds.
628. Then they missed the

tə-twít,   káw,   nakʷəm mət   tə
boy,   he's gone,   he must have

ʔácqaʔ.
slipped out.

629. ixì? uɬ axà? i? ɬəɬ-qà-qc-a?-s ixì? uɬ
629. Then   his brothers

s-ən-ċa?-ċa?r-ínk-s-əlx.
got the belly ache.

630. cù-nt-m-əlx   i? tə ylmíxʷəm: "lut   swìt
630. He told them the   king: "Don't anybody

k-s-?ácqa?-s."
go out."

631. waẏ cù-s   i? səxʷ-k̓ʷúɬ-əm-s: "xʷúy-x
631.   He told   his working man: "Go

c-ən-?ùɬxʷ-skʷ   i? sìlxʷa? i? k-ylw̓-íca?;
(and) bring in   the big   tub;

ilì?   mi kɬ-cəq-ɬt-íxʷ, swìt   yə?
right there   put it;   whoever

n̓-ċa?r̓-ínk,   ixì? ilì? mi k̓ʷúɬ-əm-s; lut
has the belly ache,   can use it; don't

swìt   k-s-?ácqa?-s."
anybody leave."

632. uɬ aɬì? waẏ k-s-ən-ma?-ìpə(n)-nt-m-əlx,
632.   They're going to tell on them,

n̓-ma?-ìp-ənt-m-əlx   axà? i? t s-kəkʕáka?,
they're going to tell on them the   birds,

boy, he's gone, he must have slipped out.
629. Then his brothers got the belly ache.
630. The king told them: "Don't anybody go out."
631. He told his working man: "Go (and) bring in the big tub; put it right
there; whoever has the belly ache, he can use it; don't anybody leave."
632. They're going to tell on them, the birds are going to tell on them,

i?   k-cəw-t-íkxt-s-əlx.
what they did to him.

633. way̓ nàx̣əmł lut   qł-nù-s-əlx
633.   And   they can't do anything

k-s-ʔac-əcqaʔ-íʔst-s-əlx.
to get out.

634. way̓ cùt   yəʔ ylmíxʷəm: "way̓ ixì? uł kʷu
634. Well, he said the king: "Now   we

c-mrím."
can get married."

635. uł ałì? way̓ ilì?   i? q̓ʷ ˤáy-l̥qs.
635.   He's there the priest.

636. cù-nt-əm   axà? i? t tkłm-ílxʷ,
636. She said to him   the   woman,

kʷə-kʷr̓ì-t tkłm-ílxʷ: "lut   a-k-s-xʷús-əska?; way̓
the Golden Woman: "Don't get in a hurry;

kʷu k-s-c-mrím-aʔx;   way̓ nàx̣əmł   kʷ
we   will get married;   but (first)

i-k-s-qʷəl-qʷíl-st-əm."
I want to talk to you."

637. way̓ uł ałì? kł-taʔkʷ?-út-əlx,   uł
637.   They were walking back and forth

c-ən-q̓əl-q̓əlxʷ-àx̣n-əm-st-əm axà? i? kʷə-kʷr̓ì-t i?
arm in arm   the Golden

tkłm-ílxʷ.
Woman.

what they did to him.
633. And they can't do anything to get out.
634. Well, the king said: "Now we can get married."
635. The priest is there.
636. The woman said to him, the Golden Woman: "Don't get in a hurry; we
    will get married; but (first) I want to talk to you."
637. They were walking back and forth arm in arm, the Golden Woman.

638. cù-nt-əm: "wáy nàx̣əmɬ kʷu
638. She said:

c-ən-maʔs-íẃs,   waẏ kʷ ƛ̓əx̣-ƛ̓x̣à-p uɬ incà?
"Our ages are different,   you are old   and I

kən xí-xw-t-əm,   uɬ lut há? a-k-s-ən-st-íls,
    am just a girl,   and don't   you think,

nínẃiʔ kʷu c-mrìm, məɬ taʔlì?   kʷ
if   we marry,   very much you

c-paʔ-paʔs-ínk.
will be sorry.

639. cəm ƛ̓i kʷu c-k̓əɬ-ƛ̓aʔ-st-íxʷ,   kʷ
639.   You'll be jealous of me, you

k̓əɬ-ƛ̓aʔ-ƛ̓aʔ-m-úɬ,   uɬ aɬì?   təl
will be jealous hearted,   because of

a-s-ƛ̓əx̣-ƛ̓x̣á-p."
your old age."

640. cùt   axà? yə? ylmíxʷəm: "wáy wníxʷ,
640. He said   the chief: "It's true,

wáy kən ƛ̓əx̣-ƛ̓x̣à-p, myàɬ   kʷu c-ən-maʔs-íẃs.
   I   am old,   too much we are unmatched.

641. uɬ   anwì? kʷ px̣-páx̣-t,   pna? c-my-st-ìxʷ yə?
641. But you   are smart, maybe you know of a

mrím-s-tṇ ʔkin x-ʔkìn-əm mi kən ɬ s-k̓ʷ-k̓ʷíy-m-əlt."
medicine   to   make   me   young again."

642. wáy taʔx̣íl-əm,
642.   She did like that,

638. She said: "Our ages are very different, you are old and I am just a
     girl, and don't you think, if we marry, you will be very sorry.
639. You'll be jealous of me, you will be jealous hearted, because of your
     old age."
640. The chief said: "It's true, I am old, we are too unmatched.
641. But you are smart, maybe you know of a medicine to make me young
     again."
642. She did like that,

c-k̓əɬ-k̓ʷƛ̓-àlqs-əm-st-s   i?   laputáy,   k̓ʷə-k̓ʷy-ùma?
she pulled out of her clothes   a   bottle,   a small

i?   laputáy.
bottle.

643.   cù-s   "way̓ axà?   síws-ənt-xʷ,   ti
643.   She told him: "Drink this,

ṇk̓ʷ-síws-ənt-xʷ,   uɬ   ixì?   kʷ   k̓ʷùɬ
drink it in one gulp,   and   then   you   will turn

?apən-ks-pìn-tk   a-k-s-my-s-k̓ʷ-k̓ʷíy-m-əlt   ixì?   uɬ
ten years   younger

kəl   s-tə-twít,   ixì?   məɬ   kʷu   pa?-pút,
towards   boyhood,   then   we   will be even,

kʷín-(n)t."
take it."

644.   way̓ ixì?   xʷíc̓-əɬt-əm,   ṇ-ɬwn-íkst-əm-s;
644.   She gave it to him,   he took it down;

swit aɬì?   mət   · naqs   ɬú-ɬ?-mən,   naqs
        maybe   one   little spoonful,   one

s-məcq̓ʷùləm-s   uɬ   ṇ-c̓sá-p.
swallow   and   it's gone.

645.   ta?x̣ìl-əm,   sitkəm-st-ìm   axà?   yə?
645.   He did like that,   he had spasms   the

ylmíxʷəm,   ɬwn-íkst-əm-s,   k̓a   ?x̣i?   kɬ-cəq-q-ínk,
king,   he let go,   he fell on his back,

ti   xʷrá·· -p.
he just   quivered.

     she pulled a bottle out of her clothes, a small bottle.
643. She told him: "Drink this, drink it in one gulp, and then you will turn
     ten years younger towards boyhood, then we will be even, take it."
644. She gave it to him, he took it down; maybe one little spoonful, one
     swallow and it's gone.
645. He did like that, the king had spasms, he let go, he fell on his back,
     he just quivered.

646. nìkxna? i? s-qìlxʷ t-kʷùp-xən i?
646. Goodness, the people rushed to him, the

s-ənkʷ-ł-yl-ylmíxʷəm-s; iwà? k-míyn-ċa?-s-əlx, iwà?
kings; they rubbed him,

x-?kí-st-s-əlx, ťi wim ixì?
they did everything,

kʷən-kʷən-ks-ənwíxʷ-əm-s-əlx uł ałì? ilì?
they held him on both sides, there was

k-səxʷ-mrím, uł ałì? nakʷà? kł-mrím-s-tṇ.
a doctor, but he didn't have medicine.

647. waỷ ixì? xʷùy-st-s-əlx i? ḳəl
647. They rushed him to

s-ən-mrím-s-tṇ, waỷ uł n-yˤìp lut ť
the hospital, but he did not

ṇ-ťəkʷ-ḳʷ-əs-pu?-ús, huy ƛ̣l-ál, n-yˤìp ƛ̣l-ál.
come to, he's dead, still dead.

648. waỷ kʷmìł aẋa? ki? c-ən-?úłxʷ aẋa? i?
648. At once comes in a

s-wi?-númt-a?x ṇta? s-qəl-tmíxʷ; waỷ
young fellow, a man;

t-x̣s-íċa?, waỷ s-wi?-númt-x.
he has a nice outfit on, he's handsome.

649. waỷ ixì? iḳlì? s-t-xʷť-p-əm-s-qìlxʷ-s aẋà?
649. She ran towards him

kʷə-kʷrì-t tkłm-ílxʷ; ṇ-st-íls: "ṇťá? waỷ
the Golden Woman; she thought: "My,

646. Goodness, the people rushed to him, the kings; they rubbed him, they did everything, they held him on both sides, there was a doctor, but he didn't have medicine.

647. They rushed him to the hospital, but he did not come to, he's dead, still dead.

648. At once a young fellow comes in, a man; he has a nice outfit on, he's handsome.

649. The Golden Woman ran towards him; she thought: "My,

mət   s—my—s—qı̀lxʷ   axà? i? ƛ̓əx̣—əx̣—ƛ̓x̣á—p—s,
they must be important people   his parents,

uɬ waẏ t—x̣s—íca?,   waẏ s—wi?—númt—x, waẏ
and   he has good clothes,   he's handsome,

ixı̀? i—k—s—qəl—tmíxʷ."
that's going to be my husband."

650. waẏ ixı̀? t—kı̀c—s   axà? i?
650.   She went to meet   the

s—qəl—tmíxʷ, uɬ ixı̀? kʷín—ks—əs,   cùt:
man,   and   they shook hands, she said:

"waẏ kʷ c—kíc—x, waẏ kʷ n̦—ƛ̓əm—p—cìn ļ
  "You got here,   you are too late at

s—máy?—xt—wìxʷ—a?x i? s—kəkˤáka?, uɬ kʷ swít,
the meeting with   the birds,   and who are you,

swı̀t a—skʷíst?"
what is your name?"

651. "t̓əxʷ ixı̀? i? c—máy?—xt—wíxʷ—əlx,   kʷa
651.   "That's what they're talking about,

i? likùk c—máy?—xt—wíxʷ, c—máya?—ɬt—s i?
the rooster talked about,   he told

cáw—t—s, ixı̀? incá?."
his life, that's me."

652. níkxna?, t̓i uɬ ixı̀?
652. Goodness,

n̦—kəlx—ús—ənt—əm,   uɬ ixı̀?
she threw her arms around his neck, and

his parents must be important people, and he has good clothes, he's
handsome, that's going to be my husband."
650. She went to meet the man, and they shook hands, she said: "You got
here, you are too late at the meeting with the birds, and who are you,
what is your name?"
651. "That's what they're talking about, the rooster talked about, he told
his life, that's me."
652. Goodness, she threw her arms around his neck, and

xp-ús-ənt-əm.
she started chewing his face.

653. cù-nt-əm, "waẏ lím-ləm-t-x, waẏ ixì? ˤapnà?
653. She said: "Thank you, now

kʷu s-c-mrím-s, lut itlì? nixʷ
we will get married, don't any more

a-k-s-wəl-wəl-cən-míst.
find excuses.

654. x̣l-àl yə? c-ən-x̣íl-əm-st-x-xʷ,
654. He's dead the one you're afraid of,

an-ylmíxʷəm, waẏ ul ixì? a-s-ən-q̇ʷíc-tn-əm."
your boss, and you'll take his place."

655. waẏ x̣lìt-s-əlx yə? q̇ʷˤáy-lqs, waẏ ixì?
655. They called the preacher,

mrím-ənt-m-əlx; waẏ wi?-s-mrím-ənt-m-əlx; waẏ
he married them; he got done marrying them;

ixì? ul sìwst-əm-st-m-əlx axà? i? t kʷə-kʷrì-t
she gave them drinks the Golden

i? t tkłm-ílxʷ lùt-əm ixì? təl l-laputáy,
Woman, not from the little bottle,

wnìxʷ-əm t síwłkʷ, yə-yˤà-t swìt axà? ł
real liquor, (to) every body in

cítxʷ, ul axà? i? s-c-?ìw-t-x
the house, and (after the) last

c-ən-x̣ƛ̣-ìks-ənt-m-əlx i? t s-ən-łs-ípna?, waẏ
they passed around cigars,

she started chewing his face.

653. She said: "Thank you, now we will get married, don't find any more excuses.

654. The one you're afraid of is dead, your boss, and you'll take his place."

655. They called the preacher, he married them; he got done marrying them; the Golden Woman gave them drinks, not from the little bottle, real liquor, (to) everybody in the house, and (after the) last they passed around cigars,

t–xƛá–p–əlx.
everybody got a treat.

656. waẏ sic   ixì? s–tə̇rq–q–áq–s–əlx;
656.   Then   they started jumping up and down;

q̇ʷəy–m–əncù··t–əlx waẏ uɬ   k–s–xəl–p–ína?–ḷx; ixì?
they danced   until daylight;

uɬ   cùt–əlx,   "waẏ kʷu px̣ʷ–m–əncút,"   waẏ
then they said,   let's scatter,"   and

px̣ʷ–m–əncút–əlx.
they scattered.

657. ixì? uɬ axà? i? tu?–twìt uɬ aɬì?
657.   And these   boys

kɬ–cəq–q–ítkʷ–əlx.
got out of trouble (lit. 'their boat came to the top').

658. cùt–əlx,   "waẏ ƛ̣l–àl   yə? ylmíxʷəm–tət,
658. They said,   "He's dead   our chief,

waẏ lut   kʷu tə k–s–ən–ma?–ìpən–(n)t–əm i? t
      we won't   be told on   by

sínca?–tət.
our brother.

659. cakʷ iwà? kʷu ɬa? n̥–ma?–ípən–(n)t–əm, uɬ axà?
659. If   even   he told on us,

kʷu t–ka?–ka?ɬís, uɬ kmìx axà? yə? ylmíxʷəm yə?
we   are three,   and only   the king

n̥–x̣íl–ənt–əm.
we've been afraid of.

everybody got a treat.
656. Then they started jumping up and down; they danced until daylight; then
     they said, let's scatter," and they scattered.
657. And these boys got out of trouble.
658. They said, "Our chief is dead, we won't be told on by our brother.
659. Even if he told on us, we are three, and we've been afraid only of the
     king.

660. cakʷ kʷu ł k-s-ən-maʔ-ìpən-(n)t-əm,   uł
660. If   he were going to tell on us,

way   la c-x?ìt   i? cáw-tət,   yə?
he would have   the first   thing we did,

n̓-malxaʔ-cìn-t-əm ł q̓əy̓-mín.
we lied   in the letter.

661. way̓ kʷu təkʷʔ-út,   way̓ xlà-p   i?
661. We   are leaving,   tomorrow is the

cáx̣ʷ-tət   mi   kʷu ł-yáʕ-p, cəx̣ʷ-xìt-əm yə?
date we put down   we'll   be back, what we told

ł?íw-tət."
our father."

662. cù-s-əlx axà? i?   s-qílxʷ k̓im   s-ilí?-s,
662. They told   the people left   there,

"way̓ łwì-łəm-t."
     "We're leaving you."

663. way̓   t̓i ixì? uł n̓-kxn-ìls-m-ənt-m-əlx
663. Well,   he wanted to go with them

axà? i? t sínca?-s-əlx.
          their youngest brother.

664. uł   lut   t̓ə kł-ylmíxʷm-əlx,
664. And they didn't   have a king (any more),

iwà?   máq-ənt-əm,   cu-nt-əm: "way̓ alà? kʷ
they tried to stop him,   they said: "You

s-ən-q̓ʷíc-tn̓-x, uł alà? way̓ kʷ t̓lá-p; anwì? way̓
took his place, and here   you stay; you

660. If he were going to tell on us, he would have the first thing we did,
     when we lied in the letter.
661. We are leaving, tomorrow is the date we put down we'll be back, what
     we told our father."
662. They told the people left there, "We're leaving you."
663. Well, their youngest brother wanted to go with them.
664. And they didn't have a king (any more), they tried to stop him, they
     said: "You took his place, stay here; you

alà? kʷ kɬ-ylmíxʷəm."
here   should be king."

665. cù-s: "lút, waẏ uɬ aɬì? c̓əxʷ-xìt-əm
665. He said: "No,   we told

ḷ?iw-tət ʕapnà? mi   kʷu ɬ-yáʕ-p,   x̣lá-p
our father today   we'll   get back, tomorrow,

t̓əxʷ.
rather.

666. uɬ   ta?lì?   ḷkʷ-ùt i? s-n-ilí?-tn̩-s, cəm̓
666. And   it's very far   his house,   we'll

kʷu ɬ-?yp-púlx,   waẏ kʷu c-?yp-púlx ki? kʷu
     have to camp,   we   had to camp   when we

c-yáʕ-p."
were on the way here."

667. k̓əm aɬi? lut   tə kɬ-ylmíxʷm-əlx,
667.   They don't   have a king any more,

kʷə-kʷr̓ì-t   yə?   ɬ yləmxʷ-wílx; waẏ
the Golden (Woman) is the one who   becomes boss;

ixì? uɬ n̩-kxn-ìls   axà? i? tkɬm-ílxʷ.
      but she wanted to go too   the woman.

668. cù-s   i? səxʷ-k̓ʷúl-əm-s, "x̣ʷúy-x ƛ̓?à-nt
668. She told   the working man,   "Go   fetch

i? s-x̣?ìm-ɬ-x̣às-t i? s-ən-kɬ-ċa?-sqáx̣a?, uɬ   axà?
the very best   horse,   and

yə? n̩-təkʷ-ki?-sqáx̣a?-tn̩, uɬ i? laprít, uɬ ixì?
a   saddle,   and a   bridle, all

should be king here."

665. He said: "No, we told our father we'll get back today, tomorrow, rather.
666. And his house is very far, we'll have to camp, we had to camp when we were on the way here."
667. They don't have a king any more, the Golden (Woman) is the one who becomes boss; but the woman wanted to go too.
668. She told the working man, "Go fetch the very best horse, and a saddle, and a bridle, all

i?   s-x?im-ɬ-x̣ás-t."
the   very best."

669. wa̓y ixì? s-x̌ʷùy-s axà? yə?
669.   He went   the

k-s-ən-ɫəws-cqáx̣a?-tņ, wa̓y c-kʷì-s i? s-x?im-ɬ-x̣às-t
barn man,   he took the very best

i? s-ən-kɬ-c̓a?-sqáx̣a?; uɬ   ixì? ņ-ɫk̓ʷ-íki?-s,
    horse;   and   he saddled it,

laprít-s,   wa̓y c-x̌ʷúy-st-s.
put the bridle on,   he brought in in.

670. uɬ aɬì? axà? wa̓y   c-?ac-əcqa?-st-s-əlx
670.   Already the others had brought out

i? kəw?áp-s-əlx, wa̓y   k-s-t-kʷəl·-íws; wa̓y
    their horses, they're already   on their horses;

ixì? sic k-?əmt-íws axà?; cù-s   axà? i?
      then she got on;   she told   the

s-qílxʷ ɫəxʷ-əm kɬ-təmxʷ-úla?xʷ: "wa̓y uɬ aɬì?
people   who lived there:

x̣̓l-àl   i? s-c-t-x̌ʷúy-əm, i-k-s-x̣ílwi?,   uɬ
"He's dead who I came to see,   my husband-to-be, and

axà? wa̓y kən ta?xʷ-ɬ-ən-q̓ʷíc-tņ,
                somebody took his place as my husband,

uɬ wa̓y ixì? kxən-(n)t-ìn   in-q̓ʷíc-tņ.
and   I'm going with my man.

671. wa̓y uɬ ɫəxʷ mnìmɬ-əmp p k̓əɬ-pa?x̣à-m t
671.   You folks   will think   about

the very best."

669. The barn man went, he took the very best horse; and he saddled it,
     put the bridle on, he brought in in.
670. The others had already brought out their horses, they're already on their
     horses; then she got on; she told the people who lived there: "The one
     I came to see is dead, my husband-to-be, and somebody took his place
     as my husband, and I'm going with my man.
671. You folks will think about

ku̱–ylmíxʷəm–p;   lut   p i–k–s–ən–k̓ʷín–xt–əm,
getting a new king; I'm not   going to pick for you,

uu̱   lut   p t̓ i–k–s–k–alá?–m̩.
and I'm not   going to stay with you.

672. uu̱   au̱ì? kʷa stim̓   alà? i–k–s–alá?–m,
672. And   for what   would I stay here,

      lut   kʷu t̓ə c–súxʷ–st–p, uu̱   lut   kʷu t̓ə
      you don't   know me,   and I'm no

      s–tm–áli?s–əmp, way̓ ƛ̓l–àl   yə? ylmíxʷəm–(m)p."
      relation to you,   he's dead   your king."

673. ixì? s–xʷúy?–s–əlx,   xʷú··y?–ɬx,
673.   They started out, they went,

      u̱–?yp–púlx–əlx,   uu̱   au̱ì? məl–m–scút–əlx;
      they camped on the way, and   they took their time;

      uu̱ au̱ì? kʷa ixì? cəx̣ʷ–xìt–s–əlx yə? ɬ?íw–s–əlx,
                   they had told   their father,

      uu̱ t̓əxʷ ixì?   c–təkʷ?–ùt–(t)n̩–s–əlx   axà?
      and   that's when   they started to come away

      i? s–xa?–x̣?ít–x, uu̱ au̱ì? kʷa t təmxʷ–úla?xʷ kə?
      the oldest ones, and   by ground

      c–xʷúy?–ɬx, axà?–m̩   au̱ì? t–k–u̱a?–m–àsqət
      they came, (while) this one   next to the sky

      əc–k–t̓əxʷt–ásqət, axà? i? u̱–sì–sənca?–s–əlx   i?
      came flying,   their little brother

      t   kəwáp–s.
      with his horse.

getting a new king; I'm not going to pick for you, and I'm not going to
stay with you.

672. And for what would I stay here, you don't know me, and I'm no relation
to you, your king is dead."

673. They started out, they went, they camped on the way, and they took
their time; they had told their father, and that's when the oldest ones
started to come away, and they came by ground, (while) this one came
flying next to the sky, their little brother with his horse.

674. s-c--ʔx̣il-x ki? ƛ̣əx̣-t-lwís,   ́uɬ ixì?
674. That's why   he gets around fast,   and then

      nix   tə́kʷ-k̇ʷ-úlaʔx,   uɬ   ti c-kxán.
      he too falls to the ground, and   he follows them.

675. waẏ k-s-x̣əl-p-ína?-ḷx,   ixì? i? kəl put
675.   When daylight comes,   it's just

      ṇ-ləšʷ-p-ùs   i? k-tə́kʷ?-út-(t)ṇ-s-əlx,
      the right time when   they left,

      ki?   ɬ-k̇əɬ-k̇ʷíƛ̣-əp-t-əlx.
      that's when   they came back in sight.

676. uɬ axà? ylmíxʷəm i? na?ɬ tkɬm-ílxʷ waẏ
676. And   the king   with his wife

      n-yšìp   c-k-ƛ̣a?-ƛ̣a?-ús-əm-st-s, aɬi?
      have been looking,

      ṇ-k̇əw-əls-ílt-m-əlx;   uɬ   axà?
      they have been lonesome for their children; and

      xs-nù-s-əlx i? s-t?íw-t-x.
      they missed the   youngest one.

677. waẏ uɬ iwà?   kʷəlst-ìɬən   yə?
677.   To no avail he had sent to search   the

      ylmíxʷəm, ƛ̣a?-ƛ̣a?-nt-ìs-əlx i? s-t?əw-t-ílt-s;
      chief,   to look for   their youngest child;

      waẏ lút, lùt   tə k-s-xʷúy-tṇ, uɬ axà?
            no,   there were no   tracks,

      ti   t-ka?-ka?ɬis ti s-xʷúy-tṇ-s.
      just three   tracks.

674. That's why he gets around fast, and then he too falls to the ground,
     and he follows them.
675. When daylight comes, it's just the right time when they left, that's when
     they came back in sight.
676. And the king with his wife have been looking, they have been lonesome
     for their children; and they missed the youngest one.
677. To no avail the chief had sent to search, to look for their youngest child;
     no, there were no tracks, just three tracks.

678. ułixìʔ kəł–kláxʷ,   ùłiʔ ťkʷ–əncùt
678.   When he got out of sight   he lay down

axàʔ iʔ s–ən–kł–ċaʔ–sqáx̣aʔ; ùłiʔ
        the horse;   and

s–ən–ťəkʷ–tán–s,   itlìʔ xʷť–ìlx   uł
there's the mark where he lay, then he got up and

ḱəł–səl–xán;   uł ałìʔ iʔ
there are no more tracks; and   that's when

k–ťəxʷt–ásqət.
he flew under the sky.

679. way̓ ł–yàʕ–p   iʔ   ƛ̓aʔ–ƛ̓aʔ–ncút–(t)ṇ–s
679.   When they got back those who were looking for

ax̀aʔ iʔ tə–twít, cùt–əlx,   "way̓ lút," way̓
        the boy,   they said,   "No,"

lut   s–c–ḱəł–páʔx̣–s, "uł ałìʔ kʷu
they can't figure it out,   "And

x–ʔkìn–əm,   mi   kʷu ťùxʷt ṇ–ʔúc–xən–(n)t–əm,
what can we do, how can we   fly   to track him,

lut   ťə k–s–ḱəł–wìk–xən–(n)t–əm ḱla ṇ–wís–t.
we can't   track him   in the sky.

680. cakʷ   axàʔ iʔ t təmxʷ–úlaʔxʷ, uł way̓
680.   If it were   on the ground,

k–s–ən–ʔùc–xən–(n)t–əm iʔ t s–xʷùy–tṇ–s iʔ t
we could follow him   by the tracks   of

s–ən–kł–ċaʔ–sqáx̣aʔ.
the horse.

678. When the horse got out of sight he lay down; and there's the mark where he lay, then he got up and there are no more tracks; and that's when he flew under the sky.

679. When those who were looking for the boy got back, they said, "No," they can't figure it out, "And what can we do, how can we fly to track him, we can't track him in the sky.

680. If it were on the ground, we could follow him by the tracks of the horse.

681. uɬ axà? atlà?   ti s-xʷùy-tn̩-s
681.   From there   there are tracks,

s-xʷìst-(t)n̩-s   i?   s-ən-kɬ-ċa?-sqáx̣a? uɬ
where he walked   the   horse   until

k̓əɬ-k̓láxʷ,   ilì? uɬ mət   t
he got out of sight, then   he must have

s-?áyx̣ʷ-t, uɬ ɬa?xʷ-sk̓ít-əm, uɬ t̓k̓ʷ-əncút.
got tired, and he rested,   and he lay down.

682. ilì?   s-t̓ək̓ʷ-tàn-s   i? ɬq̓ʷ-út-(t)n̩-s.
682. That's where he dropped down   and lay.

683. ti itlì? xʷt̓-ìlx   uɬ   ixì? c-k̓əɬ-səɬ-xàn
683.   Then   he got up and   they disappeared

i? s-xʷúy-tn̩-s; ixì? uɬ mət   n̩-wís-əlx."
the tracks;   he must have   risen high."

684. way̓   c-k-wìk-s i? ɬəɬ-s-qʷsí?-s, aɬì?
684. Well, he saw   his children,

k̓əɬ-k̓ʷìⱡ-əp-t   i? ɬəɬ-s-qʷsí?-s.
they came in sight   his children.

685. way̓ ti ɬ c-k-ʕá··ċ-əst-s, nìkxna? way̓
685.   He kept looking,   gee

xʷús-əska?.
he was anxious.

686. way̓ ti lut   i? s-k̓ɬ-ən-ɬa?-ìp-s-əlx ⱡ
686.   Before   they got to the gate   on

k̓əɬ-ʕal-mín, ixì? uɬ atlà? ɬìx̣ʷp̓-t-əlx   i?
the fence,   they all ran out

681. From there there are tracks, where the horse walked until he got out
    of sight, then he must have got tired, and he rested, and he lay down.
682. That's where he dropped down and lay.
683. Then he got up and the tracks disappeared; he must have risen high."
684. Well, he saw his children, his children came in sight.
685. He kept looking, gee he was anxious.
686. Before they got to the gate on the fence, they all ran out

la?ɬ   s-ma?-m?ím,   na?ɬ tkɬm-ílxʷ-s.
including the women folks, and   his wife.

687. huy kɬ-ən-təws-t-ìp-əlx kəl t-kəm-kn̓-íɬxʷ, waẏ
687.   They got right   to   the door,

c-ən-p-pílx.
they came in.

688. c-wík-s-əlx,   n̓ta? stím i?
688. They saw them,   what

səx-cùt-s-əlx,   ɬ s-xəl-xˤàl-t uɬ há?
kind of company have they, in the daytime and

kɬ-c̓ìk̓ʷ-əsxən?
they have a lamp?

689. n̓ta? i? s-p̓?áxʷ-s.
689. Gee,   it shines.

690. axà? k-my-my-p-ùs-əm-s-əlx   nak̓ʷəm
690. When they made out what it was,   it was

tkɬm-ílxʷ.
a woman.

691. waẏ ixì? saˤ-m-əncùt-əlx,   waẏ uɬ
691.   They got off their horses,   and

s-tək̓ʷ?-út-əlx,   uɬ axà? i? s-t?əw-t-ìlt-s
they started walking, and   their youngest son

ixì?   yə? t̓ə c-t-k̓ʷən-ks-ənwáxʷ axà? i? kəl
is the one who   is holding hands   axà? i? with

kʷə-kʷr̓ì-t i? tkɬm-ílxʷ.
the Golden Woman.

including the women folks, and his wife.
687. They got right to the door, they came in.
688. They saw them, what kind of company have they got, in the daytime
     and they have a lamp?
689. Gee, it shines.
690. When they made out what it was, it was a woman.
691. They got off their horses, and they started walking, and their youngest
     son is the one who is holding hands with the Golden Woman.

692. n̦ta? wa̦y   t-kíc-s-əlx,   uɬ ixì?
692.   Well, they went to meet them,   and

     kəɬ-təm-ʕàs-s-əlx i? s-qʷsí?-s-əlx i?   s-x?ít-x;
     they kissed   their son   the oldest one;

     ixì? uɬ itlì? k-səx-x̣à-m i?   t-k̦í-k̦a?t, wa̦y itlì?
           and then passed to   the next one,

     nixʷ ixì? kəɬ-təm-ʕás-s-əlx,   təxʷ
     also   they kissed him,

     kʷín-ks-s-əlx,   uɬ itlì? i?
     they shook hands with him   and then   the

     q̦ə?-íw̦s,   wa̦y ixì? nixʷ ?x̣íl-st-s-əlx,
     in between one,   also   the same thing,

     kʷìn-ks-s-əlx   uɬ kəɬ-təm-ʕás-s-əlx;
     they shook hands with him and kissed him;

     lìm-t-s-əlx   təl s-xʷəl-xʷál-t-s; wa̦y axà? i?
     they're glad that they're alive;   the

     s-t?íw-t-x, wa̦y uɬ ixì? ți n̦-st-ìls-əlx wa̦y
     youngest one   they thought

     ƛ̦1-ál.
     he was dead.

693. wa̦y c-k-sɫ̦-ípla?,   lut   țə ka?kìc-ɫt-s-əlx
693.   He was lost,   they never   found

     i? s-qíl-tk-s, uɬ aɬì? wa̦y myaɬ   c-psʕày-a?
         his body,   and   he was too senseless

     uɬ lut   țə k-s-ən-kəc-kn̦-áɬq-s axà?-m̦ ḷ
     and couldn't   catch up   with

692. Well, they went to meet them, and they kissed their oldest son; and
     then passed to the next one, they also kissed him, they shook hands with
     him and then the in between one, also the same thing, they shook hands
     with him and kissed him; they're glad that they're alive; the youngest
     one they thought he was dead.
693. He was lost, they never found his body, and he was too senseless and
     couldn't catch up with

s-xaʔ-xʔít;   uɬ aɬiʔ waẏ px̣-əx̣-páx̣-t-əlx,
the oldest ones;   they have sense enough,

xƛ̓-áƛ̓-əlx.
they're grown up.

694. nìkxnaʔ   ɬ lìm-t-əm-s-əlx   iʔ
694. Goodness   they were tickled (to see)

s-qʷsíʔ-s-əlx,   uɬ   waẏ   s-qəl-tmíxʷ; ƛ̓əxʷ
their youngest son, and already he's a man; but

yaʕ-mì-s-əlx   axàʔ   myàɬ   s-wiʔ-númt,   uɬ
they're backwards because he's too good looking, and

c-p̓ʔáxʷ.
he shines.

695. cù-nt-əm   axàʔ iʔ t ḻʔíw-s: "uɬ
695. He asked him   his father: "And

swìt   axàʔ iʔ a-səx̣-cút?
who is   your company?

696. yaʕ-mí-nt-əm,   s-c-ʔx̣ìl-x kiʔ síw-ənt-s-t;
696. We're backwards,   that's why   we ask you;

kʷu a-k-s-qʷaʔm-ənwíxʷ-st-əm, kʷu
give us an introduction,

a-k-səxʷ-ənwíxʷ-st-əm."
get us acquainted."

697. cú-s,   "waẏ ixìʔ   iʔ kʷə-kʷrì-t iʔ
697. He said,   "This is the Golden

tkɬm-ílxʷ; mət   c-k̓əɬ-nìxĺ-əm-st-p   ixìʔ ɬ
Woman;   maybe you've heard about her   in

the oldest ones; they have sense enough, they're grown up.

694. Goodness they were tickled (to see) their youngest son, and already he's a man; but they're backwards because he's too good looking, and he shines.

695. His father asked him: "And who is your company?

696. We're backwards, that's why we ask you; give us an introduction, get us acquainted."

697. He said, "This is the Golden Woman; maybe you've heard about her in

s-máy?-xt-wíxʷ,   mət   ka?kn-ùla?xʷ   ikli? ki?
a story,   maybe   in some other country   where

c-t́?ák̓ʷ.
she pops out (of the water).

698. ixì?   s-ta?xʷ-sípn-əmp,   ixì?   i?
698. She's your new daughter-in-law   the one

s-ənk̓ʷ-ɬ-mr·ím,   ˤapnà?   kʷu c-mrím.
I'm married to,   right now we   are married.

699. t incà?   ki? c-kʷí-n,   itlì? ùɬi?
699.   It was I who took her, then

c-xʷúy-st-ən,   ùɬi? kʷu c-mrím,   ùɬi? kʷu
I brought her,   and   we   got married,   and   we

ɬ-c-xʷúy."
came back."

700. níkxna?,   ṇta? ixì? sic t-xʷt́-əp-mí-s-əlx,
700. Goodness,   they rushed to her,

kʷìn-ks-s-əlx   axà? i? tkɬm-ílxʷ; waẏ
they shook hands with   the woman;

ṇ-kəlx-ús-s-əlx,   kəɬ-t́əm-ˤàs-s-əlx axà?
they hugged her around the neck,   they kissed her

i? t s-xa?-x̱á?-s   i? t ɬcíck-s.
    her father-in-law   her mother-in-law.

701. waẏ kən xʷíst,   waẏ
701. Well, I   am going to walk away,

c-xàr-kst-əm-st-m-ən   axà? i-s-c-ma?-máya?.
I'm talking all the time to   the one I'm teaching.

a story, maybe in some other country where she pops out (of the water).
698. She's your new daughter-in-law the one I'm married to, right now we
are married.
699. I took her and brought her, and we married, and came back."
700. Goodness, they rushed to her, shook hands with the woman; they hugged
her around the neck, her father-in-law, her mother-in-law kissed her.
701. Well, I am going to walk away, I'm talking all the time to the one I'm
teaching.

702. kən s-c-m̓a?-m̓áya?-x, u̓łi? x̣m-ìnk-s
702. I was teaching him, and then he wanted

i-k-s-captíkʷəl-xt-əm, uł ixì? ʕapnà? i?
me to tell him fairy tale stories, and then

cú-n: "t̓əxʷ captìkʷ-łt-s-ən i?
I told him: "I'll tell you the story of the

kʷə-kʷr̓ì-t i? tkłm-ílxʷ."
Golden Woman."

703. uł wa̓y axà? k-s-?asìl-s s-k-ʕac-ìw̓s,
703. And now it's been two weeks,

k-axà? i? kən n̓-c̓əy̓xʷ-ʕápəlqs-əm.
and it's now that I end my story.

704. wa̓y ixì? kən k̓wá-p.
704. Now I quit talking.

702. I was teaching him, and then he wanted me to tell him fairy tale stories, and then I told him: "I'll tell you the story of the Golden Woman."
703. And now it's been two weeks, and it's now that I end my story.
704. Now I quit talking.

APPENDIX I

[Corresponds approximately to sentences 369-514 of the text.]

705. waẏ i-s-ən-ċəpq̇-s-i̇w̓s-əm itli̇? i-s-captík^{w}ɬ,
705.   I'm going to splice   my fairy tale,

   axà? i? k^{w}ə-k^{w}ri̇-t i? tkɬm-ílx^w.
       the Golden   Woman.

706. uɬ axà? ixi̇? k^{w}ən-nù-nt-əm   i? t
706. And   he has already captured the

   tə-tẇit axà? i? k^{w}ə-k^{w}ri̇-t i? tkɬm-ílx^w i? təl
   boy   the Golden   Woman   from

   sìlx^{w}a? i? síwɬk^w.
   the big   water.

707. ixi̇? uɬ cù-nt-əm   axà? i? t k^{w}ə-k^{w}ri̇-t
707. Then   she asked him   the   Golden

   i? tkɬm-ílx^w: "uɬ χəl stím ki? k^{w}u ɬ
       Woman: "For what

   k^{w}ín-(n)t-x^w,   i? k^{w}u ɬ
   you're taking me,

   k-swít-ənt-x^w?
   (and) you tried so hard with me?

708. lùt pən-?kìn k^{w}u t̓ə c-wìk-st-s   i? t
708. Not ever   have they seen me

705. I'm going to splice my fairy tale, the Golden Woman.
706. And the boy has already captured the Golden Woman from the big water.
707. Then the Golden Woman asked him: "For what you're taking me, (and)
   you tried so hard with me?
708. Humans have never seen me;

s-qílxʷ; t anwì?   ki? kʷu ł c-my-st-ìxʷ la
humans;   (and) you   know

?kìn ki? kən ilí?;   təxʷ kən   t?àk̓ʷ   i?
where to   find me;   (that) I   come out

təl sìlxʷa? i? síwłkʷ.
of   the big   water.

709. mət   way̓ kʷ s-yəʕ̓w-p-yáw-t-x."
709. You must be   very powerful."

710. cù-s   "way̓ təxʷ kʷu s-c-kʷùlst-əm-s i?
710. He told her   "He sent me   the

      tə ylmíxʷəm, kən kł-ylmìxʷəm ki?   kʷu c-kʷúlst-s;
          king,   I   have a boss that   sent me;

      ki?   c-k̓a?-ṇt-s-ín.
      that's why I came after you.

711. ùti? kʷìn-(n)t-s-ən uł   ik̓lì? kʷ
711. And   I got you   and

      i-kł-əł-xʷúy-ṃ."
      I'm going to take you back."

712. "uł   c-?kín i? s-k̓əx-k̓xà-p-s yə? ylmíxʷəm?"
712. "And how   old is   the king?"

713. "t̓əxʷ mət   put mìw̓s i?
713.   "He might be just middle

      s-k̓əx-k̓xá-p-s."
      aged."

714. "a·· nak̓ʷəm ałì? mət   way̓ k̓íw-ḷx.
714. "Ah,   (he) might be   too old.

(and) you know where to find me; (that) I come out of the big water.
709. You must be very powerful."
710. He told her "The king sent me, I have a boss that sent me; that's why
    I came after you.
711. And I got you and I'm going to take you back."
712. "And how old is the king?"
713. "He might be just middle aged."
714. "Ah, he might be too old.

715. wa°y t anwí? ki? kʷìn-(n)t-xʷ, la?ɬ anwì?
715.   It's you that took me,   with you

      mi   kʷu c-mrím."
      (I) will   be married."

716. ixì? cù-s,   "lút, kən s-əc-k̓ʷúɬ-x,
716.   He said, "No, I   am just doing a job,

      kən kɬ-ylmìxʷəm   iklì? kən s-c-k̓ʷúɬ-x, uɬ   t
      I   have a boss for   this work,   and

      cnìɬc i? kʷu c-kʷúlst-s."
      he   sent me over."

717. uɬ cù-nt-əm   i? t kʷə-kʷr̓ì-t i? t
717. And she said to him the   Golden

      tkɬm-ílxʷ, "wa°y nìn̓wi? ixì? t incà? kən
      Woman,   "Let   me

      k̓əɬ-pa?x̣-nt-ín, məɬ wa°y nìn̓wi? la?ɬ   anwì? kʷu
      think about it,   if   (I) and you

      c-mrím."
      can get married."

718. ixì? uɬ ɬa? ɬ-yàʕ-p-əlx i? kə ylmíxʷəm,
718. That's when they got back   to the boss,

      uɬ ixì? cù-s   yə? ylmíxʷəm, "wa°y axà?
      and   he said to the boss,   "That's what

      an-x̣m-ínk, i? kʷə-kʷr̓ì-t i? tkɬm-ílxʷ."
      you want, the Golden   Woman."

719. ixì? uɬ ?ax̣əl-m-əncút,   uɬ ɬ-xʷúy   kəl
719.   And he turned around, and went back to

715. It's you that took me, with you (I) will be married."

716. He said, "No, I am just doing a job, I have a boss for this work, and
     he sent me over."

717. And the Golden Woman said to him, "Let me think about it, if (I) and
     you can get married."

718. That's when they got back to the boss, and he said to the boss, "That's
     what you want, the Golden Woman."

719. And he turned around, and went back to

s-ən-k̓ʷəl-cən-(n)cùt-(t)n̩   ł   ʔaw-s-ən-t̓áqʷ-əm, uł
the kitchen,   to lick plates,

ałì?   k-s-q̇m-íltn̩.
because he was hungry.

720. níkxna?   ł lìm-t   kʷłàx   axà? yə?
720. Gee,   he was glad (and) surprised   the

ylmíxʷəm, swìt   ałì? kʷə-kʷrì-t tkłm-ílxʷ.
king,   because of   the Golden Woman.

721. waẏ xʷìc-əxt-s   i? t kł-cítxʷ-s,
721.   He gave her a   place to stay,

qʷàm-qʷəm-t i? kł-cítxʷ-s, təxʷ i? k-s-n-ilí?-tn̩-s;
a beautiful   place   for her to stay;

ilì? k-s-ən-łq̇ʷ-út-(t)n̩, k-s-ən-cráw-əlx-tn̩, ilì?
it has a bed,   a bath,

yə-yrà-t stìm xʌ́á-p.
every   thing complete.

722. uł ixì? cù-nt-əm, "waẏ n̓in̓wi?   ixì? kən
722. And   he said,   "(I) will

x̣əlt-s-qílxʷ,   ixì? mi   kʷu
invite people (to come),   then (we) will

c-mrím.
get married.

723. k-yar-mì-nt-əm i? t i-s-ənk̓ʷ-ł-yl-ylmíxʷəm,
723. We will gather   kings like me,

cmay i-s-qʷs-qʷa?síya?, alà? i-s-qílxʷ, yə-yrà-t
all   my people,   my people, every

the kitchen, to lick plates, because he was hungry.
720. Gee, the king was glad (and) surprised, because of the Golden Woman.
721. He gave her a place to stay, a beautiful place for her to stay; it has
     a bed, a bath, everything complete.
722. And he said, "I will invite people (to come), then we will get married.
723. We will gather kings like me, all my people, my people,

swit."
body."

724. cù-nt-əm   axà? i?   t tkɬm-ílxʷ: "waẏ
724. She said to him   the   woman:

ixì?   axà? a-kɬ-cáw-t;   uɬ axà? naxəmɬ
"That's what you're going to do;   but

nàqs   i? kʷ i-k-s-cún-əm.
one thing   I'm going to say to you.

725. úc   kʷ k-s-kəkʕàka?,   tə
725. Have you got any chickens

c-tíxʷl-əm?"
that are different?"

726. "c-?kín   yə? s-kəkʕàka??"
726. "What kind of   birds?"

727. "təxʷ likùk   uɬ lipúl, kʷə-kʷrí-t;
727.   "A rooster and a hen, golden;

s-c-?xìl-x uɬ s-tìxʷl-əm   axà? i? təl
that's how   they are different   from

kʷiɬ-ət təl   s-kəkʕáka?; axà? i? kʷiɬ-ət i?
the rest of the birds;   the   other

s-kəkʕàka? uɬ lut   tə c-p̓?àxʷ c-?xiɬ t
birds   don't   shine   like

kʷə-kʷrí-t.
gold.

728. uɬ aɬì? nìnwi? c-yàʕ   i? s-qílxʷ,
728. And when they gather the people,

everybody."

724. The woman said to him: "That's what you're going to do; but one thing
I'm going to say to you.

725. Have you got any chickens that are different?"

726. "What kind of birds?"

727. "A rooster and a hen, golden; that's how they are different from the
rest of the birds; the other birds don't shine like gold.

728. And when the people gather,

ninwiʔ ɫ xƛa-p   iʔ   s-qilxʷ,   yə-yʕa-t
when   they are all there   the   people,   every

swit,   cu-nt-xʷ-əlx   iʔ   s-qilxʷ: 'la   c-xʔit   axàʔ
body,   you will tell   the   people: 'First   these

iʔ   s-kəkʕàkaʔ   k-s-may?-xt-wixʷ-aʔx-əlx,
     birds   will tell their story,

k-s-may?-ncut-aʔx-əlx;   ixiʔ   ninwiʔ
they will talk about themselves;   when

kwa-p,   ixiʔ   məɫ   kʷu   c-mrim,   ixiʔ
they are done,   then   we   will get married,

məɫ   kʷu   s-tr-ər-q-q-aq-s.'"
then   we   will jump up and down (i.e. dance).'"

729.   cut   axàʔ   ylmixʷəm,   "waẏ."
729.   He said   the chief,   "OK."

730.   waẏ ixiʔ   klaxʷ   iʔ   cx̣ʷ-asqət-s,
730.   The evening of   the   date he decided,

ixiʔ   uɫ   cu-s   axàʔ   iʔ   səxʷ-t-qʷəl-qʷəl-t-iws-əm:
            he told   the   telephone operators:

"waẏ   kʷ   t-qʷəl-qʷəl-t-iws-əm   kəl   yə-yʕa-t   iʔ   k̓
     "You   telephone   to   all   the

i-s-ənk̓ʷ-ɫ-yl-ylmixʷəm   axàʔ   ḻ   təmxʷ-ulaʔxʷ,   ɫəxʷ
kings like me   on   this earth,

iʔ   s-my-s-qilxʷ   ninwiʔ   c-kəɫ-kic-x   alaʔ.
the   important people   will (also)   get   here.

731.   uɫ   axàʔ   alaʔ   iʔ   t   ki-kaʔt,   kʷ   kʷəlst-iɫən
731.   And   those   nearby,   you   send them

when the people are all there, everybody, you will tell the people: 'First
these birds will tell their story, they will talk about themselves; when
they are done, then we will get married, then we will jump up and down
(i.e. dance).'"

729. The chief said, "OK."

730. The evening of the date he decided, he told the telephone operators:
"You telephone to all the kings like me on this earth, the important
people will (also) get here.

ixì? yə? s-xəlt-s-qílxʷ; lut   tə kɬ-ƛ̓əx-ƛ̓xà-p
      an   invitation;   there is no   old

kəm̓ k-s-k̓ʷ-k̓ʷíy-m-əlt; wa̓y̓ ti yə-yʕá-t alà?
or   young;   everybody   here

k-s-c-yaʕ-p-míx-a?x, ʕapnà? k̓láxʷ."
is going to gather,   this   evening."

732. wa̓y̓ ti lùt-i? s-k̓láxʷ-s, uɬ
732.   Before evening,

y?àʕ   i? s-qìlxʷ axà? i? təl
they started coming in the people   from

lk̓ʷ-əlkʷ-út, mət   l̩ təxʷt-lwís, aɬì?   mət
far away,   maybe on airplanes, because I guess

wa̓y̓ ta?xʷ-ɬ-təxʷt-lwís.
they had airplanes.

733. uɬ mʕan axà? i? tə-twi̓t uɬ yə?
733. And   this   boy   he

c-təxʷt-lwìs   i? t kəwáp-s,   i? kəwàp-s   wa̓y̓
has been flying   on his horse,   his horse

c-təxʷt-lwís.
has been flying around.

734. wa̓y̓ y?à···ʕ   i? s-qílxʷ, wa̓y̓ ?ayxàxa?
734. Well, they gathered the people,   a little

təl s-qá-qs-əs-c, ixì? uɬ t-xƛ̓á-p-əlx.
after dark,   everybody was in.

735. axà? i? k̓ʷəɬ-cən-(n)cút-(t)n̩, ixì?
735.   The cook

---

731. And those nearby, you send them an invitation; there is no old or young;
     everybody here is going to gather, this evening."
732. Before evening, the people started coming in from far away, maybe on
     airplanes, because I guess they had airplanes.
733. And this boy he has been flying around on his horse, his horse has been
     flying around.
734. Well, the people gathered, a little after dark, everybody was in.
735. The cook thought of it, and he told the dish washer, the boy, he said:

ṇ-łək̓ʷ-ək̓ʷ-mí-s,   uł   ixì?   cù-s   axà?   i?
thought of it,   and   he told   the

səxʷ-ən-cíw̓-m̓,   axà?   i?   tə-twít,   cùt: "uł   ƛi
dish washer,   the boy,   he said:

kʷ   qəm-qá··m-t,   sta?   k̓əł-?əys-əlscút-x,
"You   are just standing here,   go change,

k-ca?w̓-ìws-x   k̓ʷəł-kst-míst-x;   ʕapnà?
wash you face (and)   doll up;

k-s-yaʕ-mìx-a?x   ł   s-k̓láxʷ.
they are going to gather   in   the evening.

736.   way̓   ʕapnà?   mət   n-y?àʕ   i?
736.   By   now   they must be   gathered in   the

s-qílxʷ,   təl   yʕa-ł-cw-ìlxʷ-tṇ   yə?   yl-ylmíxʷəm.
people,   from   all over the world   the   chiefs.

737.   ʕapnà?   k-s-c-mrìm-a?x   yə?
737.   Tonight (lit. now)   he is getting married   the

ylmíxʷəm,   axà?   alà?   yə?   ylmìxʷəm-tət   i?   la?ł
chief,   our chief   and

kʷə-kʷr̓ì-t   tkłm-ílxʷ.
the Golden   Woman.

738.   yə-yʕà-t   swìt   x̣m-ínk-s,   na?ł   cə-cm̓-ìlt,
738.   Every   body   he wants,   young people,

la?ł   ƛ̓əx̣-əx̣-ƛ̓x̣à-p,   uł   anwí?."
      elders,   and   you."

739.   cù-s: "a··   way̓   sta?   kʷu
739.   He replied: "Ah,

"You are just standing here, go change, wash you face (and) doll up;
they are going to gather in the evening.
736. By now the people must be gathered ın, chiefs from all over the world.
737. Tonight (lit. now) the chief is getting married, our chief and the Golden
Woman.
738. He wants everybody, young people, elders, and you."
739. He replıed: "Ah,

c-qʷə́n-cín-əm-st-xʷ,   waẏ lút,   waẏ myà‍ł   kən
pity me,   no,   too much   I

k-ťəł-ł-íca?."
am dirty."

740. cù-nt-əm,   "k-ċa?ẇ-íẇs-x,   kʷəl-kst-míst-x."
740. He told him, "Wash your face, doll up."

741. cù-s: "uł ťi kən   k-ċa?ẇ-íẇs-əm uł ixì?
741. He said: "And   (if) I wash my face

i-k-s-ən-tṁ-ús-əm;   uł axà?
what good will I get out of it;

i-s-k-ťəł-ł-íca?   uł lut   kən ťə
I am dirty in the body,   and (I) don't

k-s-t-təṁ-tíṁ."
have any clothes."

742. cù-s   i? səxʷ-k̇ʷəl-cən-(n)cùt: "xʷúy-x   k̇əm
742. He told the cook: "You go,

waẏ kən s-c-ən-ťáqʷ-x."
     I   just want to lick plates."

743. waẏ ixì? ùłi? xʷúy;   ixì? ùłi?
743.   And so he went;

kíc-x,   ṇ-?úłxʷ.
he got there, he went in.

744. ?ayxàxa?   ixì? ùłi? cùt   yə?
744. In a little while   he said the

ylmíxʷəm: "há? waẏ há? p t-xƛ̇à-p i? p
chief: "Are you all here   you

pity me, no, I am too dirty."
740. He told him, "Wash your face, doll up."
741. He said: "And (if) I wash my face what good will I get out of it; I am
dirty in the body, and I don't have any clothes."
742. He told the cook: "You go, I just want to lick plates."
743. And so he went; he got there, he went in.
744. In a little while the chief said: "Are you all here you

s-qílxʷ, alà? i? p i-s-ənqs-ílxʷ?"
people,   the   local people.?"

745. cùt-əlx: "wáy̓, wáy̓, mət   kʷu t-xƛ̓á-p."
745. They said: "Yes, yes, (we) think we   are."

746. cùt: "há? la?ɬ s-cə-cm̓-ìlt la?ɬ
746. He said: "All the children and

ƛ̓əx̣-əx̣-ƛ̓x̣á-p?"
the grown ups?"

747. cùt   axà? i? k̓ʷəl̓-cən-(n)cút, "a··
747. He said   the cook,   "Ah,

na?ɬc-cá-m,   ṇ-ɬìp-t-m-ən i-səxʷ-ən-c̓íw̓-ṃ, ixì?
wait a minute, I forgot   my dish washer,

tə-twít.
the boy.

748. wim̓ c-x̣lìt-ən   uɬ   ƛ̓yá-m,
748.   I coaxed him (to come) but he wouldn't,

aɬi? s-k̓əɬ-twn̓-əls-míst-x,   aɬi? myàɬ
he thinks it's too much trouble,   he's too

k-t̓əɬ-ɬ-íc̓a?, q̓ʷəy-lscʕát.
dirty,   his clothes are dirty.

749. way̓ lùt iwà?   n-əlk̓-əmn-ìks-ən uɬ
749.   (I) tried to   force him   but

lút."
he wouldn't."

750. cù-nt-əm: "xʷúy-x," kʷùlst-s i? sxʷ-əlk̓á-m,
750. He said: "Go,"   he sent   the sheriffs,

people, the local people.?"
745. They said: "Yes, yes, we think we are."
746. He said: "All the children and the grown ups?"
747. The cook said, "Ah, wait a minute, I forgot my dish washer, the boy.
748. I coaxed him (to come) but he wouldn't, he thinks it's too much trouble,
    he's too dirty, his clothes are dirty.
749. I tried to force him but he wouldn't."
750. He said: "Go," he sent the sheriffs,

t-k-ʔəs-ʔasíl,   "xʷúy-wiʔ ƛʔá-nt-iʔ; nínwiʔ
two of them,   "Go (and) get him;   if

s-lùt-əm,   mi c-kəm-km-áxən-(n)t-p, c-əlk-ənt-ìp
he refuses,   take him by the arms,   tie him up (and)

c-xʷúyʕ-st-p;   waý kən cùt   yə-yʕà-t swít."
bring him here;   I   said every   body."

751. waý ixìʔ s-xʷúy-s iʔ   sxʷ-əlk-əlká-m; ixìʔ
751.   They went the   sheriffs;

 uɬ aɬìʔ alàʔ kɬ-čəlxʷ-xìt-s-əlx   iʔ t
and   there was a chair for him   to

k-s-ən-kɬ-mút-(t)n̩-s, waý ɬ s-t-kɬ-kaʔt-əm-s axàʔ
sit down,   very near to

yəʔ ylmíxʷəm, uɬ alàʔ   iʔ latàp ɬ
the king,   and there was a   table in

s-k-ən-qəʔ-qəʔ-íws-əm-s-əlx: axàʔ iʔ kʷə-kʷrì-t iʔ
the center of them all: the Golden

tkɬm-ìlxʷ uɬ axàʔ yəʔ ylmíxʷəm, uɬ axàʔ iʔ kəl
Woman   and axàʔ the king,   and   on

səkʷt-àqs nínwiʔ   iʔ tə-twít; uɬ
the other side there would be the boy;   and

nínwiʔ alàʔ   mi
        there (i.e. on the table) (they) will

kɬ-kʷìl·-st-s-əlx iʔ   s-kəkʕáka?; likùk   laʔɬ
place   the birds;   the rooster and

lipúl; ixìʔ məɬ mayʔ-ncút-əlx.
the hen; they   are going to tell a story.

two of them, "Go (and) get him; if he refuses, take him by the arms,
tie him up (and) bring him here; I said everybody."

751. The sheriffs went; and there was a chair for him to sit down, very near
to the king, and there was a table in the center of them all: the Golden
Woman and the king, and on the other side there would be the boy; and
there (i.e. on the table) they will place the birds; the rooster and the
hen; they are going to tell a story.

752. way kìc-s-əlx   axà? i? tə-twit;
752.   They got to where   the boy (is);

    cù-s-əlx,   "way kʷ s-c-x̣lìt-əm-s yə? ylmíxʷəm;
    they told him,   "He wants you the king;

    s-c-?kín-x uɬ lùt   y a-s-xʷúy?"
    why is it (you) have not   gone?"

753. cùt: "uɬ aɬi?   myàɬ   ʕàc-ənt
753. He said: "Because too much, look,

    i-s-t-q̇ʷəy-ʕáca?."
    I am dirty."

754. cù-s-əlx: "tanmùs   ixí?; s-cùt-x yə?
754. They said: "That's nothing;   he said the

    ylmìxʷəm tanmùs   i? x̣c-nùmt-(t)ṇ kəm iwà?
    king,   it doesn't matter   clothes   or even

    i? ƛ̣əx̣-ƛ̣x̣á-p; yə-yʕà-t swìt x̣às-t
    age;   every   body well

    k-s-k̇ə-k̇níya?-x.
    is going to listen.

755. aɬi?   k-s-c-mrím-a?x,   ʕàc-ənt
755. Because he's getting married, look,

    ylmíxʷəm-tət;   kʷu k-s-ilí?-x."
    he's our chief; we have got to be there."

756. way lùt-əm.
756.   He wouldn't.

757. ixì? kəm-kṁ-àx̣-s-əlx   uɬ
757. So   they grabbed him by the arms and

752. They got to where the boy (is); they told him, "The king wants you; why is it (you) have not gone?"

753. He said: "Because, look, I am too dirty."

754. They said: "That's nothing; the king said, it doesn't matter clothes or even age; everybody well is going to listen.

755. He's getting married, look, he's our chief; we have to be there."

756. He wouldn't.

757. So they grabbed him by the arms and

xʷúy-st-s-əlx; ṇ-ʔùɫxʷ-st-s-əlx   k̓əl
they took him; they brought him into

yləmxʷ-íɫxʷ.
the king's house.

758. kʷa ilì? i? c-kɫ-c̓àlx̣ʷ i?
758.   There   is a chair

     k-s-ən-kɫ-mút-(t)ṇ-s; cù-nt-əm   axà? i? tə-tw̓ít,
     for him to sit down;   they told   the boy,

     "kɫ-mùt-x ixí? ilì? ḷ s-ən-kɫ-mút-(t)ṇ."
     "Sit down there   on the chair."

759. uɫ aɫì? sùxʷ-ənt-əm   i? t ylmíxʷəm;
759.   He recognized him   the   king;

     "ṇta··? ixì? i? tə-tw̓ìt alà? ɫ̓əm i?
     "Oh,   that's the boy

     ɫ-sì-sənca?-s-əlx axà? i? səxʷ-k̓ʷúl-əm.
     younger brother of those   workers.

760. uɫ ixì? cùt: 'aɫì? myàɫ   kən
760. And   he said: '(I am) too

     k̓ʷə-k̓ʷy-úma?, way̓ k̓əl
     small,   (I'll go) to

     s-ən-k̓ʷəɫ-cən-(n)cút-(t)ṇ.'
     the kitchen.'

761. uɫ ixì? kʷu ɫ̓a?-ɫt-ìs   axà? i?
761. And then   he got for me those

     s-kəkˤáka?; uɫ ixì? nixʷ cnìɫc   ɫ̓a?-nt-ìs
     birds;   and   he's the one who got

they took him; they brought him into the king's house.

758. There is a chair for him to sit down; they told the boy, "Sit down there on the chair."

759. The king recognized him; "Oh, that's the boy younger brother of those workers.

760. And he said: 'I am too small, I'll go to the kitchen.'

761. And then he got those birds for me; and he's the one who got the Golden Woman."

i? kʷə-kʷrì-t i? tkɫm-ílxʷ."
the Golden Woman."

762. wáy, way ixì? c-kʷì-s yə? ḷkasàt yə?
762. Well, he took the trunk the

ylmíxʷəm; kah̓kʷ-qí-s; way ixì? kɫ-kʷìl·-st-s i?
king; he opened it; he placed down the

likùk na?ɫ i? lipúl.
rooster and the hen.

763. way kəl səkʷt-àqs i? náqs, uɫ
763. At one end one, and (the other)

akͅlà? kəl səkʷt-áqs.
at the other end.

764. uɫ ixì? cù-nt-əm: "hu-húy, p
764. And then he said: "OK, you

k-s-máy?-ncút-a?x, s-c-?xͅìl-x ki?
are going to tell about yourselves, that's why

xͅlít-ɫm-ən."
I called you."

765. way ti síl axà? i? likúk, ti
765. He's puzzled the rooster,

səl-lwís; uɫ ixì? cù-s i? tkɫm-ílxʷ-s, i?
he's puzzled; and so he told his wife, the

lipúl, "hu-húy, anwì? may?-ncút-a?x."
hen, "Go ahead, you tell the story."

766. cù-s: "lút, anwì? kʷ s-qəl-tmíxʷ,
766. She said: "No, you are the man,

762. Well, the king took the trunk; he opened it; he placed down the rooster and the hen.

763. At one end one, and (the other) at the other end.

764. And then he said: "OK, you are going to tell about yourselves, that's why I called you."

765. The rooster is puzzled, he's puzzled; and so he told his wife, the hen, "Go ahead, you tell the story."

766. She said: "No, you are the man,

anwì? c-ən-q̇a?-ìls-əm-st-x^w i? k-s-c-?íɬən-tət,
you   rustle   things to eat for us,

əc-k̓^wùɬ-st-x^w i?   s-qlàẃ i? kɬ-ən-x̣s-t-(t)án-tət,
(who) earns   the   money   to do us good,

uɬ incà? kmix ḷ cìtx^w   la n-yx^w-ùt t̓ə
and I   just in the house   (there)

c-k̓^wúɬ-st-ən; ixì? c-x^wək̓^w-əst-ín, uɬ   kən
I work;   I clean up,   and I

c-k̓^wəɬ-cən-(n)cút, kə̓m kən c-ən-q̇^wə?-ítk^w-əm.
cook,   or   I   wash clothes.

767. uɬ   anwí?, anwì? k^w k-s-xa?t-əm-scút-a?x,
767. But you,   you   are the leader,

anwì? k^w əc-x?ít."
you   are the head."

768. k-?əx^w-k^wún-m-ənt-əm;   waẏ sic cùt   waẏ.
768. She talked him into it;   then he said OK.

769. "waẏ, waẏ t̓əx^w ixì? k^wu s-cùn-əm-(m)p kən
769. "OK,   you told me to

k-s-may?-ncút-a?x;   uɬ t̓əx^w yə? ?x̣ì? təl
tell a story about myself; and   right from

in-təmx^w-úla?x^w, itlì?   mi   uɬ c-may?-nt-ìn
my country,   from there (I) will   tell

in-cáw-t.
my story.

770. waẏ kən px̣-px̣-t-wílx,   kən
770. When I   came to my senses, I

you are the one who rustles things to eat for us, earns the money to do us good; I just work in the house; I clean up, and I cook, or I wash clothes.

767. But you, you are the leader, you are the head."

768. She talked him into it; then he said OK.

769. "OK, you told me to tell a story about myself; and right from my country, from there I will tell my story.

770. When I came to my senses, I

taʔxʷ-s-puʔ-ús,   uɬ wìk-ən axàʔ i-s-k̓ʷìⱡ-t-əm, wa̓y
got my thinking,   I saw   my brothers,

t-kaʔ-kaʔɬís, yə-yʕà-t tuʔ-twít, uɬ axàʔ in-l̓ʔìw
three of them, all   boys,   and   my father

ixìʔ uɬ i-s-k̓ʷúy, ixìʔ uɬ wa̓y súxʷ-n-əlx.
     and my mother,   I got to know them.

771. aɬìʔ wa̓y kən c-px̌-px̌-t-wílx,   uɬ ixìʔ uɬ
771.   I   came to my senses, and

k̓əl s-ən-maʔ-màyaʔ-tņ kʷu maʔ-máyaʔ-ɬt-əm.
at   the school   they taught me.

772. wa̓y lùt   incàʔ i-s-t-k̓ì-k̓aʔt   uɬ
772.   (I) didn't   keep up with them

aɬìʔ kən s-tə-t̓ʔíw-t-aʔx, lùt   i-s-t-k̓ì-k̓aʔt
      I   am the youngest, couldn't keep up

iʔ k̓əl q̓əy̓-mìn ilìʔ k-s-c-my-p-nwíɬən.
with the book   to learn.

773. ixìʔ uɬ axàʔ i-s-k̓ʷìⱡ-t-əm xəⱡ-p-nù-s-əlx
773.   But   my brothers   they finished all

iʔ q̓əy̓-mín, my-p-nú-s-əlx;   cakʷ cù-s   tə
the books,   they learned them; as   they say in

n-wyápx-cən, kráčuet-m-əlx, ixìʔ uɬ ņ-px̌-m-ùs
English,   they graduated,   they finished

iʔ s-c-maʔ-máyaʔ-s-əlx.
their school.

774. wa̓y cù-s-əlx yəʔ l̓ʔíw-s-əlx,   "wa̓y   l̓ʔíw,
774.   They told   their father, "Well, father,

got my thinking, I saw my brothers, three of them, all boys, and my father and my mother, I got to know them.

771. I came to my senses, and they taught me the school.

772. I didn't keep up with them because I am the youngest, I couldn't keep up with the book to learn.

773. But my brothers they finished all the books, they learned them; as they say in English, they graduated, they finished their school.

774. They told their father, "Well, father, we're going to leave you."

way̓ ixì? ɬwín-(n)t-s-t."
   we're going to leave you."

775. cù-nt-m-əlx i? t l̓?íw-s-əlx, "uɬ
775. He said to them their father, "And

s-c-?kín-x?
why?

776. ta?lì? c-x̣s-íkst-əm-ɬm-ən;
776. Very well I have treated you;

c-tu?-tíwa?-ɬm-ən, ùɬi? p
I have babied you around, and now you

k-s-əlkʷ-ílx-a?x, kʷu k-s-ɬwín-(n)t-p."
are leaving, you are leaving me."

777. cù-s-əlx yə? l̓?íw-s-əlx, "lút, way̓
777. They told their father, "No,

wníxʷ, uɬ aɬì? x̣əl ixì? ki?
that's true, and that's why

k-s-ɬwín-(n)t-s-t.
we are leaving you.

778. uɬ aɬì? lut stìm ti k-s-my-p-nú-nt-əm,
778. Not anything we are learning,

kmìx q̓əy̓-mín; uɬ aɬì? axà? kʷu s-tu?-tìwa?-st-xʷ
just books; and   you baby us around

axà? i? kʷu a-s-qʷs-qʷa?síya?.
   your children.

779. uɬ x̣m-ìnk-tət kʷu k-s-ƛ̓a?-ƛ̓a?-s-c-k̓ʷùl̓-a?x
779. And we want to look for a job

775. Their father said to them, "And why?
776. Very well I have treated you; I have babied you around, and now you
  are leaving, you are leaving me."
777. They told their father, "No, that's true, and that's why we are leaving
  you.
778. We aren't learning anything, just books; and you baby us around, your
  children.
779. And we want to look for a job

axà? ɬ təmxʷ-úla?xʷ.
in the world.

780. ixì? kʷu təkʷ?-ùt kʷu k-əlkʷ-ákʷ, uɬ
780. When we walk out we we are going far, and

kʷu ƛa?-ƛa?-s-c-k̓ʷúɬ-əm, uɬ ixì? ṅiṅwi? kʷu
we will look for jobs, and if we

ka?kìc-əm i? t k-s-c-k̓ʷúɬ-tət, ixì? uɬ kʷu
find a job, we

s-k̓ʷúɬ-əm-s.
will work.

781. uɬ my-p-nù-nt-əm i? k-s-c-k̓ʷúɬ-tət; uɬ alà?
781. And we'll learn how to work; but

ɬ k-alà?-m-ənt-s-t uɬ lùt ixì? tə
if we stay here with you (we) will never

k-s-my-p-nú-nt-əm; uɬ aɬì? ti kmìx kʷu
learn anything; all (you do is)

s-tu?-tìwa?-st-xʷ y a-s-qʷs-qʷa?síya?, kʷu
baby us around your children, we

a-s-tu?-təw̓-ílt."
your spoiled children."

782. ixì? cù-s-əlx yə? ɬ?íw-s-əlx.
782. That's what they told their father.

783. cù-nt-m-əlx, "wáy̓, way̓
783. He told them, "Yes,

s-pu?-ús-əmp, way̓ wníxʷ."
(if) that's how you feel, that's true."

in the world.
780. When we walk out we we are going far, and we will look for jobs, and
if we find a job, we will work.
781. And we'll learn how to work; but if we stay here with you we will never
learn anything; all (you do is) baby us around your children, we your
spoiled children."
782. That's what they told their father.
783. He told them, "Yes, (if) that's how you feel, that's true."

784. wa̓y kʷùlst-s i? səxʷ-k̓ʷùl-əm-s   ɬ
784.   He sent   his man who worked   in

s-ən-ṫəws-cqáx̣a?-tn̩,   cù-s: "x̌ʷùy-x   c-ʕacà-nt
the barn,   he told him: "Go   tie

i?   s-x?im-ɬ-x̣às-t   in-kəw?áp,   in-k-?əmt-íẇs-tn̩,
the   very best   horses of mine,   my saddle horses,

ka?ɬís.
three of them.

785. uɬ   ixì? n̩-ṫək̓ʷ-ṫk̓ʷ-íkən̓-(n)t-xʷ,
785. And   put saddles on,

laprít-ənt-xʷ;   i? t s-x?im-ɬ-x̣às-t
put bridles on;   the very best

in-ṫək̓ʷ-ki?-sqàx̣a?-tn̩   in-laprít,
saddles (and)   bridles of mine,

s-k-əwp-wp-àqst-xən   kəm̓ c-k-cəw-cəw-ʕáqst-xən,
fur chaps   or   fringed chaps,

ċəl-ċl-íplx̌ən,   qəxʷ-sqáx̣a?-tn̩,   s-ṗícən-s-əlx,
spurs,   whips,   rope,

lùt   k-s-yaʕ-p-cín-s-əlx,   yə-yʕà-t   x̣ás-t,   i?
they won't   be hard up,   everything   good,   the

s-x?im-ɬ-x̣s-əlscút."
very best things."

786. ax̣à?-m̩ i? t tkɬm-ìlxʷ-s ɬ wík-s uɬ   ixì?
786.   His wife   saw,   and

cù-nt-əm: "uɬ s-c-?kín-x y a-s-x̣s-əlscùt   uɬ
asked him: "Why   your best outfits

784. He sent his man who worked in the barn, he told him: "Go tie the very
best horses of mine, my saddle horses, three of them.

785. And put saddles on, put bridles on; the very best saddles (and) bridles
of mine, fur chaps or fringed chaps, spurs, whips, rope, (so they) won't
be hard up, everything good, the very best things."

786. His wife saw, and asked him: "Why are you giving to your children your
best outfits?"

ixì? xʷìc-əɫt-xʷ-əlx   y a-s-qʷs-qʷa?síya??"
you are giving to   your children?"

787. uɫi? cù-s: "cəm ka ?kìn   ɫ
787. And he told her: "If   some place

yáʕ-p-əlx,   cəm kəm t swìt   ɫ wìk-ənt-m-əlx,
they arrive,   and   people   see them,

cəm   ti
(they will)

t-xáw-cən-m-ənt-m-əlx.
get stuck on them (lit. their lips will go dry).

788. 'ṇta? way xs-əlscút-əlx;
788. "Gee, but they have expensive things;

mət   way yəʕʷ-p-yàw-t i? ɫəx-əx-ɫxá-p-s;
(they) must be   powerful   their parents;

s-c-?xìl-x uɫ ixì? xs-əlscút-əlx.'
that's why   they have such good things.'

789. cəm   wís-ənt-m-əlx;
789. They will brag on them (speak highly of them);

uɫ axà? ɫ t-qʷəṅ-qʷṅ-íca?-ɬx,   uɫ i?
but   if they are poorly dressed, and

kəw?àp-s-əlx ɫ qʷəṅ-qʷáṅ-t, axà?
their horses   are pitiful,

ṇ-təkʷ-ki?-sqàxa?-tṇ-s-əlx ɫ kəs-kás-t, ṇta? ɫ
their saddles   ugly,   if

my-p-nù-nt-əm qa?ɫ-ylmíxʷm-əlx,   cəm
they find out their father is a king, (they) will

---

787. And he told her: "If they arrive some place, and people see them, they will get stuck on them (lit. their lips will go dry).

788. "Gee, but they have expensive things; their parents must be powerful; that's why they have such good things.'

789. They will brag on them (speak highly of them); but if they are poorly dressed, and their horses are pitiful, their saddles ugly, if they find out their father is a king, the people will say:

THE GOLDEN WOMAN

cùt-əlx i? s-qìlxʷ: 'n̓ta? mət qʷən̓-qʷàn̓-t
say the people: 'Gee, but he's pitiful

ixì? yə? ylmíxʷəm, ixì? yə? ɬ?íw-s-əlx, kəm̓
this chief, their father, or

mət way̓ ya?-yákʷ-a?, ʕàc̓-ənt i?
maybe he's very stingy, look at

s-k̓s-əlscút-s-əlx.'
what ugly outfits they have.'

790. uɬ ixì? ki? i? s-x̣s-əlscút i?
790. And that's why good outfits

xʷíc̓-ɫt-n-əlx."
I gave them."

791. way̓ uɬ ixì? c̓ək-xít-m-əlx, aɬì?
791. Then he started counting,

əc-kʷì-s i? s-ən-qláw̓-tn̩-s, uɬ aɬi?-à?
he brought over his bank, because (not)

pn-icì? uɬ way̓ k-s-ən-qláw̓-tn̩, uɬ way̓ t̓i
at that time they had (no) banks, and

cnìɬc əc-t-xt̓-əst-ìs i? s-qláw̓-s.
he himself keeps his own money.

792. uɬ way̓ t̓i kmix kʷə-kʷr̓ì-t uɬ píq-sxən;
792. And it's all gold and silver;

lut tə kɬ-q̓ʷáy-s?-ylxʷ.
(he) didn't have any green backs.

793. way̓ aɬì? təl sk̓ʷut ɬ k̓ahk̓ʷ-qì-s i?
793. On one side he opened

'Gee, but this chief is pitiful, their father, or maybe he's very stingy,
look at what ugly outfits they have.'
790. And that's why I gave them good outfits."
791. Then he started counting, he brought over his bank, because at that
time they had no banks, and he himself keeps his own money.
792. And it's all gold and silver; he didn't have any green backs.
793. On one side he opened

-253-

s-qláw̓-s;   way̓ ixì? ?asəl-?úpən-kst,   ixì?
his money;   they are twenties,

qmì-s   ɬ ka?ɬəl-lúp; qmí··-s   uɫ
he put them down in three piles; he put down until

cx̣ʷá-p;   uɫ   təx̣ʷ nix̣ʷ   t
he got enough; then   (he) also

n̓-?əyx̣ʷ-ìw̓s   t píq-sxən.
(gave them) some change in silver.

794. way̓ cù-s   i? s-x̣?ít-x: "axà? anwì? kʷ
794. Then he told the oldest one: "You

s-x̣?ít-x,   ixì? axà?   ɬík̓l-ənt-s-ən;"
are the oldest one,   this is for your lunch;"

cù-nt-əm axà? i? qə?-íw̓s: "axà? anwì?
he told   the middle one: "(I'll give) you

nix̣ʷ ɬík̓l-ənt-s-ən;"   uɫ axà? i?
also something for your lunch;" and   the

s-t?ìw-t-x,   cù-nt-əm: "ixì? axà? anwì? ixì?
youngest one, he told him: "You, this is

ɬík̓l-ənt-s-ən."
for your lunch."

795. cù-nt-m-əlx: "nak̓ʷà?   c-my-st-ìp k̓a ?k̓in
795. He told them: "(You) don't know   where

p ɬ k-s-x̣ʷúy-a?x, uɫ lut   p tə
you   are going,   and (you) don't

c-súxʷ-la?xʷ-əm kəm̓ lut   tə c-my-st-ìp i?
know the country and (you) don't   know   the

his money; they are twenties, he put them down in three piles; he put
down until he got enough; then he also (gave them) some change in
silver.

794. Then he told the oldest one: "You are the oldest one, this is for your
lunch;" he told the middle one: "I'll give you also something for your
lunch;" and the youngest one, he told him: "You, this is for your lunch."

795. He told them: "You don't know where you are going, and you don't know
the country and you don't know the

s-qílxʷ tᵊxʷ i? k–s–ən–kíc–cn–əmp.
people   when you get there.

796. uɬ   pna? cmày   p c–k–s–q̓m–íltṇ,   uɬ
796. And   (you) might   get hungry,   and

ixì? axà?   t̓íkəl–ɬm–ən.
      this is what I give you for your lunch.

797. uɬ   n̓in̓wi? ḷ tàwn   p   yáˤ–p, uɬ wày p
797. And if   to a town you get,   then you

k–s–qláw̓,   tᵊxʷ p   ?i̓ɬən   i? k̓əl
will have money,   you can eat   at

s–ən–?i̓ɬən–tṇ,   uɬ p   pùlx   i? k̓əl
an eating place, and you can camp   at

s–ən–púlx–tṇ, axà? i? kəw?àp–əmp   ṇ–p–pi̓lx–st–p i?
a hotel,   your horses you can put

k̓əl s–ən–t̓əws–cqáxa?–tṇ.
in   a barn.

798. wày p   k–s–qlàw̓ uɬ   x̣áq̓–ənt–p;
798.   You have money and you can pay for that;

nàx̣əmɬ lut   p ɬa? k–s–qláw̓,   uɬ
but   (if you) don't   have money,

cə̓m   p qʷn̓–əm–scút.
(you) will   have a bad time.

799. uɬ lut   k–s–xʷa?t–ìls–əmp   axà? ḷ
799. And don't think I gave you too much

s–qláw̓, lut   k–s–ən–st–ìls–əmp axà? p
money,   don't think that   you

people when you get there.
796. And you might get hungry, and this is what I give you for your lunch.
797. And if you get to a town, then you will have money, you can eat at
     an eating place, and you can camp at a hotel, you can put your horses
     in a barn.
798. You have money and you can pay for that; but (if) you don't have money,
     you will have a bad time.
799. And don't think I gave you too much money, don't think that you

k-s-k̓ʷúl̓-aʔx,　　　lut　　　tə　s-mìy-s
are going to work,　it isn't　　sure

xʷùs　　　　　nìn̓wi?　　ka?kìc-ənt-p　i?
that in a hurry　(you) will　get　　　　a

k-s-c-k̓ʷúl̓-əmp;　pna?　　　　cmay　p　xʷ?-ás-əsq̓ət,　ul̓
job;　　　　　　it might be　　　　　many days,　　and

cəm̓　　　　　p　k-s-q̓m-íltn̩."
(you) will　　　get hungry."

800.　cù-s-əlx　　yə?　l̓?íw-s-əlx,　　cù-nt-m-əlx　i?　t
800.　They told　　　　their father,　they told him

s-qʷs-qʷa?síya?:　"wáy̓,　way̓　lím-ləm-t-x;　way̓　axà?
the children:　　　"Thank you;　　　　　this is

i?　k-s-c̓əx̌ʷ-xít-əm-t:　　　ul̓　al̓ì?　wnìxʷ
what　we are going to tell you:　it's true that

lut　　　　tə　c-my-st-ìm　k̓a　?kìn　k̓ʷu　lə
(we) don't　know　　　　　　where　we

k-s-xʷúy-a?x,　təxʷ　ixì?　t　tanm̓s-úla?xʷ,
are going,　　　　　　　(we'll just go) anywhere,

məl̓　k̓ʷu　təkʷ?-út,　　xi?-mìx　k̓a　?kìn　k̓ʷu
　　we　will travel,　some　　　place　we

yáʕ-p,　　k̓ʷu　　sw-l̓tìlən　i?　t
will get,　(and) we　will ask　　for

k-s-ən-k̓ʷúl̓-mən-tət.
jobs.

801.　ul̓　s-c-?x̌ìl-x　ki?　c̓əx̌ʷ-xít-əm-t,
801.　And　that's why　　we are telling you,

are going to work, it isn't sure that you will get a job in a hurry; it
might be many days, and you will get hungry."

800. They told their father, the children told him: "Thank you; this is what
we are going to tell you: it's true that we don't know where we are
going, (we'll just go) anywhere, we will travel, we will get some place,
(and) we will ask for jobs.

801. And that's why we are telling you,

nak̓ʷà?   c-my-st-ìm   i?   kɬ-cáw-tət,   pna?   kʷu
(we) don't   know   what   we will do,   maybe   we

c-yaʕ-m-ìlx   kʷu   ta?xʷ-s-c-k̓ʷúɬ,   kə̓m
will be all together (when) we   get a job,   or

pna?   axà?   lút,   kʷu   px̣ʷ-x̣ʷá-m,   cə̓m   kʷu
maybe   not,   we   will scatter,   (we) might

k-nà-naqs   i?   t   k-s-ən-k̓ʷúɬ-mən-tət.
each by himself   get a job.

802.   uɬ   s-c-?x̣ìl-x   uɬ   lut   k-s-əc-my-st-ím,
802.   And   that's why   (we) don't   know,

uɬ   nàx̣əmɬ   wa̓y   kʷu   c̓əx̣ʷ-xt-(t)wíxʷ,   axà?
   but   we   will tell each other our date

i?   la?ɬ   i-s-k̓ʷíƛ̓-t-əm: lut   ixì?   c-pi?-scìɬt
   (I) and   my brothers: not   yester

s-x̣əl-x̣ʕál-t,   ƛ̓əxʷ   ʕapnà?   nín̓wi?   ƛ̓xiw-t-wílx,
day,   but   today   next year,

pùt   ṇ-ləʕ̓ʷ-p-ùs   ʕapnà?
just (when)   it's exactly   (now)

s-x̣əl-x̣ʕàl-t   mi   ɬ-c-kíc-ənt-s-t.
today (i.e. a year from now) (we) will   get back to you.

803.   uɬ   nín̓wi?   k-nàqs   ɬ   k̓áw,   uɬ   wa̓y
803.   And   if   one of us   is gone,   then

ixì?   s-ƛ̓l-əl-míx;   nàx̣əmɬ   kʷu   yə-yʕà-t   kʷu   ɬa?
     he's dead;   but   (if) we   all

c-xʷəl-xʷál-t,   wa̓y   yə-yʕà-t   kʷu   ɬ-c-yáʕ-p."
live,   then   (we) all   will come back."

we don't know what we will do, maybe we will be all together (when)
we get a job, or maybe not, we will scatter, we might each by himself
get a job.

802. And that's why we don't know, but I and my brothers will tell each other
our date: not yesterday, but today next year, just (when) it's exactly
(now) today (i.e. a year from now) we will get back to you.

803. And if one of us is gone, then he's dead; but (if) we all live, then we
all will come back."

804. ixì?   čəx̌ʷ-xìt-s-əlx yə? ḻ?íw-s-əlx.
804. That's what they told   their father.

805. cùt-əlx,   "waẏ   ixì? kʷu təkʷ?-út,"   waẏ
805. They said, "Well,   we are going,"

      t-kʷəl·-íẅs-əlx.
      they got on their horses.

806. ƛi itì?   uɬ təkʷ?-út-əlx,   uɬ aɬì?
806.   (They had) just   started,   and

      mət   s-xiƛ-la?xʷ-əxʷ   i? təmxʷ-úla?xʷ-s-əlx,
      I guess   it is level   their country,

      pùt   k-s-c-xʷùy ixì? ùɬi?   k̇əɬ-k̇láxʷ.
      quite a ways   before they get out of sight.

807. nìkxna?   axà? i?   s-t?íw-t-x,   cùt axà?
807. Goodness,   the   youngest one, said

      i?   likúk,   "axà? incá?, waẏ cù-n   in-ḻ?íw
      the   rooster, "That's me,   I said to my father

      uɬ   i-s-k̇ʷúy, cù-n-əlx   waẏ ƛi i-k-s-kxà-m
      and my mother, I told them   I want to follow

      i-s-k̇ʷíƛ-t-əm, waẏ ṇ-kxn-íls-m-ən."
      my brothers,   I want to go with them."

808. cù-nt-əm   i? t ḻ?íw-s,   "lút, waẏ k̇əm
808. He told him   his father,   "No,

      kʷu a-s-k-?am·út-əm, waẏ myàɬ   kʷ x̌ʷúp-t,
          you stay with us,   too much you are weak,

      cə̇m   ṇ-q̇a?-ils-ənt-xʷ a-s-k̇ʷíƛ-t-əm, kə̇m
      (you) will bother   your brothers,   or

804. That's what they told their father.
805. They said, "Well, we are going," they got on their horses.
806. They had just started, and I guess their country is level, it's quite a ways before they get out of sight.
807. My, the young one, the rooster said, "That's me, I said to my father and mother, I said I want to follow my brothers, I want to go with them."
808. His father told him, "No, you stay with us, you are too weak, you will bother your brothers, or

pna? k-x̣a?-ìpla?-nt-xʷ a-s-k̓ʷíx̣-t-əm, wa̓y k̓im kʷ
you may get in trouble your brothers, you

s-mút-x."
stay home."

809. wa̓y lút, ixì? s-ca-cˤáy-p-əm-s.
809. No, and he started crying.

810. ux̣ ixì? cù-s axà? i? likúk, cù-s
810. And he asked the rooster, he asked

i? lipúl: "úc wnìxʷ há? ixì? há?
the hen: "Is it true

i-s-c-qʷəl-qʷìl-t, ixì? há? in-càw-t?"
what I am saying, what I have done?"

811. axà? i? lipùl məx̣ s-ən-təkʷ-s-əncút-xt-s i?
811. The hen winked at the

likúk, cù-s, "wáy, ixì? an-cáw-t,
rooster, she said, "Yes, that's what you've done,

ixì? an-cáw-t, màtəm ilì? s-c-?x̣il-x ki?
what you've done, that's why

cù-nt-s-ən a-k-s-máya?-ṃ, t anwì? may?-nt-ìxʷ
I told you to tell your story, you tell

an-cáw-t, ux̣ ax̣ì? anwì? c-my-st-ìxʷ
your story, because you know

an-cáw-t."
what you've done."

812. wa̓y məx̣ ixì? itlì? s-ən-xc̓s-íws-əm-s.
812. And then he went on.

you might get in trouble your brothers, you stay home."
809. No, and he started crying.
810. And the rooster asked, he asked the hen: "Is it true what I am saying, what I have done?"
811. The hen winked at the rooster, she said, "Yes, that's what you've done, what you've done, that's why I told you to tell your story, you tell your story, because you know what you've done."
812. And then he went on.

813. cù-nt-əm   axà? i? t tkɫm-ìlxʷ-s yə?
813. She told him   his wife   the

ylmíxʷəm, cù-nt-əm: "waẏ, waẏ cəm
king,   she said: "(That) might

ņ-ḵəs-t-mì-s axà? i? s-qʷsí?-tət ɫ lùt-st-xʷ
do harm to   our son   if you refuse him

t n-yʕíp, n-yʕəp-əncùt lút-st-xʷ.
always,   (if) for good you refuse him.

814. pna?   cmay ņ-q̇əl-t-ùs-əs ɫ
814. (He) might   get sick   if

ņ-ḵəw-p-íls,   ņ-ƛ̣l-əl-mí-s; waẏ ixì? xi?-xi?-st-íxʷ.
he's lonesome, (maybe) die;   let him go.

815. cù-nt-xʷ axa? i? səxʷ-ḵʷùʔ-əm i?
815. Tell   the working man   (to get) the

s-x?im-ɫ-x̣ʷùp-t waẏ i? s-əc-húy-x i? t
most worthless   the done   with

s-ḵíw-ḷx,   ḵim   ƛ̣i xʷst-útya?;
age (horse), (one that) can only   walk;

ixì? mi c-ʕac-ənt-ís, ixì? məɫ ņ-ƛ̣kʷ-íki?-s,
that   he can tie,   that and put the saddle on,

kɫ-yə-yʕ-ílxʷ,   məɫ   ilì? mi
put everything on, and then

k-?əmt-íẃs-(s)t-xʷ, məɫ xʷìc̣-ənt-xʷ t   k-s-qláẇ-s,
put him on its back, and give him   some money,

axà? t ḵʷə-ḵʷy-ína?,   cəm   x̣às-t i?
        just a little, (and he) will

813. His wife told the king, she said: "That might do harm to our son if you
refuse him always, (if) you refuse him for good.

814. He might get sick if he gets lonesome, (maybe) die; let him go.

815. Tell the working man (to get) the most worthless (horse) done with age,
(one that) can only walk; that one he can tie, and put the saddle on,
put everything on, and then put him on its back, and give him some
money, just a little, and he will

s-puʔ-ús-c; uɬ lùt   ƙa ʔkìn ɬə
be happy; and (he) won't

k-s-əlkʷ-ákʷ-s, k-s-əlkʷ-əkʷ-st-ìs   axàʔ iʔ
go far,   (it won't) take him far

t   ƙìw-ḷx iʔ t s-ən-kɬ-ċaʔ-sqáx̣aʔ.
because he's old the   horse.

816. cəm   iƙlíʔ,   wi··m uc
816. (He) might (take him) there,   (he) might

ƙəɬ-ƙlàxʷ   kəm lút, məɬ tìɬ-x
get out of sight or not, then he'll just stand there

yəʔ ʔx̣ìʔ s-ən-kɬ-ċaʔ-sqax̣aʔ iʔ t s-ʔáyx̣ʷ-t.
   the horse,   he's so tired.

817. cəm   wí··m, məɬ itlìʔ ɬ-c-ṗəlƙ-ús-əm;
817. (He) will try, and then he'll come back;

lut   ɬə k-s-ən-kəc-kṅ-áɬq-s; kəm lut   ɬə
(he) won't   overtake them;   and (he) won't

k-s-ən-sìì-p-s uɬ aɬìʔ   lùt   k-s-əlkʷ-ákʷ-s."
get lost   because (he) can't go far."

818. "a··" cù-s iʔ tkɬm-ílxʷ-s, "waẏ x̣às-t
818. "Ah," he told his wife,   "It's good

iʔ kʷu ƙəɬ-paʔx̣-xít-xʷ,   waẏ
   thinking you are doing for me,

wníxʷ."
that's right."

819. cù-s   iʔ səxʷ-ƙʷúl-əm-s: "xʷùy-x
819. He told his working man: "Go

be happy; and he won't go far, the horse won't take him far because
he's old.

816. He might (take him) there, he might get out of sight or not, then the
horse'll just stand there, he's so tired.

817. He will try, and then he'll come back; he won't overtake them; and he
won't get lost because he can't go far."

818. "Ah," he told his wife, "You're doing good thinking for me, that's right."

ƛaʔ-sqàx̣aʔ,   iʔ   t   s-c-hùy-x iʔ t   s-k̓íw-ḻx,
get a horse, the one   dying   with age,

k̓əm lùt   yəʔ c-k̓ʷúl̓-əm-st-əm, wa̓y t̓i
(the one we) don't   use any more,

kmìx   c-ʔam-st-ím; ixì?   mi
(that we) just feed;   that one

c-ʕac-ənt-íxʷ.
tie up.

820. xi?-mìx   iʔ t ṇ-t̓ək̓ʷ-ki?-sqáx̣aʔ-tṇ, cakʷ
820. (Get) any old   saddle,   if

iwà? ƛəx̣-ƛx̣á-p;   xi?-mìx   t kḻ-laprít-s."
even it's an old one; (put) any old   bridle on him."

821. wa̓y ixì? s-xʷùy-s axà? iʔ səxʷ-k̓ʷúl̓-əm-s,
821.   He went   his working man,

wa̓y c-ʕac-ḻt-ìm iʔ t s-c-hùy-x iʔ t s-k̓íw-ḻx,
    he tied up   a   finished   old (horse),

k̓əm   t̓i xʷst-útyaʔ; wa̓y ṇ-t̓k̓ʷ-ìki?-s ixì?
(that) only   walks;   he saddled it

c-xʷúy-st-s;   c-kíc-st-s,   cù-nt-əm, "wa̓y
(and) brought it over; he got it there, he said,

axá?."
"Here it is."

822. cù-nt-əm   iʔ t ḻ?íw-s,   "wa̓y ixì?
822. He told him   his father,   "There's

a-kḻ-ən-k-?əmt-íw̓s-tṇ," uḻ wa̓y xʷìc-xt-s   t
your horse,"   and   he gave him some

---

819. He told his working man: "Go get a horse, the one dying with age, the one we don't use any more, that we just feed; tie up that one.

820. (Get) any old saddle, if even it's an old one; (put) any old bridle on him."

821. His working man went, tied up a finished old (horse), that only walks; he saddled it and brought it over; he got it there, he said, "Here it is."

822. His father told him, "There's your horse," and he gave him some

s-qláw-s,   waỷ   n̩-pkʷ-ɬ-ƛ́aq-naʔ-m̩.
money,   he put it in his pocket.

823. waỷ kən-xít-əm   iʔ t l̩ʔiw-s   iʔ
823.   He helped him   his father

      k-ʔəmt-íʷs,   waỷ kʷən-kʷín-ks-əs   iʔ
      get on the horse,   he shook hands with

      s-k̓ʷùy-s   uɬ yəʔ l̩ʔíw-s;   kəɬ-t̓əm-ʕás-s-əlx,
      his mother and   his father; they kissed him,

           ʔaxəl-t-əm-sqáxaʔ.
           he turned his horse around.

824. n̩t̓aʔ uɬ iwàʔ   ɬc-íʷs-əs   uɬ   iwàʔ
824.   To no avail he whipped it, and

      ɬc-ənt-ís,   uɬ iwàʔ xm-ənt-ís,   waỷ lút.
      whipped it, and even spurred it,   no.

825. uɬ aɬiʔ waỷ n-əlkʷ-kʷ-əlx-íkən,   waỷ pn-iciʔ
825. And   he's way behind them,   already

      kəɬ-k̓il·xʷ-t   iʔ s-k̓ʷíƛ-t-əm-s.
      they are out of sight   his brothers.

826. waỷ t̓i xʷst-útyaʔ,   n̩-st-ìls   "waỷ uɬ
826.   He's just walking,   he thought

      kən l̩kʷ-kʷ-əlx-íkən," wi··m̩ səp-ənt-ìs kəm̓
      "I   am way behind,"   he hit it   and

      t-xm-íc̓aʔ-s,   húy,   ixìʔ nàxəmɬ
      he spurred it, finally

      kəɬ-kláxʷ.
      he got out of sight.

money, he put it in his pocket.

823. His father helped him get on the horse, he shook hands with his mother
     and his father; they kissed him, he turned his horse around.
824. To no avail he whipped it, and whipped it, and even spurred it, no.
825. And he's way behind them, his brothers are already out of sight.
826. He's just walking, he thought "I am way behind," he hit it and he
     spurred it, finally he got out of sight.

827. ixì? uł łq̓-ìlx   i? kəwáp-s;   way̓
827.   He lay down   his horse;

    łətp-m-əncùt   axà? i?   tə-twít,
    he jumped down   the boy,

    c̓əl-l-ùla?x^w-s   ṇta? uł   la?ł
    he landed on the ground   and

    s-c̓qʷ-áqʷ-s.
    he started to cry.

828. uł ʕím-t-əm-s   i? kəwáp-s,   uł ixì?
828. And he got angry at   his horse,

    k-sṗ-íc̓a?-s; way̓ səṗ-ənt-í··s,   huy uł
    he hit it;   he hit it on the body   and

    k-səṗ-qí-s;   ixì? uł
    he hit it on the head;

    t-x̣?ən-cən-mìst-m-ənt-əm axà? i? t kəwáp-s,
    he tried to stop him   his horse,

    cù-nt-əm: "way̓, way̓ kʷu c-qʷn̓-íkst-əm-st-xʷ, way̓
    he said: "Have pity on me,

    ałi? kən s-c-hùy-x   i? t   s-k̓íw-łx.
    I   am to the limit   with old age.

829. way̓ ixì? uł kən c̓əs-p-ískit   uł
829.   My breath is all out of me and

    iti? i-s-ən-c̓a?-c̓a?xʷ-s-c̓ím, uł alà? i? kən
    I am so weak boned,   and here   I

    tk̓ʷ-əncùt i? kən łq̓-ílx.
    lay down,   I lay down.

827. His horse lay down; the boy jumped down, he landed on the ground and he started to cry.

828. And he got angry at his horse, he hit it; he hit it on the body and he hit it on the head; his horse tried to stop him, he said: "Have pity on me, I am to the limit with old age.

829. My breath is all out of me and I am so weak boned, and here I lay down, I lay down.

830. way̓ lut kʷu a-k-s-k-səp̓-qín,   pna?
830.   Don't   hit me on the head, (you) might

kʷu k-sp̓-ùs-ənt-xʷ   ixì? u⁴ cəm   sic kən
   hit me in the eye   and (I) might then

knəm-p-qín, kən t̓əkʷ-p-ús."
get blind,   bust my eye."

831. t̓i kʷm̓i⁴ təl s-k-ən-wìs-t-əm-s ki?
831.   At once from above

c-qʷəl-qʷíl-st-əm;   cù-nt-əm: "way̓ ?uyá?,
something spoke to him; it said: "Listen,

c-qʷn̓-ìkst-əm-st-xʷ an-kəwáp; way̓ t incà? mi
have pity on   your horse;   I   will

n̓-qʷən̓-mí-nt-s-ən."
pity you."

832. iwà? s-ta?χ̣ìl-x   ?əks-wìx qʷàm-qʷəm-t
832.   He did like that, there was a beautiful

s-ən-k⁴-ċa?-sqáχa?, xʷəm   t̓i s-k̓ə⁴-q̓əy̓-ncút.
horse,   as pretty as a picture.

833. n̓ta? i? n̓-t̓əkʷ-ki?-sqàχa?-tn̓ síc,   u⁴
833. Gee, the saddle   brand new, and

i? laprít-s, u⁴ ilì? k-s-k-cəw-cəw-ʕáqst-xən ilì?
   its bridle, and   fringed chaps

c-k-⁴áxʷ-p.
hanging there.

834. cù-nt-əm: "xʷús-t-x, xʷús-t-x, xʷs-xʷús-əlx,
834. He said: "Hurry,   hurry,   hurry,

830. Don't hit me on the head, you might hit me in the eye and I might then get blind, bust my eye."
831. At once from above something spoke to him; it said: "Listen, have pity on your horse; I will pity you."
832. He did like that, there was a beautiful horse, pretty as a picture.
833. Gee, the saddle brand new, and its bridle, and fringed chaps hanging there.
834. He said: "Hurry, hurry, hurry,

nàxəmɫ y a-s-k̓ʷiλ-t-əm mət wa̓y λáxʷ-t, kəm̓
or   your brothers might   be dead, or

mət   uc pənh-íws-ənt-əm.
(we) might   be in time.

835. ti kʷ məl-mìl-ɬx   uɫ k̓m-íp-st-m-əlx,   wa̓y
835. If you take your time   they'll be dead,

yà-p-əlx ɬ n̓-ʔəɫn-aʔ-s-qílxʷ-tn̓, ilìʔ
they got to the man eater,   there

k-s-púlx-aʔ-x-əlx;   xʷùs-t-x kʷ i-s-cún-əm,
they are going to camp; hurry up   I am telling you,

kʷu c-t-xa-xa-p-ús-əm-st-xʷ."
(and) you keep staring at me."

836. wa̓y ɫq̓-ìlx   iʔ s-ən-kɫ-ċaʔ-sqáxaʔ, wa̓y
836.   He lay down the horse,

t-xʷt̓-əp-mì-s ixìʔ s-k-ʔəmt-íws-c.
he jumped to it and he got on.

837. uɫ cù-nt-əm: "lut t̓ a-k-s-k̓ín-t; wa̓y
837. And he told him: "Don't   get scared;

cù-nt-s-ən   kʷ k-sy-m-scút-aʔx, kʷ
I'm telling you   do your best,

k-ċən-ċən-á-m, kʷ t-kʷən-kʷní-m; uɫ nìn̓wiʔ lut
hold on tight,   hang on;   and   don't

a-k-s-k̓ín-t, uɫ kʷ n̓-ċíp-ċəp-s-əm.
be uneasy,   and kʷ shut your eyes tight.

838. tə   n-wìs-t mi kən k-s-xy̓-ús-t-aʔx, t
838. Through the air   I   am going to go,

or your brothers might be dead, or we might be in time.
835. If you take your time they'll be dead, they got to the man-eater, they
are going to camp there; hurry up I am telling you, you keep staring
at me."
836. His horse lay down, he jumped to it and he got on.
837. And he told him: "Don't get scared; I'm telling you do your best, hold
on tight, hang on; and don't be uneasy, and shut your eyes tight.
838. Through the air I am going to go,

ṇ-ła?-m-ink-s   i?   t   s-t-k̓m-ásqət."
right next to   the   sky."

839.   ixí?   ṇ-wis-əlx.
839.   And so he went up in the air.

840.   uł   waẏ   c-?x̣íł   t   wnixʷ   t
840.   (It feels) like   really

s-ən-wa?-wa?s-xən-mix   i?   s-ən-kł-ća?-sqáx̣a?,   uł
it left the ground   the   horse,   and

wa?-wil·   i?
he was weaving from side to side   the

s-ən-kł-ća?-sqáx̣a?,   lut   tə   s-q̓ˤà-p-s
horse,   (it) didn't   move

c-?x̣íł   t   ṇ-xa?-cín;   łíq̓ʷ-ət   i?
as (when)   it moves forward;   one can tell when   a

s-ən-kł-ća?-sqàx̣a?   ła?   c-qíc-əlx.
horse   is running.

841.   ti   kʷmíł   uł   ṇ-wis-əlx;   uł   ałi?
841.   All at once   it rose;

ṇ-ćip-ćəp-s-əm   uł   iwà?   k-ćí-ćəx̣ʷ-s-əm,   sta?
he shut his eyes   and   tried to   peek,

waẏ   wnixʷ   s-c-ən-wa?s-mix-əlx;   waẏ   ti   ilì?
       sure enough they're up in the air;

uł   ł-ən-ćíp-ćəp-s-əm,   təx̣ʷ   ł-ən-qʷ-qʷál-qʷəl-s-əm,
and   he shut his eyes,   he shut them lightly,

waẏ   x̣ʷúy?-ḷx.
       they went.

right next to the sky."
839. And so he went up in the air.
840. (It feels) like the horse really left the ground, and the horse was
     weaving from side to side, it didn't move as (when) it moves forward;
     one can tell when a horse is running.
841. All at once it rose; he shut his eyes and tried to peek, sure enough
     they're up in the air; and he shut his eyes, he shut them lightly, they
     went.

842. uɬ   lut   ṫəxʷ ṫə c-my-st-ìn ɬ k̓ʷìnx
842. And (I) don't   know   at what time

     ki? tək̓ʷ-k̓ʷa?-t-í?st-əlx, náxəmɬ waẏ q̓sà-p-i? i?
          they got started,   but   he's way

     s-n-əlk̓ʷ-k̓ʷ-əlx-íkəṅ-s.
     behind.

843. waẏ ?anwì-s waẏ c-?x̣ìɬ t s-ṫək̓ʷ-k̓ʷ-ùla?x̣ʷ
843.   He felt   as if   they hit the ground

     ɬ   təmx̣ʷ-úla?x̣ʷ; waẏ ṫək̓ʷ-k̓ʷ-úla?x̣ʷ-əlx, waẏ
     (on the ground);   yes they hit the ground,

     t-x̣ʷp-x̣ʷp-ús-əm;   waẏ wìk-s i? təmx̣ʷ-úla?x̣ʷ.
     he opened his eyes; he saw the country.

844. cù-nt-əm   axà? i? t kəwáp-s: "waẏ ṫi
844. He told him   his horse:

     kʷ   x̣ʷs-x̣ʷús-əlx,   lut
     "You do things in a hurry, don't

     a-k-s-q̓ʷ-q̓ʷíl-q̓ʷəl-t-əm, uɬ nixʷ lut
     waste time,   and   don't

     a-k-s-ən-ɬíp-t-əm axà? i? c̓əx̣ʷ-c̓x̣ʷ-ənt-s-ín;
     forget   what   I'm going to preach to you;

     kʷu ṇ-ləʕ̓ʷ-úɬt-xʷ,   i? lùt-i? t x̣àxʷ-t
          do exactly as I tell you,   not yet   dead are

     y a-s-k̓ʷìx̣-t-əm, pùt-i?   c-x̣ʷəl-x̣ʷál-t-əlx,
        your brothers, (they) are still alive,

     waẏ pənh-íẉs-ənt-əm.
          we're in time.

842. And I don't know at what time they got started, but he's way behind.
843. He felt as if they hit the ground; yes they hit the ground, he opened
     his eyes; he saw the country.
844. His horse told him: "You do things in a hurry, don't waste time, and
     don't forget what I'm going to preach to you; do exactly as I tell you,
     your brothers are not yet dead, they are still alive, we're in time.

845. uł nàxəmł lut a-k-s-ən-łip-t-əm i?
845.   But   don't forget   what

ċəxʷ-ċxʷ-ənt-s-ín, ṇ-ləˤʷ-ùs-ənt-xʷ i? ċəxʷ-ənt-s-ín,
I'm telling you,   do exactly as   I tell you,

ixì? mi   p   xʷəl-xʷál-t."
and (you) will all pull through."

846. wa̓y cù-s   i? lipúl-s: "há? ixì? há?
846. Then he said to the hen:

i-s-c-qʷəl-qʷìl-t?"
"Am I telling it right?"

847. cù-nt-əm   i? t lipúl, "wa̓y, ixì?
847. She told him the   hen, "Yes,

a-s-c-qʷəl-qʷíl-t,   wa̓y ixì? an-cáw-t;"
you're telling it right,   that's what you did;"

itlì? ł-qʷəl-qʷíl-t.
then he'd talk more.

848. cù-nt-əm   axà? i? t kəwáp-s: "nìṅwi? cəm
848. He told him   his horse:

ti   k̓ì-k̓a?t i? k-s-c-xʷúy-tət,   uł wa̓y ałì?
"Just a little   ways we are going,   and

t̓əxʷ-xʷ-əl-m-úla?xʷ, wa̓y k-s-ən-kʷa?c-míx-a?x;   cəm
it's changing,   it's going to be night; when

kʷu kə(ł)-ł?íq̓ʷ   ilì? c-wíx,   ixì?
we   come in sight there will be a house, that's

ṇ-?əłn-a?-s-qílxʷ-tṇ, pə-ptwínaxʷ, uł cəm wa̓y kʷu
the man-eater's,   an old lady, and when   we

845. But don't forget what I'm telling you, do exactly as I tell you, and you
will all pull through."
846. Then he said to the hen: "Am I telling it right?"
847. The hen told him, "Yes, you're telling it right, that's what you did;" then
he'd talk more.
848. His horse told him: "We're going just a little ways, and it's changing,
it's going to be night; when we come in sight there will be a house,
that's the man-eater's, an old lady, and when we

k̓əɫ-k̓ʷƛ̓à-p   məɫ   waẏ   kʷu
come in sight

c-wah-ənt-ìm   i?   t   k-kəw?áp-a?,   ixì?
they are going to bark at us   the   dogs,   they

aɫì?   i?   s-t-kʷəƛ̓-kʷƛ̓-ùs-tn̩-s   kəm̓   t̓ən-t̓ìna?-s   axà?
        are her eyes   and   her ears

n̩-?əɫn-a?-s-qílxʷ-tn̩.
(for) the man-eater.

849.   uɫ   waẏ   cəm̓   t̓i   əc-k-ʕàc̓-əst-əm-s
849.   And   she won't take her eyes off you

i?   t   n̩-?əɫn-a?-s-qílxʷ-tn̩;   alà?   kʷ
the   man-eater;   when   you

c-k̓ɫ-ən-k̓a?t-ìp   məɫ   c-ɫx̌ʷpá-m,   ixì?   uɫ
get close to the door   she'll run out,

míla?-n̩t-s,   cəm̓   cù-nt-s: '?à··msəm
she'll start baiting you,   she'll   tell you: 'Poor

s-ən-?íma?t,   waẏ   kʷ   c-kìc-x   kʷu   kíc-ənt-xʷ;   waẏ
grandchild,   you   got here   got to me;

t̓i   x̌às-t   kʷ   ɫ   púlx,   kʷu   n̩-pùlx-m-ənt-xʷ
   it's best   you   camp,   you camp with me

s-ən-?íma?t.'
grandchild.'

850.   cù-nt-xʷ: 'wáẏ,   waẏ   kən   s-ən-sìì-p-x
850.   You'll tell her: 'Yes,   yes   I   got lost

uɫ   lut   t̓ə   c-my-st-ìn   k̓a   ?kìn   kən   ɫ
and   (I) don't   know   where   I

come in sight the dogs are going to bark at us, they are her eyes and
her ears (for) the man-eater.

849. And the man-eater won't take her eyes off you; when you get close to
the door she'll run out, she'll start baiting you, she'll tell you: 'Poor
grandchild, you got here to me; it's best you camp, you camp with me
grandchild.'

850. You'll tell her: 'Yes, yes I got lost and I don't know where I

s–əc–xʷúy–x; uɬ way kən ṇ–x̣íɬ itlì? ɬ
was going; and I got scared to

i–k–s–xʷúy; uɬ alà? c–wìk–ɬt–s–ən c–wìx an–cítxʷ,
go on; and then I saw here your house,

i? kʷ in–xa?–x?ít; way kən púlx, ninwi?
my grandmother; yes, I will camp, and

ḷ s–x̣əl–x̣ʕàl–t mi itlì? kən xʷúy.'
in the daytime (I) will travel on.'

851. cəm cù–nt–s i? t pə–ptwínaxʷ: 'way,
851. She'll tell you the old lady:

way lím–ləm–t–x,' cəm ninwi? xʷìc̓–əɬt–s i?
'Oh, thank you,' (she) will give you the

laklí; cù–nt–əm, 'ixì? yə? cwìx, i?
key; she'll say, '(See) that building, the

s–ən–ɬəws–cqáx̣a?–tṇ, uɬ aɬì? c–laklí–st–ən,
barn, I always lock it,

cəm kən c–náq̓ʷ–əq̓ʷ, aɬì?
(they) might steal from me,

kɬ–psʕày–a? axà? ḷ təmxʷ–úla?xʷ.
there are lots of no good people here on earth.

852. uɬ way ilì? kɬ–ən–twìs–t s–ən–kɬ–c̓a?–sqáx̣a?,
852. There there are horses,

uɬ k̓im nàqs i? s–ən–tìɬ–x–tṇ–s yə?
and (there is) still one stall that's

c–x̣áq, uɬ ixì? ilì? mi kʷ
empty, and that's where (you) will

was going; and I got scared to go on; and then I saw here your house,
my grandmother; yes, I will camp, and in the daytime I will travel on.'
851. The old lady'll tell you: 'Oh, thank you,' she will give you the key; she'll
say, '(See) that building, the barn, I always lock it, they might steal from
me, there are lots of no good people here on earth.
852. There there are horses, and (there is) still one stall that's empty, and
that's where you will

ṇ-təł-x-sqáx̣aʔ-m̓.　ixìʔ　məł　n̓in̓wiʔ　iʔ　x̌ʷùy-st-x̌ʷ
put your horse,　　ixìʔ　　　　　　　　　you take there

y　an-kəwáp.'"
your horse.'"

853.　uł　cù-nt-əm　　　iʔ　t　kəwáp-s:　　"kʷu
853.　And　he told him　　　his horse:

x̌ʷùy-st-x̌ʷ　　　kʷu　ṇ-ʔúłx̌ʷ-st-x̌ʷ;　cəm̓　alàʔ
"You take me,　　put me there;　　as soon as

k̓ł-ən-k̓ahk̓ʷ-ìp-ənt-x̌ʷ　məł　sy-m-əncʕàt　　　　　iʔ
you open the door　　they'll start fussing　the

s-kəkʕákaʔ　məł　ṇ-p̓ʔàx̌ʷ　　　　yəʔ　ʔx̣iʔ　iʔ
birds,　　and　it will light up　　　　the

s-ən-t̓əws-cqáx̣aʔ-tṇ;　uł　ixìʔ　　iʔ　c̓ík̓ʷ-əsxən,　uł
barn;　　　　　　that's　　her lamp,　and

ixìʔ　　nix̌ʷ　s-t-k̓ʷəƛ̓-k̓ʷƛ̓-ús-tṇ-s,　uł　ixìʔ　nix̌ʷ
that's　also　her eyes,　　　　and

k̓əł-ləx̌ʷ-ncùt-(t)ṇ-s　ax̣àʔ　iʔ　ṇ-ʔəłn-aʔ-s-qílx̌ʷ-tṇ.
they warn　　ax̣àʔ　the　man-eater.

854.　cəm̓　wìk-ənt-x̌ʷ　　cəm̓　　　kʷ
854.　When　you see that　(it) will

ṇ-p̓aʔ-p̓aʔx̌ʷ-ús,　　cəm̓　nàx̣əmł　t-qʷaʔm-ús-m-ənt-x̌ʷ,
shine in your eyes,　　but　　you'll get used to it,

uł　wìk-ənt-x̌ʷ　　kʷə-k̓ʷrì-t　　　iʔ　s-kəkʕákaʔ."
and　you'll see that　they are golden　　birds."

855.　"t̓əx̌ʷ　ixìʔ　　incàʔ　laʔł　anwíʔ　ax̣àʔ
855.　"And　that's　me　　and　you,　(and) that's why

put your horse, you take there your horse.'"
853. And his horse told him: "You take me, put me there; as soon as you
open the door the birds'll start fussing, and the barn will light up; that's
her lamp, and that's also her eyes, and they warn the man-eater.
854. When you see that (it) will shine in your eyes, but you'll get used to
it, and you'll see that they are golden birds."
855. "And that's me and you, (and) that's why

i? kən əc-máy?-ncút."
I   am telling the story."

856. waý ilì?   ki? i? tə-twit axà? i?
856.   Right then   the boy,   the

səxʷ-ən-cíw-m, waý ilì? c-?x̣ìɬ   t s-qíɬ-t-x:
dish washer,   just like   he woke up:

"waý ixì?   in-càw-t axà? i? likùk
    "That's my story   the rooster

əc-máy?-ncút;"   ņ-ɬək̓ʷ-ək̓ʷ-mì-s yə-yˁà-t ixì? i?
is telling about;" he thought of   all

cáw-t-s.
he's done.

857. "waý ixì?   incà? nak̓ʷəm k̓ʷu
857.   "That's me

əc-máy?-st-ís."
he's telling a story about."

858. waý ixì? ņ-tìɬ-x-st-s i? kəwáp-s;
858.   So   he put up   his horse;

cù-nt-əm   i? t xa?-x?ít-s: "nìnwi?   axà?
he told him   his grand mother: "As soon as

kən ɬ-ən-?ùɬxʷ ņ-cíx̣-xt-m-ən,   ƛ̓əxʷ
I   go back in I'll warm something up for you,

k̓ʷúɬ-cən-(n)t-s-ən, uɬ nìnwi?   waý ɬ
I'll cook for you,   and (I) will have

i-k-s-p̓i?q-ìltən mi   kʷ ɬ-c-kíc-x; uɬ ixì?
everything ready when you get back;   and then

I am telling the story."

856. Right then the boy, the dish washer, just like he woke up: "That's my
story the rooster is telling about;" he thought of all he's done.

857. "That's me he's telling a story about."

858. So he put up his horse; his grand mother told him: "As soon as I go
back in I'll warm something up for you, I'll cook for you, and I will have
everything ready when you get back; and then

nàx̌əmɬ   kʷu   ɬ-xʷíc-əɬt-xʷ   in-laklí."
          you give me   my key."

859. cù-nt-əm   i?   t   kəwáp-s: "cù-nt-xʷ: 'waẏ
859. He said   his horse: "You tell her:

      lut   kʷ   ƚ   i-kɬ-əɬ-xʷíc-əɬt-əm,   uɬ   aɬi?   kən
      '(I) won't   give it back to you,   because   I

      s-qʷim̓-m̓-x   təl   i-s-k̓ʷ-k̓ʷíy-m-əlt,   ùɬi?   kən
      got scared   because   I am so little,   and   I

      qʷim̓-m̓   ɬ   i-k-s-ən-slí-p.
      got scared   to   get lost.

860. ùɬi?   kən   c-ʕ̓ʷimst   uɬ   ta?lí?   k-s-kʷàɬ-t
860. And then I   hurried   and   very much he sweat

      in-kəwáp;   uɬ   cəm̓   ɬ   siwst-əm-st-ən   kəm̓   ?am-t-ìn   t
      my horse;   and   if   I water it   or   feed it

      lawàn   ɬ   s-k-s-kʷáɬ-t-s,   uɬ   aɬi?   cəm̓
      oats   while he is sweating,   that will

      n̓-kəs-t-mí-s;   uɬ   nixʷ   axá?   lut   ƚ
      be bad for him; and another thing, (I) didn't

      ən-k̓ʷíxʷ-kn̓-n̓,   lut   ƚə   kɬ-tx-ílxʷ-ən.
      unsaddle him,   (I) didn't   comb him.

861. uɬ   aɬi?   cəm̓   n̓-skʷ-ìkən   cəm̓   ilí?
861.   Because (he) might   get a sore back

      c-k-s-kʷàɬ-t   ɬa?   n̓-k̓ʷíxʷ-kən-n̓;
      (if) while he's sweating   I take the saddle off;

      nàx̌əmɬ   ilí?   sa?ƚ-s-kʷàɬ-t
      but   (when) the sweat dries off

      you give me my key."

859. His horse said: "You tell her: 'I won't give it back to you, because I got
     scared because I am so little, and I got scared to get lost.

860. And then I hurried and my horse sweat very much; and if I water it
     or feed it oats while he is sweating, that will be bad for him; and
     another thing, I didn't unsaddle him, I didn't comb him.

861. Because he might get a sore back if I take the saddle off while he's
     sweating; but (when) the sweat dries off

ʔayxáxaʔ,   uɬ ixìʔ sic
in a little while,   then

n̓–k̓ʷíxʷ–kən̓–n̓;   ixìʔ mi   sic
I'll take the saddle off;   then (I) will

sìwst–əm–st–ən kəm̓ ʔam–t–ìn t lawán; uɬ
water him   and feed him   oats;   and

lut   t̓ə k–s–ən–k̓əs–t–mì–s uɬ lut   t̓ə
(that) won't   harm him   and (he) won't

k–s–ən–skʷ–íkən̓–s; ixìʔ mi   sic kɬ–tx–ílxʷ–əm;
get a sore back;   then (I) will   comb him;

ixìʔ n̓ìn̓wiʔ ɬ wiʔ–s–k̓ʷúl̓–n̓,   mi sic
       when   I get done working it,   then

ɬ–xʷìc̓–əɬt–s–ən   an–laklí, cəm̓
I'll give you back   your key,

xàr–kst–m–ənt–s–ən   itìʔ ɬaʔ ɬ–x̣lìt–ɬt–s–ən
(or) I'd be bothering you   asking again for

an–laklí.'
your key.'

862. lut   kʷu a–k–s–ən–k̓ʷíxʷ–kn̓–əm,   lut
862. Don't   take the saddle off me, don't

a–k–s–k̓ʷɬà–m iʔ laprít; uɬ ilìʔ kən
take off   the bridle;

c–kɬ–yə–yʕ–ílxʷ,   way̓ ti   mi kʷu
leave everything on me,   just

n̓–ʕac–ənt–íxʷ.
tie me there.

in a little while, then I'll take the saddle off; then I will water him and
feed him oats; and (that) won't harm him and he won't get a sore back;
then I will comb him; when I get done working it, then I'll give you back
your key, (or) I'd be bothering you asking you again for your key.'
862. Don't take the saddle off me, don't take off the bridle; leave everything
on me, just tie me there.

863. waỷ ałì? cəṁ   taʔlì? p kł–cáw–t   mi
863.   (You) will   quite   a time have

   p łíx̣ʷp̓–ət,   nak̓ʷà? t̓ùl   ixì? yə?
     getting away,   she's quite fierce   the

   ṇ–ʔəłn–aʔ–s–qílxʷ–tṇ, nìnẁi?   taʔlì? p
   man-eater,   (you) will   quite

   kł–cáw–t.
   a time have.

864. uł nìnẁi? kʷu ła? ṇ–k̓ʷíxʷ–kən–(n)t–xʷ
864. And if   you take the saddle off me

   uł lut   a–k–s–t–k̓ì–ka?t kʷu ł
     (you) won't   have time to

   a–kł–ł–ən–tk̓ʷ–ik̓ṇ–əm, kʷu ł a–kł–əł–laprít–əm, mi
   put the saddle on me,   (and) the bridle,

   uł c–k–c̓əl–mí–łəm–s; uł axà? myàł kʷ
   and she'll be there; and   you

   x̣ʷúp–t;   axà?–ṃ y a–s–k̓ʷìλ–t–əm waỷ x̣λ–áλ,
   are not able;   your brothers   are grown,

   uł ałi? waỷ wi?–s–ən–k̓ʷəxʷ–ki?–sqàx̣a?–ṃ–əlx   uł
           they already took the saddles off

   nàx̣əmł waỷ sy–sy–ús–əlx.
   but   they are smart.

865. waỷ cəṁ   ṇ–łìp–t–əm–s axà? i?
865. Then (she) will forget   the

   pə–ptwìnaxʷ   i? laklí–s; ixì? kʷ
   old lady (about) the key;   when you

863. You will have quite a time getting away, the man-eater's quite fierce,
    you will have quite a time.
864. And if you take the saddle off me you won't have time to put the saddle
    on me, (and) the bridle, and she'll be there; and you are not able; your
    brothers are grown, they already took the saddles off but they are smart.
865. Then the old lady will forget about the key; when you

wiʔ-cìn   məł cù-nt-s,   'waẏ kʷ
get done eating   she'll say to you,

i-s-kíw-lx-st-əm,   kʷ i-s-màyaʔ-łt-əm y
'I'll take you upstairs,   I'll show you

a-k-s-ən-łq̇ʷ-út-(t)ṇ.'"
where you are going to sleep.'"

866. cù-s,   "waẏ."
866. He said, "I'll do it."

867. waẏ wníxʷ,   ti   kəl-k̇ʷíλ-əp-t-əlx,
867.   Sure enough, as soon as they came in sight,

waẏ ti lut   s-ək-s-c-xʷúy-s, waẏ c-wìx
          (they) hadn't gone far,   there was

iʔ cítxʷ, waẏ c-k-ċík-əs, waẏ c-ən-ṗʔáxʷ, waẏ
a house,   it's lit up,   it's bright,

ałìʔ uł k-saʕ-ús-əs.
          and the sun had gone down.

868. nìkxnaʔ iʔ k-kəwʔàp-aʔ c-sy-m-əncʕát,
868. Gee   the dogs   made a big fuss,

c-wah-ənt-ís-əlx.
they barked.

869. waẏ ti təł-m-əncùt   ik̇lìʔ kəl
869.   He went straight for

cítxʷ,   uł k̇ł-ən-łaʔ-íp,   uł ti
the house,   got up to the house, and just

put   k̇ł-ən-łaʔ-ìp   uł c-łx̣ʷp̀à-m   iʔ
as soon as he got to the door   she came out the

get done eating she'll say to you, 'I'll take you upstairs, I'll show you
where you are going to sleep.'"
866. He said, "I'll do it."
867. Sure enough, as soon as they came in sight, they hadn't gone far, there
    was a house, it's lit up, it's bright, and the sun had gone down.
868. Gee the dogs made a big fuss, they barked.
869. He went straight for the house, got up to the house, and just as soon
    as he got to the door the old lady

pə-ptwínaxʷ: "waẏ s-ən-ʔíma?t kʷu c-kíc-ənt-xʷ,
old lady: "Oh, grandchild,   you got here,

pna? kʷ s-c-ən-slí-p-x kəm mət   kʷu
maybe you are lost   or   maybe

a-s-ən-k̇əw-p-ìls-əm   ùłi? kʷu c-t-xʷúy-m-ənt-xʷ;
you get lonesome for me and so   you came to see me;

waẏ lìm-ləm-t-x uł kʷu c-kíc-ənt-xʷ; waẏ alà? kʷu
    thank you   for   coming;

ṇ-púlx-m-ənt-xʷ,   məł k̇ʷən-k̇ʷənx-àsq̇ət
camp with me,   and (stay) a few days (until)

xi?-mìx kʷ ła?xʷ-ískit, mət   təl   łkʷ-ùt   kʷ
whenever you get rested, I guess from far away you

łə c-xʷúy-x."
come."

870. cù-s,   "waẏ, ałì? lut   łə
870. He told her, "Yes,   (I) don't

c-my-st-ìn axà? i? təmxʷ-úla?xʷ; uł cəm   kən
know   this   country;   and (I) will

slì-p   axà? ḷ s-ən-kʷə-kʷ?àc ł i-k-s-xʷy-lwís.
get lost   in the night   if I travel around.

871. uł ta?lì?   kən ṇ-x̣ìł ałì?   kən
871. And (I'm) very   scared because I

s-k̇ʷə-k̇ʷíy-m-əlt; waẏ alà? kən púlx."
am little;   here I   will camp."

872. cù-nt-əm, "waẏ kʷìn-(n)t-xʷ in-laklí,
872. She said,   "Take   my key,

said: "Oh, grandchild, you got here, maybe you are lost or maybe you get lonesome for me and so you came to see me; thank you for coming; camp with me, and (stay) a few days (until) whenever you get rested, I guess you come from far away."

870. He told her, "Yes, I don't know this country; and I will get lost in the night if I travel around.

871. And I'm very scared because I am little; I will camp here."

872. She said, "Take my key,

ikli?　　　　　i?　s-ən-ṫəws-cqáx̌a?-tṇ,"　c̓q̓ʷ-əstúɫt-əm,
over there is　the　barn,　　　　　　　　she pointed,

"aɫi?　　　n-yˤip　c-laklí-st-ən　aɫi?
"because　always　I lock it,　　because

kɫ-psˤay-a?　　　　axà?　ɬ　təmx̌ʷ-úla?x̌ʷ,　cəṁ　kən
there are bad people　　in　the world,

c-náq̓ʷ-əq̓ʷ,　　　　s-c-?x̌ìl-x　ki?　əc-laklì-st-ən　i?
they steal from me,　that's why　　I always lock　the

s-ən-ṫəws-cqáx̌a?-tṇ;　uɫ　ilì?　kən
barn;　　　　　　　and　there　I

k-s-ən-kʷúm-m-ən,　　　ɬ　an-ṫək̓ʷ-ki?-sqàx̌a?-tṇ　ɬ
have a place to put away　your saddle (and)

an-laprít;　　təxʷ　ilì?　k-ɫìxʷ-p-ənt-xʷ
your bridle;　　　hang them up,

c-k-c̓l-álqʷ.
there are some pegs.

873. uɫ　way̓　　ilì?　kɫ-ən-ṫwìs-t
873. And　already　there　are

s-ən-kɫ-c̓a?-sqáx̌a?,　uɫ　k̓im　　　　neqs-lùp　ilì?
horses there,　　　but　there's still　one stall

c-ən-x̌áq;　ilì?　mi　　　　ṇ-?ùɫxʷ-st-x-xʷ　an-kəwáp.
empty;　　there　(you) will　put　　　　your horse.

874. uɫ　ilì?　kən　kɫ-tx-ylxʷ-sqáx̌a?-tṇ,
874. And　　I　have something to comb your horse,

kɫ-tx-ìlxʷ-ənt-xʷ　an-kəwáp,　　kʷ　ɫ
you can comb　　　your horse,

over there is the barn, she pointed, "because always I lock it, because
there are no good people in the world, they steal from me, that's why
I always lock the barn; and there I have a place to put away your saddle
(and) your bridle; hang them up, there are some pegs.

873. And already there are horses there, but there's still one stall empty;
you will put your horse there.

874. And I have something to comb your horse, you can comb your horse,

wiʔ-s-ən-kʷəxʷ-kiʔ-sqàx̣aʔ-m̩   məɫ
when you get done taking off the saddle and

wiʔ-s-ʔam-t-íxʷ; uɫ ixì? uɫ kʷúl-cən-(n)t-s-ən,
feeding him; and then   I'll cook for you,

cìx-ɫt-s-ən   y a-k-s-c-ʔíɫən."
I'll warm for you   something to eat."

875. cù-s, "wáy̓," uɫ ixì? kʷì-s i? laklí,
875. He said, "OK," and then he took the key,

way̓ s-xʷùy-s i? kəl s-ən-ɫəws-cqáx̣aʔ-tn̩.
and went   to the barn.

876. ɫi alà?   kɫ-ən-k̓ahk̓ʷ-ìp-s alà?
876.   The minute he opened the door

sy-m-əncˤàt   i? likùk i?
they started making a fuss the rooster, the

s-kəkˤáka?.
birds.

877. way̓ qʷím̓-m̩;   iwà? s-taʔx̣il-x   uɫ
877.   He got startled;   he went like that

aɫì? n̩-p̓aʔ-p̓aʔxʷ-ús,   way̓ lut   ɫə
because it shone in his eyes,   (he) couldn't

k-my-my-p-ùs-əm-s uɫ aɫì?
make out what they were because

n̩-p̓aʔ-p̓aʔxʷ-ús.
they shone in his eyes.

878. ixì? sic t-qʷaʔm-ús-əm-s, há?
878.   Then he got used to them, what is

when you get done taking off the saddle and feeding him; and then I'll
cook for you, I'll warm for you something to eat."
875. He said, "OK," and then he took the key, and went to the barn.
876. The minute he opened the door the rooster, the birds started making
a fuss.
877. He got startled; he went like that because it shone in his eyes, he
couldn't make out what they were because they shone in his eyes.
878. Then he got used to them, what is

s-c-ʔkin-x̓?
the matter?

879. nak̓ʷ-əm axà? i? təl s-kəkˁàka? kə?
879. It's from those chickens that

c-p̓ˁáx̌ʷ, uɬ k-əlkʷ-ák̓ʷ; n̓ta? la n-yx̌ʷ-ùt
it shines, and it goes a long ways; gee, inside

uɬ taɬ-t s-c-ʔx̌iɬ t s-x̌əl-x̌ˁál-t.
it's just like daylight.

880. way̓ t̓i ilì? ˁac-ənt-ìs i? kəwáp-s,
880. He tied his horse,

lut t̓ə síwst-əm-st-s; way̓ laklí-s ixì?
(he) didn't water it; he locked and

ɬəɬ-x̌ʷúy-s.
went back.

881. ɬ-kíc-x, way̓ c-wi?-s-kɬ-sàl
881. He got back, and there is already on the table

i? k-s-c-ʔíɬən-s.
his meal.

the matter?
879. It's from those chickens that it shines, and it goes a long ways; gee,
    inside it's just like daylight.
880. He tied his horse, he didn't water it; he locked and went back.
881. He got back, and his meal is already on the table.

APPENDIX II

[Corresponds approximately to sentences 421-431 of the text.]

882. "waẏ kʷ s-x̣lìt-əm-s   i? tə ylmíxʷəm."
882.   "He wants you the   king."

883. "sta? lút; c-ən-k̓əs-k̓s-ùs-(s)t-ṇ yə? ylmìxʷəm
883. "Heck no;   I'm too ugly for   the   king

kəm̓ i? s-qílxʷ, cəm̓   kʷu c̓a?x-m-ís;
or   the people, (they) will   get ashamed of me;

waẏ myàɬ   kən k-t̓əɬ-ɬ-íc̓a?, axà? kən
     (I am) too   dirty,   I'm just

səxʷ-k̓ʷúl-əm-s."
his working boy."

884. cu-nt-əm-əlx,   "lút," waẏ ixì?
884. They told him,   "No,"

kəm̓-km̓-àx̣-s-əlx   uɬ c-xʷùy-st-s-əlx uɬ
they grabbed him by the arms and they took him   and

ṇ-?úɬxʷ-st-s-əlx;   uɬ waẏ ilì? c-kɬ-c̓àlxʷ
they brought him in; and   there was a chair

s-ən-kɬ-mút-(t)ṇ-s.
for him to sit down.

885. waẏ ixì? x̣s-t-wìlx   axà? i? kʷə-kʷrì-t
885.   Then it was satisfied   the   Golden

882. "The king wants you."
883. "Heck no; I'm too ugly for the king or the people, they will get ashamed
     of me; I am too dirty, I'm just his working boy."
884. They told him, "No," they grabbed him by the arms and they took him
     and they brought him in; and there was a chair for him to sit down.

i? tkɫm-ìlxʷ   i?   s-pu?-ús-c,   uɫ   aɫì?   wa̓y̓   k̓əl
Woman's   heart,

tə-twìt   i?   x̣m-ínk-s;   n̩-st-ìls: "uɫ   aɫì?
the boy   she likes;   she thought:

mìnà   təl   tanm̓ùs   wa̓y̓   mət
"I guess it isn't   for   nothing   he must be

s-yə̓ʕʷ-p-yáw-t-x,   ki?   kʷu   kʷən-nú-s;   lut
powerful,   that's why   he caught me;   no

swìt   kʷu   t̓ə   c-wík-st-s,   uɫ   t   cnìɫc   kʷu
body   has ever seen me,   but   he

wík-s   ùɫi?   kʷu   kʷí-s.
saw me   and   he took me.

886.   wa̓y̓   mət   sy-sy-ùs   ixí?   wa̓y̓
886.   (He) must   be very smart   even

s-tə-tw̓ít-s.
as young as he is.

887.   uɫ   axà?   ylmíxʷəm,   ixì?   iwà?   t̓əxʷ
887.   And   this   king,   even if

ylmíxʷəm,   uɫ   lut   i-k-s-k-tím,
he is a king,   (I) won't   get anything out of him,

wa̓y̓   ɫəx̣-ɫəx̣-p-út-əm;   wa̓y̓   t̓i   axà?   i?   k̓əl
he's too old;   way   for

tə-tw̓ìt   i-s-pu?-ús."
the young boy   I'll go."

888.   wa̓y̓   ƛlá-p-əlx.
888.   They all settled down.

885. Then the Golden Woman's heart was satisfied, she likes the boy; sh
     thought: "I guess it isn't for nothing he must be powerful, that's wh
     he caught me; nobody has ever seen me, but he saw me and he too
     me.
886. He must be very smart even as young as he is.
887. And this king, even if he is a king, I won't get anything out of hir
     he's too old; I'll go for the young boy."
888. They all settled down.

APPENDIX III

[Corresponds approximately to sentences 521-538 of the text.]

889. waẏ ixì? ti wi?-cìn   uł   ixì?
889.   He got done eating and   then

   t-k̓əw-ḷx-ús-ənt-əm;   waẏ wìk-s   ti
   she took him upstairs;   he saw that

   nəqs-ìłca?   yə? ṇ-wís-t,   waẏ ilì? ki?
   it's all one room the   upstairs,

   c-kł-xк̓-m-ìlx   i?   s-ən-łq̓ʷ-út-(t)ṇ.
   they are all in a row   the beds.

890. níkxna? axà? sˤaẏ   i? s-k̓ʷíк̓-t-əm-s;
890. My,   they are noisy   his brothers;

   ixì? ta?xʷ-s-c-mrəm-mrìm ixí? uł
         they all have women   and

   s-c-pu?-?əcki?-scút-a?x-əlx,   s-c-?íckṇ-a?x-əlx.
   they are playing with their women, they're playing.

891. axà? i? s-x?ìt-x   waẏ
891.   The oldest one is already

   k-s-ənk̓ʷ-əł-łq̓ʷ-lút,   uł axà? itlì? i? t
   in bed with a partner, and

   k̓ì-ka?t   uł ixì? nixʷ k-s-ənk̓ʷ-əł-łq̓ʷ-lút,
   the next one   also has a bed partner,

889. He got done eating and then she took him upstairs; he saw that it's
     all one room the upstairs, the beds are all in a row.
890. My, his brothers are noisy; they all have women and they are playing
     with their women, they're playing.
891. The oldest one is already in bed with a partner, and the next one also
     has a bed partner,

tkɬm-ílxʷ,   uɬ   axà?   i?   qə?-ìẇs   ixì?
a woman,   and   the in between one

k-s-ənkʷ-əɬ-ɬqʷ-lút,   yə-yʕà-t   s-wi?-wi?-númt-x.
has a bed partner,   they're all good looking.

892. uɬ   axà?   ɬ   k-s-ən-ɬqʷ-út-(t)ṇ-s,   i?
892. And   in his bed,

cáqʷ-s-ənt-əm,   ixì?   ti   kmìx   k-náqs.
she pointed,   there's only one person.

893. cù-nt-əm: "ixì?   axà?   a-kɬ-cìtxʷ
893. She said: "That's   your place,

a-k-s-ən-ɬqʷ-út-(t)ṇ;   waẏ   ixì?   wi?-s-máya?-ɬt-s-ən,
your bed;   now   I'm done showing you,

uɬ   waẏ   kən   ?aw-s-púlx,   kən   ?áyxʷ-t;"   ixì?
and I   am going to bed,   I   am tired;"   and

ɬ-sàxʷ-t   axà?   i?   pə-ptwínaxʷ.
she went down   the   old lady.

894. waẏ   uɬ   aɬì?   c-?xìɬ   tə
894.   Just like

yìxʷ-ús-ənt-əm,   uɬ   ṇ-ɬìp-t-əm-s   i?   laklí-s,
they covered her face,   and she forgot   her key,

lut   tə   ɬ-xlít-s.
she didn't   ask for it back.

895. waẏ   ti   xʷùs-əska?-m-ənt-əm   axà?   i?   t
895.   She was in a hurry

k-s-ənkʷ-əɬ-ɬqʷ-lút-s,   "waẏ   xʷs-ma?-cín-m-ənt-əm."
his bed partner,   "Hurry!"

a woman, and the in between one has a bed partner, they're all good
looking.
892. And in his bed, she pointed, there's only one person.
893. She said: "That's your place, your bed; now I'm done showing you, and
I am going to bed, I am tired;" and the old lady went down.
894. Just like somebody covered her face, and she forgot her key, she didn't
ask for it back.
895. His bed partner was in a hurry, "Hurry!"

896. cù-s: "lút, waẏ t̓əxʷ k̓əɬ-ʔím-ənt-xʷ,
896. He said to her: "Wait a minute,

   uɬ waẏ kən k-s-k̓aʔkín-aʔx."
   where am I going?."

897. cù-nt-əm   i? t kəwáp-s: "waẏ t̓i axà?
897. He had told him   his horse:

   an-t-qəl-tk-ìc̓a?   y a-s-x̣íƛ-xən,   uɬ mət uc
   "Your top clothes,   your trousers,   maybe

   t̓əxʷ y an-lasmís,   lut   a-k-s-xʷt-əlscút,   waẏ t̓i
   your shirt,   don't   take them off,

   kmix an-q̓ə?-xán; uɬ ixì? k-s-mi?-máy?-t-s,
   only   your shoes;   go through the motions,

   ninwi? nàx̣əmɬ ɬəxʷ-p-ənt-ìxʷ   y a-k-s-ɬq̓-əlx-álqs,
       but   put on top of them   your night shirt,

   uɬ axà? k-ɬəxʷ-p-ìna?-n̓t-xʷ y a-s-t-təm̓-tím̓;
       put it over   your clothes;

   lut   t̓ə k-s-mi?-nù-ɬt-s-əlx i? t
   she won't   know the difference   the

   n̓-?əɬn-a?-s-qílxʷ-tn̓.
   man-eater.

898. uɬ ixì? ninwi? t̓i lut k-s-q̓ə-q̓sá-p-i?-s,
898. And   don't make it to long,

   məɬ t-x̣?ən-cən-mìst-m-ənt-xʷ   y a-s-ənkʷ-əɬ-ɬq̓ʷ-lút,
       tell her to leave you alone   your bed partner,

   cù-nt-xʷ, 'wáẏ, waẏ   kʷu cí?-skʷ,   waẏ
   tell her,   'Please   leave me alone,

896. He said to her: "Wait a minute, I'm not going anywhere (lit. where am I going?.)."

897. His horse had told him: "Your top clothes, your trousers, maybe your shirt, don't take them off, only your shoes; go through the motions, but put your night shirt on top of them, put it over your clothes; the man-eater won't know the difference.

898. And don't make it to long, tell your bed partner to leave you alone, tell her, 'Please leave me alone,

aɬìʔ   lut   ƛ i-s-qʷʔám,
because (I) am not   used to this kind of business,

i-s-xʷy-lwìs   i-s-k-ʔəmt-íws   waẏ kən
I've been traveling around,   riding around,   I

ʔáyx̣ʷ-t,   kən k-ʔəyx̣ʷ-t-íws; kən k-s-ɬaʔxʷ-iskit-aʔx,
am tired,   saddle weary;   I   want to rest,

kən k-s-ʔítx.'
    (and) sleep.'

899. uɬ   aɬìʔ cəm ʕay-ʕay-ìnk-ənt-s   uɬ
899. And   She'll tickle your belly   and

xp-ús-ənt-s,   lut k-s-kəmʔ-íkxt-əm-s, uɬ   ixìʔ
chew your face,   she'll do everything, but

ƛiʔ   kʷ s-c-qʷìl-əm-s xʷùs   kʷ
(she's) just   faking you   in a hurry

k-s-ʔítx-aʔx;   waẏ məɬ ixìʔ k̓ʷaʔ-k̓ʷùɬ-ənt-xʷ
to put you to sleep;   and then play

kʷ x̣ʷáq̓ʷ-əlqs-əm, kʷ ʔət-ʔətx-àyaʔ kʷ
  snore,   you play sleep

x̣ʷáq̓ʷ-əlqs-əm, wim   k-s-qs-qs-ìnk-ənt-s
(and) snore,   for nothing she'll scratch your belly

axàʔ iʔ t a-s-ənkʷ-əɬ-ɬq̓ʷ-lút, məɬ cəm cniɬc nixʷ
       your bed partner,   and   she   also

k-s-ʔítx.
will get sleepy.

900. kʷ   sy-m-scùt   lut   a-k-s-ʔítx,   waẏ
900. You do your best (and) don't fall asleep,

because I am not used to this kind of business, I've been traveling
around, riding around, I am tired, saddle weary; I want to rest, (and)
sleep.'

899. And She'll tickle your belly and chew your face, she'll do everything,
but she's just faking you to put you to sleep in a hurry; and then play
snore, you play sleep (and) snore, for nothing your bed partner'll scratch
your belly, and she also will get sleepy.

900. You do your best (and) don't fall asleep,

cə̇m ƛ̇i kʷ   ʔìtx   ixì? uⱡ p   n̦-ċəs-p-úla?xʷ
if   you sleep   you are all goners,

yə-yˁà-t p   ƛ́áxʷ-t;   huy mət ƛ̇i c-t-xⱡ̇-əst-ís,
all   dead ducks;   watch her close,

waẏ ƛ̇i   x̣ʷàq̇ʷ-əlqs-əm   uⱡ   nìn̦wi? iwà?
       as soon as she starts snoring and

yr-ənt-ìxʷ   uⱡ lut   k-s-yum̦-míst-ș, ixì? mi
you push her and (she) won't even move,   then

kʷ   xʷⱡ̇-ílx, məⱡ qìⱡ-ənt-xʷ-əlx axà? y
you jump up   and wake up

a-s-k̇ʷíƛ̇-t-əm."
your brothers."

if you sleep you are all goners, all dead ducks; watch her close, as soon
as she starts snoring and you push her and she won't even move, then
you jump up and wake up your brothers."

APPENDIX IV

[Corresponds approximately to sentences 544-552 of the text.]

901. ul   put   k̓lá-p-əlx,   wa'y
901. And just as they settled down,

   c-k̓əl-nixəl-lx tla   yxʷ-út   ti c-xʷt-ilx
   they heard   from downstairs   someone get up

   təl s-ən-lq̓ʷ-út-(t)n̦; wa'y k-cik-s-ənt-əm i?
   from the bed;   she lit   the

   cikʷ-əsxən; wa'y ixi? s-c-t-kíw-lx-s,   wa'y
   lamp;   she was coming up the steps,

   lut   s-ən-ləx-cín-s, ti kmix tə
   it wasn't too loud,

   c-xək-xk-ilx   i? t s-ən-t-kíw-lx-tn̦, ul ali?
   something rubbing   on the stairs   because

   k-k̓a?l-i?st cəm k̓əl-ql-əl-t-numt i? tu?-twit.
   she sneaks   (not to) wake up the boys.

902. "ul   cəm ninwi?   wik-lt-p c-kʷis-kʷs-(s)t-s
902. "And   (you) will see that she's holding

   axà? i? t-xr-ikst-(t)n̦ i? cikʷ-əsxən, ul axà? kəl
   a   dangling   lantern,   and   in

   sk̓ʷùt   kl-ən-sp-ùs-tn̦ c-kʷis-kʷs-(s)t-s,
   the other (hand) a sword   she is holding,

901. And just as they settled down, they heard someone get up from the
bed downstairs; she lit the lamp; she was coming up the steps, it wasn't
too loud, something rubbing on the stairs, something that was coming
up, because she sneaks (not to) wake up the boys.

902. "And you will see that she's holding a dangling lantern, and in the other
(hand) she is holding a sword,

ixì? məł axà? xa?t-əm-st-ìs i? s-x?ít-x waẏ uł
    and   she comes to   the oldest,

ałì?   k̓li? yə? c-k-cəhá-m,   ixì? məł
because   she faces him,   and

ŋ-xl-ús-əs,   məł itlì? łt̓àp   i?
she'll chop his head off, and   it'll come off

ca?sì-qən-s i? təl s-qíl-tk-s, uł ti ilì?
his head   from his body,   and

xʷrà··-p   i? s-qíl-tk-s, łət̓-ła?t̓àp
it will quiver   his body,   jump up and down

məł   cə̓m k̓l-əl-p-íłca?."
and then   it will stop."

[Corresponds to sentences 559-560 of the text.]

903. "uł ixì? t̓i kmìx   c-łìxʷ-p-ənt-xʷ
903.   "(You will) just slip on

an-q̓ə?-xán; uł ałì? miǹà   lut kł-púts-əlx
your shoes; but (they) probably   have boots

k-s-x̣ƛ̓-x̣iƛ̓-xən-m-əlx i? q̓ə?-xán-s-əlx,
leg high   boots,

ixì?   ałì? ḷ s-k-?əmt-íws, yə?
that's what (they use)   on horseback,   that

c-cə̓m-cm-ípa?łxən, i? kł-ws-ws-xən-cín-xən, yə?
have sharp heels, that have a high top,   that

and she comes to the oldest, because she faces him, and she'll chop his
head off, and his head'll come off from his body, and his body will quiver,
jump up and down and then it will stop."

903. "You (will) just slip on your shoes; but they probably have boots, leg
high boots, that's what (they use) on horseback, the ones that have sharp

lut   tə   kɬ-k-ɬˤaʔx̣-ikən-(n)t-əm,   ixiʔ   t
don't   have lace,   that's what   in

ən-qʷəl-qʷil-tṇ-tət   yəʔ   c-ʔùm-st-əm   iʔ   t
our language   we call

n-ws-ws-t-ipɬxən   t   q̇aʔ-xán,   uɬ   axàʔ   iʔ   t
high heeled   shoes,   and   in

s-wyàpix   ixiʔ   púts."
English   boots."

[Corresponds approximately to sentences 107-114 and 590-598 of the text.]

904.   axàʔ   iʔ   s-x̣ʔit-x   əc-x̣ʔít,   uɬ
904.   The   oldest   took the lead,   and

ʔaw-t-p-àɬq-əlx   axàʔ   iʔ   k̇ʷiλ-ət;   waẏ   iʔ
they are following him   the   others;   the

s-tə-t?iw-t-aʔx   axàʔ   c-ʔíw-t,   kɬ-cáw-t,
youngest one   is way behind,   trying,

qc-c-əlx-iʔpustxən   iʔ   t   s-ən-k̇aʔt-kṇ-áɬq.
stumbling   to   keep up.

905.   waẏ   kɬ-ən-caʔ-íp-əlx,   waẏ
905.   They knocked on the door,

c-kɬ-ən-q̇ʔ-íp,   iʔ   s-yləmxʷ-iɬxʷ.
there's a sign on the door,   it was the   king's house.

906.   waẏ   kɬ-ən-caʔ-íp-m-əlx,
906.   They knocked at the door,

heels, that have a high top, that don't have lace, that's what in our
language we call high heeled shoes, and in English boots.

904. The oldest took the lead, and the others are following him; the youngest
one is way behind, trying, stumbling to keep up.
905. They knocked on the door, there was a sign on the door, (it was) the
king's house.
906. They knocked at the door,

k̓ɬ–ən–k̓ahk̓ʷ–ìp–ɬt–m–əlx   i?   tə   ylmíxʷəm;
he opened the door for them   the   king;

cù–nt–m–əlx: "t̓i   s–my–s–qìlxʷ   ḷ?íw–m̓p,   uɬ
he said: "Important people   is your father,

t̓i   ḷ   təm̓–tm̓–ùt–(t)n–əmp   uɬ   wa̓y̓   súxʷ–ɬm–ən."
just   by   your clothes   I can tell."

907.   cù–s–əlx: "wa̓y̓,"   ?ùm–la?xʷ–s–əlx
907.   "That's right,"   they named the place

tla   ?kìn   t   təmxʷ–úla?xʷ,   mət   təl
from   where (they were),   the country,   maybe

kíwa,   minà   təl   ņ–ca?líwm,   cù–nt–m–əlx,   "wa̓y̓
Kewa,   not   from   Inchelium,   they told him,   "A big

sìlxʷa?   táwn."
"A big   town."

[Corresponds approximately to sentences 121–125 and 607–607 of the text.]

908.   "wa̓y̓   t̓əxʷ   iwà?   kən   q̓xʷ–ìls   ixì?   k̓əl
908.   "I wish   I   could

s–k̓ʷúl–ɬxʷ–əm,   uɬ   kʷa   anwì?   kʷ   ylmíxʷəm,
do house building,   and   you   are the boss,

kʷa   c–my–st–ìxʷ   lut   nàqs   ixì?   t̓ə
     you know that   not   the same thing

c–k̓ʷùl–st–s   k̓əm   i?   t–k–?əs–?asíl,   uɬ   wa̓y̓
can do   two people,   it's got to be

the king opened the door for them; he said: "Your father is important
people, just by your clothes I can tell."
907. "That's right," they named the place from where (they were), the
country, maybe Kewa, not from Inchelium, they told him, "A big town."

908. "I wish I could do house building, and you are the boss, you know that
two people cannot do the same thing,

ƛi   k-nàqs   kɫ-ylmíxʷəm,   uɫ   waẏ   axà?
just   one person   to be boss,   and

incà?   iḱlì?   i?   t-ḱɫ-ḱa?t   i?   ḱəl
I (will take)   what's   close   to

s-ḱʷúɫ-ɫxʷ-əm,   i?   s-míƛ-əɫxʷ-əm.
house building,   house painting.

909. kʷa   ʕác-ənt,   úc   wi?-st-ìp   sic   i?
909. Because,   look,   whenever   you finish   a new

cítxʷ,   kəm   i?   s-ən-ƛəws-cqáx̣a?-tṇ,   məɫ   axà?   i?
house,   or   a   barn,   then   the

səxʷ-mìƛ-əɫxʷ-əm   ixí?   uɫ   ixì?   s-míƛ-əɫxʷ-əm-s,   lut
painter   has to paint it,   not

axà?   i?   səxʷ-ḱʷùɫ-əɫxʷ-əm   ƛə   c-míƛ-əɫxʷ-əm,
       the   carpenter   that does the painting,

put   la   ?ḱìn   yaʕ-p-cín,   ki?
only   when   they get hard up,

yaʕ-p-cn-(n)ù-nt-əm   ki?   c-míƛ-əɫxʷ-m-əlx."
(they get hard up)   that   they will paint."

it's got to be just one person to be boss, and I (will take) what's close
to house building, house painting.

909. Because, look, whenever you finish a new house, or a barn, then the
painter has to paint it, it's not the carpenter that does the painting,
only when they get hard up will they paint."

APPENDIX V

[Corresponds approximately to sentences 130-137 of the text.]

910. "waẏ iwà?   χm–ìnk–ən axà? i?
910.   "(I) would have liked

   s–k̓ʷúl–əłxʷ–əm uł axà? i? s–mík̓–əłxʷ–əm, uł ałi?
   carpentry   or   house painting,   but

   qʷən̓–cìn   kən s–t?ìw–t–x   uł ałi?
   it's a pity that I   am the youngest and

   xa?ìt–t–əlx   axà? i? s–xa?–x?ít–x.
   got first choice   the oldest ones.

911. ixì? kʷí–s–əlx;   uł lut   kʷu
911.   They took them; and it can't be

   k–s–t–k–?əs–?asìl–s ļ nàqs   s–c–k̓ʷúl; uł ałi?
   two of us   at the same job;   because

   ylmìxʷəm   ļ?íw–tət,   uł cəm̓ kʷu ła?
   he's a king   our father, and   when

   ł–yàʕ–p   uł kʷu síw–ənt–əm: 'uł stim̓ i?
   we get back   he'll ask us: 'What

   s–c–my–p–nw–íłn–əmp?'
   did you learn?'

912. waẏ ti χàs–t   kʷu ła? c–pχʷà–m
912.   It's better that we   diversify

910. "I would have liked carpentry or house painting, but it's a pity that
   I am the youngest and the oldest ones got first choice.
911. They took them; and two of us can't be at the same job; because our
   father is a king, and when we get back he'll ask us: 'What did you learn?'
912. It's better that we diversify

i?   k–s–my–p–nwiłən–tət;   way̓   tᶿxʷ   s–ta?–ł–wl–wlím,
what   we learn;   blacksmithing,

ixì?   i–k–s–c–k̓ʷúl."
that's   my job."

913.   cù–nt–əm   i?   t   ylmíxʷəm: "way̓   kli?   k̓əl
913.   He told him   the   king: "Way   to

s–pùƛ–əm–s   yə?   c–ən–x̣q–íws   ilì?   ki?
the other end of   the   open place   that's   where

c–wíx,   uł   ałì?   ixì?   c–x̣q–úla?xʷ,
he lives,   because   there's lots of room there,

kʷa   ałì?   axà?   lut   tᶿ   c–xʷək̓ʷ–xʷàk̓ʷ–ət   i?
     because   it's never   clean   the

s–ən–ta?–ł–wl–wlím–tn̩.
blacksmith's.

914.   kʷa   ilì?   s–c–yaʕ–l̩scùt–x   i?
914.   He's always having come in

s–c–k̓ʕaw–míst–x;   uł   s–c–?x̣il–x   ki?   ł
hired freight;   and   that's why   at

s–t–k̓m–áx̣ən,   uł   ałì?   ta?lì?
the other end (he is),   because

łq̓–ùla?xʷ   yə?   c–x̣q–úla?xʷ."
there is a wide place   with nothing on."

what we learn; blacksmithing, that's my job."

913. The king told him: "Way to the other end of the open place that's where
he lives, because there's lots of room there, because the blacksmith's is
never clean.

914. He's always having hired freight come in; and that's why he is at the
other end, because there is a wide place with nothing on."

[Corresponds to sentences 146-147 of the text.]

915. "way̓ p   ƚa?xʷ-iskit-əm,   x̣là-p   mi   p
915. "Now you   rest,   tomorrow (you) will

   k̓ʷúl-əm;   way̓ ti   p ƚ-xʷùy   i? k̓əl
   go to work; just   go back   to

   cítxʷ-əmp   məƚ ilì? k̓əƚ-?ìm-ənt-p i? lw-lìw-ļx,
   your house and then wait for   the bell,

   ixì? t̓i   lìw-kst-əm ixì?   uƚ way̓ p
       just when   it rings   that's   when you

   k-s-?əƚ-?íƚn-a?x."
   will eat."

[Corresponds to sentences 154-156 of the text.]

916. cù-nt-əm   i? tə ylmíxʷəm-s, i?   t
916. He told him   his boss,   the

   k̓ʷəl-cən-(n)cút: "nàx̣əmƚ anwì? cəm̓   kʷ
   cook: "But   you   will be

   c-?íw-t,   aƚì?   kʷa n̓ìn̓wi? wi?-wi?-cín
   the last one, because   when   they finish eating

   i? s-c-k̓ʷúl-x, ixì? uƚ kʷ ṇ-cíw̓-ṃ;   uƚ   axà?
   the working men, then   you wash dishes; and

   nixʷ kʷ məl-mìl-ļx   kʷ
        you take your time

   wi?-s-ən-cíw̓-ṃ,   uƚ cəm̓ kʷ k-slíp-əm,
   when you finish washing,   you   can get wood,

915. "Now you rest, tomorrow you will go to work; just go back to where
   you're supposed to stay and then wait for the bell, just when it rings
   that's when you will eat."

916. His boss told him, the cook: "But you will be the last one, because when
   the working men finish eating, then you wash dishes; you take your

ɫəxʷ kʷ kaʔm-ìsəlp̓-əm x̌əl x̌lá-p."
pack wood   for tomorrow."

[Corresponds to sentences 215-220 of the text.]

917. "waẏ t incà? c-xʷúy-st-m-ən,   lut   kʷu
917.   "I   will take you over, don't

a-k-s-ʔax̣l-íkst-əm, uɫ a-k-s-k̓ʷùɫ-əm
guide me,   and (don't) fix

an-ʕac-sqáx̣aʔ-tn̩.
your reins and bridle.

918. uɫ ti   waẏ kən x̌là-p məɫ kʷ
918.   As soon as   I   stop   you

k-təɫ-x-ìws l ən-ɫək̓ʷ-ki?-sqáx̣aʔ-tn̩, uɫ aɫì?
stand   on the saddle,   because

k̓əɫ-twì-st-xʷ   cəm ilì? kʷ ɫ k-ʔəmt-ìws;
you can't reach if   you stay on the saddle;

kʷ   k-təɫ-x-ìws nàx̣əmɫ put k̓əɫ-kíc-ənt-xʷ-əlx.
(if) you stand   you'll reach them.

919. ixì? məɫ c-kəm̓-ɫt-ìxʷ-əlx   i?
919.   Then you'll grab them by

s-c̓u-c̓u-xán-s-əlx; waẏ ti   kʷ ɫ c-k-ʔəmt-ìws
their feet;   the minute you   straddle

ak̓là? kʷ c-t-xəm·-uʔs-áka?st,
       you will have them one in each hand,

time and when you finish washing dishes you can get wood, pack wood
for tomorrow."

917. "I will take you over, don't guide me, and (don't) fix your reins and
bridle.
918. As soon as I stop you stand on the saddle, because you can't reach if
you stay on the saddle; (if) you stand you'll reach them.
919. Then you'll grab them by their feet; the minute you straddle you will

kɫ-íẃs-ənt-xʷ-əlx,   k̓ə n-sək̓ʷət-ɫnìwt i? náqs, uɫ
separate them,   to one side   one,   and

k̓ə n-sək̓ʷət-ɫnìwt i? náqs; uɫ la?ɫ
to the other side   the other; and about that time

i-k-s-ɫx̣ʷpá-m."
I'll run out."

[Follows sentence 230 of the text.]

920. "waẏ ak̓là? kən k-s-k-?əm-?əmt-íẃs-a?x,
920.   "I   am going for a little ride,

    mət   ʕày-t in-kəwàp t   sáq̓ʷ,
    he must be tired my horse from doing nothing,

    ?ayxàxa?   mi kən ɫ-c-kíc-x."
    in a little while I   will be back."

[Corresponds to sentences 231-233 of the text.]

921. ixì? s-xʷùy-s i? k̓əl s-ən-k̓ʷəɫ-cən-(n)cùt-(t)ṇ
921. So   he went to the kitchen

    ɫ k-?aw-s-ən-t̓áqʷ-əm.
    to lick plates.

922. uɫ aɫì? captík̓ʷəl-s-əlx,   uɫ aɫì?
922. And   that's fairy tales for you,

have them one in each hand, separate them, to one side one, and to
the other side the other; and about that time I'll run out."

920. "I am going for a little ride, my horse must be tired from doing nothing,
in a little while I will be back."

921. So he went to the kitchen to lick plates.
922. And that's fairy tales for you,

ƛàx̣–t   i?   s–ma?–máy?,   uɬ   wáy
it travels fast   news,   and

c–təm–s–ču–ču–x̣án;   uɬ   wáy   c–my–st–ìs–əlx   i?   t
it has no feet;   and   already   they know

s–k̓ʷíƛ–t–əm–s   k̓əl   cítxʷ.
his brothers   at   the bunk house.

[Corresponds to sentences 234-236 of the text.]

923.   "wáy   i–k–s–cùn–əm   yə?   ylmíxʷəm,   nìnẁi?   ɬ
923.   "I'm going to ask   the   king,   if

x̣m–ìnk–s   i?   kʷə–kʷrì–t   i?   tkɬm–ílxʷ;   ilì?   ļ
he likes   the   Golden   Woman;   in

nəqs–lùp   kə?   c–t̓?ák̓ʷ;   lut
one place (only)   she comes up;   it isn't

s–qʷày–s   t   swìt   t̓ə   c–wík–st–əm;   uɬ   nìnẁi?
very often   people   see her;   and   if

ɬ   an–x̣m–ìnk,   uɬ   wáy   ƛa?–ɬt–s–ìn
   you want her,   I'll get her for you

a–kɬ–náx̣ʷ–nəx̣ʷ."
for your wife."

924. aɬì?   lut   mət   t̓ə   kɬ–tkɬm–ìlxʷ
924. Because (he) doesn't   maybe   have a wife

axà?   yə?   ylmíxʷəm.
       the   king.

news travels fast and it has no feet; and already his brothers at the
bunk house know.

923. "I'm going to ask the king, if he likes the Golden Woman; in one place
(only) she comes up; it isn't very often (that) people see her; and if
you want her, I'll get her for you for your wife."

924. Because maybe the king doesn't have a wife.

925. uɬ   aɬì? pna? iwà? ɬa? kɬ–tkɬm–ílxʷ,   uɬ
925. And   even if he had a wife,

    aɬì? s–wyápix,   uɬ waỳ k–s–xʷək̓ʷ–əncút–a?x.
          he's a white man,   and   he can get a divorce.

925. And even if he had a wife, he's a white man, and he can get a divorce.

Organization of the Glossary

Entries are listed according to the following alphabetical order:

ʔ   a   c   c̓   č   æ   e   ə   h   k   k̓   kʷ   k̓ʷ   l   i   ł   ƛ̓
m   m̓   n   n̓   o   p   p̓   q   q̓   qʷ   q̓ʷ   r   r̓   s   t   t̓   u
w   w̓   x   xʷ   x̣   x̣ʷ   ʕ   ʕ̓   ʕʷ   ʕ̓ʷ .

č, æ, e, o occur only in loans.

Each entry is listed in **bold face**, and is accompanied by a simple gloss in *italics*. Grammatical comments, usually of allomorphy, are added, as are cross-references, and, for the lexical morphemes, cognates from other Interior Salish languages.[*]

The parenthesized number indicates the total occurrences of that morph in the text. Occurrences of the morph by sentence number follow, except for morphs of very high frequency, where they are omitted.

[*]The sources of the cognates are listed in the bibliography.

Glossary

ʔác– reduplicative allomorph of ʔácqaʔ *go out* (q. v.). (10) 5, 93, 105, 220, 401, 560, 561, 566, 633, 670.

ʔácqaʔ *go out.* Cr acqeʔ, Ka ʔócqeʔ, Sh (ʔə)ʔúcqe. (12) 14, 27, 54, 129, 143, 148, 223, 502, 628, 630, 631.

ʔam *feed.* Only root in Cv that transitivizes with –t and not –nt. Cr em(–t), Ka ʔem̓, Sh mt. (13) 60, 67, 201, 207, 475, 507, 513, 517, 519, 819, 860, 861, 874.

ʔámsəm *poor, pityful.* Used as an expression of commiseration. (1) 849.

ʔam·út (√ʔamut) *sit.* Ka ʔemút, Sh ʔəmút. Cf. mut. (3) 20, 465, 808.

ʔanwí *feel.* Ka ʔenwé. (5) 47, 86, 90, 215, 843.

ʔapən stressless allomorph of ʔúpən *ten* (q. v.) in compounds. (1) 643.

ʔasəl stressless allomorph of ʔasíl *two* (q. v.) in compounds. (1) 793.

ʔasíl *two.* Ka ʔesél, Sh seséle. (5) 320, 703, 750, 908, 911.

ʔaw₁ *go.* Usually the first root member of a compound. Cr igʷ, Ka ʔew, probably Sh ʔəwit. (11) 25, 208, 418, 518, 519, 530, 719, 893, 904, 921.

ʔaw₂ as in k̓əɫ–ʔaw–cn–íʔst *do by mistake, make a mistake.* (4) 100, 103, 167.

ʔax̌əl = ʔax̌l *act a certain way, do like.* Cf. ʔx̌íl. Cr ax̌il, Ka ʔax̌íl, Sh x̌il–m. (2) 719, 823.

ʔax̌l = ʔax̌əl *act a certain way, do like.* Cf. ʔx̌íl. (4) 45, 427, 493, 917.

ʔayx̌áxaʔ *in a little while, a while after.* Cf. ixíxiʔ. (7) 67, 78, 450, 734, 744, 861, 920.

ʔáyx̌ʷ–t *tire(d).* Ka ʔayx̌ʷ–t. (10) 63, 240, 241, 390, 522, 532, 681, 816, 893, 898.

ʔəckiʔ stressless allomorph of ʔíckn̓ *play* (q. v.) before s. (1) 890.

ʔəks–wíx *be standing in a place.* Cf. wíx. Ka ʔečs–wíš. Cf. Sh c–w?ex. (5) 39, 487, 507, 512, 832.

ʔəkʷ stressless allomorph of ʔúkʷ *bring, carry.* (q. v.). (1) 243.

ʔəɫ– reduplicative allomorph of ʔíɫn *eat* (q. v.). (1) 915.

ʔəɬn stressless allomorph of ʔíɬn *eat* (q. v.) in the form ṇ-ʔəɬn-
aʔ-s-qílxʷ-tṇ *cannibal, man-eater.* (31) 41, 51, 52, 54, 81, 158,
166, 169, 177, 191, 194, 196, 210, 218, 227, 342, 489, 500, 511, 548,
560, 571, 625, 835, 848, 849, 853, 863, 897.

ʔəɬxʷ stressless allomorph of ʔúɬxʷ *enter* (q. v.). (3) 300, 529, 578.

ʔəm— reduplicative allomorph of ʔam·út *sit* (q. v.). (18) 24, 26, 55, 73, 100,
103, 167, 335, 347, 471, 503, 517, 524, 576, 577, 920.

ʔəm stressless allomorph of ʔúm *name, call* (q. v.). In the construction
kəɬ-ʔəm-cín *agree.* (1) 347.

ʔəmt stressless allomorph of ʔam·út *sit* (q. v.). (31) 12, 23, 24, 26, 40,
42, 43, 48, 217, 222, 223, 272, 448, 471, 479, 488, 491, 495, 561, 670,
784, 815, 822, 823, 836, 898, 903, 918, 919, 920.

ʔəs— reduplicative allomorph of ʔasíl *two* (q. v.). (4) 455, 750, 908, 911.

ʔəsəl stressless allomorph of ʔasíl *two* (q. v.). (1) 455.

ʔət— reduplicative allomorph of ʔítx *sleep* (q. v.). (8) 76, 77, 79, 530, 535,
899.

ʔətx stressless allomorph of ʔítx *sleep* (q. v.). (5) 77, 79, 83, 542, 899.

ʔəxʷ₁ as in ʔəxʷ-kʷú-kst *coax, beg.* Ka čuxʷkun-. (1) 354.

ʔəxʷ₂ as in k-ʔəxʷ-kʷún *coax, beg.* Ka ʔexʷkún. (2) 418, 768.

ʔəx̣t stressless allomorph of √ʔux̣t *baby, infant.* Ka ʔox̣ʷt. (1) 467.

ʔəys stressless allomorph of ʔíys *(ex)change* (q. v.). Cf. ʔəyxʷ. (2) 84,
735.

ʔəyxʷ *change.* Cf. ʔəys, ʔíys. (1) 793.

ʔəy̓x̣ʷ stressless allomorph of ʔáyx̣ʷ-t *tire(d)* (q. v.). (1) 898.

ʔic (problematic) *shake.* (1) 536.

ʔíck allomorph of ʔíckṇ *play* (q. v.) before s. (2) 72, 528.

ʔíckṇ *play.* (1) 890.

ʔíɬən = ʔíɬn *eat.* Ka ʔiɬn, Sh ʔiɬn. (13) 18, 70, 146, 147, 421,
457, 514, 766, 797, 874, 881, 915.

ʔím as in kɬ-ʔím *wait (for).* (9) 55, 73, 74, 100, 103, 167, 896, 915.

ʔíma?t as in s-ən-ʔíma?t *grandchild.* Sh ʔimc. (7) 503, 524, 576,
577, 849, 869.

ʔískʷl (problematic) *throw down.* (1) 102.

ʔítx *sleep.* Ka ʔitš, Sh ʔitx, ʔətix. (13) 76, 79, 457, 532, 534,
535, 536, 898, 899, 900.

ʔíw as in c-ʔíw-t *last, final.* Ka ecé?ut, Sh ʔəwit. (3) 655, 904, 916.

ʔíwl *wave (of water).* Ka ʔiwl, Sh (?) ʔiwl. (1) 319.

ʔíys *(ex)change.* Cf. Ka ʔey *change,* Sh ʔey, ʔəyxʷ. Cf. ʔəys.
(1) 541.

ʔkí allomorph of ʔkín *indefinite interrogative root* (q. v.) before s. (1) 646.

ʔkín *indefinite interrogative root.* Ka čeń, Sh ken. (44) 5, 17, 96, 97, 99, 149, 195, 205, 264, 305, 438, 442, 444, 456, 457, 469, 493, 515, 570, 573, 588, 597, 625, 641, 679, 708, 712, 726, 752, 775, 786, 787, 795, 800, 815, 850, 878, 896, 906, 909.

ʔkn stressless allomorph of ʔkín *indefinite interrogative root* (q. v.). (1) 316.

ʔu– reduplicative allomorph of √ʔux̣t *baby, infant.* Cf. ʔəx̣t. (1) 467.

ʔuc₁ as in ʔuc–kl–áp *run down(stairs).* Cf. Sh kelépem. (1) 95.

ʔuc₂ as in n–ʔúc–xn *follow.* (5) 224, 477, 560, 679, 680.

ʔúkʷ *bring, carry.* Ka ʔukʷ, Sh ʔukʷ. (8) 181, 185, 208, 226, 240, 245, 291, 353.

ʔúlus *gather, be together.* (2) 323, 460.

ʔúɬxʷ *enter.* Ka ʔuɬxʷ, Sh ʔuɬxʷ. (12) 183, 391, 429, 604, 631, 648, 743, 757, 853, 884, 858, 873.

ʔúm *name, call.* Sh ʔəm(e)t. (7) 152, 191, 234, 436, 597, 903, 907.

ʔúpən as in ʔúpən–kst *ten.* Cr upən(čt), Ka ʔupn, Sh ʔup–əkst. (3) 16, 455, 793.

ʔuyá? possibly ʔuyá *interjection listen!* (1) 831.

ʔx̣í? in the construction yə? ʔx̣í? *there* (usually not translated): (13) 310, 329, 338, 436, 478, 533, 537, 552, 769, 816, 853. In the construction ƙa ʔx̣í? *(towards) there:* (1) 645.

ʔx̣íl *act a certain way.* Cf. ʔax̣l. (31) 31, 39, 42, 68, 173, 208, 346, 378, 391, 448, 485, 541, 568, 571, 616, 625, 642, 645, 674, 692, 696, 727, 764, 788, 801, 802, 832, 872, 914.

ʔx̣íɬ as in c–ʔx̣iɬ t *like, as.* Cf. ʔáx̣l, ʔx̣í?. (24) 45, 121, 131, 216, 286, 301, 313, 343, 381, 383, 408, 495, 567, 580, 614, 622, 627, 727, 840, 843, 856, 879, 894.

ʔyp– *on the way* (lexical prefix). (3) 666, 673.

a– allomorph of an– *2nd sg possessive your* (q. v.) before s, ɬ, and kɬ– *unrealized aspect.* (160)

a·· interjection. (11) 135, 288, 353, 399, 473, 601, 609, 714, 739, 747, 818.

–a?–₁ compound connective (as in n–ʔəɬn–a?–s–qílxʷ–tn). (26) 41, 51, 52, 55, 80, 158, 166, 177, 191, 196, 210, 218, 227, 342, 500, 511, 548, 560, 571, 625, 835, 848, 849, 853, 868, 897.

–a?–₂ diminutive infix, on roots and suffixes. (5) 73, 100, 103, 167, 849.

–a? suffix of uncertain meaning. In the forms k–kwáp–a?, ɬqáqc–a?, k–cíkʷ–a? psˤáy–a?, yákʷ–a?: (24) 54, 80, 81, 88, 121, 131, 139, 194, 207, 465, 466, 488, 500, 501, 526, 538, 541, 558, 607, 629, 693, 789, 851, 872.

–á? *negative* suffix (aɫi?-á?, nak̇ʷ-á?), always stressed. (5) 169, 791, 795, 801, 863.

–a?x *inchoative* suffix. (76)

–áka?st *diminutive of* –ákst, –íkst, *hand* (lexical suffix) (q. v.). (1) 919.

ak̇lá? *deictic particle* to here. (6) 15, 38, 431, 763, 919, 920.

–ák̇ʷ *stressed reduplicative allomorph of* √lakʷ *far, distant.* (14) 267, 307, 343, 345, 356, 357, 359, 366, 379, 780, 815, 817, 879.

–ál *stressed reduplicative allomorph of* √x̌al *still, lifeless.* (11) 162, 207, 302, 475, 647, 654, 658, 670, 672, 692.

alá? *here.* Cf. ilí?. (48) 24, 26, 38, 39, 59, 61, 104, 130, 149, 279, 324, 331, 335, 410, 411, 440, 465, 471, 664, 671, 672, 723, 730, 731, 737, 744, 751, 759, 781, 829, 849, 850, 853, 869, 871, 876.

–áli?s *relative* (lexical suffix). (1) 672.

–álqs *clothing, dress* (lexical suffix). Ka –alqs, Sh –eɬqs. (4) 523, 642, 897.

–álqʷ *cylindrical object* (lexical suffix). Ka –alqʷ, Sh –elqʷ. (1) 872.

aɫí? *because.* (196)

–áɫq *back, behind* (lexical suffix). Ka –aɫq *race.* In construction with –kṅ-áɫq: (3) 693, 817, 904. In construction with –(i)p-aɫq: (1) 904.

–áx̌ *stressed reduplicative allomorph of* √xax̌ *grow, complete.* (3) 92, 693, 864.

an– *2nd sg possessive, your.* (44)

anwí? *probably* anwí *you sg.* Ka anwí?, Sh ?–nwi?. (51)

–áp *bottom, base* (lexical suffix). Cf. –íp. (1) 95.

–áq *stressed reduplicative allomorph of* √t̓raq *jump.* (3) 414, 656, 728.

–áqs₁ *food* (lexical suffix). Ka –aqs. (7) 416, 451, 751, 763.

–áqs₂ *point, nose, end* (lexical suffix). Ka –aqs, Sh –eqs. (3) 283, 751, 763.

–áqs₃ *wages, cost* (lexical suffix). (2) 451, 763.

–áqst-xən *leg* (lexical suffix). Ka –aqst-šn, Sh –eqst-xṅ. (3) 12, 448, 785.

–áqʷ *stressed reduplicative allomorph of* √c̓aqʷ *cry.* (8) 21, 204, 254, 255, 319, 466, 485.

–ás– *stressed reduplicative allomorph of* –asq̓ət *day, sky* (lexical suffix) (q. v.). (1) 799.

–ásq̓ət *day, sky* (lexical suffix). Ka –asq̇t, Sh –esq̇t. (14) 48, 151, 224, 273, 281, 348, 491, 498, 673, 678, 730, 838, 869.

–átkʷ *free variant of* –ítkʷ *water* (lexical suffix) (q. v.). (1) 290.

aṫlá? *from there.* Cf. iṫlí?. (4) 17, 456, 681, 686.

–áw stressed reduplicative allomorph of √x̣aw̓ *dry.* (1) 519.

axá? deictic particle *this.* Cf. ixí?. (438)

–áx̣ allomorph of –áx̣n *arm* (lexical suffix) (q. v.) before s. (3) 428, 757, 884.

–áx̣ən = –áx̣n *arm* (lexical suffix). Ka –ax̣n, Sh –ex̣n. (7) 366, 368, 379, 423, 637, 750, 914.

–áya? *pretend, not real* (lexical suffix). Ka –áye?, Sh –eẏe. (5) 77, 79, 899.

–áya?–qən *top of the head* (lexical suffix). (2) 72, 525.

c–1 *cislocative* prefix.

c–2 *actual aspect* prefix.

–c1 allomorph of –s *3rd possessive, his, her, its* (q. v.), after s.

–c2 reduplicative allomorph of x̣əc *hundred* (q. v.). (1) 16.

ca– reduplicative allomorph of cʕáy *cry out* (q. v.). (1) 809.

–cá stressed reduplicative allomorph of nałcá *forget* (q. v.). (2) 420, 747.

ca? *hit, knock on.* Ka (?) cu?, Sh (?) cu?. (6) 110, 183, 384, 590, 905, 906.

ca?líwm as in ņ–ca?líwm *Inchelium* (place name). (1) 906.

ca?ps plural allomorph of √c?ups *younger sister.* (1) 73.

ca?x̣ allomorph of cíx̣ *hot* (q. v.). (1) 348.

cah *face, in front of.* Cf. cəh. In the forms k–cah, ņ–cah: (3) 84, 444, 577.

cakʷ particle *if, should.* (14) 91, 266, 329, 357, 375, 410, 424, 611, 620, 659, 660, 680, 773, 820.

captíkʷ allomorph of captíkʷəl *tell a tale, a fictional story* (q. v.) before ł. (1) 702.

captíkʷəl *tell a tale, a fictional story.* (2) 702, 922.

captíkʷł *tale, fictional story.* (5) 1, 43, 611, 612, 705.

cáw as in cáw–t *what one does.* Ka cut, Sh cuwət. (36) 221, 261, 344, 346, 381, 432, 445, 446, 447, 613, 614, 617, 618, 619, 620, 623, 624, 626, 651, 660, 724, 769, 801, 810, 811, 847, 856, 863, 904.

cə– reduplicative allomorph of cm̓ *small* (q. v.). (2) 738, 746.

cəh as in k–cəh–íkst *right hand (side).* Ka čch–ikst. Cf. cah. (1) 88.

cəh as in cəh–xn–mí–nt *be on a good track* (misshearing?). (2) 319, 320.

cəhá allomorph of cah *face, in front of* (q. v.). (1) 902.

cəm̓ particle *maybe, might.* Cf. cmáy. (105)

–cən1 = –cn lexical suffix (?). Problematic in t–x̣?ən–cən–míst *stop, prevent.* (6) 36, 304, 483, 531, 828, 898.

−cən₂ = −cən stressless allomorph of −cín *mouth, food, language* (lexical suffix) (q. v.). (24) 61, 140, 141, 405, 412, 418, 419, 445, 611, 653, 719, 735, 742, 747, 760, 766, 773, 787, 858, 874, 916, 921.

cəq *put down, place, rest.* Ka caq, Sh ceq. (4) 448, 631, 645, 657.

cəq (problematic) *squirm around, hit, throw.* Ka cq̓, Sh cq̓. (4) 721, 360, 428.

cəw₁ stressless allomorph of √cˁaw *fringe.* Ka co, Sh cuˁw. (8) 12, 448, 785, 833.

cəw₂ stressless allomorph of cáw (cáw−t) *what one does* (q. v.). (1) 632.

cəw̓ *repeat.* (4) Ka cew̓. 250, 358, 620.

−cí− allomorph of −cín *mouth, food, language* (lexical suffix) (q. v.) before s. (4) 210, 250, 358, 620.

cí? *leave alone, not bother.* (2) 533, 898.

−cín *mouth, food, language* (lexical suffix). In the constructions wi?cín *finish eating,* məlχa?−cín *misrepresent,* ƛ̓əx̣−cín *loud,* k̓ɫ?əm−cín *agree:* (15) 62, 95, 147, 155, 235, 258, 333, 347, 521, 660, 865, 889, 901, 916. In the construction yaˁ−p−cín *hard up:* (7) 10, 176, 177, 330, 331, 785, 909. In the construction qʷən̓−cín *pity(ful):* (8) 37, 139, 246, 249, 427, 467, 739, 910. In the construction qʷən̓−s−cín *beg for:* (1) 296). In the construction q̓əm−s−cín *wish for:* (4) 20, 226, 288, 353. In the construction n̩−ƛ̓əm−p−cín *be late:* (1) 650. In the construction x̣ʷs−ma?−cín *hurry:* (1) 895). In the construction n̩−xa?−cín *forward:* (1) 840. In the construction yaˁ−cín *shore:* (1) 265.

−cín−xən *ankle* (lexical suffix). (1) 903.

citx̣ʷ *house.* Ka citx̣ʷ, Sh citx̣ʷ. (23) 65, 119, 136, 154, 155, 199, 389, 391, 400, 401, 409, 500, 655, 721, 766, 850, 867, 869, 893, 909, 915, 922.

cíx *warm.* Cf. cix̣. (1) 874.

cíx̣ *hot.* Cf. cix. (1) 858.

ckʷ as in n̩−ckʷ−ískit *groan.* (√ckʷ *pull*). Ka ckʷ, Sh ckʷ. (2) 536.

cmáy *maybe, possibly.* Cf. cəm̓. (10) 267, 278, 457, 472, 561, 617, 723, 796, 799, 814.

cm̓ *small.* Ka cm̓, Sh cm. (2) 738, 746.

−cn = −cən stressless allomorph of −cín *mouth, food, language* (lexical suffix) (q. v.). In the construction −cn−ítkʷ *shore:* (9) 234, 264, 280, 282, 295, 319, 335, 350. For various other constructions cf. −cín. (13) 100, 103, 167, 243, 281, 348, 541, 795, 909.

cniɫc *he, she, one.* (12) 169, 245, 534, 539, 543, 624, 626, 716, 761, 791, 885, 899.

cp *bat the eye.* Ka cap, Sh cíp̓. (1) 48.

–cqáx̣a? allomorph of –sqáx̣a? *animal* (lexical suffix) after s. (22) 31, 59, 91, 93, 105, 201, 216, 506, 508, 559, 560, 567, 578, 669, 784, 797, 851, 853, 872, 875, 909.

cqʷ reduplicative allomorph of cˤiqʷ *featherless, bare.* (1) 321.

cú allomorph of √cún ~ √cút *say, tell* (q. v.) before transitive affixes (–nt, –st). (223)

cún allomorph of √cút *say, tell* (q. v.) before middle affix. (10) 13, 76, 118, 210, 262, 520, 724, 769, 835, 923.

cút allomorph of √cún *say, tell* (q. v.) in intransitive forms. Ka cu. (58)

cw (problematic) *dwell.* Cf. cwíx. Sh (?) cw–eɫxʷ *to build a house.* (2) 400, 736.

cwíx (problematic) *building.* Cf. cw. Sh (?) w?ex. (1) 851.

cxʷ *glad.* Sh cexʷ. (1) 502.

cx̣ʷá *stock, pile.* (3) 15, 455, 793.

–cˤát allomorph of –cút *reflexive* with pharyngeal-shifting roots. (1) 96.

cˤáw *bathe.* Ka caw. (5) 62, 148, 721.

cˤáy *cry.* Ka caá, Sh cˤ–ep–m. (1) 809.

cˤíqʷ *featherless, bare.* (1) 321.

c̓a?–₁ stressless reduplicative allomorph of c̓ár *sour, ache.* (1) 629.

c̓a?–₂ stressless reduplicative allomorph of c̓a?xʷ *weak* (q. v.). (1) 829.

c̓a? as in s–ən–kɫ–c̓a?–sqáx̣a? *horse.* Ka sənč̓ɫc̓a?sqáx̣e?. (26) 23, 25, 33, 39, 40, 45, 49, 59, 321, 468, 475, 480, 487, 646, 668, 669, 678, 680, 681, 815, 816, 832, 836, 840, 852, 873.

–c̓a? stressless allomorph of –íc̓a? *(body) cover, surface* (lexical suffix) (q. v.). (3) 18, 321, 646.

c̓a?kn interrogative indefinite root *whatever.* Probably further analyzable √?kin (q. v.). (1) 264.

c̓a?r *sour, ache.* Ka c̓er, Sh c̓al–t. (2) 629, 631.

c̓a?sí–qən *head.* (2) 552, 902.

c̓a?x *shame.* Ka c̓e?eš, Sh c̓ex. (1) 883.

c̓a?xʷ (doubtful) *weak.* (1) 829.

c̓álx̣ʷ *points extend.* (In the construction kɫ–c̓álx̣ʷ *chair.*) (3) 429, 758, 884.

c̓áɫt *cold.* Ka c̓al–t, Sh c̓eɫ. (2) 322, 329.

c̓áqʷ *point.* Ka c̓oqʷ. (1) 892.

c̓aw allomorph of c̓íw *wash.* (3) 735, 740, 741.

c̓áx̣ʷ *promise.* Ka c̓ox̣ʷ. (4) 301, 307, 483, 661.

čəḱ *count.* (2) 14, 791.

čəl₁ = čl *point, protrusion.* In the construction čəl–čl–íp̓łxən *spurs.* Ka čl. (3) 12, 31, 785.

čəl₂ *stand (on the ground).* Ka čil, Sh čl. (2) 827, 864.

čəlx̣ʷ *stressless allomorph of* čálx̣ʷ *points extend* (q. v.). (1) 751.

čəm *sharp point.* Sh čm. (1) 903.

čən *stressless allomorph of* √cˤan *tight.* Ka čan. (1) 837.

čənˤá *allomorph (in middle forms) of* √cˤan *tight.* (1) 837.

čəp *as in* n̩–čip–s *shut the eye.* Cf. čp. Ka čip. (8) 44, 46, 494, 497, 837, 841.

čəpq́ *glue, join.* (2) 611, 705.

čəs *stressless allomorph of* čsá *gone, finished* (q. v.). (3) 535, 829, 900.

čəx̣ʷ = čx̣ʷ *stressless allomorph of* čax̣ʷ *promise* (q. v.). (16) 7, 151, 318, 334, 459, 618, 661, 665, 673, 800, 801, 802, 804, 844.

čəx̣ʷ *peek* (√cix̣ʷ). (4) 498, 548, 550, 841.

čəyx̣ʷ–ˤápəlqs *the end of the story.* (1) 703.

či– *reduplicative allomorph of* čəx̣ʷ *peek* (q. v.). (4) 498, 548, 550, 841.

čiḱ *light (as lamp).* Cf. čik̓ʷ. (3) 574, 867, 901.

čik̓ʷ *as in* k–čik̓ʷ–a? *left hand side.* Ka ččik̓ʷe?. (1) 88.

čik̓ʷ *lamp, light.* Cf. čik̓. (17) 78, 89, 216, 545, 548, 550, 555, 568, 574, 688, 853, 901, 902.

čim *bone.* Ka s–čom, Sh s–čem. (1) 829.

čint *say what?* Ka ?eči(n̩). (1) 193.

čip *bat (the eye).* Ka čip. (8) 44, 46, 494, 497, 837, 841.

čiw *wash.* Ka čew, Sh čew. (11) 140, 154, 155, 238, 241, 412, 735, 747, 856, 916.

čl = čəl *point, protrusion.* (4) 12, 31, 785, 872.

čm = čəm *sharp point.* Sh čm. (1) 903.

čqʷ *as in* čqʷ–áqʷ *cry out.* Ka čqʷ(e). (8) 21, 204, 254, 255, 319, 466, 485, 827.

čqʷ *stressless allomorph of* čáqʷ *point* (q. v.). (1) 872.

čsá *gone, finished.* Ka čs. (1) 644.

ču *as in* s–ču–xán *foot.* (4) 919, 922.

čx̣ʷ = čəx̣ʷ *stressless allomorph of* čáx̣ʷ *promise.* Ka čox̣ʷ. (7) 277, 334, 343, 347, 730, 844.

əc–₁ *actual aspect prefix.* (13) 191, 208, 213, 466, 509, 588, 614, 673, 767, 802, 855, 856, 904. In construction with –st transitives: (8) 369, 534, 613, 766, 802, 849, 857, 872. In construction with s–...–x progressive: (12) 37, 48, 114, 154, 246, 249, 370, 474, 625, 716, 815, 850. In construction with s−...−s, not clearly understood: (4) 7, 204, 383, 441.

əc−₂   cislocative prefix. (1) 791.

−əcqaʔ   stressless allomorph of ʔácqaʔ go out (q. v.) in reduplicated forms. (10) 5, 93, 105, 220, 401, 560, 561, 566, 633, 670.

−əc̓   reduplicative allomorph of ʕác̓ look (q. v.). (1) 383.

−əh   reduplicative allomorph of cah face, in front of (q. v.). (1) 444.

ək−₁ = k−   allomorph of kⱡ− unrealized aspect (q. v.) before s. (2) 32, 456.

ək−₂ = k−   allomorph of kⱡ− have (q. v.) before s. (4) 18, 331, 580, 867.

−ək   stressless reduplicative allomorph of xl·ák turn. (1) 234.

əkⱡ−   unclear prefix, with cáw−t possibly have. (2) 344, 346.

−əkʷ = −kʷ   stressless reduplicative allomorph of √lakʷ far. (1) 815.

−ək̓ʷ   stressless reduplicative allomorph of ⱡk̓ʷ (as in n̩−ⱡək̓ʷ−mí) remember. (4) 419, 421, 735, 856.

−əl   stressless reduplicative allomorph of √x̣̓al still, lifeless. (13) 162, 171, 205, 209, 221, 257, 305, 345, 441, 459, 472, 475, 531.

əlk̓   stressless allomorph of √lak̓ tie. (5) 423, 520, 749, 750, 751.

əlk̓á   allomorph of √lak̓ tie in middle forms. Ka lič̓, Sh lk̓. (3) 425, 750, 751.

əlkʷ   stressless allomorph of √lakʷ far. Ka lkʷu. (23) 265, 267, 307, 343, 345, 356, 357, 359, 364, 366, 379, 732, 776, 780, 815, 817, 825, 842, 869, 879.

−əlqs   in the construction x̌ʷáq̓ʷ−əlqs snore. (11) 77, 78, 85, 533, 534, 542, 543, 550, 899, 900.

−əls   stressless allomorph of −íls feelings, thinking (q. v.). (8) 232, 370, 391, 406, 471, 477, 676, 748.

−əlscút = −lscút appurtenances (lexical suffix). Ka −elscút. (12) 448, 553, 585, 592, 735, 785, 786, 788, 789, 790, 897.

−əlt   stressless allomorph of −ílt child (lexical suffix) (q. v.). (6) 467, 641, 643, 731, 859, 871.

−əlx₁   plural number suffix.

−əlx₂   stressless allomorph of −ílx motion (q. v.).

−əlxʷ   stressless allomorph of −ílxʷ body, cover (lexical suffix) (q. v.). (1) 255.

əⱡ−   (once) again, back (directional prefix). (10) After unrealized prefix kⱡ−əⱡ: (8) 163, 156, 243, 339, 516, 711, 859, 864. Not clear in 79.

əⱡ = ⱡ   subordinating particle. (1) 331.

−əⱡ− = −ⱡ−   compound connective. (8) 22, 79, 403, 891, 895, 898, 899, 901.

−əⱡ   stressless reduplicative allomorph of qíⱡ awake(n) (q. v.). (2) 81, 901.

–əɬt = **–ɬt** *ditransitive* suffix. (34) 58, 60, 65, 68, 118, 126, 127, 136, 137, 141, 181, 213, 239, 243, 268, 287, 289, 293, 352, 449, 506, 516, 605, 609, 610, 644, 786, 851, 858, 859, 861.

–əɬxʷ stressless allomorph of **–íɬxʷ** *house* (lexical suffix) (q. v.). (13) 124, 126, 607, 608, 610, 908, 909, 910.

–əm₁ = **–m** *middle voice* suffix.

–əm₂ = **–m** stressless allomorph of **–ím** *1 pl transitive.*

–əm₃ = **–m** stressless allomorph of **–ím** *transitive indefinite subject.*

–əm₄ = **–m** stressless allomorph of **–úm** *2nd sg object* suffix.

–əmn stressless allomorph of **–mín** *instrumental* suffix (q. v.). In ṇ–cq̓–əmn–íls: (1) 71. In n–əlk̓–əmn–íks: (1) 749.

–əmp = **–ṃp** *2nd pl possessive* suffix. (32) 9, 11, 17, 18, 113, 149, 200, 201, 432, 457, 542, 564, 594, 671, 672, 698, 769, 783, 795, 797, 799, 800, 906, 911, 915.

–əms stressless allomorph of **mús** *four* (k–mus–əms *four persons*). (6) 2, 89, 111, 145, 524, 552.

ən– = **ṇ–** = **n–** *locative* prefix.

–ən = **–n** stressless allomorph of **–ín** *1st sg transitive subject* suffix.

–əncút *reflexive.* Segmentable **–nt–cút**. (42) 38, 82, 84, 103, 153, 186, 215, 221, 228, 310, 315, 337, 359, 365, 404, 414, 415, 440, 444, 448, 469, 502, 556, 559, 574, 577, 587, 593, 619, 656, 678, 719, 811, 925.

–əncʕát allomorph of **–ncút** with pharyngeal shifting roots. (7) 508, 509, 563, 567, 853, 868, 876.

ənk̓ʷ = **nk̓ʷ** *one.* Bound root. Ka nk̓ʷu?, Sh nk̓ʷu?. (28) 22, 71, 72, 74, 79, 150, 400, 402, 403, 526, 527, 531, 539, 540, 543, 558, 646, 698, 723, 730, 891, 895, 898, 899.

ənqs stressless allomorph of **náqs** *one.* (1) 744.

–ənt = **–nt** *transitive* suffix.

ənx̣ʷ = **nəx̣ʷ** stressless allomorph of **nax̣ʷ** *wife* (q. v.). (2) 218, 396.

–əp₁ stressless reduplicative allomorph of **slap** *mistake* (q. v.). (1) 50.

–əp₂ = **–p** *non-control* suffix. (4) 381, 675, 684, 867.

–ənwáxʷ = **–(ə)nwíxʷ** *reciprocal* suffix. Cf. **–twíxʷ**. (2) 379, 691.

–ənwíxʷ = **–(ə)nwáxʷ** *reciprocal* suffix. Cf. **–twíxʷ**. (4) 414, 646, 696.

–əp not clear with the root **xʷt̓** (in the form **xʷt̓–əp** *jump (to), rush.* (4) 91, 558, 700, 836.

–əq̓ʷ stressless reduplicative allomorph of **náq̓ʷ** *steal.* (2) 851, 872.

–ər̓– reduplicative allomorph of **tər̓q** *jump, kick* (q. v.). (2) 414, 728.

(–)əs– allomorph of **s–** *absolutive* prefix (q. v.). (7) 7, 72, 74, 150, 402, 459, 647.

–əs₁ = **–s** stressless allomorph of **–ís** *3rd transitive subject* pronoun (q.

v.). (25) 22, 95, 100, 118, 127, 137, 141, 188, 244, 280(?), 283, 472, 541, 552, 574, 576, 577, 605, 610, 650, 814, 823, 824, 867, 902.

—əs₂ stressless reduplicative allomorph of qs₁ *dark* (q. v.). (1) 734.

—əs₃ stressless reduplicative allomorph of x̣ás *good* (q. v.). (1) 461.

—əska? morpheme of uncertain meaning in the construction xʷús–əska? *hurry* (cf. xʷús). (3) 636, 685, 895.

—əsq̓ət stressless allomorph of –ásq̓ət *day, sky* (lexical suffix) (q. v.). (1) 799.

—əst₁ affix of unclear meaning, possibly related to –cút *reflexive,* and/or –í?st *reflexive* (q. v.). In the construction k̓əⱡ–kʷís–əst *envy:* (3) 157, 159. In the construction k–mílkʷ–əst–m–ənt *rub against:* (1) 529.

—əst₂ = –st *transitive* suffix. (8) 213, 214, 349, 558, 766, 791, 849, 900.

—əstúⱡt = –stúⱡt– *redirective ditransitive* suffix. Cf. –úⱡt. (1) 872.

—əsxən stressless allomorph of –ísxn *rock(s), small round object(s)* (lexical suffix) (q. v.). (13) 78, 87, 88, 216, 545, 548, 555, 568, 574, 688, 853, 901, 902.

—ət = –t *stative* suffix. (9) 377, 425, 557, 727, 840, 863, 904, 913.

—ətx reduplicative allomorph of ?ítx *sleep* (q. v.). (5) 76, 530, 535.

əwp = up = wp stressless allomorph of √wap *thick growth.* Cf. wp. (3) 12, 448, 785.

əwt stressless allomorph of wtán *put in* before ⱡ. (1) 514.

əwxʷ = wxʷ *stare at.* (1) 583.

əwʕí = wʕí unclear. *Move fast.* (1) 516.

əx– prefix of uncertain function in the construction əx–?kín. (2) 205, 316.

—əx suffix of uncertain function in the construction ilí?–x–əx *wait a minute,* in which –x–əx may be viewed as a diminutive imperative. (2) 186, 243.

—əxn = –xn = –xən stressless allomorph of –xán *foot, leg* (lexical suffix) (q. v.). (1) 357.

—əxt = –xt stressless allomorph of –xít *ditransitive* suffix (q. v.). (8) 23, 62, 137, 142, 199, 477, 605, 721.

—əxʷ₁ stressless reduplicative allomorph of súxʷ₁ *leave (pl.)* (q. v.). (2) 94, 106.

—əxʷ₂ stressless reduplicative allomorph of –úla?xʷ *land, earth* (lexical suffix) (q. v.). (1) 806.

—əx̣₁ stressless reduplicative allomorph of √ƛ̓ax̣ *grow.* Cf. ƛ̓x̣á. (16) 20, 160, 162, 205, 257, 375, 436, 465, 592, 593, 649, 738, 746, 788.

—əx̣₂ stressless reduplicative allomorph of pax̣₁ *think* (q. v.). (1) 693.

há? *interrogative* particle. (33) 96, 99, 161, 189, 190, 195, 205, 257, 340, 375, 410, 438, 570, 601, 618, 638, 688, 744, 746, 810, 846, 878.

háht *laugh.* (1) 528.

hə— reduplicative allomorph of hu? *catch cold.* Ka ho?. (1) 289.

həł— *group of* (lexical prefix). (2) 363, 612.

hu— reduplicative allomorph of húy in the construction hu–húy *okay.* (6) 120, 367, 432, 606, 764, 765.

hú? *catch cold.* Ka ho?. (1) 289.

humá? interjection of unclear meaning. (1) 38.

húy *hinish.* Ka hoy, Sh he?éy (?). (41)

i— allomorph of in— *1st sg possessive, my* (q. v.) before s, ł and kł— *unrealized* aspect. (141).

i? *article.* Cf. yə?, y. (1091).

—i? probably —y *transitive imperative pl* suffix.

—i?pustxən (segmentable —i?pust-xən) *step* (lexical suffix). Ka —épu?sčən. (1) 904.

—i?st *reflexive (?)* suffix. Ka —i(st). Cf. —míst. (14) 79, 100, 103, 119, 165, 167, 233, 336, 536, 560, 626, 633, 842, 901.

—icí? as in pn–icí? *at that time.* (2) 791, 825.

—íca? *(body) cover, surface* (lexical suffix). Ka —íce?, Sh —íce?. (25) 18, 33, 67, 237, 303, 323, 329, 381, 480, 518, 529, 592, 631, 648, 649, 739, 741, 748, 789, 826, 828, 883, 897.

—íkən = —íkn̓ *back (anatomy)* (lexical suffix) (q. v.). Ka —ičn, Sh —ikn. (14) 12, 64, 220, 221, 223, 512, 518, 785, 825, 826, 842, 861, 903.

—íki? allomorph of —íkn̓ *back (anatomy)* (lexical suffix) (q. v.) before s or ł. (8) 26, 272, 470, 476, 478, 669, 815, 821.

—íkn̓ = —íkən *back (anatomy)* (lexical suffix) (q. v.). (2) 104, 864.

—íks allomorph of —íkst *hand* (lexical suffix) (q. v.) before —nt *transitive.* (3) 414, 655, 749.

—íkst *hand* (lexical suffix). Cf. —íkxt. Ka —ečst, Sh —eks(t). (28) 16, 45, 87, 88, 155, 156, 200, 300, 304, 361, 362, 364, 377, 389, 439, 461, 486, 493, 536, 549, 644, 645, 776, 828, 831, 902, 917.

—íkxt *manipulation* (lexical suffix). Cf. —íkst. (2) 632, 899.

iḱlí? deictic particle *to there.* Cf. aḱlá?. (32) 98, 108, 126, 128, 136, 141, 153, 247, 264, 280, 366, 425, 444, 507, 514, 563, 588, 589, 604, 610, 615, 649, 697, 711, 716, 816, 869, 872, 908.

—íl allomorph of —íls *feeling, thinking* (q. v.) before ł. (1) 439.

−íla?t diminutive of −ílt *child* (lexical suffix) (q. v.). (2) 467.

ilí? *there.* Cf. alá?. (104)

−íls *feelings, thinking.* Ka −e(ls). (61) 10, 19, 20, 22, 24, 71, 113, 120, 121, 130, 171, 194, 200, 201, 225, 227, 265, 268, 269, 297, 301, 313, 314, 331, 332, 335, 369, 376, 379, 438, 463, 464, 467, 472, 477, 512, 554, 570, 578, 585, 592, 600, 638, 649, 663, 667, 692, 766, 799, 807, 808, 814, 826, 869, 885, 908.

−ílt *child* (lexical suffix). Ka −elt, Sh −iɬe. (7) 26, 676, 677, 691, 738, 746, 781.

−íltən *stomach* (lexical suffix). Ka −elt, Sh −eltn. (4) 719, 796, 799, 858.

−ílx *motion.* Ka −ilš, Sh −elx. In the following constructions: ɬq̓−ílx *lie down:* (14) 33, 76, 83, 84, 85, 90, 481, 484, 537, 541, 543, 827, 829, 836; ?ətx−ílx *go to sleep:* (2) 83, 542; yaʕ−m−ílx *get together:* (5) 144, 154, 162, 441, 801; k−əlkʷ−ílx *go off a way:* (2) 356, 364; n̓−q̓a?−ílx *have business:* (1) 594; xʷt̓−ílx *get up:* (7) 484, 536, 538, 678, 683, 900, 901; xk−ílx *make noise by rubbing:* (2) 547, 901; ɬkʷ−ílx *leave:* (1) 776; kɬ−xx̣−m−ílx *be in a row:* (1) 189.

−ílxʷ *body, cover* (lexical suffix). Cf. ylxʷ. In the construction tkɬm−ílxʷ *woman:* (77). In the constructions: kɬ−yə−yʕ−ílxʷ *body coverings:* (4) 64, 512, 815, 862; c̓a?kn−ílxʷ *whatever color:* (1) 264; yʕa−ɬ−cw−ílxʷ−tn̓ *all tribes:* (2) 400, 736; s−nəqs−ílxʷ *compatriot:* (2) 410, 744; kɬ−tx−ílxʷ *curry:* (4) 519, 860, 861; q̓ʷay−s?−ylxʷ *greenback:* (1) 792.

−íɬca? *inside, body* (lexical suffix). Ka −eɬc̓e?, Sh eɬc̓e. (3) 548, 889, 902.

−iɬən = −íɬn as in kʷəlst−íɬən *send somebody.* Cf? −ɬtíɬən. (3) 423, 677, 731.

−íɬp *tree, plant* (lexical suffix). Often in place names. Ka −eɬp, Sh −eɬp. (1) 611.

−íɬxʷ *house* (lexical suffix). Ka −eɬxʷ, Sh −eɬxʷ. (15) 53, 108, 109, 126, 145, 182, 380, 391, 412, 588, 590, 687, 757, 905.

−ím₁ *3rd transitive subject* pronoun with plural object. (13) 19, 41, 117, 158, 159, 160, 167, 199, 489, 645, 821, 848.

−ím₂ *middle* suffix of (di)transitives with possessive inflection. (6) 211, 249, 259, 490, 620.

−ím₃ *1st pl transitive subject* pronoun. (7) 214, 460, 599, 800, 801, 802, 819.

in− *1st sg possessive, my.* (44) 57, 66, 131, 140, 191, 192, 288, 294, 301, 315, 317, 334, 335, 389, 445, 449, 505, 515, 516, 603, 608, 610, 611, 618, 621, 670, 769, 770, 784, 785, 807, 810, 850, 856, 858, 860, 872, 920.

−ín *1st sg transitive subject* pronoun. (27) 1, 16, 67, 122, 132, 179, 248, 277, 370, 371, 493, 519, 670, 710, 717, 766, 769, 842, 844, 850, 860, 861, 870, 923.

−ína? *ear, quantity, surface* (lexical suffix). Ka −éne?, Sh −ene. (11) 23, 215, 271, 477, 520, 565, 627, 656, 675, 815, 897.

incá? probably incá *I*. First person sg independent pronoun. (30)

−ínk *stomach* (lexical suffix). In the construction x̣m−ínk *like, love*: (35). In construction with other roots: (27) 76, 84, 202, 206, 208, 224, 225, 254, 256, 258, 260, 273, 472, 528, 529, 531, 537, 540, 541, 543, 629, 631, 638, 645, 838, 899.

−íp₁ *2nd pl transitive subject* pronoun. (9) 10, 84, 200, 423, 456, 476, 750, 795, 909.

−íp₂ *door* (lexical suffix). Cf. −áp. Ka −ep. (26) 53, 59, 109, 110, 126, 175, 183, 186, 237, 244, 384, 453, 507, 508, 567, 578, 590, 604, 686, 687, 849, 853, 869, 876, 905, 906.

−íp₃ not understood in the construction x̣m−íp *be late*: (4) 488, 489, 492, 835. In the construction penh−íp *be on time*: (1) 499.

−ípa?ɬxən diminutive form of −ípɬxən *heel* (lexical suffix) (q. v.). (1) 903.

−ípə(n) not understood in the construction n̩−ma?−ípən *tell on*: (4) 632, 658, 659, 660. (The underlying form is probably −ipń, with −ń lost before −nt *transitive*. In the third person transitive, with −nt regularly Ø, the suffix surfaces as −ípi?, hinting to ń → i? /_s. Cf. Ka nmiyépən *I accuse him.* Note that Vogt reports "Ka esənme?ipəńcú *he accuses himself.* Phonetics not entirely clear."). Cf. −ípi?.

−ípi? not understood in the construction n̩−ma?−ípən *tell on*, where in the third person transitive n → i? /_s. Cf. −ípən. (1) 252.

−ípla? *handle, manipulate* (lexical suffix). Ka −éple?, Sh −iple?. (9) 162, 167, 333, 391, 465, 468, 626, 693, 808.

−ípɬxən (segmentable −ípɬ−xn) *heel* (lexical suffix). Sh −eple?−xn. (4) 12, 31, 785, 903.

−ípna? *lip(s)* (lexical suffix). Sh −epne. (3) 404, 414, 655.

−íps *neck* (lexical suffix). Sh −eps. (16) 262, 264, 269, 271, 282, 287, 299, 310, 335, 338, 340, 349, 350, 352, 357, 358.

−ís *3rd transitive subject* pronoun. (62) 15, 34, 54, 125, 136, 137, 167, 169, 175, 182, 204, 210, 213, 255, 259, 334, 347, 349, 449, 450, 452, 453, 454, 470, 471, 475, 477, 482, 500, 502, 514, 555, 558, 559, 613, 615, 616, 623, 627, 677, 761, 791, 793, 815, 824, 826, 828, 857, 868, 880, 883, 900, 902, 922.

−ísəlṗ *wood* (lexical suffix). Sh −esíṗ. Cf. slíṗ. (4). 140, 154, 568, 916.

−ískit *pharynx* (lexical suffix). Sh −eske. (5) 536, 829, 869, 898, 915.

−ísxən *rock(s), small round object(s)* (lexical suffix). Ka −esšn, Sh −esxṅ. (1) 28.

−ít *1st pl transitive subject* pronoun. (1) 343.

ití? deictic particle *then; from where, from whom.* (7) 290, 433, 443, 615, 806, 829, 861.

−ítkʷ *water* (lexical suffix). Ka −etkʷ, Sh −et−kʷe. Cf. −átkʷ. In the construction −cn−ítkʷ *shore*: (9) 234, 264, 280, 282, 295, 319, 335, 350; elsewhere: (8) 285, 289, 295, 300, 354, 657, 766.

itlí? deictic particle *from there.* Cf. atlá?. (36) 80, 89, 107, 120, 232, 233, 329, 333, 436, 446, 449, 454, 484, 527, 541, 542, 552, 580, 611, 653, 678, 683, 692, 699, 705, 769, 812, 817, 847, 850, 891, 902.

iwá? probably iwá particle *to no avail, even though.* (59) 33, 34, 66, 132, 220, 223, 224, 266, 288, 296, 304, 307, 310, 317, 329, 334, 353, 354, 357, 359, 370, 375, 400, 410, 421, 424, 467, 469, 480, 536, 646, 659, 664, 677, 749, 754, 820, 824, 832, 841, 877, 887, 900, 908, 910, 925.

−íwt *place, position.* Ka −ewt, Sh −ewt. (4) 1, 401, 433, 440.

−íws *middle, center* (lexical suffix). Ka −ews, Sh −ews. With the meaning *on horseback* with the stems ṇ−k−?əmt−, k−tkʷ−, t−kʷəl·−, k−?əyx̣ʷ−t−: (41) 12, 23, 24, 26, 30, 40, 42, 43, 48, 94, 105, 217, 222, 223, 272, 448, 462, 471, 479, 488, 491, 495, 561, 569, 579, 670, 784, 805, 815, 822, 823, 836, 898, 903, 918, 919, 920. With extended meanings in various other constructions: (31) 15, 73, 130, 218, 396, 407, 491, 527, 582, 611, 638, 640, 692, 703, 730, 735, 740, 751, 741, 793, 794, 812, 824, 834, 844, 891, 913, 918, 919.

ixí? deictic particle *that.* Cf. axá?. (588)

ixíxi? *in a little while, a while after.* Cf. ?ayxáxa?. (3) 90, 284, 351.

−íxʷ *2nd sg transitive subject* pronoun. (39) 12, 26, 49, 53, 60, 64, 79, 196, 197, 214, 253, 279, 289, 293, 328, 331, 345, 353, 355, 369, 443, 474, 513, 537, 538, 631, 639, 641, 708, 811, 814, 819, 862, 874, 897, 900, 908, 919.

k−₁ with numerals prefix meaning *person.*

k−₂ allomorph of kɬ− *unrealized* prefix before s.

k−₃ allomorph of kɬ− *have* prefix before s or ɬ.

k−₄ *resultive* prefix, affects the meaning of the root it is prefixed to. In the construction k−waẏ *well, so.*

k—ᶜ reduplicative (diminutive) allomorph of kəw?áp—a? *dogs* (plural) (q. v.).

ka?— reduplicative allomorph of ka?ɬís *three*. (7) 3, 14, 659, 677, 770.

ka?kíc *find*. Probably analyzable as ka?—kíc. (3) 693, 799, 780.

ka?ɬəl— allomorph of ka?ɬís *three* in the construction ka?ɬəl—lúp *three piles*. (3) 15, 454, 793.

ka?ɬís *three*. (7) 3, 12, 14, 659, 677, 770, 784.

ka?m *carry plural objects*. (3) 140, 154, 916.

kcn as in n̩—kcn—íkn̩ *overtake someone*. Cf. Ka čc—n—wexʷ. Cf. kəc. (5) 104, 220, 221, 223, 478.

kə? allegro speech variant of ki? relative particle *that, which* (q. v.). (3) 673, 879, 923.

kəc allomorph of kcn (q. v.) when the following morpheme is unstressed, as in the constructions n̩—kəc—kn̩—wíxʷ *overtake one another,* n̩—kəc—kn̩—aɬq *catch up*. Cf. kic. (3) 144, 693, 817.

kəkʕáka as in s—kəkʕáka? *bird, chicken*. (43)

kəlqʷ unclear form, possibly k—lqʷ. In the construction kəlqʷ—íkst *touch the arm*. (1) 377.

kəlx stressless allomorph of √kilx *hand*. (3) 75, 652, 700.

kəm? unclear in the construction kəm?—íkxt *do things*. (1) 899.

kəm̩₁ = km̩ stressless allomorph of km̩á *take plural objects* (q. v.).

kəm̩₂ conjunctive particle *or*. (55)

—kən̩ stressless allomorph of —íkn̩ *back (anatomy)* (lexical suffix) (q. v.). (6) 144, 518, 519, 861, 864.

kət̩ = kt̩ *cut off*. Sh kit̩. (4) 95, 96, 100, 101.

kəw— reduplicative allomorph of kəwík *ghost*. Sh (?) qʷy. (1) 572.

kəw?áp plural allomorph of kəwáp *horse* (q. v.) in the form k—kəw?áp—a? *dogs*. (15) 54, 199, 200, 452, 500, 501, 566, 585, 670, 784, 789, 797, 848, 868.

kəwáp *horse*. Bound morpheme, must be accompanied by a possessive affix. (53) 32, 35, 60, 66, 203, 205, 254, 255, 256, 260, 271, 272, 301, 303, 304, 307, 311, 312, 315, 334, 335,343, 478, 481, 482, 483, 486, 507, 516, 561, 673, 733, 827, 828, 831, 844, 848, 852, 853, 858, 859, 860, 873, 874, 880, 897, 920.

kəwík *ghost somebody*. Cf? Sh qʷy. (1) 572.

ki? relative particle *that, which*. Cf. kə?. (77)

kíc *reach somebody*. Ka čic, Sh kic. (23) 51, 60, 78, 162, 203, 255, 324, 325, 327, 357, 358, 425, 650, 692, 752, 795, 802, 821, 849, 869, 918. In the construction kíc—x *arrive*. Ka čicš, Sh kicx. (28) 24, 27, 60, 61, 75, 181, 226, 238, 243, 270, 316, 317, 357, 457, 471, 477, 514, 543, 579, 610, 650, 693, 730, 743, 849, 858, 881, 920.

kíl *follow, chase*. Sh kel. (1) 478.

kip unclear. Possibly k—yp. *Dark (?).* (1) 408.

kíw *yes.* (1) 399.

kíwa *Kewa* (place name). (1) 906.

kł as in ʔuc—kł—áp *run downward.* (1) 95.

kł—₁ *unrealized aspect* prefix. (37) 18, 26, 65, 79, 119, 153, 186, 199, 209, 221, 228, 243, 255, 302, 339, 375, 448, 451, 452, 456, 457, 516, 664, 671, 711, 721, 766, 820, 822, 859, 864, 893, 908, 923.

kł—₂ directional prefix *down, under.* (41) 12, 61, 70, 174, 255, 280, 285, 381, 402, 429, 431, 433, 512, 514, 519, 523, 589, 591, 631, 637, 645, 657, 751, 758, 815, 860, 861, 862, 874, 881, 884, 889. In the construction s—ən—kł—ća?—sqáχa? *horse:* (25) 23, 25, 33, 39, 40, 45, 49, 59, 468, 475, 480, 487, 668, 669, 678, 680, 815, 816, 832, 836, 840, 852.

kł—₃ *have* prefix. (43) 2, 31, 64, 78, 98, 148, 191, 395, 524, 547, 575, 623, 646, 664, 667, 670, 688, 710, 716, 724, 731, 792, 801, 851, 852, 863, 872, 873, 874, 902, 903, 904, 924, 925.

kł (√kił) *separate.* Sh kił. (1) 919.

kłá as in c—t—kłá—m *another, the next.* Cf? ła?. (2) 607.

kmátəm interjection *certainly.* (1) 620.

kmíx *only.* Ka čmiš. (23) 275, 659, 778, 781, 819, 892, 903. 47, 48, 178, 417, 470, 475, 498, 513, 530, 536, 599, 766, 792, 897, 901.

km = kəm stressless allomorph of kma *take plural objects* (q. v.). (7) 200, 423, 428, 449, 750, 757, 884.

kmá *take plural objects.* (1) 262.

kma? interjection *it is not.* Probably related to kəm *or* (q. v.). (3) 307, 422, 427.

knəm as in knəm—p—qín *blind.* Ka čnm—p—qín. (1) 830.

—kn = —kən stressless allomorph of —íkn *back (anatomy)* (lexical suffix) (q. v.). (9) 53, 64, 512, 687, 693, 817, 860, 862, 904.

kráčuet (English) *graduate.* (1) 773.

—ks allomorph of —íkst in construction with the root kʷín, kʷən—ks— *hold, shake hands:* (11) 310, 337, 368, 379, 414, 646, 650, 691, 692, 700, 823. In the construction ʔapən—ks—pín—tk *ten years:* (1) 643.

—kst stressless allomorph of —íkst *hand* (lexical suffix) (q. v.). (14) 16, 261, 290, 354, 363, 370, 455, 701, 735, 740, 793, 861, 915.

kt = kət *cut off* (q. v.). (4) 95, 96, 100, 101.

kutpáy (English) *good bye.* (2) 106, 579.

kxá allomorph of kxán *follow* (q. v.) in the middle construction kxá—m. (1) 807.

kxán *follow.* Sh (?) kxep. (1) 674.

kxən = kxn stressless allomorph of kxán *follow* (q. v.). (4) 365, 371, 670.

kxn = kxən stressless allomorph of kxán *follow* (q. v.). (5) 19, 463, 663, 667, 807.

ǩ– reduplicative allomorph of ǩaʔl *surreptitiously, easy* (q. v.). (3) 79, 536, 901.

ǩ locative particle *to*. (2) 84, 730.

ǩa allomorph of ǩ locative particle *to*. In the construction ǩa ʔkín *to where?*: (13) 442, 444, 456, 469, 493, 588, 787, 795, 800, 815, 850, · 896. In the construction ǩa ṇwíst *upward*: (1) 521. In the construction ǩa ʔxíʔ *where*: (1) 645.

ǩaʔ allomorph of ǩat *near* (q. v.) before c. (1) 295.

ǩaʔít *near*. Ka čit, Sh ǩiʔt. Cf. ǩat. (2) 41, 581.

ǩaʔkn stem based on the construction ǩa ʔkín (q. v.). (1) 697.

ǩaʔl as in ǩ–ǩaʔl–íʔst *surreptitiously, easy*. (3) 79, 536, 901.

ǩaʔs allomorph of ǩás *bad* (q. v.). In the construction ṇ–ǩaʔs–íls *be angry, mean*. (1) 438.

ǩaʔt allomorph of ǩát *near*. (17) 151, 274, 527, 538, 606, 692, 731, 751, 772, 848, 849, 864, 891, 904, 908.

ǩahkʷ *open*. Ka čehkʷ. (15) 59, 110, 183, 384, 431, 453, 507, 508, 567, 590, 762, 793, 853, 876, 906.

ǩáma? *pine needles*. Ka čem–e?, Sh ǩeme. (1) 323.

ǩás *bad*. Ka čes, Sh ǩis–t. (1) 789.

ǩát *near*. Ka čit, Sh ǩiʔt. Cf. ǩaʔít. (1) 39.

ǩáw *gone*. Ka čúu. (9) 7, 154, 163, 317, 441, 575, 578, 628, 803.

ǩə–₁ reduplicative allomorph of ǩníya? *listen* (q. v.). (3) 411, 418, 754.

ǩə–₂ reduplicative allomorph of ǩat *near* (q. v.). (1) 228.

ǩə allomorph of ǩ locative particle *to*. (12) 41, 166, 207, 237, 259, 333, 537, 541, 543, 718, 919.

ǩəl locative particle *(in)to*. (81)

ǩəl· unclear form in the construction ǩəl·–íʔst *work (?)*. (1) 119.

ǩəlxʷ stressless allomorph of ǩláxʷ *disappear, late, dark*. (q. v.). Ka čluxʷ, Sh ǩəluxʷ. (4) 56, 443, 504, 580.

ǩə(ɬ)– allomorph of ǩəɬ– (q. v.). (1) 848.

ǩəɬ– = ǩɬ– directional prefix that derives stems as follows: ǩəɬ–pa(ʔ)x *plan, think*: (16) 4, 165, 172, 233, 236, 468, 473, 481, 615, 616, 671, 679, 717, 818; ǩəɬ–ǩláxʷ *out of sight*: (12) 17, 32, 279, 443, 356, 478, 678, 681, 806, 816, 825, 826; ǩəɬ–ɋəy̓ *write down*: (2) 49, 832; ǩəɬ–táq *lay down*: (1) 576; ǩəɬ–ʔím *wait for*: (3) 74, 896, 915; ǩəɬ–təm *suck, kiss*: (6) 75, 692, 700, 823; ǩəɬ–ʕal *fence*: (1) 686;

k̓əɬ-ʔətx-númt *fall asleep:* (3) 76, 530, 535; k̓əɬ-níxəl *hear (about):* (12) 78, 196, 247, 253, 324, 326, 391, 544, 546, 570, 697, 901; k̓əɬ-qɬ-əɬ-t-númt *be awakened:* (2) 81, 901; k̓əɬ-ʔíys *change (place):* (2) 84, 541; k̓əɬ-ʔanwí *hear, feel:* (3) 86, 90, 215; k̓əɬ-ʔaw-cn-íʔst *by mistake:* (2) 100, 167; k̓əɬ-ɬəp-m-əncút *do oneself wrong:* (1) 103; k̓əɬ-ɬʔíq̓ʷ *appear:* (1) 848; k̓əɬ-síw *ask:* (1) 108; k̓əɬ-k̓ʷís-əst *be envious:* (2) 157, 159; k̓əɬ-xʷíl *throw away:* (1) 161; k̓əɬ-wík *see:* (1) 679; k̓əɬ-səl *disappear:* (2) 678, 683; k̓əɬ-my-p-númt *find out:* (1) 223; k̓əɬ-k̓ʷínxʷ *answer:* (1) 243; k̓əɬ-q̓má *wish for:* (1) 246; k̓əɬ-kíc(-x) *reach:* (6) 316, 317, 357, 358, 730, 918; k̓əɬ-twín *fall short:* (4) 329, 370, 748, 918; k̓əɬ-ʔəm(t) *sit down:* (1) 355; k̓əɬ-ʔəm-cín *agree:* (1) 347; k̓əɬ-ʔəxʷ-k̓ʷú-kst *coax:* (1) 354; k̓əɬ-k̓ʷíƛ *appear:* (6) 381, 580, 642, 675, 684, 867; k̓əɬ-tək̓ʷ *put down:* (1) 454; k̓əɬ-ʔəɬxʷ *crawl under:* (1) 529; k̓əɬ-ƛaʔ *jealous:* (2) 639; k̓əɬ-ləxʷ *instruct:* (3) 537, 538, 853.

k̓əm₁ = k̓m *surface, bulk.* In composition with various affixes assumes a variety of meanings. Ka čim, čem, Sh k̓em. (5) 53, 687, 819, 821, 908.

k̓əm₂ particle *except.* Probably related to k̓im *except.* (7) 60, 308, 346, 474, 667, 742, 808.

k̓əs stressless allomorph of k̓ás *bad* (q. v.). (10) 22, 301, 314, 472, 517, 789, 813, 860, 861, 883.

k̓ət allomorph of k̓at *near* (q. v.). (1) 228.

k̓əw₁ stressless allomorph of k̓áw *gone* (q. v.). (6) 7, 312, 472, 676, 814, 869.

k̓əw₂ stressless allomorph of k̓íw *climb* (q. v.). (2) 375, 889.

k̓i- reduplicative allomorph of k̓aʔt *near* (q. v.). In the construction k̓i-k̓at *near.* (12) 527, 538, 606, 692, 731, 751, 772, 848, 864, 891, 908.

k̓íl·xʷ in the construction k̓əɬ-k̓íl·xʷ-t *disappear.* In ablaut relationship with k̓láxʷ (q. v.). (2) 478, 825.

k̓im *except.* Sh k̓éməɬ. (11) 20, 340, 349, 464, 465, 470, 662, 808, 815, 852, 873.

k̓im *dark.* Ka čim. (2) 216, 545.

k̓in *afraid.* (4) 494, 516, 837.

k̓it *near.* Cf. k̓aʔt. (2) 291, 354.

k̓iw *climb.* In the construction k̓íw-əlx *old.* Ka čew-lš, Sh k̓ew-lx. (15) 23, 25, 32, 37, 468, 469, 474, 484, 714, 815, 819, 821, 828. In the construction t-k̓íw-əlx *climb:* (12) 78, 86, 96, 98, 521, 547, 559, 570, 574, 865, 901.

k̉la   variant of k̉l = k̉əl locative particle *(in)to.* (2) 239, 679.

k̉lá?   variant of ak̉lá? deictic particle *to here* (q. v.). (2) 364, 427.

k̉láxʷ   *disappear, late, dark.* Ka člxʷ, Sh k̉əluxʷ. Cf. k̉íl·xʷ. (27) 17, 32, 40, 49, 107, 127, 154, 155, 238, 264, 272, 274, 279, 408, 456, 461, 481, 678, 681, 730, 731, 732, 735, 806, 816, 826.

k̉lí?   variant of ik̉lí? deictic particle *to there.* (3) 146, 902, 913.

k̉ɬ–   = k̉əɬ–   Directional prefix that derives stems as follows: k̉ɬ–ən–k̉ahk̉ʷ *open:* (12) 59, 110, 183, 384, 453, 507, 508, 567, 590. k̉ɬ–ən–k̉m–íp *door:* (1) 53. k̉ɬ–ən–ɬa? *be next to:* (5) 109, 590, 686, 869. k̉ɬ–ən–ca? *knock on:* (6) 110, 183, 384, 590, 905, 906. k̉ɬ–ən–q̉ə? *stick on:* (2) 126, 604. k̉ɬ–ən–t̉ɬ *seal:* (2) 175, 237. k̉ɬ–ən–t̉l *open:* (3) 186, 188, 244. k̉ɬ–wk(–cút) *see:* (2) 220, 223. k̉ɬ–yíxʷ *envy:* (1) 232. k̉ɬ–ən–?əɬxʷ *lock in:* (1) 578. k̉ɬ–ən–t̉əws *stand next to:* (1) 687. k̉ɬ–ən–k̉a?t *get close to:* (1) 849.

k̉m   = k̉əm *surface, bulk.* In composition with various affixes assumes a variety of meanings. (7) 48, 53, 224, 273, 498, 838, 914.

k̉níya?   *listen.* (3) 411, 418, 754.

k̉s   = k̉əs stressless allomorph of k̉ás *bad* (q. v.). (4) 281, 400, 789, 883.

k̉wá   allomorph of k̉áw *gone* (q. v.) in the construction k̉wá–p *stop talking.* (2) 704, 728.

k̉ʕáw   *hire, pray.* Ka čaw. (1) 914.

kʷ   *2nd sg intransitive subject* pronoun. (222)

–kʷ   stressless reduplicative allomorph of √lakʷ *far.* (3) 825, 826, 842.

kʷ?ác   as in s–ən–kʷ–kʷ?ác *evening.* Cf. kʷá?c. Ka kʷkʷ?ec. (3) 57, 505, 870.

kʷ?aɬ   inceptive allomorph of kʷáɬ *warm, sweat* (q. v.). Sh c–kʷel. (1) 323.

kʷa   interjection (24) 167, 177, 210, 212, 216, 234, 369, 393, 421, 612, 614, 625, 651, 672, 673, 758, 908, 909, 913, 914, 916.

kʷa?–   reduplicative allomorph of kʷ?aɬ *warm up (from being cold)* (q. v.). 323.

–kʷa?–   reduplicative infix of təkʷ?–út *walk* (q. v.). 842.

kʷa?c   stressless allomorph of kʷ?ác *late, dark* (q. v.) in the constructions kʷa?c–núxʷ, kʷa?c–míx. (2) 516, 848.

kʷáɬ   *warm, sweat.* Ka kʷiɬ. Cf. kʷ?aɬ. (6) 519, 519, 860, 861.

kʷə–₁   reduplicative allomorph of kʷrí *gold(en)* (q. v.). (58).

kʷə–₂   reduplicative allomorph of kʷím (q. v.). (1) 577.

kʷə–₃   reduplicative allomorph of kʷ?ác *evening* (q. v.). (3) 57, 505, 870.

kʷəl·   = kʷl· stressless allomorph of kʷíl *sit.* In the construction kʷəl·–íws the l is always long. Cf. kʷíl. (7) 94, 105, 462, 569,

579, 670, 805.

kʷəlst stressless allomorph of kʷúlst *send* (q. v.). (6) 387, 391, 423, 468, 677, 731.

kʷəl stressless allomorph of kʷál *warm, sweat.* (2) 66, 516.

kʷəƛ̓ = kʷƛ̓ *face; eye(s)* (reduplicated). (4) 501, 511, 848, 853.

kʷən = kʷn stressless allomorph of kʷín *take* (q. v.). (34) 219, 266, 267, 278, 310, 336, 337, 343, 358, 368, 371, 372, 373, 376, 377, 379, 390, 414, 493, 494, 497, 548, 646, 691, 706, 823, 837, 885.

kʷən· allomorph of kʷín *take* (q. v.) in the construction kʷən·–í?st *(manage to) catch.* Reasons for long n not clear. (1) 336.

kʷər̓ = kʷr̓ stressless allomorph of kʷr̓í *gold(en).* (1) 28.

kʷi allomorph of kʷín *take* before the *first* (−n) and *third* (−s) transitive endings. (15) 117, 125, 282, 299, 310, 338, 430, 607, 669, 762, 791, 885, 875, 911.

kʷíl₁ *red.* Ka kʷil. (3) 263, 348, 349.

kʷíl₂ *sit.* (2) 367, 368.

kʷíl· allomorph of kʷíl₂ (with -C2 reduplication ?) *sit* (q. v.). (4) 366, 402, 751, 762.

kʷím̓ form of uncertain meaning. (1) 577.

kʷín *take.* Ka kʷen, Sh kʷen. Cf. kʷís. (16) 264, 288, 290, 368, 529, 615, 643, 650, 692, 700, 707, 711, 715, 823, 872.

kʷínxʷ *answer.* Ka kʷenxʷ. (1) 243.

kʷís₁ *hold.* Cf. kʷín *take.* (3) 88, 902.

kʷís₂ as in k̓əɬ–kʷís *envy.* (2) 157, 159.

kʷl stressless allomorph of kʷíl *sit* (q. v.). In the construction kʷl–íwt *sit, stay:* (4) 1, 401, 433, 440.

kʷl· stressless allomorph of kʷíl (with -C2 reduplication ?) *sit* (q. v.). (2) 94, 105.

kʷƛ̓ = kʷəƛ̓ *face; eye(s)* (reduplicated). (5) 47, 501, 511, 848, 853.

kʷm̓iɬ *suddenly.* (11) 17, 35, 205, 324, 486, 499, 544, 570, 648, 831, 841.

kʷni allomorph of kʷín *take* (q. v.). In middle forms: (6) 303, 369, 493, 494, 497, 837. In the construction kʷni–útya? *grab:* (3) 299, 307, 358.

kʷr̓ stressless allomorph of kʷr̓í *gold(en)* (q. v.). (1) 28.

kʷr̓í *gold(en).* Ka kʷri. (60).

kʷs stressless allomorph of kʷís *hold* (q. v.). (3) 88, 902.

kʷu₁ unclear form in the construction ?əxʷ–kʷú–kst *coax, beg.* Cf. kʷun. (1) 354.

kʷu₂ *1st pl intransitive subject* proclitic.

kʷu₃ *1st sg/pl object* proclitic.

kʷúkʷ unclear. (1) 196.

k̓ʷúlst *send.* Ka k̓ʷul(st). (14) 127, 137, 141, 166, 333, 473, 596, 605, 610, 710, 716, 750, 784.

k̓ʷúm *store, keep.* Ka k̓ʷum. (1) 872.

k̓ʷún *unclear.* In the construction ʔəxʷ–k̓ʷún *coax.* Cf. k̓ʷuı. (2) 418, 768.

k̓ʷúp *as in* t–k̓ʷúp–xn *rush.* Cf. Ka k̓ʷup, Sh k̓ʷup. (1) 646.

k̓ʷ– reduplicative allomorph of k̓ʷíy *small* (q.v.). (4) 641, 643, 731, 859.

–k̓ʷı allomorph of t̓ək̓ʷ (C2 reduplication) *lie on* (q. v.). (9) 49, 274, 277, 327, 499, 647, 674, 843.

–k̓ʷz allomorph of ɬək̓ʷ (C2 reduplication) *remember* (q. v.). (2) 617, 624.

k̓ʷaʔ– reduplicative *diminutive* allomorph of k̓ʷúl *work, make, do.* (1) 899.

k̓ʷaʔ particle possibly meaning *until.* (3) 186, 243, 518.

k̓ʷác *strong.* (2) 345, 359.

k̓ʷə– reduplicative *diminutive* allomorph of k̓ʷíy *small* (q. v.). (10) 20, 23, 139, 463, 464, 477, 642, 760, 815, 871.

k̓ʷəc– reduplicative allomorph of k̓ʷác *strong* (q. v.). (2) 345, 359.

k̓ʷəl stressless allomorph of k̓ʷúl *work, make, do* (q. v.). (16) 140, 141, 412, 418, 419, 719, 735, 740, 742, 747, 760, 766, 916, 921.

k̓ʷəƛ stressless allomorph of k̓ʷƛá *pull out* (q. v.). Cf. k̓ʷíƛ. (7) 79, 80, 300, 536, 539, 559.

k̓ʷən– reduplicative allomorph of k̓ʷínx *indefinite number* (q. v.). (1) 869.

k̓ʷənx stressless allomorph of k̓ʷínx *indefinite number* (q. v.). (1) 869.

k̓ʷəxʷ stressless allomorph of k̓ʷíxʷ *unravel, peel off* (q. v.). (3) 564, 864, 874.

k̓ʷíƛ *rest, remainder, same kind; appear.* Ka k̓ʷíƛt, k̓ʷƛi. Cf. k̓ʷəƛ.
With first meaning: (42) 20, 41, 44, 50, 52, 59, 71, 155, 210, 231, 242, 252, 258, 333, 377, 389, 437, 464, 478, 490, 499, 528, 537, 542, 556, 727, 770, 773, 802, 807, 808, 825, 834, 844, 864, 890, 900, 904, 922.
With second meaning: (4) 381, 675, 684, 867.

k̓ʷín *pick (out).* Ka k̓en, Sh k̓ʷen. (1) 671.

k̓ʷínx *indefinite number.* Ka k̓ʷinš, Sh k̓ʷinx. (4) 16, 445, 842.

k̓ʷít *step over.* (1) 540.

k̓ʷíxʷ *unravel, peel off.* (9) 64, 512, 518, 519, 860, 861, 862, 864.

k̓ʷíy *small.* Ka k̓ʷuyum, Sh koy (key?) ky, ke?. (5) 641, 643, 731, 859, 871.

k̓ʷɬáx *surprise(d).* (1) 720.

k̓ʷƛ stressless allomorph of k̓ʷíƛ *appear* (q. v.). (1) 642.

ꞣʷƛ̓á₁ allomorph (ablaut relationship) of k̓ʷiƛ̓ appear (q. v.), probably with singular meaning. (2) 580, 848.

ꞣʷƛ̓á₂ pull out, take off. Probably related to k̓ʷiƛ̓ appear (q. v.). (2) 212, 862.

k̓ʷúɬ work, make, do. Ka. k̓uɬ, Sh k̓ʷul. (112)

k̓ʷúy as in s–k̓ʷúy man's mother. Ka s–k̓ʷuy, Sh k̓úy̓e. (5) 22, 467, 770, 807, 823.

k̓ʷy stressless allomorph of k̓ʷiy small (q. v.). (9) 20, 23, 139, 463, 464, 477, 642, 760, 815.

l = ɬ locative particle (before V) in, at. (9) 74, 190, 265, 356, 526, 655, 827, 872.

ɬ = l locative particle (before C) in, at. (83)

ɬʔiw man's father. Ka lʔew, Sh lew̓e uncle. (35)

la allomorph of l locative particle before ʔkín, c–xʔít, n–yxʷ–út. (13) 17, 97, 457, 562, 573, 660, 708, 766, 879, 909.

laʔɬ = naʔɬ conjunctive particle with, and. (22) 50, 204, 303, 374, 400, 403, 433, 485, 686, 715, 717, 737, 738, 746, 751, 802, 827, 855, 919.

–laʔxʷ stressless allomorph of –úlaʔxʷ land, earth (lexical suffix) (q. v.). (11) 152, 191, 234, 335, 428, 436, 578, 597, 795, 806, 907.

laklí key (French la clef). (24) 52, 58, 60, 65, 68, 71, 213, 214, 506, 515, 520, 851, 858, 861, 865, 872, 875, 880, 894.

laprít bridle (French la bride). (15) 12, 39, 64, 448, 487, 566, 668, 669, 785, 820, 833, 862, 864, 872.

laputáy bottle (French la boutaille). (3) 642, 655.

lasmís shirt (French la chemise). (1) 897.

latáp table (French la table). (3) 402, 431, 751.

lawán oats (French l'avoine). (6) 67, 507, 517, 519, 860, 861.

ləm stressless allomorph of lím glad, thank(ful) (q. v.). (8) 159, 328, 388, 589, 653, 800, 851, 869.

ləxʷ warn, instruct. Cf? Sh leꭓ. (4) 277, 537, 538, 853.

ləꞓʷ (√líꞓʷ) fit. Ka loꞓʷ, Sh? liꞓʷ. (6) 175, 318, 675, 802, 844.

likúk [likʷúk, likók] rooster (French le coq). (23) 218, 395, 431, 433, 435, 436, 445, 612, 613, 617, 619, 626, 618, 651, 727, 751, 762, 765, 807, 810, 811, 856, 876.

–lílx unclear. Probably an allomorph of –ílx motion (q. v.) with plural reference. (1) 556.

lím glad, thank(ful). Ka lem, Sh lem. (17) 28, 54, 159, 328, 341, 388, 502, 589, 653, 692, 694, 720, 800, 851, 869.

lipúl   *hen* (French *la poule*).   (18) 218, 395, 431, 433, 434, 445, 446, 612, 618, 619, 727, 751, 762, 765, 810, 811, 846, 847.

líw   *ring, bell*.   (2) 915.

ḷkasát   *case, money box* (French *la cassette*).   (2) 431, 762.

ḷkʷ (√lakʷ)   *far, distant*.   Ka lkʷu.   (5) 112, 390, 666, 732, 826.

–ḷqs = –əlqs   stressless allomorph of –álqs *clothing, dress* (lexical suffix) (q. v.).   (2) 635, 655.

–ḷscút = –əlscút   *appurtenances* (lexical suffix).   Ka –elscút.   (1) 914.

–lscʕát   pharyngeal allomorph of –lscut *appurtenances* (lexical suffix) (q. v.).   (1) 748.

–lúp   *pile, place* (lexical suffix).   (4) 15, 454, 461, 793, 873, 923.

lút   *not*.   (264)

lw   stressless allomorph of líw *ring, bell* (q. v.).   (1) 915.

–lwís   *iterative* suffix.   Ka –luís.   (13) 57, 273, 319, 390, 505, 674, 732, 733, 765, 870, 898.

–ḷx₁ = –əlx, –lx   *plural number* suffix.

–ḷx₂   stressless allomorph of –ílx *motion* (q. v.).   521, 889.

–ḷxʷ = –əlxʷ = –lxʷ   stressless allomorph of –ílxʷ *body, cover* (lexical suffix) (q. v.).   (3) 263, 282, 349.

–lxʷ = –ḷxʷ, –əlxʷ   stressless allomorph of –ílxʷ *body, cover* (lexical suffix) (q. v.).   (1) 263.

láx̣   as in s–láx̣–t   *friend, partner*.   Ka (s)ḷax̣t.   (1) 163.

ł–   directional prefix *back, again*.   Cf. łəł–.

ł = łə   *subordinating particle*.

ł?₁   stressless allomorph of łá? *near* (q. v.).   Ka łe?.   (2) 234, 319.

ł?₂ (√łu?)   *spoon*.   (1) 644.

ł?íq̓ʷ   inceptive allomorph of łíq̓ʷ *perceptible* (q. v.).   Ka łaq̓ʷ.   (1) 848.

ła?₁   *near*.   (17) 84, 109, 264, 273, 280, 491, 531, 537, 540, 541, 543, 590, 673, 686, 838, 869.   In the construction na–łá? *the other side*.   Ka łe?.   (1) 275.

ła?₂   particle *when*.   (25) 92, 160, 169, 189, 221, 241, 244, 245, 252, 317, 494, 511, 531, 623, 659, 718, 798, 803, 840, 861, 864, 911, 912, 925.

ła?–   reduplicative allomorph of ła?t́ *wet* (q. v.).   (1) 289.

ła?t́ (√łat̓)   *wet*.   Sh łat̓.   (1) 289.

ła?t́áp   diminutive allomorph of łt́ap *jump off* (q. v.).   (1) 902.

ła?xʷ   *breathe*.   (6) 155, 390, 681, 869, 898, 915.

ɬác *pat, stroke.* Ka ɬc, Sh ɬec. (2) 204, 502.

ɬáxʷ *hang.* Sh ɬuxʷ. (1) 833.

ɬc (√ɬac) *soak(ed), drip.* Ka ɬc(a), Sh ɬac. (1) 346.

ɬcíck *mother-in-law.* Probably further segmentable. Ka ɬcecč, Sh ɬcəcek. (1) 700.

ɬc̓ *whip.* (2) 824.

ɬə–1 reduplicative allomorph of ɬˤac *soak(ed), drip* (q. v.). (1) 346.

ɬə–2 reduplicative allomorph of ɬˤat̓ *wet* (q. v.). (1) 266.

ɬə = ɬ subordinating particle. (10) 252, 469, 480, 491, 493, 625, 800.

ɬəc stressless allomorph of ɬác *pat, stroke* (q. v.). (1) 255.

ɬəc̓ allomorph of ɬc̓ *whip* (q. v.). (2) 34, 36.

ɬək̓ʷ *remember.* Ka ɬk̓ʷk̓ʷ, Sh ɬək̓ʷ. (8) 64, 419, 421, 617, 624, 735, 856.

ɬəɬ–1 directional prefix *back again.* Cf. ɬ–. (7) 90, 198, 200, 222, 553, 880.

ɬəɬ–2 plural prefix. (8) 131, 194, 207, 488, 558, 629, 684.

–ɬəm = –ɬm stressless allomorph of –ɬúləm *2nd pl transitive object* suffix (q. v.). (5) 201, 439, 662, 864.

ɬəp̓ *disgusted.* (3) 103, 314, 315.

ɬəq̓ʷ = ɬq̓ʷ *lie down.* Cf. ɬq̓2. Ka ɬq̓ʷu, Sh ɬq̓ʷut. (5) 71, 79, 558.

ɬət̓ reduplicative allomorph of ɬt̓áp *jump off* (q. v.). (1) 902.

ɬət̓p stressless allomorph of ɬt̓ap *jump off* (q. v.). (1) 827.

ɬəxʷ stressless allomorph of ɬíxʷ *hang, drape over, slip on* (q. v.). (2) 897.

ɬik̓– reduplicative allomorph of ɬik̓tá *sob* (q. v.). (2) 205, 255.

ɬik̓tá *sob.* (2) 205, 255.

ɬíp *disappear, forget.* Ka ɬep, Sh ɬep. (9) 49, 50, 71, 338, 614, 747, 844, 865, 894.

ɬíq̓ʷ *perceptible.* Ka ɬaq̓ʷ. Cf. ɬʔíq̓ʷ. (1) 840.

ɬíxʷ *hang, drape over, slip on.* Ka ɬxxʷ (?), Sh ɬuxʷ. (2) 872, 903.

ɬíx̣ʷp̓ *escape, run out.* Ka ɬx̣up̓, Sh ɬx̣ʷ–up. Cf. ɬx̣ʷp, ɬx̣ʷp̓á. (5) 425, 557, 686, 863.

–ɬm = –ɬəm stressless allomorph of –ɬúləm *2nd pl transitive object* suffix (q. v.). (8) 10, 112, 439, 764, 776, 796, 906.

ɬm̓ *respect.* (2) 22, 467.

–ɬníwt *side* (lexical suffix). (2) 919.

ɬq̓1 (√ɬaq̓–t) *wide.* Ka ɬaq̓, Sh ɬeq̓. Cf. ɬq̓ *lie down.* (1) 914.

ɬq̓2 *lie down.* Ka ɬq̓, Sh ɬeq̓. Cf. ɬq̓ʷ. (19) 33, 72, 76, 83, 84, 85, 90, 481, 484, 523, 525, 537, 541, 543, 827, 829, 836.

ɬq̓ʷ = ɬəq̓ʷ *lie down.* Ka ɬq̓ʷ. Cf. ɬq̓. (27) 62, 70, 71, 74, 148, 522, 523, 526, 527, 531, 539, 540, 543, 682, 721, 865, 889, 891, 892, 893,

895, 898, 899, 901, 914.

ɫs   *stink*. In the construction s‑ən‑ɫs‑ípna? *cigar*. (3) 404, 414, 655.

—ɫt   *ditransitive* suffix. (66) 4, 26, 27, 49, 62, 66, 70, 71, 79, 88, 110, 117, 132, 136, 167, 175, 179, 181, 183, 185, 199, 210, 211, 226, 228, 240, 248, 249, 253, 259, 291, 328, 331, 353, 384, 470, 476, 514, 522, 590, 595, 599, 614, 620, 623, 631, 651, 761, 771, 790, 821, 850, 861, 865, 874, 893, 902, 906, 919, 923.

—ɫtíɫən = —ɫtíɫn   *question, information* (lexical suffix). Cf. —íɫən, —nwíɫən. (1) 800.

—ɫtíɫn = —ɫtíɫən   *question, information* (lexical suffix). Cf. —íɫən, —nwíɫən. (2) 405, 587.

ɫtáp   *jump off*. (2) 552, 902.

ɫu—   reduplicative allomorph of √ɫu? *spoon*. Cf. ɫ?. Ka ɫu?‑mn. (1) 644.

—ɫúləm   *2nd pl transitive object* suffix. (3) 201, 530, 535.

ɫwí   allomorph of ɫwín *leave* (q. v.) before ɫ. (1) 662.

ɫwín   *leave*. Sh ɫwel. (5) 437, 438, 774, 776, 777.

ɫwn   stressless allomorph of ɫwín *leave* (q. v.). (6) 361, 362, 364, 644, 645.

—ɫxʷ   stressless allomorph of —íɫxʷ *house* (lexical suffix) (q. v.). (8) 116, 118, 603, 604, 607, 908.

ɫx̣ʷp   *escape* (in the construction ɫx̣ʷp‑nú the p is not glottalized). Ka ɫx̣ʷp. Cf. ɫíx̣ʷp̓, ɫx̣ʷpá. (3) 306, 312, 477.

ɫx̣ʷpá   *escape*. Cf. ɫx̣ʷp, ɫíx̣ʷp̓. (9) 93, 105, 450, 563, 569, 578, 849, 869, 919.

ɫʕa?x̣   *lace (?)*. (1) 903.

ɫʕac   *soak(ed), drip*. Ka ɫca, Sh ɫac. (1) 308.

ɫʕat̓   *wet*. Sh ɫat̓. (1) 266.

ƛ̓?a   allomorph of ƛ̓a? *look for* (q. v.) in middle and transitive imperative constructions. (6) 192, 333, 362, 440, 668, 750.

ƛ̓a?   *look for*. Ka ƛ̓u?. In transitive constructions: (22) 179, 196, 197, 211, 214, 248, 249, 253, 259, 289, 293, 353, 355, 369, 370, 477, 677, 710, 761, 923. In constructions with lexical suffixes or —míx: (12) 17, 114, 167, 465, 495, 676, 808, 819. In compounds: (3) 600, 779, 780. In construction with kəɫ—, with the meaning *jealous*: (2) 639. In reflexive constructions: (2) 679.

ƛ̓áq   as in ƛ̓áq‑na? *pocket*. Ka ƛ̓áqne?. (4) 29, 219, 822.

ƛ̓áw̓   *extinguish*. (2) 78, 545.

ƛ̓áxʷ   *die, kill*. (7) 44, 50, 329, 489, 834, 844, 900.

ƛ̓áx̣   *fast*. Ka ƛ̓ax̣. (1) 922.

ƛ̓əm = ƛ̓m   *past*. (3) 43, 650, 759.

ƛ̓əw̓ = ƛ̓w̓   stressless allomorph of ƛ̓áw̓ *extinguish* (q. v.). (1) 78.

ƛ̓əxʷ = ƛ̓xʷ stressless allomorph of ƛ̓áxʷ *die, kill* (q. v.). (7) 81, 167, 530, 535, 538, 542.

ƛ̓əx̣₁ stressless allomorph of ƛ̓áx̣ *fast* (q. v.). (1) 674.

ƛ̓əx̣₂ *loud.* (2) 95, 901.

ƛ̓əx̣₃ stressless allomorph of √ƛ̓ax̣ *grow.* Cf. ƛ̓x̣á. (28) 20, 160, 162, 205, 257, 375, 400, 410, 436, 437, 465, 592, 616, 638, 639, 640, 649, 712, 713, 731, 738, 746, 754, 788, 820, 887.

ƛ̓l stressless allomorph of √ƛ̓al *motionless, lifeless.* Cf. ƛ̓lá. (26) 162, 171, 205, 207, 209, 221, 257, 302, 305, 345, 441, 459, 472, 475, 531, 647, 654, 658, 670, 672, 692, 803, 814, 902.

ƛ̓lá *motionless, lifeless.* In the construction ƛ̓lá-p *stop.* Cf. ƛ̓l. Ka ƛ̓il, Sh t̓il. (8) 188, 408, 415, 612, 664, 888, 901, 918.

ƛ̓m = ƛ̓əm *past.* (4) 488, 489, 492, 835.

ƛ̓w̓ = ƛ̓əw̓ stressless allomorph of ƛ̓áw̓ *extinguish* (q. v.). (1) 555.

ƛ̓xʷ = ƛ̓əxʷ stressless allomorph of ƛ̓axʷ (q. v.). (3) 41, 158, 489.

ƛ̓xʷú *win.* Ka ƛ̓xʷu, Sh t̓xʷ–um. (1) 17.

ƛ̓x̣á (√ƛ̓ax̣) *grow* Sh t̓əx̣. (28) 20, 160, 162, 205, 257, 375, 376, 400, 410, 436, 437, 465, 592, 616, 638, 639, 640, 649, 712, 713, 731, 738, 746, 754, 788, 820.

−m₁ = −əm₁ *middle voice* suffix.

−m₂ = −əm₂ stressless allomorph of −ím *1st pl transitive subject* pronoun.

−m₃ = −əm₃ stressless allomorph of −ím *transitive indefinite subject* pronoun.

−m₄ = −əm₄ stressless allomorph of −úm *2nd sg object* suffix.

−m = −m = −əm (q. v.).

−m̓ allomorph of qʷím̓ (C2 reduplication) *afraid* (q. v.). (3) 859, 877.

m̓ʔán *mid-afternoon.* (1) 348.

m̓ʔím *women (plural).* Ka mʔem. (5) 71, 83, 525, 528, 686.

ma?− reduplicative allomorph of mʔim in the construction s−ma?−m̓ʔím *women.* (6) 71, 83, 252, 525, 528, 686.

ma?₁ unclear in the construction n̓−ma?−íp *tell on.* Probably related to ma? (q. v.). (6) 252, 632, 658, 659, 660.

ma?₂ *interjection.* (2) 186, 243.

−ma? unclear suffix in the constructions ʔúkʷ−ma?, xʷs−ma?−cín. (1) 208.

ma?s *unmatched, different (ages).* (2) 638, 640.

málkʷ *complete, round.* Ka milk̓ʷ, Sh mlk̓ʷ. (1) 307.

málx̣a? *tell falsehood.* (5) 164, 301, 302, 305, 660.

mánxʷ smoke (tobacco). Ka menxʷ, Sh s-menx. (1) 404.

máq stop, keep from. (1) 664.

mátəm interjection. (1) 811.

məcq́ʷúləm mouthful, swallow. (1) 644.

məl₁ in the construction məl-qn-úps eagle. Ka mlqnups. (5) 320, 323, 328, 358, 363,

məl₂ stressless allomorph of míl slow. (6) 91, 489, 578, 673, 835, 916.

məlk̇ʷ stressless allomorph of málk̇ʷ complete, round (q. v.). Ka milk̇ʷ, Sh mlk̇ʷ. (1) 407.

məlχa? stressless allomorph of málχa? tell falsehood (q. v.). (10) 162, 207, 210, 235, 258, 333, 542, 543, 550.

məɬ conjunction and. (101)

—mən stressless allomorph of —mín instrumental suffix (q. v.). (6) 149, 448, 474, 644, 800, 801.

mət dubitative particle maybe. (66)

—mi— transitive stem formative suffix. (37) 17, 22, 36, 64, 149, 156, 287, 301, 314, 319, 320, 323, 327, 361, 419, 421, 467, 472, 483, 486, 517, 617, 624, 694, 696, 700, 723, 735, 813, 814, 831, 836, 856, 860, 861.

mi future particle. (101)

mil slow. (5) 91, 489, 578 835, 916.

míla? bait. Sh ml lure. (2) 524, 849.

mílk̇ʷ as in k-mílk̇ʷ-əst-m-ənt rub against somebody. Cf? málk̇ʷ complete, round. (1) 529.

miɬ paint, rub. Ka miɬ, Sh (?) meɬ. (11) 124, 126, 607, 608, 610, 908, 909, 910.

—mín instrumental suffix. (22) 72, 117, 118, 125, 181, 185, 186, 243, 250, 437, 440, 599, 605, 610, 660, 686, 772, 773, 778.

miná probably not. (7) 161, 363, 374, 376, 885, 903, 907.

—mist intransitive reflexive suffix. Cf? —i?st. (22) 36, 81, 278, 291, 304, 360, 361, 370, 428, 437, 477, 483, 484, 531, 653, 735, 740, 748, 828, 898, 900, 914. Unstressed (5) 91, 278, 329, 465, 518, 560.

—míx₁ in the construction (s—)xi?-míx any/some time, place, thing. (2) 200, 800, 820, 869.

—míx₂ one who is ...ing. (22) 66, 81, 114, 162, 205, 257, 305, 408, 412, 441, 459, 495, 516, 538, 542, 731, 735, 803, 840, 841, 848.

míy₁ know, be sure. Ka miy. Cf. my. (10) 252, 266, 307, 341, 343, 356, 536, 586, 610, 799.

míy₂ place on top of. (1) 283.

míyn rub. (1) 646.

mnímɬ plural independent pronoun stem. (3) 564, 598, 671.

—mp = —əmp 2nd pl possessive suffix. (2) 149, 906.

mrəm   stressless allomorph of mrím *spouse, marry* (q. v.). (1) 890.

mr·im   perfective allomorph of mrím *spouse, marry* (q. v.). (4) 22, 374, 403, 698.

mrím₁   *spouse, marry.* (18) 392, 403, 413, 615, 617, 621, 634, 636, 638, 641, 653, 655, 698, 699, 715, 717, 722, 728, 737, 755, 890.

mrím₂   *medicine.* Ka mali, mari, Sh mlam. (3) 646, 647.

mús₁   in the construction mús–kst *take a chance.* Cf. ṁs. (3) 261, 370.

mús₂   *four.* Ka mus, Sh mus. (7) 2, 89, 111, 145, 262, 524, 552.

mút   *sit.* Cf. Ka ?emút, Sh mut. Cf. ?am·út. (15) 20, 174, 283, 429, 431, 464, 465, 591, 751, 758, 808, 884.

my₁   *know.* Ka miy. Cf. míy. (66) 1, 6, 10, 16, 17, 57, 122, 127, 132, 137, 141, 146, 156, 160, 169, 182, 223, 231, 440, 443, 456, 460, 493, 500, 505, 558, 563, 581, 599, 600, 602, 605, 608, 620, 626, 627, 641, 690, 772, 773, 778, 781, 789, 795, 800, 801, 802, 811, 842, 850, 870, 877, 908, 911, 912, 922.

my₂   *superlative* (in compounds). (13) 2, 160, 327, 375, 377, 448, 592, 593, 643, 649, 730, 906.

myáł   *too much.* (15) 20, 60, 240, 464, 616, 640, 693, 694, 739, 748, 753, 760, 808, 864, 883.

mˤan   *interjection.* (2) 178, 733.

–m̓   unclear. Apparent reduplicative allomorph of stím *what* (q. v.). (1) 438.

ma?–₁   reduplicative allomorph of máya? *teach* (q. v.). Cf. may?. (14) 3, 5, 118, 163, 599, 604, 701, 702, 771, 773.

ma?–₂   reduplicative allomorph of may? *tell* (q. v.). Cf. máya? (1) 922.

may?   *tell.* Unstressed in the constructions may?–ncút: (21) 156, 332, 402, 403, 411, 412, 413, 418, 432, 434, 436, 612, 613, 617, 728, 751, 764, 765, 769, 855, 856; may?–xt–wíxʷ: (7) 367, 625, 650, 651, 697, 728; and normally in all other transitive constructions (with –nt, –st, –łt): (5) 613, 623, 769, 811, 857, 922. Stressed in the constructions mi?–máy?, ma?–máy? (3) 568, 897, 922.

máya?   *teach.* Cf. may?. In intransitive constructions: (13) 3, 5, 118, 163, 599, 604, 701, 702, 771, 773, 811; in transitive constructions: (16) 4, 62, 70, 71, 113, 132, 209, 447, 595, 599, 614, 651, 771, 865, 894.

mi?–   reduplicative allomorph of mya? in the construction mi?–mya?–ncút *experience.* (4) 6, 122, 156, 603.

mi?   unclear in the constructions mi?–ncút: (1) 160; mi?–nú–łt: (1) 897; mi?–máy?: (2) 568, 897.

miws   unclear, probably further segmentable, *middle.* (1) 713.

ṁs stressless allomorph of √ṁus *hope*. Cf. mus₁. (1) 341.

ṁú– reduplicative allomorph of ṁs *hope* (q. v.). (1) 341.

ṁya? as in ṁi?–ṁya? *experience*. Cf. máya?, ṁay?. (4) 6, 122, 156, 603.

n– *locative* prefix.

–n stressless allomorph of –ín *1st sg transitive subject* pronoun.

na– allomorph of n– *locative* in the construction na–ɬá? *other side* (q. v.). Cf. ɬa?₁. (1) 275.

ná– reduplicative allomorph of naqs *one* (q. v.) in the construction ná–naqs *alone*. (1) 801.

–ná *transitive* suffix in the form ?am–ná– *feed*. (2) 513, 517.

–na? stressless allomorph of –ína? *ear, cover* (lexical suffix) (q. v.). (4) 29, 219, 822.

na?ɬ conjunctive particle *with*. (5) 612, 676, 686, 738, 762.

na?ɬc stressless allomorph of na?ɬcá–m *forget*. (2) 420, 747.

na?ɬcá *forget*. (1) 421.

nákʷá? emphatic negative *indeed not*. Cf. nákʷəm. (10) 169, 341, 456, 460, 483, 505, 646, 795, 801, 863.

nákʷəm emphatic evidential *indeed*. Cf. nakʷá?. (21) 48, 189, 194, 210, 245, 273, 285, 298, 320, 324, 326, 509, 576, 577, 613, 628, 690, 714, 857, 879.

náqs *one*. (30) 15, 80, 89, 120, 262, 263, 326, 329, 441, 454, 459, 541, 644, 724, 763, 801, 803, 852, 892, 908, 911, 919.

náqʷ *steal*. Ka naqʷ, Sh nqʷ–um. (3) 228, 851, 872.

náxəmɬ *however*. (45)

náxʷ *wife*. Ka noxʷ, Sh nuxʷ. (1) 923.

–ncút *reflexive* suffix. (48) 6, 18, 55, 122, 140, 141, 156, 160, 212, 332, 402, 403, 411, 412, 413, 418, 419,432, 434, 436, 503, 603, 612, 613, 617, 625, 719, 728, 735, 742, 747, 751, 760, 764, 765, 766, 769, 832, 853, 855, 856, 916, 921.

nəqs stressless allomorph of náqs *one* (q. v.). (8) 145, 410, 461, 467, 548, 873, 889, 923.

nəxʷ = nxʷ = ənxʷ stressless allomorph of náxʷ *wife* (q. v.). (1) 923.

níkxna? interjection. (15) 28, 39, 381, 388, 391, 487, 646, 652, 685, 694, 700, 720, 807, 868, 890.

nís *gone*. Sh nes. (5) 274, 300, 310, 346.

níw *wind blows*. Ka neẇ, Sh s–new–t. (4) 47, 283, 319.

níxəl = níxl *hear, understand.* (11) 78, 205, 257, 408, 533, 534, 544, 546, 570, 901.

níxl = níxəl *hear, understand.* (8) 196, 247, 253, 324, 326, 391, 412, 697.

nixʷ particle *also.* (32) 12, 23, 72, 80, 121, 131, 326, 478, 484, 511, 518, 529, 534, 541, 562, 599, 653, 674, 692, 761, 793, 794, 844, 853, 860, 891, 899, 916.

ṇk̓ʷ– *one* (bound root in compounds only). Ka nk̓ʷu?, Sh nk̓ʷu?. (5) 1, 7, 150, 459, 643.

–nt– *transitive* suffix. (254)

ṇt̓a? interjection. (34) 104, 159, 227, 286, 314, 322, 381, 383, 385, 409, 466, 480, 487, 578, 583, 592, 648, 649, 688, 689, 692, 700, 759, 788, 789, 824, 827, 833, 879.

–nú– transitivizing suffix *manage to.* (51) 127, 132, 141, 162, 169, 171, 221, 231, 267, 278, 306, 312, 325, 343, 345, 358, 371, 372, 373, 376, 377, 390, 440, 469, 477, 480, 484, 500, 599, 600, 605, 626, 628, 633, 676, 706, 773, 778, 781, 789, 885, 897. Cf. –nún–

–númt intransitive suffix of unclear meaning, possibly *reflexive completive.* (23) 81, 363, 400, 530, 535, 563. 76, 383, 524, 530, 535, 558, 648, 649, 891. 754, 901. 91, 223, 286, 694.

–nún– allomorph of –nú– *manage to* (q. v.) in possessive constructions. (3) 266, 339, 608.

–núxʷ *span of time* (lexical suffix). (6) 56, 294, 355, 504, 516, 580.

–nwíɬən *information* (lexical suffix). Cf. –íɬən, –ɬtíɬən. (8) 6, 132, 156, 160, 602, 772, 911, 912.

–ṇwís *high, up.* Ka nwist. (1) 521.

–nwíxʷ *reciprocal* suffix. Cf. –ənwíxʷ, –ənwáxʷ, –twíxʷ.

–nxʷ unclear in the construction tká–nxʷ *in contact.* (2) 297, 344.

níṇwi? *if and when, in a while.* (109)

p proclitic subject pronoun *you pl.*

–p *non control* suffix.

pa?–₁ reduplicative allomorph of pín *fold* (q. v.). (1) 175.

pa?–₂ reduplicative allomorph of pút *just, exactly, even* (q. v.). (1) 643.

pa?–₃ reduplicative allomorph of pa?s *think* (q. v.); in the construction pa?–pa?s–ínk *feel bad.* (10) 202, 206, 208, 225, 254, 256, 258, 260, 472, 638, 643.

pa?s *think.* Cf. Ka pupusenč. (10) 202, 206, 208, 225, 254, 256, 258, 260, 472, 638.

páʔx̣ *think.* Cf. pax̣. Stressed in the construction k̓əⱡ–páʔx̣: (3) 4, 236, 679.

paʔx̣ stressless allomorph of páʔx̣ *think* (q. v.). Cf. pax̣. (8) 165, 233, 468, 473, 615, 616, 717, 818.

paʔx̣á allomorph of páʔx̣ *think* in middle constructions. Cf. pax̣. (3) 165, 233, 671.

páx̣₁ *think.* Ka pax̣. Cf. paʔx̣(á). (4) 160, 172, 641, 693.

páx̣₂ *rub, strike against.* Ka pax̣, Sh pex̣. (1) 568.

pǽsčər *pasture* (English). (1) 201.

pə–₁ reduplicative allomorph of ptwínax̣ʷ *old woman* (q. v.). (35) 54, 71, 73, 78, 86, 90, 93, 95, 106, 166, 167, 213, 220, 223, 410, 424, 502, 514, 520, 524, 530, 548, 551, 552, 553, 560, 563, 569, 570, 578, 848, 851, 865, 869, 893.

pə–₂ reduplicative allomorph of psʕáy *feeble minded* (q. v.). (1) 465.

pə–₃ reduplicative allomorph of pʕás *baby chick* (q. v.). (1) 323.

pəlx stressless allomorph of pílx *enter* (q. v.). (1) 582.

pən allomorph of penh *time* (q. v.). In the construction pən–ʔkín *some time.* Cf. pín₁. (3) 5, 625, 708.

pənh *time.* Ka pen, Sh pen. Cf. pín₁. (4) 491, 499, 834, 844.

–pəs reduplicative allomorph of pʕás *baby chick* (q. v.). (1) 323.

pət? allomorph of pút *just, exactly, even* (q. v.) in the construction pət?–íls *respect feelings.* (2) 10, 439.

pi?– *during* (lexical prefix). In the construction pi?–scíⱡt *yesterday.* Ka spi?scé?. (1) 802.

píl *flat, open* (country). (1) 443.

pílx *enter.* Ka pilš. (7) 52, 110, 111, 591, 594, 687, 797.

pín₁ *time;* in the construction s–pín–tk *year.* Cf. pənh. (5) 7, 150, 459, 643.

pín₂ *fold.* (1) 175.

píq *white.* Ka piq, Sh piq, peq. (3) 477, 792, 793.

pk̓ʷ *pour something solid.* Ka puk̓ʷ, Sh pək̓ʷ. (3) 29, 458, 822.

–pla? stressless allomorph of –ípla? *handle, manipulate* (lexical suffix) (q. v.). (4) 55, 437, 503, 588.

pⱡ̓ stressless allomorph of púⱡ̓ *complete, finish, come to the end* (q. v.). Ka puⱡ̓əm, Sh puⱡ̓. (4) 3, 154, 163, 773.

pn in the construction pn–icí? *at that time.* Cf. pənh, pín. (2) 791, 825.

pna? dubitative particle *maybe.* (22) 176, 187, 246, 267, 278, 440, 457, 461, 465, 472, 561, 617, 641, 796, 799, 801, 808, 814, 830, 869, 925.

psʕáy *feeble minded.* (6) 139, 465, 466, 693, 851, 872.

ptwínax̣ʷ as in pə–ptwínax̣ʷ *old woman.* (35) 54, 71, 73, 78, 86, 90,

93, 95, 106, 166, 167, 213, 220, 223, 410, 424, 502, 514, 520, 524, 530,
548, 551, 552, 553, 560, 563, 569, 570, 578, 848, 851, 865, 869, 893.

pu?–   *spouse* (lexical prefix). (1) 890.

pu?   as in s–pu?–ús *heart*. Ka s–p?us, Sh (?) pus–mn. (16) 9, 11,
62, 172, 184, 236, 406, 479, 598, 615, 647, 770, 783, 815, 885, 887.

púl   *kill*. Ka puls. (6) 170, 311, 315, 317, 482, 503.

púlx   *camp, spend the night*. (26) 56, 57, 59, 128, 147, 166, 212, 230, 268,
270, 499, 504, 505, 553, 666, 673, 797, 835, 849, 850, 869, 871, 893.

púƛ   *complete, finish, come to the end*. Ka puƛ, Sh put. (5) 5, 188, 437,
440, 913.

pút   *just, exactly, even*. Ka put, Sh put. (28) 7, 85, 93, 105, 121, 131,
216, 265, 266, 280, 286, 343, 357, 364, 367, 381, 383, 440, 446, 459,
579, 675, 713, 802, 869, 901, 909, 918. In the construction pút–əm:
(1) 422; in the construction pút–i? *still*: (5) 19, 139, 213, 298, 346;
in the construction pa?–pút *even*: (1) 643; in the construction
ņ–pút–əls *satisfied*: (1) 391.

púts   *boots* (English). (2) 903.

puw   stressless allomorph of √pʕaw *make noise*. Cf ? pw *beat a drum*.
(1) 96.

px̣   stressless allomorph of páx̣ɪ *think* (q. v.). (9) 160, 571, 641, 693, 770,
771.

px̣ʷ   stressless allomorph of px̣ʷá *scatter, diversify* (q. v.). (5) 153, 461, 656,
801.

px̣ʷá   *scatter, diversify*. (1) 912.

pʕás   *baby chick*. (1) 323.

p̓?áx̣ʷ   *shine*. Ka p̓exʷ. (19) 216, 285, 286, 381, 383, 508, 509, 563, 567,
689, 694, 727, 853, 867, 879.

p̓a?–   reduplicative allomorph of p̓?áx̣ʷ *shine* (q. v.). (4) 385, 854, 877.

p̓a?x̣ʷ   stressless allomorph of p̓?axʷ *shine* (q. v.). (6) 285, 381, 385, 854,
877.

p̓əlk̓   (√plák̓) *turn back*. (2) 186, 817.

p̓i?q = p̓yq   (√p̓yaq) *ready to eat, ripe*. Ka p̓yaq. (1) 858.

p̓ícən   *rope*. Ka s–p̓eč–n. (1) 785.

–q–   reduplicative infix of √tˀraq *kick, dance*. Cf. təˀrq. (5) 204, 414, 656,
728.

—q₁ reduplicative allomorph of cəq *put down, place, rest* (q. v.). (2) 645, 657.

—q₂ reduplicative allomorph of təq *fool, trick* (q. v.). (1) 339.

—q₃ allomorph of —qín *head* (lexical suffix) (q. v.). before s. (1) 204.

qá—₁ reduplicative allomorph of qc₁ in the construction ł—qá—qc—a? *older brother* (q. v.). (13) 80, 81, 121, 131, 194, 207, 488, 526, 538, 541, 558, 607, 629.

qá—₂ reduplicative allomorph of qs₁ *dark* (q. v.). (2) 408, 734.

qá—₃ reduplicative allomorph of qc₃ *trot.* (1) 480.

qa?ł— lexical prefix *children, family.* (4) 151, 323, 448, 789.

qám *stand.* (1) 735.

qáp *cap.* Sh qp—em. (1) 72.

qc₁ as in ł—qá—qc—a? *older brother.* Ka łqáqce?. Sh qé?ce *father.* (13) 80, 81, 121, 131, 194, 207, 480, 488, 526, 538, 541, 558, 607, 629.

qc₂ *draw back.* Ka qc(i). (1) 310.

qc₃ *trot.* Ka qec—lš. (2) 480, 904.

qəl₁ as in s—qəl—tmíxʷ *man.* Ka sqltmixʷ. Cf? qíl₁, qíl₂. (9) 22, 326, 434, 467, 648, 649, 650, 694, 766.

qəl₂ as in t—qəl—p—məncút *squirm.* (1) 359.

qəl₃ = ql stressless allomorph of qíl—t *top, step on* (q. v.). (2) 43, 897.

qəm₁ = qm *satisfied.* (3) 171, 325, 554.

qəm₂ stressless allomorph of qam *stand* (q. v.). (1) 735.

—qən = —qn stressless allomorph of —qín *head* (lexical suffix) (q. v.). (18) 72, 79, 80, 85, 101, 102, 212, 409(?), 451, 502, 525, 536, 552, 559, 576, 902.

qəxʷ *whip.* Ka qixʷ, Sh qixʷ. (3) 31, 34, 785.

—qí stressed allomorph of —qín *head* (lexical suffix) before s. (9) 34, 303, 311, 431, 482, 539, 762, 793, 828.

qíc *trot.* Ka qec. (1) 840.

qíl₁ in the construction s—qíl—tk *body.* Ka qel. (10) 267, 307, 335, 344, 383, 519, 552, 693, 902.

qíl₂ *top, step on.* Ka ql—t, Sh qelt. (4) 87, 98, 547, 575.

qílxʷ *Indian, person.* Ka s—qélixʷ, Sh qlmuxʷ, qelmxʷ. (79)

qíł *awak(en).* Ka qíł, Sh qíł. () 538, 541, 556, 617, 622, 624, 856, 900.

—qín *head* (lexical suffix). (13) 36, 80, 286, 298, 308, 346, 383, 444, 494, 536, 559, 830.

—qína?—xən *diminutive* allomorph of —qín—xən *toe* (lexical suffix). (3) 266, 298, 308.

qípc   *spring time.* Ka qepc, Sh s-qepc. (1) 3.

ql = qəl   *stressless allomorph of* qíl-t   *top, step on* (q. v.). (1) 295.

qláw̓   *beaver, money.* Ka s-qlew̓, Sh s-qlew̓. (27) 14, 16, 17, 18, 23, 28, 29, 286, 449, 453, 458, 477, 766, 791, 793, 797, 798, 799, 815, 822.

qɫ₁   *reduplicative allomorph of* qíɫ *awak(en)* (q. v.). (3) 81, 556, 901.

qɫ₂   *able.* (4) 469, 480, 484, 633.

qm = qəm   *satisfied.* (3) 225, 268, 379.

qmí   *put something down.* (3) 219, 793.

−qn = −qən   *stressless allomorph of* −qín   *head* (lexical suffix) (q. v.). (11) 39, 72, 79, 320, 323, 328, 358, 363, 525, 539, 543.

qp   *as in* qp-qín-tŋ *hair.* (2) 286, 383.

qs₁   *dark.* (2) 408, 734.

qs₂   *scratch, tickle.* Sh qəs-qis. (8) 408, 528, 529, 531, 899.

qʕay   *vise-like.* (1) 359.

q̓a?   *in the construction* q̓a?-íls   *bother, business.* (16) 20, 113, 120, 121, 130, 200, 201, 269, 331, 332, 369, 464, 512, 594, 766, 903.

q̓áy̓   *write.* Ka q̓ey̓, Sh q̓ey̓. (11) 175, 176, 180, 181, 189, 190, 239, 244, 245, 252.

q̓ə−   *reduplicative allomorph of* q̓sá-p-i?   *long time ago.* (1) 898.

q̓ə?   *insert. In the construction* q̓ə?-xán   *shoes:* (4) 448, 451, 897, 903. *In the construction* k̓ɫ−ən−q̓ə?-íp   *a sign on the door:* (3) 126, 604, 905. *In the construction* q̓ə?-íws   *middle one:* (7) 15, 130, 527, 692, 751, 794, 891.

q̓əl−   *reduplicative allomorph of* q̓əlxʷ *hook* (q. v.). (4) 366, 368, 379, 637.

q̓əl   (√q̓il−t) *sick.* (4) 22, 472, 814.

q̓əlxʷ   *hook.* (4) 366, 368, 379, 637.

q̓əm   *as in* n−q̓əm-s-cín *wish for.* Ka č̓ɫ−q̓mi. (4) 210, 226, 288, 353.

q̓əx   *stressless allomorph of* q̓íx *stingy of* (q. v.). Cr q̓ex Ka q̓ixt. (1) 353.

q̓əy̓ = q̓y̓   *stressless allomorph of* q̓áy̓ *write* (q. v.). (32) 49, 117, 118, 125, 136, 141, 175, 181, 185, 186, 189, 210, 235, 243, 246, 250, 259, 437, 440, 599, 604, 605, 610, 660, 772, 773, 832.

q̓íx   *stingy of.* Sh q̓ix, Cr q̓ex. (2) 353, 421.

q̓l   *drape around.* Ka s−q̓l-eps *necklace.* (16) 262, 264, 269, 271, 282, 287, 299, 310, 335, 338, 340, 349, 350, 352, 357, 358.

q̓ɫ   *match.* Cf? Sh q̓eɫ *braid.* (1) 526.

q̓m   *stressless allomorph of* q̓má *wish for* (q. v.). Ka s−q̓m-eɫt-n, Sh q̓m-eltn. (3) 719, 796, 799.

qmá   *wish for.* (1) 246.

qsá   as in q̓sá–p–i?   *long ago.* Ka q̓sípi?, Sh q̓?es. (4) 149, 408, 842, 898.

q̓xʷ   *wish.* Ka q̓exʷ. (1) 908.

q̓y = q̓əy̓ stressless allomorph of q̓áy̓ *write* (q. v.). (2) 175, 237.

q̓yá   allomorph of q̓áy̓ *write* (q. v.) in middle constructions. (8) 174, 175, 210, 236, 237, 259, 609.

q̓ʕa   *move.* Sh q̓ʕ, q̓ʕeʕ. (1) 840.

qʷ–1   reduplicative allomorph of qʷál̓ *shut lightly* (q. v.). (1) 841.

qʷ–2   reduplicative allomorph of qʷíl̓ *waste time* (q. v.). (1) 844.

qʷ?ál̓   allomorph of qʷíl1 *talk* (q. v.). (2) 625.

qʷ?ám   *accustomed.* Ka qʷe?m. (1) 898.

qʷa?–1   reduplicative allomorph of qʷ?ál̓ (√qʷil) *talk* (q. v.). (2) 625.

qʷa?–2   reduplicative allomorph of qʷa?m *accustomed* (q. v.). (1) 440.

qʷa?m   stressless allomorph of qʷ?ám *accustomed* (q. v.). (5) 156, 440, 696, 854, 878.

qʷa?síya?   as in s–qʷs–qʷa?síya?   *children.* Cf. qʷsí. (10) 320, 328, 331, 439, 451, 723, 778, 781, 786, 800.

qʷác   *hat.* Ka qʷac–qn. (15) 72, 79, 80, 85, 101, 102, 451, 525, 536, 539, 543, 559, 576.

qʷál̓   *shut lightly.* (1) 841.

qʷám   *beautiful, excellent.* Ka qʷem, Sh qʷem. (6) 39, 479, 487, 721, 832.

qʷán̓   *pity(ful).* Ka qʷin, Sh qʷn–qʷen–t. (2) 789.

qʷáy   *often.* Ka qʷey. (1) 923.

qʷáy̓   *downhill.* (3) 96, 559, 570.

qʷəc   stressless allomorph of qʷác *hat* (q. v.). (5) 72, 85, 101, 102, 576.

qʷəl   stressless allomorph of qʷíl *talk* (q. v.). (27) 35, 49, 190, 205, 210, 251, 252, 259, 407, 434, 445, 446, 486, 611, 636, 730, 810, 831, 846, 847, 903.

qʷəl̓1   stressless allomorph of qʷál̓ *shut lightly* (q. v.). (1) 841.

qʷəl̓2   stressless allomorph of qʷíl̓ *waste time* (q. v.). (1) 844.

qʷəm   stressless allomorph of qʷám *beautiful, excellent* (q. v.). (6) 39, 479, 487, 721, 832.

qʷən̓ = qʷn̓ stressless allomorph of qʷán̓ *pity(ful)* (q. v.). (24) 22, 36, 37, 139, 246, 249, 287, 291, 296, 323, 361, 427, 467, 483, 486, 739, 789, 831, 910.

qʷíl1   *talk.* Ka qʷel, Sh qʷel. (21) 35, 49, 190, 205, 210, 251, 252, 259, 434, 445, 446, 486, 611, 636, 810, 831, 846, 847, 903.

qʷíl₂ *deceive.* Ka qʷil, Sh qʷil. (1) 899.

qʷíl *waste time.* (1) 844.

qʷím *afraid.* (2) 859, 877.

qʷń = qʷən stressless allomorph of qʷán *pity(ful)* (q. v.). (6) 304, 486, 789, 798, 828, 831.

qʷńa allomorph of qʷán *pity(ful)* *(q. v.).* in —míst reflexive forms. (2) 291, 361.

qʷs–₁ reduplicative allomorph of qʷaʔsíyaʔ *children* (q. v.). (10) 320, 328, 331, 439, 451, 467, 723, 778, 781, 786, 800.

qʷs–₂ reduplicative allomorph of qʷsíʔ *son* (q. v.). (1) 467.

qʷsíʔ *son.* Ka s–qʷseʔ, Sh qʷseʔ. Cf. qʷaʔsíyaʔ. (9) 2, 22, 467, 477, 684, 692, 694, 813.

qʷʕáw *crazy, drunk.* Ka qʷew, qʷaw. (2) 404, 465.

qʷʕáy *blue.* Ka qʷay, Sh qʷiy, qʷey. (1) 263.

q̓ʷáy *unclear.* (1) 792.

q̓ʷəʔ *as in* q̓ʷəʔ–ítkʷ *wash clothes.* Ka n–q̓ʷetkʷ. (1) 766.

q̓ʷəł stressless allomorph of q̓ʷił *do one's best* (q. v.). (1) 564.

q̓ʷəx̣ *nail (anatomy).* Ka q̓x̣ʷ, Sh q̓ʷəx̣. (3) 298, 308, 346.

q̓ʷəy₁ *dance.* Ka q̓ʷəy̓, Sh q̓ʷey. (3) 404, 414, 656.

q̓ʷəy₂ stressless, apharyngeal allomorph of q̓ʷʕáy *black, soiled* (q. v.). (2) 748, 753.

q̓ʷíc *replace.* (4) 654, 664, 670.

q̓ʷíł *do one's best.* Ka q̓ʷiłq̓ʷł–t. (1) 564. 1 564.

q̓ʷʕáy *black, soiled.* Ka q̓ʷay. (5) 263, 281, 282, 635, 655.

rétyo *radio (English).* (1) 407.

s– *absolutive* prefix. (2361)

–sʔ– *unclear in the form* q̓ʷay–sʔ–ílxʷ *green back.* (1) 792.

–s *3rd possessive, his, her, its.*

sá– reduplicative allomorph of sq̓t *rain* (q. v.). (3) 319, 329.

saʔp *water animal.* (1) 290.

saʔt *dry off.* (2) 518, 861.

saʔx̣ *cool off.* (1) 67.

sál *set (of table).* (1) 881.

sáq̓ʷ *inactive.* (1) 920.

sáx̣ʷ *downstairs.* Sh səsúx̣ʷ. (5) 90, 524, 553, 893.

saʕ *descend.* (3) 587, 691, 867.

–scút *reflexive* suffix. Cf. –ncút. (11) 37, 215, 314, 316, 564, 673, 767, 798, 837, 890, 900.

scíɬt *yesterday.* Ka spiːscé. (1) 802.

səʔst stressless allomorph of síwst *drink* (q. v.). Ka sust, Sh (?) t–sw–suʔt. (1) 507.

səkʷət = səkʷt stressless allomorph of skʷút *half, across* (q. v.). (2) 919.

səkʷt = səkʷət stressless allomorph of skʷút *half, across* (q. v.). (5) 87, 549, 751, 763.

səl₁ stressless allomorph of sál *set (of table)* (q. v.). (3) 61, 70, 514.

səl₂ as in n̥–səl–səl–p–ús *dizzy.* Ka sl. Cf. síɬ *puzzled.* (5) 494, 497.

səlxʷaʔ stressless allomorph of sílxʷaʔ *big (sg)* (q. v.). (2) 451.

səɬ₁ *clear, no tracks.* (2) 678, 683.

səɬ₂ stressless allomorph of síɬ *puzzled* (q. v.). Cf. səl *dizzy.* (1) 765.

səncaʔ stressless allomorph of síncaʔ *younger brother* (q. v.). (11) 157, 158, 159, 160, 171, 175, 181, 560, 565, 673, 759.

səp = sp hít with a club. Ka sp(i), Sh sp. (10) 34, 303, 311, 471, 482, 826, 828, 830.

səxʷ– = sxʷ– lexical prefix *person who.* Distribution unclear, probably stylistic variant. (44) 12, 14, 23, 25, 116, 118, 126, 136, 141, 199, 201, 412, 418, 420, 421, 448, 450, 473, 562, 603, 604, 607, 610, 631, 646, 668, 696, 730, 735, 742, 747, 759, 784, 815, 819, 821, 856, 883, 909.

səx̣₁ *accompany.* Ka sax̣. Cf. səx̣ *pass.* (3) 381, 688, 695.

səx̣₂ *pass.* Ka (?) sax̣, Sh six̣. Cf. səx̣ *accompany.* (1) 692.

sí– reduplicative allomorph of síncaʔ *younger brother.* (11) 157, 158, 159, 160, 171, 175, 181, 560, 565, 673, 759.

síc *new.* Ka síc. (28) 50, 68, 112, 169, 187, 315, 320, 364, 367, 375, 414, 518, 543, 553, 617, 656, 670, 700, 768, 830, 833, 861, 878, 909.

sílxʷaʔ *big (sg.).* (13) 1, 2, 107, 234, 247, 274, 276, 338, 344, 631, 706, 708, 907.

síɬ *puzzled.* Ka sl. Cf. səl *dizzy.* (2) 433, 765.

síncaʔ *younger brother.* Ka sínceʔ, Sh sínce. (3) 154, 658, 663.

sípn *daughter-in-law.* Sh sepn. (1) 698.

sítkəm *spasm.* Unclear. (1) 645.

síw *ask.* Ka sew, Sh sew. (6) 108, 191, 445, 588, 696, 911.

síwɬkʷ *water.* Ka sewɬ–kʷ, Sh séwɬ–kʷe. (32) 234, 247, 266, 267, 274, 275, 276, 294, 297, 298, 307, 308, 309, 338, 342, 343, 344, 345, 355, 356, 357, 359, 364, 366, 507, 655, 706, 708.

síws(t) *drink.* Ka sus. síws in –nt transitive constructions only;

síwst in intranstitive or −m−st constructions: (10) 66, 67, 404, 414, 517, 519, 655, 860, 861, 880.

−sk̓it   stressless allomorph of −ísk̓it pharynx (lexical suffix) (q. v.). Distribution not clear. (3) 155, 390, 681.

skʷ   swell, swollen. Ka sukʷ(ú). (3) 518, 861.

−skʷ   imperative suffix. (2) 631, 898.

skʷíst   name. Ka s−kʷes−t. (5) 1, 175, 190, 210, 650.

sk̓ʷút   half, across. (5) 83, 431, 793, 902.

sláp   in the construction sláp−əp mistake. Ka sli−pp. (1) 50.

slíp   wood. (2) 140, 916.

sl̓   stressless allomorph of sl̓í lose, disappear (q. v.). (3) 224, 626, 693.

sl̓í   lose, disappear. Cf. səl̓. (7) 504, 516, 817, 850, 859, 869, 870.

spúm   fur. Ka s−pum. (1) 321.

sp̓ = səp̓   hit with a club. (12) 33, 78, 87, 88, 89, 303, 480, 549, 828, 830, 902.

−sqáx̣a?   domestic animal (lexical suffix). Ka −sqáx̣e?, Sh sqéx̣e?. (59) 12, 23, 25, 31, 33, 34, 39, 40, 45, 49, 59, 91, 92, 104, 194, 207, 448, 450, 468, 475, 480, 487, 494, 507, 564, 566, 668, 669, 678, 680, 681, 785, 789, 815, 816, 819, 820, 823, 832, 833, 836, 840, 852, 864, 872, 873, 874, 917, 918.

sq̓t   (√sq̓it)   rain. (3) 319, 329.

−st₁   transitive. (221)

−st₂   intransitive reflexive (?) as in k̓ʷul̓−st.

sta?   interjection. (7) 416, 422, 427, 735, 739, 841, 883.

stím   what. Ka tem, Sh s−tem. (35) 10, 113, 115, 120, 123, 130, 133, 138, 176, 184, 205, 256, 266, 297, 323, 330, 331, 369, 372, 440, 474, 572, 594, 599, 602, 606, 672, 688, 707, 721, 778, 911.

sumíx   power, spirit. Possibly analyzable s−wmíx. Ka sumés̆, Sh səmex. (1) 177.

súxʷ₁   leave (pl.). Sh sxʷup. (3) 94, 106, 579.

súxʷ₂   recognize. Ka suxʷ, Sh suxʷ. (6) 430, 672, 759, 770, 795, 906.

sw   stressless allomorph of síw ask (q. v.). (3) 437, 587, 800.

swít   who. Ka swet. (32) 1, 132, 197, 227, 278, 329, 400, 410, 424, 466, 560, 599, 630, 631, 644, 650, 655, 695, 707, 720, 723, 728, 738, 750, 754, 787, 885, 923.

sx   miss. (1) 628.

−sxən = −əsxən   stressless allomorph of −ísxən rock(s), small round object(s) (lexical suffix) (q. v.). (3) 477, 792, 793.

sxʷ− = səxʷ−   person who (lexical suffix). Distribution unclear, probably stylistic variant. (3) 425, 750, 751.

sy₁   smart, powerful. Ka sy. (23) 169, 215, 220, 309, 334, 341, 344, 346,

564, 837, 864, 886, 900.

sy₂   stressless apharyngeal allomorph of sʕáy *make noise* (q. v.). (8) 508, 509, 528, 563, 567, 853, 868, 876.

sʕáy   *make noise.* Ka say. (1) 890.

t—₁   allomorph of k— *resultive* and *person* (with numerals) before (back)-velars.

t—₂   reduplicative allomorph of tím *things, clothes* (q. v.). 448, 451, 741, 897.

t = tə   *agentive instrumental* particle.

—t₁   *stative* suffix.

—t₂   unclear suffix in the construction xí—xw—t—əm *girl* (q. v.). (3) 410, 424, 638.

t?əw   stressless allomorph of t?íw *youngest, last one* (q. v.). (3) 26, 677, 691.

t?íw   *youngest, last one.* Ka t?ew—t. (23) 15, 19, 21, 72, 74, 91, 138, 139, 158, 160, 202, 241, 244, 463, 527, 529, 676, 692, 772, 794, 807, 904, 910.

ta?—   reduplicative allomorph of t?íw *youngest, last one* (q. v.). (1) 527.

ta?   *pound, hammer.* Ka te?, Sh te?. (4) 134, 136, 912, 913.

ta?kín   *how.* Stem based on √?kin *indefinite interrogative* (q. v.). (1) 149.

ta?kʷ?   *repetitive-diminutive* allomorph of tkʷ? *walk* (q. v.). (1) 637.

ta?lí?   *(very) much.* (24) 63, 95, 167, 168, 197, 215, 278, 390, 391, 408, 439, 455, 532, 560, 638, 666, 776, 860, 863, 871, 914.

ta?m   *clear of snow.* Cf. təm. (1) 3.

ta?xʷ   *obtain, get.* Ka tixʷ, Sh txʷ. (10) 17, 271, 456, 457, 670, 698, 732, 770, 801, 890.

ta?x̣il   *turn around.* Stem based on √?ax̣l *act a certain way, do like* (q. v.). (6) 39, 42, 642, 695, 832, 877.

táɬ   *straight, sure.* Cf. tiɬ. (2) 381, 879.

tám   *clouds.* Ka tim, Sh tem. (1) 224.

—tán   *instrumental* suffix. Cf. —tən, —tn̩. (6) 151, 209, 475, 678, 682, 766.

tanms   stressless allomorph of tanmús *insignificant* (q. v.). (1) 800.

tanmús   *insignificant.* (10) 158, 161, 169, 374, 376, 443, 533, 754, 885.

táq   *wave, touch with the hand.* Ka tq, Sh tq. (2) 106, 579.

táwn   *town* (English). (16) 1, 2, 107, 108, 266, 298, 308, 436, 457, 580, 581, 582, 585, 797, 906.

tə = t   *agentive instrumental* particle.

təkʷ—   reduplicative allomorph of təkʷ? *walk* (q. v.). (7) 5, 11, 17, 440, 600, 842.

təkʷ?   *walk.* Ka tkʷ?u. (19) 5, 11, 17, 269, 440, 443, 462, 589, 600, 661,

673, 675, 691, 780, 800, 805, 806.

təl *cislocative* particle *from.* (62) 5, 78, 90, 93, 105, 112, 159, 169, 205, 257, 265, 267, 307, 315, 329, 343, 345, 356, 357, 359, 364, 366, 372, 381, 400, 436, 437, 443, 449, 475, 486, 496, 509, 552, 560, 570, 571, 599, 639, 655, 692, 706, 708, 727, 732, 734, 736, 769, 793, 831, 859, 869, 879, 885, 901, 902, 906.

təlxʷ stressless allomorph of tílxʷ *difficult* (q. v.). (2) 484, 519.

təɬ stressless allomorph of tíɬ *straight, stand* (q. v.). (5) 593, 852, 869, 918.

təm *have not.* Ka tam. Cf. taʔm. (1) 922.

təmxʷ *land, country.* Sh tmixʷ. (30) 5, 18, 48, 227, 234, 277, 329, 342, 355, 372, 407, 440, 443, 492, 496, 498, 600, 670, 673, 680, 769, 779, 806, 843, 851, 870, 872, 906.

təm̓₁ stressless allomorph of túm̓ *woman's mother.* (1) 324.

təm̓₂ = tm̓ stressless allomorph of tím̓ *things, clothes* (q. v.). Cf. stím̓. (6) 448, 451, 741, 897, 906.

təm̓₃ *clouds.* (1) 224.

−tən = −tņ ~ −tn *instrumental* suffix. Cf. −tán. (5) 8, 166, 212, 286, 309.

təq *fool, trick.* (1) 339.

tərq (√tŕaq) *jump, kick.* Ka teɬq̓. (1) 656.

−tət *first pl. possessive* suffix. (49)

təw *buy.* Ka téu. (1) 18.

təw̓− = tuʔ stressless reduplicative allomorph of tíwaʔ *baby somebody* (q. v.). (1) 781.

tíkɬ *bottom, below.* (2) 90, 553.

tíl− reduplicative allomorph of tílxʷ *difficult* (q. v.). (1) 519.

tílxʷ *difficult.* Sh tlxʷ *lose courage.* (1) 252.

tíɬ *upright.* Cf? Ka čɬeʔ, Sh tɬeʔ *lean.* Cf. táɬ−t. (8) 32, 38, 60, 481, 512, 816, 852, 858.

tím̓ as in t−təm̓−tím̓ *clothes* (cf. stím̓): (5) 448, 451, 741, 897; in the construction k−tím̓ *obtain things:* (1) 887.

tíwaʔ as in tuʔ−tíwaʔ−st *baby somebody.* Cf. twít boy. (4) 599, 776, 778, 781.

tk as in pín−tk *time, year:* (5) 7, 150, 459, 643. In the construction s−qíl−tk *body:* (11) 267, 307, 335, 344, 383, 519, 552, 693, 897, 902.

tká *touch.* (2) 297, 344.

tkɬm as in tkɬm−ílxʷ *woman.* (78)

tkʷú as in tkʷú−p−xən *run.* (2) 329, 566.

tla allomorph of təl *cislocative* particle *from* (q. v.). (4) 546, 597, 901, 906.

tm as in s-tm-áli?s *relative*. (1) 672.

tmíxʷ as in s-qəl-tmíxʷ *man*. (9) 22, 326, 434, 467, 648, 649, 650, 694, 766.

tm̓ = təm̓ stressless allomorph of tím̓ *things, clothes* (q. v.). (1) 741, 906.

−tn = −tn̩ = −tən *instrumental* suffix. Cf. −tán. (183)

tr̓ reduplicative allomorph of tər̓q *jump, kick* (q. v.). (2) 414, 728.

tu? = təw̓ reduplicative allomorph of twít *boy* (q. v.). (16) 2, 59, 458, 575, 579, 585, 586, 592, 599, 657, 770, 776, 778, 781, 901.

túm̓ *woman's mother*. Ka tum̓, Sh túme *aunt*. (1) 324.

twí allomorph of twín̓ *short* before s. (1) 918.

twín̓ *short*. Cf. Ka ntu·tewín̓šən *she got short on her lap (?)*. (1) 329.

twít = tw̓ít *boy*. Cf. tíwa?. Ka ttwit, Sh twit *to grow up*. (37) 377, 381, 430, 592, 615, 617, 622, 657. 2, 59, 169, 229, 297, 301, 332, 376, 378, 386, 387, 400, 421, 424, 425, 430, 472, 479, 485, 575, 585, 586, 603, 628, 679, 747, 827, 856, 885.

−(t)wíxʷ *reciprocal* suffix. Cf. −wíxʷ, −nwíxʷ. (1) 802.

−twíxʷ *reciprocal* suffix. Cf. −wíxʷ, −nwíxʷ. (1) 343.

twn̓ stressless allomorph of twín̓ *short* (q. v.). (2) 370, 748.

tw̓ít = twít *boy*. (37) 28, 32, 36, 184, 188, 189, 193, 202, 238, 244, 254, 287, 352, 361, 363, 379, 410, 458, 466, 483, 495, 579, 613, 614, 626, 643, 706, 733, 735, 751, 752, 758, 759, 770, 886, 887, 901.

tx *comb*. Sh tx. (7) 204, 519, 860, 861, 874.

tx̣ʷ *straight*. Ka tox̣ʷ, Sh tux̣ʷ. (2) 444, 472.

ṫ = ṫə *emphatic particle*. Cf. ṫi, ṫəxʷ. (27) 66, 91, 289, 293, 294, 336, 339, 353, 362, 364, 427, 435, 493, 505, 516, 517, 518, 558, 564, 647, 671, 837, 859, 860, 898.

ṫ?ák̓ʷ *resultive (?)* allomorph of √ṫakʷ *lie, come to rest, appear*. Cf. ṫəkʷ. (6) 234, 284, 351, 697, 708, 923.

ṫa?− reduplicative allomorph of ṫa?k̓míx *virgin*. (1) 524.

ṫa?k̓míx *virgin*. Probably further segmentable. Ka s-ṫič-m-iš. (1) 524.

ṫa?l as in n̩-ṫa?l-íls *settle one's feelings, come to*. (2) 24, 313.

ṫáq *lie, throw*. Ka ṫaq, Sh ṫeq. (1) 576.

ṫáq (?) *stretch*. (1) 357.

ṫáqʷ *lick*. Sh ṫeqʷ. (9) 412, 416, 417, 420, 421, 426, 719, 742, 921.

ṫə = ṫ *emphatic particle*. (87)

ṫək *be marked, go by a mark*. Cf(?) Sh ṫək-xen *make tracks*. (1) 72.

ƛ̓əkʷ = ƛ̓k̓ʷ ? (q. v.).   In the construction n–ƛ̓əkʷ–s–əncút *wink:* (2)
619, 811; in the construction ƛ̓əkʷ–p–ús *eye bursts:* (1) 830.

ƛ̓əkʷ = ƛ̓k̓ʷ (√ƛ̓akʷ) *lie, come to rest, appear.* Cf. ƛ̓ʔák̓ʷ.   (26) 12, 39,
49, 91, 92, 104, 274, 277, 327, 448, 450, 487, 499, 566, 647, 668, 674,
678, 682, 785, 789, 820, 833, 843, 872, 918.

ƛ̓əl as in s–ƛ̓əl–s–qílxʷ *earth people.* Cf. Sh s–ƛ̓l–sqéləxʷ *soul.*
Cf. ƛ̓l. (2) 331.

ƛ̓əł *dirty.* Ka ƛ̓ił. (4) 739, 741, 748, 883.

ƛ̓əm (√ƛ̓um) *suck.* Ka ƛ̓əm, Sh ƛ̓um.   (7) 75, 529, 692, 700, 823.

ƛ̓ən– reduplicative allomorph of ƛ̓ína? *ear* (q. v.). (3) 501, 511, 848.

ƛ̓əp = ƛ̓p *corner, edge.* (1) 283.

ƛ̓əq stressless allomorph of ƛ̓aq *lie, throw* (q. v.). (1) 559.

ƛ̓əqʷ *unclear.* Hatch. (1) 320.

ƛ̓əws stressless allomorph of ƛ̓wís *stand.* (1) 687.   In the construction
s–n–ƛ̓əws–cqáx̣a?–tn *barn:* (20) 59, 91, 93, 105, 201, 216, 506,
508, 559, 560, 567, 578, 669, 784, 797, 851, 853, 872, 875, 909.

ƛ̓əxʷ– reduplicative allomorph of ƛ̓íxʷl *different.* (1) 848.

ƛ̓əxʷ *evidential particle.* Cf. ƛ̓i, ƛ̓(ə).   (87)

ƛ̓əxʷt stressless allomorph of ƛ̓úxʷt *fly* (q. v.). (6) 273, 678, 732, 733.

ƛ̓í– reduplicative allomorph of ƛ̓əqʷ *hatch* (q. v.). (1) 320.

ƛ̓i *evidential particle.* Cf. ƛ̓əxʷ, ƛ̓(ə).   (151)

ƛ̓íc *stroke, pat.* (1) 255.

ƛ̓íkəl = ƛ̓íkl *grub, lunch.* Ka ƛ̓ečl.   (2) 514, 796.

ƛ̓íkl = ƛ̓íkəl *grub, lunch.* (4) 17, 794.

ƛ̓ík̓ʷət *lake.* (1) 234.

ƛ̓ína? *ear.* Ka ƛ̓éne?, Sh ƛ̓éne. (3) 501, 511, 848.

ƛ̓íx *come ashore (from the water).* (7) 265, 266, 297, 335, 356.

ƛ̓íxʷl *different.* Ka ƛ̓ixʷl, Sh ƛ̓ixʷəł. (2) 725, 727.

ƛ̓k̓ʷ = ƛ̓əkʷ ? (q. v.).   In the construction n̩–ƛ̓k̓ʷ–ús–ənt *blind someone.*
(1) 36.

ƛ̓k̓ʷ = ƛ̓ək̓ʷ (q. v.) (√ƛ̓akʷ) *lie, come to rest, appear.* Cf. ƛ̓ʔák̓ʷ. (21)
12, 15, 26, 30, 38, 64, 272, 454, 470, 476, 512, 669, 678, 681, 785, 815,
821, 829, 864.

ƛ̓l *cut open.* Ka ƛ̓l(i), Sh ƛ̓l. Cf. ƛ̓əl. (3) 186, 188, 244.

ƛ̓ł *glue, seal.* Ka ƛ̓eł, Sh ƛ̓eł. (2) 175, 237.

ƛ̓p = ƛ̓əp *corner, edge.* (1) 283.

ƛ̓sá *full, packed.* (1) 409.

ƛ̓úl *tame.* (2) 341, 863.

ƛ̓úxʷt *fly.* Ka ƛ̓uxʷt, Sh ƛ̓uxʷt. (3) 48, 272, 679.

ƛ̓wís *stand.* (2) 852, 873.

ƛ̓x̣iw *a year from.* (2) 440, 802.

ƚyá   *refuse.* (1) 748.

−u?s   stressless allomorph of −íẃs (q. v.). (1) 919.

uc   *dubitative interrogative* particle. (13) 177, 387, 393, 445, 491, 557, 560, 725, 810, 816, 834, 897, 909.

−úla?xʷ   *land, earth* (lexical suffix). Ka −úle?xʷ, Sh −uⱡəxʷ.   (59) 1, 3, 5, 17, 48, 49, 57, 146, 227, 234, 274, 277, 295, 327, 329, 342, 348, 355, 372, 407, 408, 440, 443, 492, 496, 498, 499, 505, 507, 535, 600, 670, 673, 674, 680, 697, 730, 769, 779, 800, 806, 827, 843, 848, 851, 870, 872, 900, 906, 913, 914.

uⱡ   conjunctive particle *and.* (916)

úⱡi?   conjunctive particle *and then.* Further analyzable uⱡ−i?.   (35) 38, 158, 163, 167, 199, 208, 305, 437, 484, 485, 509, 516, 526, 568, 588, 678. 711, 743, 744, 776, 787, 806, 860, 869, 885. 438, 516, 536, 568, 699, 702.

−úⱡt   *redirective ditransitive* suffix.   Cf. −(ə)stúⱡt.   (3) 277, 387, 844.

−úm   *2nd sg object* suffix. (3) 520, 531, 602.

−úma?   suffix of indeterminate meaning, in the construction k̓ʷə−k̓ʷy−úma? *small.* (6) 20, 139, 463, 464, 642, 760.

up = wp   = əwp (√wap)   *thick growth.* (1) 448.

−úps   *tail* (lexical suffix).   In the construction məl−qn−úps *eagle:* (5) 320, 323, 328, 358, 363.

−ús   (lexical suffix).   In the following constructions: s−pu?−ús *heart, wish:* (16) 9, 11, 62, 172, 184, 236, 406, 479, 598, 615, 647, 770, 783, 815, 885, 887; sy−sy−ús *smart, powerful:* (9) 169, 220, 309, 334, 341, 344, 346, 864, 886; n̓−pƛ̓−m−ús *finish:* (4) 3, 154, 163, 773; ƛa?−ús *look around:* (3) 17, 495, 676; ?axl−ús *turn away:* (1) 427; pəlk̓−ús *turn back:* (1) 817; xy̓−ús *go in:* (1) 838; t−k̓əw−ⱡx−ús *go up(stairs):* (1) 889; k̓əw−p−ús *out of sight:* (1) 312; k̓əⱡ−k̓əlxʷ−ús *out of sight:* (1) 443; xʷst−ús *walk off:* (1) 428; kⱡ−xn̓−ús *sun set:* (1) 280; k−saʕ−ús *sun set:* (1) 867; n̓−ʕac−ús *trap:* (1) 503; n̓−tm̓−ús *worthless:* (1) 741; t−qʷa?−m−ús *be used to:* (1) 878; n̓−q̓əlt−ús *get sick:* (4) 22, 472, 814; n̓−ləʕ̓ʷ−p−ús, n̓−ləʕ̓ʷ−ús *come true, fit:* (3) 318, 675, 802; n̓−my−p−ús, k−my−p−ús *make something out:* (3) 581, 690, 877; sⱡ−ús *lose someone:* (1) 224; with the meaning *head, eye, face, neck* in construction with various roots: (39) 36, 47, 75, 78, 87, 88, 89, 95, 96, 100, 101, 216, 385, 400, 449, 494, 497, 501, 511, 552, 558, 576, 577, 583, 652, 700, 830, 835, 843, 848, 853, 854, 877, 894, 899, 902.

–út suffix of uncertain meaning. In the construction tkʷʔ–út *walk:* (19) 5, 11, 17, 269, 440, 443, 462, 589, 600, 637, 661, 673, 675, 691, 780, 800, 805, 806. In the costruction xʷəst–út *walk:* (1) 480. In the construction ɬq̇ʷ–út *lie on:* (12) 62, 70, 71, 74, 148, 682, 721, 865, 889, 892, 893, 901. In the construction lkʷ–út *far:* (8) 112, 265, 390, 522, 523, 666, 732, 869, In the construction tx̣ʷ–m–út *straight:* (1) 472 In the construction ƛ̣x̣–ƛ̣x̣–p–út *too old:* (1) 887. In the construction yx̣ʷ–út *below:* (5) 546, 562, 766, 879, 901.

–útyaʔ *approximating* (lexical suffix). (7) 299, 307, 358, 478, 815, 821, 826.

uyáʔ interjection *listen.* (3) 22, 483, 486.

wʔ = uʔ stressless variant of wiʔ *finish* (q. v.). (3) 155, 200, 389.

wʔas allomorph of wís *high* (q. v.). in a-ablaut grade, *completive* aspect. (1) 496.

waʔ–₁ reduplicative allomorph of waʔs *high* (q. v.). (3) 45, 495, 840.

waʔ–₂ reduplicative allomorph of wíl *weave from side to side* (q. v.). (1) 840.

waʔl *puzzle.* (2) 570, 585.

waʔs a-grade allomorph of wís *high* (q. v.). (5) 45, 495, 840, 841.

wah *dog bark.* Ka wewe. (4) 54, 500, 848, 868.

wáy interjection *well, finished, yes.* Related to wiʔ *finish* (q. v.). (951)

wérhaws *warehouse (English).* (1) 449.

wəl unclear. *Find excuses.* Probably related to wíl· *weave from side to side* (q. v.). (2) 653.

wəypáy allomorph of wyapy–x *white man.* Cf. wyápix.(2) 368, 379.

wiʔ *finish.* (58) 19, 60, 61, 62, 64, 85, 94, 95, 105, 147, 155, 175, 186, 238, 243, 286, 310, 347, 348, 363, 383, 400, 403, 413, 450, 514, 521, 524, 537, 541, 559, 569, 648, 649, 655, 694, 861, 864, 865, 874, 881, 889, 891, 893, 909, 916.

–wiʔ probably –wy *intransitive imperative pl* suffix. (7) 110, 423, 432, 556, 750.

wik *see.* Ka wič, Sh wik. (31) 13 48, 88, 105, 112, 274, 275, 331, 381, 391, 430, 498, 508, 580, 679, 684, 688, 708, 770, 786, 787, 843, 850, 854, 885, 889, 902, 923.

wíl· *weave from side to side.* Sh wel *tilted.* (1) 840.

–wílx *developmental* suffix. (10) 25, 37, 440, 471, 571, 667, 770, 771, 802. 885.

wim particle *to no avail.* (14) 360, 418, 420, 428, 467, 471, 482, 531, 646, 748, 816, 817, 826, 899.

wís *high.* Ka wis *long,* Sh wis *high.* (17) 38, 45, 299, 300, 336, 358, 406, 486, 491, 679, 683, 789, 831, 838, 839, 841, 889.

–wít unclear suffix, probably meaning *step.* (1) 43.

wíx *dwell, live.* Cf. ʔəks–wix *stand.* (13) 1, 39, 108, 487, 507, 512, 588, 610, 832, 848, 850, 867, 913.

–wíxʷ *reciprocal* suffix. Cf. –nwixʷ, –twixʷ. (10) 144, 336, 367, 461, 625, 650, 651, 697, 728.

wk stressless allomorph of wík *see.* (3) 220, 223, 461.

wl reduplicative allomorph of wlím *iron* (q. v.). (4) 134, 136, 912, 913.

wlím *iron.* Ka u·lu·lím, Sh s–wl–wlilm. (4) 134, 136, 912, 913.

wníxʷ *true.* Ka unéxʷ, Sh wnexʷ. (16) 24, 189, 190, 258, 496, 618, 640, 655, 777, 783, 800, 810, 818, 840, 841, 867.

wnxʷ stressless allomorph of wníxʷ *true* (q. v.). (2) 520, 565.

wp = up = əwp *thick growth.* Ka wp, Sh wup. (3) 12, 507, 785.

wr̥ *fire, burn.* Ka wr(i), wer(i), Sh wl–em. (3) 323, 329, 568.

ws stressless allomorph of wís *high* (q. v.). (4) 903.

wt = ut allomorph of wtán *put in* (q. v.) in transitive forms. (3) 28, 453, 591.

–wt stressless allomorph of –wít *step* (q. v.). (1) 295.

wtan *put in.* (3) 15, 298, 523.

wxʷ = əwxʷ *stare at.* (1) 583.

wyápix *white man.* Ka suyápi, Sh swyepmx. Cf. wəypáy. (5) 583, 584, 585, 903, 925.

wyápx allomorph of wyápix *white man.* (1) 773.

wˤi–mst unclear. *Move fast.* (1) 516.

–x₁ *intransitive imperative.* 214

–x₂ suffix of unclear function: with kíc: *arrive;* with tíɫ: *stand.*

xʔím superlative root in compounds, with basic meaning of *limit.* (13) 12, 37, 448, 668, 669, 784, 785, 815.

xʔít *first.* Ka šʔit, Sh xʔit. In the constructions: s(–xaʔ)–xʔít–x *oldest one*: (19) 3, 15, 78, 89, 114, 174, 236, 239, 526, 552, 601, 673, 692, 693, 794, 891, 902, 904; c–xʔít(–iʔ) *(at) first* (6) 17, 155, 325, 346, 660, 728; əc–xʔít *take the lead* (2) 767, 904; xaʔít–ət *go first*: (1) 910; xaʔ–xʔít *grandmother*: (2) 850, 858.

xaʔ– reduplicative allomorph of xʔit *first* (q. v.). (6) 3, 673, 693, 850, 858, 910.

xaʔ *move forward,* probably related to xʔít. (1) 840.

xaʔít completive (?) allomorph of xʔít *first* (q. v.). (1) 910.

xaʔt stressless completive allomorph of xʔít *first* (q. v.). (3) 602, 767, 902.

–xán *foot, leg* (lexical suffix). Ka –šin, Sh –xen. (12) 45, 448, 451, 495, 678, 683, 897, 903, 919, 922.

xár   as in   xár–kst *bother someone.* Cf? Sp šer.   (2) 701, 861.

xək = xk   *rub(bing noise).* (2) 547, 901.

xəl = xl   *chop, cut off.* Ka šil, Sh xl *bite.* (3) 558, 576, 577.

xəlk   stressless allomorph of xl·ák *turn, go around* (q. v.).   (1) 327.

xəƛ̓   stressless allomorph of xƛ̓á *finish, complete* (q. v.).   (2) 599, 773.

xəm·   *hold, have between.* Sh xm–em.   (1) 919.

–xən = –xn = –əxn   stressless allomorph of –xán   *foot, leg* (lexical
   suffix) (q. v.).   Cf. –(ˤ)áqst–xən, –qín–xən, –cín–xən.
   (33) 12, 31, 224, 266, 298, 308, 319, 320, 329, 346, 448, 477, 560, 646,
   679, 680, 785, 833, 840, 897, 903, 904.

xi–   reduplicative allomorph of xw *girl* (q. v.).   (3) 410, 424, 638.

xi?₁   as in   xi?–míx *whatever, whenever.*   (5) 200, 800, 820, 869.

xi?₂   *let go.* (2) 814.

xi?t   *rush, hurry.* (1) 91.

xíƛ̓   *level, flat.* Sp šiƛ̓.   1 806.

–xít   *ditransitive* suffix.   (34) 7, 14, 28, 30, 43, 61, 70, 141, 151, 189, 235, 246,
   318, 341, 345, 448, 459, 468, 473, 514, 591, 604, 618, 661, 665, 673,
   751, 791, 800, 801, 804, 818, 823.

xk = xək   *rub(bing noise).* (2) 547, 901.

xl = xəl   *chop, cut off.* (6) 552, 558, 576, 577, 902.

xl·ak   *turn, go around.* (1) 234.

xƛ̓   stressless allomorph of xƛ̓á *finish, complete* (q. v.). (7) 92, 406, 414, 655,
   693, 864, 889.

xƛ̓á   *finish, complete.* (17) 39, 85, 89, 148, 400, 401, 406, 410, 431, 542, 552,
   655, 721, 728, 734, 744, 745.

xƛ̓út   *rock.* (1) 283.

xm   *spur.* (3) 33, 824, 826.

xṇ   unclear. *Set (of sun).* (1) 280.

–xn = –xən stressless allomorph of –xán   *foot, leg* (lexical suffix) (q. v.).
   (1) 566.

xp   *chew.* (2) 652, 899.

xr   *hang, dangle.* Sp šer (šal), Sh xal.   (1) 902.

xs   *miss, feel the absence.* (2) 162, 676.

–xt   stressless allomorph of –xít *ditransitive* suffix (q. v.).   (12) 367, 619,
   625, 650, 651, 671, 728, 802, 811, 822, 858.

xt̓   stressless allomorph of xt̓á *care for, look after* (q. v.). (6) 81, 213, 214,
   349, 791, 900.

xt̓á   *care for, look after.* Sp šƛ̓.   (1) 266, 465, 562.

xt̓s   *continue doing.* (1) 812.

xw   *girl.* Sp šew, Sh xew̓.   (3) 410, 424, 638.

xy̓ = xi? (?) *go through.* (1) 838.

–xˤán pharyngeal allomorph of –xán *foot, leg* (lexical suffix) (q. v.). (1) 289.

–xʷ– reduplicative infix of t̓íxʷl *different* (q. v.). (1) 848.

–xʷ₁ allomorph (C2 reduplication) of súxʷ *leave* (q. v.). (1) 579.

–xʷ₂ stressless allomorph of –íxʷ *2nd sg transitive subject* suffix.

xʷ? stressless allomorph of xʷ?ít *many* (q. v.). (1) 799.

xʷ?ít *many.* Ka xu?ít, Sh xʷ?it. (2) 455, 613.

xʷa?t *completive (?)* allomorph of xʷ?ít *many.* (1) 799.

xʷák̓ʷ *clean, extricate, pull out.* (1) 913.

xʷál *alive.* Ka xulxʷil, Sh xʷl–xʷel–t. (9) 7, 169, 441, 459, 561, 692, 803, 844.

xʷár *shiver, quiver, shake.* Sp xʷer(í). Cf. xʷrá. (3) 322.

xʷək̓ʷ stressless allomorph of xʷák̓ʷ *clean, extricate, pull out* (q. v.). Sh xʷuk̓ʷ, Sp xʷuk̓ʷ. (3) 766, 913, 925.

xʷəl stressless allomorph of xʷál *alive* (q. v.). (21) 7, 158, 159, 160, 169, 328, 331, 441, 459, 490, 561, 692, 803, 844.

xʷəm interjection (?) *pretty.* (1) 832.

xʷəs reduplicative allomorph of xʷíst *walk* (q. v.). (1) 31.

xʷíc *give.* Sp xʷicš, Sh xʷic. (47) 10, 23, 58, 60, 62, 65, 68, 118, 126, 127, 136, 137, 141, 142, 181, 199, 213, 239, 243, 268, 287, 289, 293, 352, 449, 477, 506, 516, 605, 609, 610, 644, 721, 786, 790, 815, 822, 851, 858, 859, 861.

xʷíp *spread out, unfold, open.* Ka xʷep, Sh xʷep. (1) 335.

xʷíst *walk.* Ka xʷist, Sh xʷəset. (5) 33, 470, 484, 681, 701.

xʷp stressless allomorph of xʷíp *spread out, unfold, open* (q. v.). (5) 264, 282, 350, 843.

xʷrá *shiver, quiver, shake.* Cf. xʷár. Ka xʷer(í). (2) 645, 902.

xʷs stressless allomorph of xʷús *hurry, fast* (q. v.). (7) 92, 488, 564, 568, 834, 844, 895.

xʷst stressless allomorph of xʷíst *walk* (q. v.). (11) 289, 295, 319, 354, 428, 478, 480, 815, 821, 826.

xʷt₁ *take away, off.* (2) 553, 897.

xʷt₂ as in xʷt–xʷt–íls *quick temper.* (4) 301, 314.

xʷt̓ *jump, run.* Sp xʷt̓(i). (15) 91, 469, 484, 536, 538, 556, 558, 578, 579, 649, 678, 683, 700, 836, 900, 901.

xʷús *hurry, fast.* Sh xʷ?us. (18) 40, 92, 457, 488, 541, 556, 564, 568, 636, 685, 799, 834, 835, 844, 895, 899.

xʷúy *go.* Ka xʷuy, Sh xʷuy. (114)

xʷúy? allomorph of xʷúy *go* (q. v.) of unclear function. (17) 107, 147, 153,

380, 590, 673. 107, 109, 153, 274, 379, 499, 580, 673, 841.

x̣ʷy   stressless allomorph of x̣ʷúy *go* (q. v.). (4) 57, 390, 505, 870, 898.

—x̣₁   reduplicative allomorph of páʔx̣ *think* (q. v.). (2) 165, 233.

—x̣₂   reduplicative allomorph of q̓íx̣ *stingy of* (q. v.). (1) 421.

x̣ʔən   *stop.* Sp x̣en(í) *tell, warn.* (6) 36, 304, 483, 531, 828, 898.

x̣a—   reduplicative allomorph of x̣aˤ *stare at.* (1) 835.

—x̣á   reduplicative allomorph of səx̣ *pass* (q. v.). (1) 692.

x̣aʔ₁   *powerful, important.* Sh x̣əx̣eʔ. (4) 178, 227.

x̣aʔ₂   as in s—x̣aʔ—x̣áʔ *father-in-law.* Sp s—x̣aʔx̣éʔ. (2) 700.

x̣aʔs   *completive (?)* allomorph of x̣ás *good* (q. v.). (2) 416, 627.

x̣am·   unclear form. *Noise?* (1) 324.

x̣áq   *open, empty.* (3) 60, 852, 873.

x̣áq̓   *pay.* Ka x̣aq̓, Sh x̣eq̓. (1) 798.

x̣ás   *good.* Ka x̣es. (27) 12, 40, 161, 172, 236, 287, 352, 448, 469, 473,
     475, 504, 585, 668, 669, 754, 784, 785, 815, 818, 849, 912.

x̣áw   *dry.* Sh x̣ew—t. (1) 787.

x̣aˤ   *stare.* (1) 835.

x̣c   *ready.* Ka x̣c, Sh x̣c. (7) 19, 82, 415, 556, 559, 574, 754.

x̣c̓íʔ   *stick (of wood).* Sh s—x̣c̓ey. (1) 303.

x̣ə—   reduplicative allomorph of x̣c̓íʔ *stick (of wood)* (q. v.). (1) 303.

x̣əc   *hundred.* Sh x̣ec—p—qiqn—kst. Cf. x̣c *ready.* (1) 16.

x̣əl₁   reduplicative allomorph of x̣ˤál *day(light)* (q. v.). (18) 8, 151, 154,
     264, 271, 440, 459, 567, 656, 675, 688, 802, 850, 879, 916.

x̣əl₂   particle *for the reason, because.* (7) 158, 369, 422, 520, 572, 707, 777.

x̣əlt   stressless allomorph of x̣lít *ask* (q. v.). (4) 407, 422, 722, 731.

x̣əl̓   stressless allomorph of x̣íl *fear* (q. v.). Cf. x̣íɬ. (4) 294, 355.

x̣íl   *fear.* Ka x̣el. Cf. x̣íɬ. (7) 46, 227, 325, 327, 355, 654, 659.

x̣ílwiʔ   *husband.* Sh x̣élwiʔ. (1) 670.

x̣íɬ   *fear.* Cf. x̣íl. (5) 44, 490, 493, 850, 871.

x̣íƛ̓   *climb.* Sh s—x̣et̓—m—xn, Sp s—x̣ƛ̓i—šn *trousers.* (2) 897, 903.

x̣lá   allomorph of x̣ˤál *day(light)* in the construction x̣lá—p *morrow.* (10)
     127, 153, 197, 262, 269, 519, 661, 665, 915, 916.

x̣lít   *ask.* Ka x̣alít, Sh x̣lit. (14) 66, 146, 400, 412, 420, 421, 426,
     655, 748, 752, 764, 861, 882, 894.

x̣ƛ̓   stressless allomorph of x̣íƛ̓ *climb* (q. v.). (1) 903.

x̣m   as in x̣m—ínk *like.* Sp x̣m—enč. (35) 10, 11, 57, 66, 115, 131, 140,
     179, 191, 192, 197, 210, 248, 288, 293, 294, 375, 378, 387, 505, 530,
     602, 603, 606, 608, 615, 621, 702, 718, 738, 779, 885, 910, 923.

x̣q   stressless allomorph of x̣áq   open, empty (q. v.).   (3) 913, 914.

x̣s   stressless allomorph of x̣as   good (q. v.).   (21) 17, 149, 156, 439, 448, 461,
      471, 477, 585, 592, 648, 649, 766, 776, 785, 786, 788, 790, 885.

x̣w̓   stressless allomorph of x̣áw̓   dry (q. v.).   (1) 519.

x̣yáɬnəx̣ʷ   sun.   (3) 280, 381.

x̣ʕal   day(light).   (14) 8, 151, 154, 264, 440, 459, 567, 688, 802, 850, 879.

x̣ʷʔ   as in x̣ʷʔ-íɬp   Colville.   (1) 611.

-x̣ʷá   reduplicative allomorph of px̣ʷá   scatter, diversify (q. v.).   (2) 461, 801.

x̣ʷáq̓ʷ   as in x̣ʷáq̓ʷ-əlqs   snore.   Sh x̣ʷuq̓ʷl-əqs.   (11) 77, 78, 85,
      533, 534, 542, 543, 550, 899, 900.

x̣ʷəl   stressless allomorph of x̣ʷíl   discard (q. v.).   (1) 405.

x̣ʷíl   discard.   Ka x̣ʷel.   (3) 161, 242, 315.

x̣ʷp   stressless allomorph of x̣ʷúp   worthless (q. v.).   (2) 815, 864.

x̣ʷúp   worthless.   Ka x̣ʷupt, Sh s-x̣ʷup-t.   (7) 19, 23, 91, 564, 808, 815,
      864.

y   allomorph of iʔ   article (q. v.) before V.   (27) 23, 44, 70, 226, 249, 330, 396,
      488, 499, 522, 531, 752, 781, 786, 834, 844, 852, 864, 865, 874, 897,
      898, 900.

yʔáʕ   (people) gather.   (4) 408, 732, 734, 736.

yʔáʕʔ   completive allomorph of yʔáʕ   (people) gather (q. v.) (equivalent of
      -C2 reduplication ?).   (1) 408.

yaʔ   reduplicative allomorph of yákʷ-aʔ   stingy (q. v.).   (1) 789.

yákʷ   stingy.   Sp yukʷ(é).   (1) 789.

yáɬ   crowd.   (1) 624.

yáw   reduplicative allomorph of yáʕw   strong, strength (q. v.).   (7) 158, 229,
      370, 377, 709, 788, 885.

yáx̣aʔ   watch.   (1) 418.

yáʕ   arrive.   (30) 7, 8, 53, 107, 109, 151, 153, 155, 160, 162, 199, 215, 264,
      277, 380, 408, 440, 444, 450, 452, 459, 661, 665, 666, 679, 718, 728,
      731, 787, 797, 800, 803, 835, 911.

yaʕ₁   as in yaʕ-cín   shore.   (1) 265.

yaʕ₂   as in yaʕ-p-cín   in trouble.   (8) 10, 176, 177, 330, 331, 785, 909.

yáʕ   gather.   (13) 144, 154, 162, 172, 236, 400, 401, 412, 441, 723, 735, 801,
      914.

yaʕ̓   as in ya̓ʔ-mí-   be backward.   (2) 694, 696.

yáʕw   strong, strength.   Sp yoʔ, yuʔ, Sh yʕw-yuʕw.   (1) 268.

yə—₁ reduplicative allomorph of yˁá *all* (q. v.). (36) 2, 10, 64, 72, 73, 227, 267, 335, 383, 400, 410, 418, 424, 448, 451, 512, 525, 526, 620, 655, 721, 723, 728, 730, 731, 738, 750, 754, 770, 785, 803, 815, 856, 862, 891, 900.

yə—₂ reduplicative allomorph of yáxa? *watch* (q. v.). (4) 64, 418, 815, 862.

yə? *article.* Cf. i?, y. (146)

yəˁw stressless allomorph of yáˁw *strong, strength* (q. v.). (7) 158, 229, 370, 377, 709, 788, 885.

yíxʷ *envy.* Sp yuxʷ. (1) 232.

yl— reduplicative allomorph of ylmíxʷəm *chief* (q. v.). (7) 400, 402, 410, 646, 723, 730, 736.

yləmx̌ʷ stressless allomorph of ylmíxʷəm *chief* (q. v.). (13) 108, 109, 126, 182, 380, 391, 412, 588, 590, 667, 757, 905.

ylmíxʷəm = ylmíxʷm *chief, boss.* Sp ?ilmíxʷm. (120)

ylmíxʷm = ylmíxʷəm *chief, boss.* (4) 2, 664, 667, 789.

ylw̓ *tub.* (1) 631.

—ylxʷ allomorph of —ílxʷ *body, cover* (lexical suffix) (q. v.). The y is unclear. (1) 874.

yl̓ *grab.* Cf? Ka yal, yel, Sh yel, yal *be wound around.* (1) 217.

yl̓xʷ *cover.* Cf. —ylxʷ. (1) 894.

yr *push.* (1) 900.

yu?— reduplicative allomorph of yáˁw (q. v.) in the construction yu?—yáˁw—t *strength.* (1) 268.

yum̓ *move.* Cf? Ka yí?u (ií?u?), Sh yw *lively.* (1) 900.

yw *strong.* Probably related to yáˁw *strong, strength.* (4) 215, 216.

yx̌ʷ *(be)low.* Sp yšut, Sh yuxʷ. (9) 215, 221, 224, 502, 546, 562, 766, 879, 901.

yˁ stressless allomorph of yˁá *all* (q. v.). (4) 64, 512, 815, 862.

yˁá *all.* Sp ya?. (36) 2, 10, 64, 72, 73, 227, 267, 335, 383, 400, 410, 424, 448, 451, 525, 526, 620, 655, 721, 723, 728, 730, 731, 738, 750, 754, 770, 785, 803, 856, 891, 900. Unstressed in yˁa—ł—cw—ílxʷ—tṇ *all over the world:* (1) 736.

yˁəp stressless allomorph of n—yˁíp *always* (q. v.). (1) 813.

yˁíp as in n—yˁíp *always.* (10) 154, 291, 296, 311, 472, 621, 647, 676, 813, 872.

ˁac *tie.* Sp ˁac, (h)ac, Sh ˁec. (19) 12, 26, 53, 64, 279, 468, 470, 474, 476, 494, 503, 513, 703, 815, 819, 821, 862, 880, 917.

ˁacá allomorph of ˁac *tie* (q. v.) in transitive imperative forms. (2) 25, 784.

ʕác   *look.* Cf. ʕac̓x̣.   (21) 118, 127, 137, 141, 186, 188, 243, 244, 264, 383, 448, 558, 592, 605, 610, 685, 753, 755, 789, 849, 909.

−ʕáca?   pharyngeal allomorph of −íca? *body (cover), surface* (lexical suffix) (q. v.).   (1) 753.

ʕácəx̣   *look.* Sp ?ac̓x̣, ʕac̓x̣. Cf. ʕac̓.   (1) 38.

−ʕálx   pharyngeal allomorph of −ílx *motion* (q. v.).   (1) 528.

−ʕám   pharyngeal allomorph of −m *middle* suffix (q. v.).   (1) 48.

−ʕáp   pharyngeal allomorph of −p *non control* (q. v.).   (1) 346.

−ʕápəlqs   pharyngeal allomorph of −ápəlqs *story* (lexical suffix).   (1) 703.

ʕapná?   *now.*   (17) 5, 68, 127, 151, 391, 440, 459, 653, 665, 698, 702, 731, 735, 736, 737, 802.

−ʕáqst   pharyngeal allomorph of −áqst in the construction −ʕáqst−xən *leg* (lexical suffix) (q. v.).   (4) 12, 448, 785, 833.

−ʕás   pharyngeal allomorph of −ús *face, fire, eye* (lexical suffix) (q. v.).   (7) 75, 529, 692, 700, 823.

ʕáy   *tired.*   (1) 920.

ʕay   *tickle.*   (4) 76, 899.

ʕím   *anger.* Sp ʕaymt, ?aymt, Sh ʕey.   (3) 167, 168, 828.

ʕal   *fence.*   (1) 686.

ʕáw̓   *(let) loose.*   (1) 494.

ʕʷímst   unclear, probably further analyzable.   *Hurry.*   (1) 860.

Bibliography

Allison, S. S. 1892. "Account of the Similkameen Indians of British Columbia." *Journal of the Anthropological Institute of Great Britain and Ireland*, XXI, No. 3, pp. 305-318.

Bascom, William 1954. "Four functions of folklore." *Journal of American Folklore* 67:333-49.

Boas, Franz, ed. 1930. *The Salishan tribes of the Western Plateaus.* 45th annual report of the Bureau of American Ethnology, 1027-28. Washington, D. C.

Carlson, Barry F., n. d. *Spokane dictionary.* MS.

Carriere, J. M. 1937. *Tales from the French folklore of Missouri.* Northwestern University, Evanston and Chicago.

Degh, Linda 1965. *Folktales of Hungary.* University of Chicago Press.

Dorrance, Ward A. 1935. *The survival of French in the old district of Saint Genevieve.* The University of Missouri Studies, Vol. 10, No. 2.

Dorson, Richard, A. ed. 1972. *Folklore and folklife. An introduction.* University of Chicago Press.

Fahey, John 1974. *The Flathead Indians.* University of Oklahoma Press.

Greenway, John 1964. *Literature among the primitives.* Folklore Associates, Inc. Hatboro.

Hebert, Yvonne M. 1982. *Transitivity in (Nicola Lake) Okanagan.* University of British Columbia PhD dissertation.

Hymes, Dell 1977. "Discovering oral performance." *New Literary History* 8:431-57.

Jacobs, Melville 1959. *The Content and style of an oral literature. Clackamas Chinook myths and tales.* University of Chicago Press.

Jacobsen, William H. Jr. 1976. "Noun and verb in Nootkan." In *The Victoria conference on Northwestern languages, Victoria, B. C., Nov. 4-6.* Edited by Barbara S. Efrat. B. C. Provincial Museum, Heritage Record No. 4.

Kashube, Dorothea 1978. *Crow texts.* Native American Texts Series No. 2. University of Chicago Press.

Kinkade, M. Dale 1981. *Dictionary of the Moses Columbian language.* Colville Confederated Tribes.

———— 1983. "Salish evidence against the universality of 'noun' and 'verb'." *Lingua* 60:25-40.

Krohn, Kaarle 1971. *Folklore methodology formulated by Julius Krohn and expanded by Nordic researchers.* University of Texas Press.

Kuipers, Aert 1968. "The categories verb-noun and transitive-intransitive in English and Squamish." *Lingua* 21:610-26.

———— 1973. *The Shuswap language.* Mouton.

Mattina, Anthony 1973. *Colville grammatical structure.* University of Hawaii PhD dissertation.

———— 1980. "Imperative constructions in Colville-Okanagan and and in the other languages of the Interior." *Glossa* 14:212-32.

———— 1982. "The Colville-Okanagan transitive system. *International Journal of American Linguistics* 48:421-35.

Maud, Ralph, ed. 1978. *The Salish people. The local contribution of Charles Hill-Tout.* Volume I. *The Thompson and the Okanagan.* Talonbooks, Vancouver.

McClendon, Sally 1980. "The rhetorical structure of Eastern Pomo." Paper delivered at the Conference on American Indian Languages, American Anthropological Association, Washington D. C.

No author 1965. *Colville termination. Hearings before the subcommittee on Indian affairs of the committee on interior and insular affairs. House of representatives, eighty-ninth congress, first session on H. R. 5925 and S. 1413 to provide for the termination of federal supervision over the property of the Colville tribe and individual members thereof and H. R. 6331 to provide members of the Colville Confederated tribes with full citizenship and to provide for vesting each tribal member with his equal cash share representing his equity in all reservation assets of the Colville Confederated tribes in the state of Washington.* Hearings Held in Washington, D. C., June 18 and August 13, 1965, Spokane, Wash., November 3, 1965, and Nespelem, Wash., November 4 and 5, 1965. Serial No. 89-23.

Purl, Douglas C. 1974. "Blue Jay and Wolf." Paper presented at the IX International Conference on Salish languages, Vancouver, B. C.

Raufer, Sister Maria Ilma, 0. P. 1966. *Black robes and Indians on the last frontier. A story of heroism.* Bruce Publishing Co., Milwaukee.

Reichard, Gladys 1947. *An Analysis of Coeur d'Alene Indian myths.* Memoirs of the American Folklore Society vol. 41. Philadelphia.

Sebillot, Paul 1904-7. *Le Folklore de France.* Editions G.-P. Maisonneuve et Larose, Paris. Reprinted 1968.

Silko, Leslie Marmon 1981. *Storyteller.*

Speare, Jean E., ed. 1973. *The Days of Augusta.* J. J. Douglas Ltd., Vancouver.

Spier, Leslie ed. 1938. *The Sinkaietk or Southern Okanagon of Washington.* General Series in Anthropology No. 6, Menasha, Wisconsin.

Thompson, Laurence C. and M. Terry Thompson forthcoming. *The Thompson language.* British Columbia Provincial Museum, Victoria.

_____ 1981. "Control hierarchy in Salish lexicons." Paper delivered at the Conference on American Indian Languages, American Anthropological Association, Los Angeles.

Thompson, Stith 1955. *Motif index of folk literature.* Revised edition. Indiana University Press, Bloomington.

Thompson, Stith 1961. *The types of the folktale.* Second revision. Helsingin Liikekirjapaino Oy, Helsinky.

Vogt, Hans 1940. *The Kalispel language.* Det Norske Videnskaps Akademi i Oslo.

Watkins, Donald 1970. *A Description of the phonemes and position classes in the morphology of Head of the Lake Okanagan (Salish).* University of Alberta PhD dissertation.

Weinhold, Karl 1896. *Weitschrift des Vereins für Volkskunde.* Berlin, Verlag von A. Asher & Co.

Witherspoon, Gary 1978. "Language in culture and culture in language." *International Journal of American Linguistics* 46:1-13.

Woodbury, Hanni 1980. "Cohesive and grammatical functions of selected Onondaga particles." Paper delivered at the Conference on American Indian Languages, American Anthropological Association, Washington D. C.